About Research & Education Association

Founded in 1959, Research & Education Association (REA) is dedicated to publishing the finest and most effective educational materials—including software, study guides, and test preps—for students in middle school, high school, college, graduate school, and beyond.

REA's Test Preparation series includes books and software for all academic levels in almost all disciplines. Research & Education Association publishes test preps for students who have not yet entered high school, as well as high school students preparing to enter college. Students from countries around the world seeking to attend college in the United States will find the assistance they need in REA's publications. For college students seeking advanced degrees, REA publishes test preps for many major graduate school admission examinations in a wide variety of disciplines, including engineering, law, and medicine. Students at every level, in every field, with every ambition can find what they are looking for among REA's publications.

REA presents tests that accurately depict the official exams in both degree of difficulty and types of questions. REA's practice tests are always based upon the most recently administered exams, and include every type of question that can be expected on the actual exams.

REA's publications and educational materials are highly regarded and continually receive an unprecedented amount of praise from professionals, instructors, librarians, parents, and students. Our authors are as diverse as the fields represented in the books we publish. They are well known in their respective disciplines and serve on the faculties of prestigious high schools, colleges, and universities throughout the United States and Canada.

We invite you to visit us at *www.rea.com* to find out how "REA is making the world smarter."

Acknowledgments

Foundational material was provided by William H. Barber, Ed.D., Midwestern State University, Wichita Falls, Texas; M. C. Camerer, Ed.D., Midwestern State University, Wichita Falls; Betty J. Conaway, Ph.D., Baylor University, Waco, Texas; Sharon Feaster, Ed.D., LeTourneau University, Longview, Texas; Donna Owens, M.A., University of Texas at Tyler; and Pauline Travis, Ph.D., Southwestern Oklahoma State University, Weatherford. We would also like to thank Larry B. Kling, Vice President, Editorial, for his overall direction; Pam Weston, Vice President, Publishing, for setting the quality standards for production integrity and managing the publication to completion; John Paul Cording, Vice President, Technology, for coordinating the design, development, and testing of REA's TEST*ware*® software; Amy Jamison, Reena Shah, and Dipen Patel, Project Managers, for their software design contributions and tireless testing efforts; Christine Reilley, Senior Editor, for her editorial contributions; Anne Winthrop Esposito, Senior Editor, for coordinating revisions; Diane Goldschmidt, Associate Editor, for post-production coordination; Christine Saul, Senior Graphic Artist, for creation of artwork; Caragraphics, for coordinating pre-press electronic file mapping; and Network Typesetting, for page composition.

The Best Test Preparation for the

TExES

Texas Examinations of Educator Standards

PPR

Pedagogy & Professional Responsibilities
Tests for EC–4, 4–8, 8–12, and EC–12

With CD-ROM for Windows® –
REA's Interactive TEST*ware*® for the TExES PPR

Stephen C. Anderson, Ph.D.
Tarleton State University
Killeen, Texas

Deborah Jinkins, Ph.D.
Tarleton State University
Killeen, Texas

Stacey L. Edmonson, Ed.D.
Sam Houston State University
Huntsville, Texas

Gail M. Platt, Ph.D.
South Plains College
Levelland, Texas

Steven A. Harris, Ed.D.
Tarleton State University
Killeen, Texas

Luis A. Rosado, Ph.D.
University of Texas at Arlington
Arlington, Texas

Research & Education Association
Visit our website at
www.rea.com

Research & Education Association
61 Ethel Road West
Piscataway, New Jersey 08854
E-mail: info@rea.com

The Best Test Preparation for the TExES PPR
Texas Examinations of Educator Standards
Pedagogy and Professional Responsibilities Tests for EC–4, 4–8,
8–12 and EC–12
With CD-ROM for Windows®
REA's TEST*ware®* for the TExES PPR

Printed in the United States of America

Library of Congress Control Number 2006927995

International Standard Book Number 0-7386-0068-7

Windows® is a trademark of Microsoft Corporation.

 REA® and TEST*ware®* are registered trademarks
of Research & Education Association, Inc.

CONTENTS

About the Authors

Stephen C. Anderson is an assistant professor of curriculum and instruction at Tarleton State University – Central Texas, where he has taught since 1999. He currently teaches undergraduate courses in teacher education and graduate courses in curriculum and instruction. His work experience includes teaching in the Georgetown, Texas, public schools from 1984 to 1999. Dr. Anderson studied abroad in Lima and Huancayo, Peru in 1976 and 1978, as an exchange student and researcher. He holds a doctorate from the University of Texas at Austin and is the author of *J. W. Edgar: Educator for Texas*.

Stacey Edmonson is an assistant professor of educational leadership at Sam Houston State University in Huntsville, Texas. She has experience in Texas public schools as a teacher, principal, and director of special programs. She has also worked extensively with the State Board for Educator Certification on the principal's certification examination. Dr. Edmonson has been an executive board member of the Texas Professors of Educational Administration, and she serves the Education Law Association as the Southwest Region representative for the School Law Reporter. She teaches courses in qualitative research, school law, advanced instructional theory, and research methodologies. She holds an Ed.D. in Educational Administration, with minors in psychology and special education, from Texas A&M University – Commerce.

Steven A. Harris is assistant professor and coordinator of the Tarleton Model for Accelerated Teacher Education (TMATE) post-baccalaureate program at Tarleton State University in Killeen, Texas. He holds a doctorate in education administration from the University of North Texas, where his graduate research has been lauded as a landmark study of Texas teacher attrition as it relates to the different categories of teacher preparation programs. He has successfully worked as an elementary teacher, secondary English teacher, gifted and talented program director/teacher, elementary school, high school, and central office administrator, technology director, and grant writer.

Deborah Jinkins is an assistant professor of curriculum and instruction in reading and writing at Tarleton State University, where she has taught since 2000. She has served as a K–12 public school educator, principal, and central office administrator for 20 years in addition to service at the Texas Education Agency and with one of the Department of Education's regional research labs, Southwest Educational Development Lab (SEDL) in Austin, Texas. She leads in the creation and establishment of two unique school programs: Project LEAP, an alternative school for drop-outs and at-risk high school students, and NYOS Charter School (Not Your Ordinary School). She co-authored *The Character of Leadership: Political Realism and Public Virtue in Non-Profit Organizations* and serves on the editorial board for Reading Psychology. She received a bachelor's degree in Elementary Education from Howard Payne University, a master's degree in Educational Administration and Supervision from Texas Woman's University, and her Ph.D. from Texas A&M University, College Station.

Gail M. Platt is the director of the Teaching and Learning Center and Title III Projects at South Plains College in Levelland, Texas. She holds a Ph.D. degree in human development and a master's degree in English from Texas Tech University. She has been vice-president of the Texas Community College Teachers Association (2000-2001 and 2002-2003) and is president-elect (2003-2004). She is also a past president of the Texas chapter of the College Reading and Learning Association (1994-95) and was an original member of the Texas Academic Skills Council (1987-90), which was instrumental in developing the Texas Academic Skills Program (TASP) in Texas. In 1999, Dr. Platt was named Developmental Educator of the Year in Texas. She has published numerous articles and is a frequent speaker at state, national, and international conferences.

Luis A. Rosado is the director of the Center for Bilingual Education Program at the University of Texas at Arlington. He holds degrees from the University of Puerto Rico, Boston State College, and Texas A & M University-Kingsville. He has published in the areas of parental involvement, cross-cultural communication, and Spanish linguistics. Recent publications include articles in the *National Forum of Educational Admininstation and Supervision Journal*. Dr. Rosado has 21 years of teaching experience at the elementary, high school, and college levels. He has taught in Puerto Rico, Massachusetts, and Texas.

TExES

Texas Examinations of Educator Standards

Introduction

Passing the TExES PPR Tests

INSTALLING REA's TEST*ware*®

SYSTEM REQUIREMENTS

Pentium 75 MHz (300 MHz recommended) or a higher or compatible processor; Microsoft Windows 98 or later; 64 MB available RAM; Internet Explorer 5.5 or higher.

INSTALLATION

1. Insert the TExES TEST*ware*® CD-ROM into the CD-ROM drive.
2. If the installation doesn't begin automatically, from the Start Menu, choose the RUN command. When the RUN dialog box appears, type d:\ setup (where D is the letter of your CD-ROM drive) at the prompt and click OK.
3. The installation process will begin. A dialog box proposing the directory "Program Files\REA\TExES" will appear. If the name and location are suitable, click OK. If you wish to specify a different name or location, type it in and click OK.
4. Start the TExES TEST*ware*® application by double-clicking on the icon.

REA's TExES TEST*ware*® is **EASY** to **LEARN AND USE**. To achieve maximum benefits, we recommend that you take a few minutes to go through the on-screen tutorial on your computer.

TECHNICAL SUPPORT

REA's TEST*ware*® is backed by customer and technical support. For questions about **installation or operation of your software**, contact us at:

Research & Education Association
Phone: (732) 819-8880 (9 a.m. to 5 p.m. ET, Monday–Friday)
Fax: (732) 819-8808
Website: http://www.rea.com
E-mail: info@rea.com

Note to Windows XP Users: In order for the TEST*ware*® to function properly, please install and run the application under the same computer-administrator level user account. Installing the TEST*ware*® as one user and running it as another could cause file access path conflicts.

Introduction

Passing the TExES PPR Tests

ABOUT THIS BOOK & TEST*ware*®

Inside this book you will find a concise, targeted topical review along with a series of practice exams that accurately simulate the Pedagogy and Professional Responsibilities (PPR) tests of the Texas Examinations of Educator Standards battery. These exams are known by the acronym *TExES*, which is pronounced much like *Texas*. The book presents material relevant to the Pedagogy and Professional Responsibilities tests known as PPR EC–4, PPR 4–8, PPR 8–12, and PPR EC–12. REA's subject review is designed to provide you with the information and strategies needed to pass these exams. This book contains four full-length practice tests based on the most recently administered TExES PPR tests. You are given five hours to complete the actual test, so we do likewise for our practice tests. REA's model tests contain every type of question that you can expect to encounter on the TExES PPR tests. Following each practice test, you will find an answer key with detailed explanations designed to help you master the material.

The practice tests in this book and software package are included in two formats. They are in printed form in this book, and in TEST*ware*® format on the enclosed CD. **We recommend that you begin your preparation by first taking the practice exams on your computer.** The software provides timed conditions and instantaneous, accurate scoring, which make it easier to pinpoint your strengths and weaknesses.

ABOUT THE TEST

Who takes the test and what is it used for?

The TExES is taken by individuals seeking teacher certification in Texas. If you meet any one of the following criteria, you are eligible to take the test:

- Completed an approved educator preparation program at a Texas college or university

- Enrolled in an alternative certification program and in the second semester of a one-year internship

- Fully certified in another state or country other than the U.S. and seek certification in Texas

- Enrolled in the last semester of an educator preparation program at a Texas college or university on the date that the test is administered

- Hold a current one-year certificate issued by the Texas Education Agency

- Are a post-baccalaureate student eligible to take a test

- Are enrolled in a program at a Texas university in the spring semester before a summer completion on the date of the test administration

- Hold a valid Texas classroom certificate and a bachelor's degree, and seek additional certification

What is the format of the TExES PPR?

Each Pedagogy and Professional Responsibilities (PPR) test contains approximately ninety multiple-choice questions designed to assess your knowledge of the information described in the competencies included in our review sections. Eighty of the items are scored and about ten of the questions are experimental or pilot questions (that will not be included in your score). You will be given four choices (A, B, C, or D) from which to select the best answer to each item.

You'll find three different kinds of multiple-choice questions on the TExES:

- Some of the questions are so-called single-answer items; these questions are direct or require a sentence completion and address a single competency.

- Some questions are cluster items, which are preceded by a short passage or scenario. Your answer will be based on the information presented in the passage, not on your own experiences. It will need to be based on careful analysis of the event or situation, solving a problem presented in the passage or making a decision based on the information you are given.

- Finally, the test may contain one or more Teacher Decision Sets that present situations that a teacher could potentially face while on the job. The Teacher Decision Sets (TDS) start with a stimulus or general scenario. One or two questions are based on the original scenario and then further stimuli are presented that lead to more questions. These further stimuli stem from the original stimulus. Generally, the TDS will contain two or more stimuli and three to twelve questions in total. The questions may address competencies from all domains of the test. All of the questions are about general principles and concepts in education.

What is the difference between the different versions of the test?

The competencies tested on the four versions of the TExES Pedagogy and Professional Responsibilities tests are identical. There is no difference in subject matter—only the scenarios are placed in different, age-appropriate settings. These different settings address the developmental differences in individuals at various ages and the breadth and depth of content appropriate to those individuals.

The TExES framework is designed to provide greater specificity by focusing on content areas for those who wish to teach in kindergarten through grade four and by providing a broader assessment (in terms of both breadth and depth of knowledge) for those teaching grades eight through twelve. The TExES testing program is aligned with, and thus serves as good preparation for teaching the state curriculum in Texas, the Texas Essential Knowledge and Skills (TEKS).

Which test should I take?

The TExES PPR is more specific than previous certification exams. The version of the test you take depends on the level of certification you seek and the level of students you most want to teach. If you want to teach younger students (kindergarten through fourth grade), you should take the PPR EC–4. If you want to teach grades four through eight, you should take the PPR 4–8. You should take the PPR 8–12 if you're planning to teach grades eight through twelve. If you seek all-level certification, you should take the PPR EC–12.

In addition to the Pedagogy and Professional Responsibilities test appropriate for the level you wish to teach, you will need to take a content-specific test. Both the Texas State Board for Educator Certification (SBEC) and your school can provide you with a complete list of all available content-specific tests.

While you are not required to take both the TExES PPR test and a content-area test on the same day, it is recommended that you do so. Do consider, however, that each test session is five hours[†] long.

Who administers the test?

The TExES is developed and administered by National Evaluation Systems, Inc., (NES) in cooperation with the Texas State Board for Educator Certification (SBEC). A test development process was designed and is implemented to ensure that the content and difficulty level of the test are appropriate and based on a state aim of aligning the school curriculum from grade to grade, from kindergarten through college.

[†]The TExES PPR tests are considered half-session tests. Taking two half-session tests in a single session will give you five hours for *both*. Consult your registration bulletin for details.

When should the TExES PPR be taken?

The test should be taken just before or after graduation for those seeking certification right out of school. The TExES is a requirement to teach in Texas, so if you are planning on being an educator, you must take and pass this test.

If you don't do well on the TExES, don't panic! You can take it again, and in fact many candidates do. A score on the TExES that does not match your expectations should not change your plans about teaching.

When and where is the test given?

The TExES is usually administered six times a year at several locations throughout Texas. The usual testing day is Saturday, but the test may be taken on an alternate day if a conflict, such as a religious obligation, exists.

The TExES Registration Bulletin offers information about test dates and locations, as well as registration information and how to make testing accommodations for those with special needs. To receive a registration bulletin, contact:

TExES Program
National Evaluation Systems, Inc.
P.O. Box 140467
Austin, TX 78714-0467
Phone: (512) 927-5151 or (800) 523-7088
TDD: (512) 926-1248

Registration bulletins are also available at education departments of Texas colleges and universities.

The Texas State Board for Educator Certification (SBEC) can be reached at (888) 863-5880 or (512) 469-3008 or via e-mail at sbec@sbec.state.tx.us. You can also find information about the test and registration on the SBEC website at http://www.sbec.state.tx.us.

Is there a registration fee?

To take the TExES, you must pay a registration fee. If you are using the registration form, all fees must be paid in full by personal check, cashier's check, or money order payable to NES. All payments must be made in U.S. dollars. Cash will not be accepted. If you are registering via the Internet or phone during the emergency registration period, payment must be made by VISA or MasterCard.

HOW TO USE THIS BOOK

About the Review Sections

The reviews in this book are designed to help you sharpen the basic skills needed to approach the TExES, as well as provide strategies for attacking the questions. By using the reviews in conjunction with the practice tests, you will be better prepared for the actual test.

Each chapter covers a separate domain. The reviews extensively discuss the competencies contained in the domain and include sample questions based on each competency. They will give you a better understanding of what the TExES measures.

You have learned most of what you need to succeed on the test through your schooling. The classes you took should have provided you with the knowledge necessary to make important decisions about situations you will face as a teacher. Our topical review is designed to help you fit the information you have acquired into specific competencies. Reviewing your class notes and textbooks along with studying our domain reviews will give you an excellent start towards passing the TExES.

When should I start studying?

It is never too early to start studying for the TExES. The earlier you begin, the more time you will have to sharpen your skills. Do not procrastinate! Cramming is *not* an effective way to study, since it does not allow you the time needed to learn the test material.

The importance of careful reading and critical thinking cannot be overlooked in preparing for the TExES. Set aside regular periods of time each day for prolonged reading in order to develop the reading stamina required for successfully completing this type of test. Consider and explore different reading methods to find those that are most effective for you. For example, you should skim material and then summarize main ideas and key details in your own words. You should also practice scanning text to locate specific answers or examples. Practice until you have developed flexibility in your reading and have a repertoire of strategies to use as the situation demands.

You should have plenty of time in which to complete the TExES, but be aware of the amount of time you spent on each question so that you allow enough time to complete the test. Although speed is not very important, a steady pace should be maintained when answering the questions. The practice tests will help you prepare for this task.

What do I study first?

Read over the competency reviews and the suggestions for test-taking. Studying the competencies thoroughly will reinforce the basic skills you need to do well on the exam. Within the review section of this book, the competencies are broken down into a competency statement and a description of what the competency covers. Make sure to take the practice tests to become familiar with the format and procedures involved with taking the actual TExES.

To best utilize your study time, follow our TExES PPR Study Schedule located in the front of this book. The schedule is based on a seven-week program, but can be condensed to four weeks if necessary.

How should I study for the TExES PPR?

It is very important for you to choose the time and place for studying that works best for you. Some individuals set aside a certain number of hours every morning to study, while others choose to study at night before going to sleep. Others study during the day, while waiting in line, or even while eating lunch. Only you can determine when and where your study time will be most effective. Be consistent and use your time wisely; work out a study routine and stick to it.

Consider a visit to your local college or university learning resources center or academic support center to explore your individual learning style. It would also be a good opportunity to discover what kind of support is offered to individuals planning to take the TExES.

When you take the practice tests, try to make your testing conditions as much like the actual test as possible. Turn your television and radio off and sit down at a quiet table free from distraction.

As you complete each practice test, score your test and thoroughly review the explanations to the questions you answered incorrectly; however, do not review too much at any one time. Concentrate on one problem area at a time by reviewing the question and explanation and studying our review until you are confident that you completely understand the material.

Keep track of your scores so that you will be able to gauge your progress and discover general weaknesses in particular sections. You should carefully study the reviews that cover your areas of difficulty, as this will build your skills in those areas.

TExES PPR STUDY SCHEDULE

The following study course schedule* allows for thorough preparation to pass the TExES Pedagogy and Professional Responsibilities (PPR) tests. Since this is a suggested seven-week course of study, you may want to use more time to study the TExES review and other supplementary materials. Be sure to keep a structured schedule by setting aside ample time each day to study. Depending on your schedule you may find it easier to study through the weekend. No matter which schedule works best for you, however, the more time you devote to studying for the TExES, the more prepared and confident you will be on the day of the actual test.

*Note that each of this book's practice tests is based on a unique TExES PPR test. While these model tests will tend to build on each other, readers are advised to take into account the subject matter they most want to focus on.

Week	Activity
1	Take one TEST*ware* practice test as a diagnostic exam. Your score will be an indication of your strengths and weaknesses. Review the explanations for the questions you answered incorrectly.
2	Study REA's TExES Review. Highlight key terms and information. Take notes on the important educational theories and key educators, as writing will aid in your retention of information.
3 and 4	Review your references and sources, and the references given in this book. Consult your education textbooks. Use any other supplementary material which your counselor or the Texas Education Agency suggests.
5	Condense your notes and findings. You should have a structured outline detailing specific facts. You may want to use index cards to aid you in memorizing important facts and concepts. Take a second full-length TEST*ware* practice exam. Review the explanations for the questions you answered incorrectly.
6	Test yourself using the index cards. You may want to have a friend or colleague quiz you on key facts and items. Take a third full-length TEST*ware* practice exam. Review the explanations for the questions you answered incorrectly.
7	Study any areas you consider to be your weaknesses by using your study materials, references, and notes. Take the fourth TEST*ware* practice test. Again review the explanations for the questions you answered incorrectly. You may retake any of the other practice exams provided in this book.

SCORING THE TExES PPR

How is the TExES PPR scored?

While the exact number of test items varies from test to test, the TExES PPR features about 90 questions. No matter how many questions are on a specific form of the test, however, only 80 of them will be scored. The other questions are included for developmental purposes only. This is a way for National Evaluation Systems to try out new questions.

Your raw score for the TExES is determined by totaling the number of correct answers. Your raw score will then be converted into a scaled score between 100 and 300. You must earn a scaled score of 240 in order to pass the test. The scaled score is not a set percentage of items answered correctly because no two forms of a TExES test are exactly identical. A scaled score makes up for these differences in order to maintain fairness for all test-takers. Thus, the number of correct answers needed may vary; while on one test 53 correct answers may equate to a scaled score of 240, you might need 57 correct answers on another version of the same test. Roughly spoken, you need about 70% of correct answers in order to pass the test (though this may be as low as 65% on one test, and as high as 72% on another).

How do I calculate my score for the practice tests?

The practice tests in this book contain ninety questions so that you can get a good feeling of how much time you have available for each question on the actual exam. (Remember, you don't know which questions *won't* be scored so you have to answer each question on the actual exam.)

For the practice tests in this book, you need to answer 70% of all questions correctly in order to get a passing score. To figure out if you have achieved this, simply count the number of questions you answered correctly. If you have answered more than 63 questions correctly, you have passed the test.

If your score is not as high as you expected, don't worry. With each practice test, you are building skills to do well on the TExES PPR.

When will I receive my score report and what will it look like?

Your score report should arrive about four weeks after you take the test. If you have not received your test results two weeks after the score report mailing date noted on the test registration bulletin, contact NES at (800) 523-7088.

Unofficial score report information is available on the Internet at www.texes. nesinc.com. You can access your unofficial score after 5 p.m. central time on the score report mailing date of each test administration.

A copy of your score report is sent to the institution indicated on your registration form and to the SBEC. If you need an additional copy of your score report after two months past the test administration date, you can obtain one for $15 by calling NES for up to five years after the test date.

TExES PPR TEST-TAKING TIPS

Although you may not be familiar with tests such as the TExES, this book will help acquaint you with this type of examination and help alleviate your test-taking anxieties. Listed below are ways to help you become accustomed to the TExES, some of which may be applied to other tests as well.

• *Get comfortable with the format of the TExES.* When you are practicing, simulate the conditions under which you will be taking the actual test. Stay calm and pace yourself. After simulating the test only once, you will boost your chances of doing well, and you will be able to sit down for the actual TExES with much more confidence.

• *Read all of the possible answers.* Just because you think you have found the correct response, do not automatically assume that it is the best answer. Read through each choice to be sure that you are not making a mistake by jumping to conclusions.

• *Use the process of elimination.* Go through each answer to a question and eliminate as many of the answer choices as possible. By eliminating two answer choices, you have given yourself a better chance of getting the item correct since there will only be two choices left from which to make your guess. Do not leave an answer blank; it is better to guess than not to answer a question on the TExES.

• *Work quickly and steadily.* You will have five hours to complete the test, so work quickly and steadily to avoid focusing on any one problem too long. Taking the practice tests in this book will help you learn to budget your precious time.

• *Learn the directions and format of the test.* Familiarizing yourself with the directions and format of the test will not only save time, but will also help you avoid nervousness (and the mistakes caused by getting nervous).

• *Develop reading stamina.* Reading for four or more hours at one sitting requires a good deal of stamina. Practice reading for longer stretches. Practice various reading strategies: skimming for main ideas and general information, scanning for details and specific information, and careful reading for memory. Upon completing a passage, think back and summarize what you have read. Be sure you are reading to understand ideas and concepts, not merely reading the words.

• *Be sure that the answer circle you are marking corresponds to the number of the question in the test booklet.* Since the test is multiple-choice, it is graded by machine, and marking one wrong answer can throw off your answer key and your score. Be extremely careful.

THE DAY OF THE TEST

Before the Test

On the day of the test, you should wake up early (after a decent night's rest, we hope) and have a good breakfast. Make sure to dress comfortably, so that you are not distracted by being too hot or too cold while taking the test. Plan to arrive at the test center early. This will allow you to collect your thoughts and relax before the test, and will also spare you the anguish that comes with being late. You should arrive at the test center at 7:30 a.m. for the morning administration, or 1:30 p.m. for the afternoon session.

Before you leave for the test center, make sure that you have your admission ticket and two forms of identification (e.g., driver's license), one of which must contain a recent photograph, your name, and signature. You will not be admitted to the test center without proper identification.

You must bring several No. 2 pencils with erasers, as none will be provided at the test center.

If you would like, you may wear a watch to the test center. However, you may not wear one that makes noise, because it may disturb the other test takers. No dictionaries, textbooks, notebooks, calculators (save for Mathematics Test 17, for which you may bring your own calculator, so long as it is one of the brands and models specified in the TExES bulletin), briefcases, or packages will be permitted. Drinking, smoking, and eating are prohibited.

During the Test

The TExES is administered in one sitting with no breaks. Procedures will be followed to maintain test security.

Once you enter the test center, follow all of the rules and instructions given by the test supervisor. If you do not, you risk being dismissed from the test and having your scores cancelled.

When all of the materials have been distributed, the test instructor will give you directions for filling out your answer sheet. Fill out this sheet carefully since this information will be printed on your score report.

During the test, be sure to mark only one answer per question, erase unwanted answers and marks completely, and fill in answers darkly and neatly.

After the Test

When you finish your test, hand in your materials and you will be dismissed. Then, go home and relax—you deserve it!

TExES

Texas Examinations of Educator Standards

Chapter 1

Domain I:
Designing Instruction

Chapter 1

DOMAIN I:
Designing Instruction and Assessment to Promote Student Learning

Regardless of the age of the students or the discipline taught, teachers must understand learners. Benjamin Bloom (1976) has suggested that students' cognitive entry skills and intelligence (or IQ) account for about 50 percent of what students achieve academically; 25 percent can be attributed to the quality of instruction students receive; the remaining 25 percent can be attributed to affective characteristics of the students. Those affective characteristics include such things as the learner's personality, self-concept, locus of control, attitudes, level of anxiety, and study habits. Therefore, although it is important that teachers acquire and utilize effective teaching techniques and provide quality instruction to students, it can be argued that it is even more important in terms of educational outcomes that teachers understand cognitive and affective factors that influence student performance.

The traditional view of education saw the learner as a *tabula rasa*, a blank slate, upon which the teacher wrote knowledge. In this model, the student was assumed to be an empty vessel; he or she came into the classroom knowing nothing. It was the teacher's responsibility, as the expert, to impart knowledge or to fill the empty vessel.

Today, cognitive psychologists have corrected this faulty notion. Educators now recognize that students bring to the classroom an array of personal characteristics and experiences upon which they base their present knowledge and acquire new understanding. Those characteristics and experiences may or may not be congruent to the teacher's background; nonetheless, they constitute a knowledge base for the learner. Therefore, the teacher's role is to activate the learner's prior knowledge and help the student connect new information with what is already known. Thus, in today's educational model, the student is seen as an active learner who brings much to the classroom.

The effective teacher, then, must go beyond assuming the role of a "sage on the stage." The effective teacher must be more than just an expert who has mastered a discipline or body of knowledge. The effective teacher must be a facilitator of learning; an effective teacher empowers students to learn for and by themselves. The effective teacher, in other words, is a "guide by the side" of students, assisting them in the process of learning and enhancing that process for students.

In preparing for the TExES, prospective teachers will be required to answer a series of questions assessing their ability *to design instruction and assessment to promote student learning.* This domain will include questions that address the following four competencies:

001. The teacher understands human development processes and applies this knowledge to plan instruction and ongoing assessment that motivate students and are responsive to their developmental characteristics and needs.

002. The teacher understands student diversity and knows how to plan learning experiences and design assessments that are responsive to differences among students and that promote all students' learning.

003. The teacher understands procedures for designing effective and coherent instruction and assessment based on appropriate learning goals and objectives.

004. The teacher understands learning processes and factors that impact student learning and demonstrates this knowledge by planning effective, engaging instruction and appropriate assessments.

In the pages that follow, each of these competencies will be addressed at some length. An example of the kind of question that might be used to assess the competency will also be presented and discussed. Although the competencies are listed separately and will be addressed separately, it is important to remember that these competencies are interconnected and intricately interrelated; thus, theories of human development are important in evaluating environmental and contextual factors, which in turn affect the educator's view of diversity, which in turn affects the teacher's instructional practices, which in turn play a significant role in influencing motivation in the classroom. Teachers must consistently address issues of instruction and assessment in regard to developmental ages/stages of learners, motivating learners, diversity of learning and other characteristics/factors described in various competencies of the TExES.

COMPETENCY 001

The teacher understands human development processes and applies this knowledge to plan instruction and ongoing assessment that motivate students and are responsive to their developmental characteristics and needs.

This competency relates to the importance of teachers having a basic understanding of the principles of human development in its many dimensions: physically, mentally or cognitively, emotionally, and socially. It is also important that teachers appreciate a dynamic and interactive view of human development. This approach to understanding human development is one which recognizes that human beings do not develop in a vacuum. People exist in an environment that, friendly or unfriendly, supportive or nonsupportive, evokes and provokes reactions from individuals; moreover, it is not a one-way street with the environment doing all the driving. People also act in certain ways to shape and form their environment. There is a constant interaction or interplay between people and their environments. Thus, effective teachers must be sensitive to and knowledgeable of both personal characteristics of students and characteristics of their environment.

Student Development and Maturation

A teacher does not have to be an expert in anatomy and physiology to see the physical changes that accompany students' growth and maturity. Teachers must also be aware of the multiplicity of issues affecting physical growth and maturation. For example, teachers must take into account the role of proper nutrition, adequate rest and physical activity, and the undue influence of drug abuse on students' academic performance and social interactions.

Many studies have underscored the importance of good nutrition in providing the foundation for academic success. For this reason, school breakfast and lunch programs provide free meals to students with limited financial resources. For some students, these free meals may be their only source of nutrition. Too often, children consume too much fast food – dense in simple carbohydrates and refined sugars – and not enough of the nutrients and vitamins required for building strong bones and maintaining muscle tone.

Likewise, studies have consistently demonstrated that today's children are prone to lead sedentary lifestyles – spending many hours in front of the television and computer screen or playing video games – and lack the physical activity and exercise required for good health. Physical education and other school activities then assume an even more important role in the school day.

Children need enough sleep to be able to stay awake and participate in their classes. Concentration and focus are lacking when students are tired. Their immunity breaks down and they are less resistant to illnesses when they lack sufficient sleep and rest. Because many families are hard-pressed to provide adequate supervision at home, children may stay up too late. High school students are often working at jobs where they are required to work late hours, meaning they do not get the rest they need in order to be prepared for the school day. Teachers need to be aware of these factors and anticipate remedies or ways to address these issues with children's parents and caretakers. Often, parenting education programs provided through the local school districts are aimed at addressing these issues.

The Problems of Substance Abuse

Another problem that merits the teacher's attention is the effect of drug use. This can take many forms. A child may show developmental delays (cognitively, socially, physically, and psychologically) because of prenatal drug abuse by parents. Mothers who drink alcohol during pregnancy may give birth to infants with fetal alcohol syndrome (FAS). These individuals have a distinct pattern of facial abnormalities, growth retardation, and evidence of central nervous system dysfunction. Even those who do not have the characteristic facial abnormalities and growth retardation associated with FAS have brain and other neurological deficits such as poor motor skills, hand-eye coordination problems, and complex behavioral and learning problems, including difficulties with memory, attention, and judgment. The National Organization on Fetal Alcohol Syndrome provides extensive information about individuals with FAS and effective strategies for working with these individuals.

Alcohol consumption itself causes a number of marked changes in behavior. Even low doses significantly impair judgment and coordination. Low to moderate doses of alcohol also increase the incidence of aggressive acts. Moderate to high doses of alcohol cause marked impairment of higher mental functions, severely altering a person's ability to learn and remember information. Very high doses cause respiratory depression and death. If combined with other depressants of the central nervous system, much lower doses of alcohol will produce the more significant effects just described. Repeated use of alcohol can lead to dependence. Sudden cessation of alcohol intake is likely to produce withdrawal symptoms, including severe anxiety, tremors, hallucinations, and convulsions. In fact, alcohol withdrawal can be life-threatening. On the other hand, long-term consumption of large quantities of alcohol, particularly when combined with poor nutrition, can also lead to permanent damage to vital organs such as the brain and the liver.

In a nationwide study conducted 1997 by the U.S. Centers for Disease Control and Prevention, over 79 percent of students in grades 9 – 12 reported that they have had at least one alcoholic drink during their lifetime. Nearly one-third of these students indicated that they had their first drink (more than a few sips) before the age of 13.

Moreover, almost 6 percent of students said that they had at least one alcoholic drink on school property on one of the 30 days preceding their participation in the national survey. Almost 17 percent of the students surveyed said that they had driven a vehicle one or more times after drinking alcohol during the 30 days before participating in the study.

This same study revealed that over 47 percent of high school students had used marijuana during their lifetime. The study also found that:

- 8.2 percent used some form of cocaine

- 3.1 percent used some form of illegal steroids

- 2.1 percent injected illegal drugs

Seventeen percent reported other illegal drug use, including LSD (lysergic acid diethylamide), PCP (phencyclidine), "ecstasy" (methylenedioxymethamphetamine), "speed" (amphetamine), "ice" (methamphetamine), or heroin.

Children whose parents are using illegal drugs or who use illegal drugs themselves will also often present troubling behaviors that disrupt classrooms and the learning of others, not to mention the negative effects on their own academic progress. Drug use impairs judgment, reaction time, and reduces inhibitions. Faulty thinking can quickly lead to conflict or violence; for example, drug use may contribute to a student escalating a conflict that would have been taken in stride if the student had not been under the influence. Drug use is directly tied to violence in the schools since drug sales and related activities also contribute to school violence. Disputes between rival dealers, between dealers and buyers, and even between rival gangs can set the stage for fighting and other acts of violence. Students involved in drug-related activities may be more likely to carry weapons. Efforts to prevent drug abuse can have an impact on decreasing school conflict and violence.

Teachers must take note of warning signs and symptoms of drug use and, while safeguarding issues of student confidentiality, be prepared to make a referral to the school counselor(s) or psychologist when an intervention is required. The Center for Substance Abuse Prevention lists the following individual risk factors for drug abuse:

- Rebelliousness

- Friends who engage in the problem behavior

- Favorable attitudes about drug use

- Early initiation of the problem behavior

- Negative relationships with adults

- Risk-taking propensity/impulsivity

Combined with these individual risk factors are peer group risk factors (such as peer pressure), family risk factors (including family history of risky behaviors, family conflict, family management problems, parental attitudes and involvement in drug use), school risk factors (such as early and persistent antisocial behaviors, academic failure beginning in elementary school, and low school commitment), community risk factors (including availability of drugs, community law/norms favorable to drug use, extreme economic and social deprivation, transition and mobility, and low neighborhood attachment and community disorganization), and, finally, social risk factors (impoverishment, unemployment/underemployment, discrimination, and pro-drug messages in the media).

Warning Signs for Violence

Experts tend to agree that drug use (including alcohol use) and other high-risk behaviors are inextricably linked to violence. Because of events like the Columbine shootings, teachers must be ever vigilant. Some of the common warning signs that students could be at risk for violent behavior are listed below:

- History of being violent toward his/her peers

- Access to firearms

- Involved in drinking alcohol or taking other drugs

- Caregivers have a history of drug/alcohol involvement

- Peer group reinforces antisocial behaviors

- Learned attitudes accepting aggressive behaviors as "normal" and an effective way to solve problems

- High level of violence in the home, in the neighborhood, and in the media

- School history that includes aggressive and disruptive classroom behavior

- Poor school achievement, poor school attendance, and numerous school suspensions

- Difficulty with social skills and poor peer relations

- Difficulty controlling his/her impulses and emotions

- History of parental rejection, inconsistent discipline, and lack of supervision

Of course, the parallel between these warning signs of potentially violent behavior and those of potential drug use is obvious. Often, although not always, the students with drug problems are the same ones with a proclivity for violent behavior.

Even though there is no precise way to predict when a person will become violent, there are some "triggers" that should cause teachers to be alert and pay close attention. These include the following:

- Irrational beliefs and ideas

- Verbal, nonverbal, or written threats or intimidation

- Fascination with weaponry and/or acts of violence

- Expressions of a plan to hurt himself or others

- Externalization of blame

- Unreciprocated romantic obsession

- Taking up much of teacher's time with behavior or performance problems

- Fear reaction among fellow students or family

- Drastic change in belief systems

- Displays of unwarranted anger

- New or increased source(s) of stress at home or school

- Inability to take criticism

- Feelings of being victimized

- Intoxication from alcohol or other substances

- Expressions of hopelessness or heightened anxiety

- Productivity and/or attendance problems

- Violence towards inanimate objects

- Stealing or sabotaging projects or equipment

- Lack of concern for the safety of others

When teachers observe these warning "triggers," they must be increasingly aware of the possibility of a crisis situation. Experts on coping with school crises say educators must accept reality. Violence can occur—it can happen to you and your school—and that while teachers and administrators must be alert and aware, safety is an "inside issue" and must involve a committed student body, faculty/staff, and community.

If a crisis does occur, there are certain things that teachers should do as part of the school response team. These include the following:

- Providing accurate information to students

- Leading class discussions to give everyone the opportunity to express his/her feelings, ideas, and concerns

- Dispelling rumors by truthfully answering questions

- Modeling appropriate responses of care and concern

- Giving permission for a range of emotions

- Identifying students who need counseling

- Providing activities to reduce trauma and express emotions through artwork, music, and writing

- Setting aside curriculum as needed

- Discussing funeral procedures including customs and etiquette

- Encouraging parents to accompany their children to funerals (Southeastern Regional Vision for Education, 2002)

Teachers can either be part of the solution or part of the problem. Armed with information and taking the time to contemplate their role in a crisis, teachers can provide students with important support and guidance in worst-case scenarios.

School Safety

Suggestions for ways schools can ensure safety and combat drug use are provided by the U. S. Department of Education in its publication for *Creating Safe and Drug-Free Schools: An Action Guide*. Among the recommendations are the following:

- Establish a team of educators, students, parents, law enforcement, juvenile justice officials, and community leaders to develop a plan for a safe and drug-free school

- Ensure that students are engaged in schoolwork that is challenging, informative, and rewarding

- Establish, publish, publicize, and enforce policies that clearly define acceptable and unacceptable behavior with zero tolerance for weapons, violence, gangs, and use or sale of alcohol and drugs

- Take immediate action on all reports of drug use or sales, threats, bullying, gang activity, or victimization

- Create an environment that encourages parents and other adults to visit the school and participate in activities

- Encourage staff to treat students and each other with respect

- Involve youth in policy and program development

- Offer programs that teach peaceful, nonviolent methods for managing conflict to students, their families, and school staff

- Work with the media to increase public awareness of safety issues

Although the concepts presented in this section have to do with student behaviors, these ideas are also integral to Competency 005, which deals with creating safe environments for learning. This, again, is an example of how teaching is not simply a set of discrete skills, but the interplay and interconnectedness of skills, abilities, attitudes, and competencies that allow teachers to deal successfully with all elements of teaching effectiveness.

Physiological Development

Even though a pre-school child may have trouble grasping pencils or crayons in a manner to facilitate handwriting, most two-year-olds can grasp crayons sufficiently to make marks on papers and, therefore, enjoy the creative excitement of art. Thus, physiological changes play a significant role in the development of children as they increase their control of bodily movements and functions and refine their motor skills. Their ability to engage in simple to complex classroom and playground activities increases as they develop. Classroom and playground activities must be adjusted and adapted in order to be developmentally appropriate for the skill levels of the children.

As students enter junior high or begin their secondary education, they again experience important physiological changes with the onset of puberty. With puberty comes changes in primary sexual characteristics and the emergence of secondary sexual characteristics. In addition to bodily characteristics, there is a change in bodily feelings and an increase in sex drive.

Girls, on average, reach maturational milestones before boys. Physical changes may cause embarrassment to both females and males when they draw unwelcome attention; moreover, these changes almost always create some discomfort as adolescents find the body they were familiar and comfortable with to be quite different, sometimes seemingly overnight.

David Elkind has noted two developmental characteristics of adolescence that share a relationship to the physiological changes accompanying maturation. These two characteristics are the *imaginary audience* and the *personal fable*. Adolescents, preoccupied with their own physiological changes, often assume that others are equally intrigued by these changes in appearance and behavior. They may feel that others are staring at them, watching their every move, scrutinizing their behavior for one misstep, or their appearance for any flaws. If everyone is watching, then it is imperative to be, to act, and to look just right. In today's culture, that means wearing the right clothes and having all the right brand names and status symbols. Because of adolescents' sensitivity to attention (especially the wrong kind of attention – that is, not fitting in, not being "right"), it is especially important that teachers of this age group be aware of the *imaginary audience* phenomenon and be sensitive to social interactions in the classroom. It, indeed, is important that teachers not contribute to creating unwanted attention or to stigmatizing or stereotyping students.

Personal fable refers to the belief that "my life is different from everyone else's; therefore, no one can understand how I feel or what I think. No one has ever felt or thought what I feel and think." This out-of-focus view tends to support both a feeling of isolation (which may be precipitated by the changing sensations from a body that is undergoing biological changes) and a willingness to engage in risky behavior (thinking that only others have car accidents when they drive dangerously or only other girls get pregnant when they have unprotected sexual relations—"It won't happen to me.").

In sum, these two characteristics of adolescence are examples of how physical changes accompany, and perhaps even evoke, emotional and cognitive changes as individuals grow and mature. Both phenomena of *imaginary audience* and *personal fable* have emotional features (fear of rejection, fear of isolation, fear of difference, shame, guilt from increased sexual feelings, frustration, and so forth) and both describe a feature of adolescent cognitive ability: the ability to think about one's self as an object of one's own and other's thought. The developmental epistemologist Jean Piaget explained that this way of thinking represents the cognitive stage of formal operations.

Cognition is a term commonly used to refer to all the processes whereby knowledge is acquired; the term can be used to cover very basic perceptual processes—such as smell, touch, sound, and so forth—to very advanced operations, such as analysis, synthesis, and critical thinking.

Theories of Cognitive Development

Until his death in 1980, Jean Piaget was a predominant figure in the field of cognitive psychology. It is safe to postulate that perhaps no other single individual has had greater influence on educational practices than Piaget. Basically, his theory of cognitive development is based on the notion that cognitive abilities (or one's ability to think) are developed as individuals mature physiologically and they have opportunities to interact with their environment. Piaget described these interactions as the *equilibration* of *accommodation* and *assimilation* cycles or processes. In other words, when individuals (who, according to Piaget, are innately endowed with certain cognitive predispositions and capabilities) encounter a new or novel stimulus, they are brought into a state of *disequilibrium.*

That is a way of saying that they are thrown off balance; they do not know or understand that which is new or unfamiliar. However, through the complementary processes of *accommodation* (or adjusting prior knowledge gained through former experiences and interactions) and *assimilation* (fitting together the new information with what has been previously known or understood), individuals come to know or understand that which is new. Once again, individuals are returned to a state of *equilibrium* where they remain until the next encounter with an unfamiliar something. For Piaget, this is how learners learn.

Piaget also predicted that certain behaviors and ways of thinking characterize individuals at different ages. For this reason, his theory is considered a *stage* theory. *Stage* theories share the common tenet that certain characteristics will occur in predictable sequences and at certain times in the life of the individual.

According to Piaget, there are four stages of cognitive development, beginning with the *sensorimotor* stage describing individuals from birth to around the age of two. The second stage, *preoperational* (describing cognitive behavior between the ages of two and seven), is characterized by egocentrism, rigidity of thought, semilogical reasoning, and limited social cognition; some cognitive psychologists have observed that this stage seems to describe how individuals think more in terms of what they can't do than what they can do. This stage describes the way that children in pre-school and kindergarten go about problem-solving; also, many children in the primary grades may be at this stage in their cognitive development.

The next two stages, however, may be most important for elementary and secondary school teachers since they describe cognitive development during the times that most students are in school. The third stage, *concrete operations,* is the beginning of operational thinking and describes the thinking of children between the ages of seven and eleven. Learners at this age begin to decenter. They are able to take into consideration viewpoints other than their own. They can perform transformations, meaning that they can understand reversibility, inversion, reciprocity, and conservation. They can group items into categories. They can make inferences about reality and engage in inductive reasoning; they increase their quantitative skills and can manipulate symbols if given concrete examples with which to work. This stage of cognitive development is the threshold to higher-level learning for students.

Finally, *formal operations* is the last stage of cognitive development and opens wide the door for higher-ordered, critical thinking. This stage describes the way of thinking for learners between the ages of 11 and 15 and, for Piaget, constitutes the ultimate stage of cognitive development (thus also describing adult thinking). Learners at this stage of cognitive development can engage in logical, abstract, and hypothetical thought; they can use the scientific method, meaning they can formulate hypotheses, isolate influences, and identify cause-and-effect relationships. They can plan and anticipate verbal cues. They can engage in both deductive and inductive reasoning, and they can operate on verbal statements exclusive of concrete experiences or examples. These cognitive abilities characterize the highest levels of thought.

Another theoretical approach to understanding human development is offered by Erik Erikson, another important stage theorist, who described psychosocial development. For each of eight stages, he identified a developmental task explained in terms of two polarities. For the purposes of this discussion, only those stages describing school-age individuals will be included.

According to Erikson, pre-schoolers and primary school-aged children must be able to function in the outside world independently of parents. When children are able to do this, they achieve a sense of *initiative*; when children are not able to move away from total parental attachment and control, they experience a sense of *guilt*. Thus, this stage of psychosocial development is the stage of initiative versus guilt. The child's first venture away from home and into the world of school has considerable significance when viewed in light of this theory; it is imperative that teachers assist students in their first experiences on their own, away from parental control. Teachers must plan and structure activities that will allow each student to have some control over his or her environment, to make some decisions, and to experience a sense of accomplishment. This can be done by allowing students to select between two choices of activity to demonstrate a skill, to put away materials in the appropriate place, and to work on a self-selected project.

Erikson's next stage of development is one involving a tension between *industry* and *inferiority*. For example, if the child who enters school (thus achieving initiative) acquires the skills (including academic skills such as reading, writing, and computation, as well as social skills that include playing with others, communicating with others, and forming friendships, and so forth) that enable her or him to be successful in school, then the child achieves a sense of industry; failure to achieve these skills leads to a sense of inferiority. Teachers must individualize instruction and structure activities that will allow each student to experience a measure of success.

Identity Achievement and Diffusion

Around the time students enter junior high, they begin the developmental task of achieving *identity*. According to Erikson, the struggle to achieve identity is one of the most important developmental tasks and one which creates serious psychosocial problems for adolescents. For example, even the individual who has successfully achieved all the important developmental milestones (such as initiative and industry) now finds him- or herself in a state of flux: Everything (body, feelings, thoughts) is changing. The adolescent starts to ask, "Who am I?" Erikson believed that if adolescents find out what they believe in, what their goals, ideas, and values are, then they attain identity achievement; failure to discover these things leads to identity diffusion.

By the time many students reach high school, they are entering the stage of young adulthood, for Erikson a psychosocial stage characterized by the polarities of *intimacy* and *isolation*. Individuals at this stage of development begin to think about forming lasting friendships, even marital unions. Erikson would argue that many psychosocial problems experienced by young adults have their origin in the individual's failure to achieve identity during the preceding stage; the young person who does not know who he or she really is cannot achieve true intimacy.

For the classroom teacher, knowledge of psychosocial stages of human development can result in greater effectiveness. For example, the effective teacher realizes the importance of helping students achieve skills necessary to accomplish crucial developmental tasks. According to Erikson's theory, teachers of elementary school-aged learners would do well to focus on teaching academic and social skills, helping students gain proficiency in skills that will enable them to be productive members of society. On the other hand, secondary school teachers would do well to keep in mind, as they engage students in higher-ordered thinking activities appropriate to their stage of cognitive development, that students have pressing psychological and social needs in their struggle to achieve identity and to attain intimacy.

By understanding key principles of human development in its multiple dimensions, effective teachers provide students with both age-appropriate and developmentally appropriate instruction. This, in sum, is the best instruction. It is instruction that addresses all the needs of students—their physical, emotional, and social needs, as well as their cognitive (or intellectual) needs.

Stage Theories and Individual Variation

Although stage theorists (such as Piaget and Erikson) expect certain cognitive and psychosocial changes to occur in predictable patterns at predictable times in an individual's lifespan, there is always individual variation. That means, for example, that although most children are ready to begin learning to read around the age of six, there will be some children who start to read before that age and some who will not be ready to read until they are older. This does not mean that there is anything wrong with those individuals who develop at a slightly different trajectory. However, when individuals advance faster than their peers or lag substantially behind them, there will be psychological and social factors for teachers to consider. In these cases, it will be important for teachers to be observant of these patterns of individual difference and to be able to tailor instructions to meet the needs of individuals who may differ from the group as a whole.

Developmental Delays

Some students, however, do have developmental problems and/or learning disabilities. Specific laws (such as ADA and IDEA, both discussed as part of Competency 013) address the special education needs of these students.

Teachers may be uncertain or anxious when they encounter students with learning disabilities and/or special needs. In such cases, some very basic points can be helpful.

These include the following:

- Use a normal tone of voice. Do not raise your voice or slow your speech unless the student asks you to do so.

- Offer to shake hands with the student. It is acceptable to use your left hand if that is what the student offers you.

- Look directly at the student when speaking to the student, not at the aide or parent who is accompanying the student.

- Talk and maintain eye contact with the student, not the interpreter, if the student is using one.

- Treat a wheelchair as the student's personal space. Do not lean on the wheelchair or attempt to move it unless the student asks you to do so.

- Ask before attempting to help. If the student wants help, ask how you can be of assistance without presuming to know what is needed.

- Offer your arm to guide a student with a vision impairment. Do not steer the student or put your arms around the student.

In providing assistance to students with disabilities it is important to keep in mind that physical and intellectual abilities are not necessarily linked. However, some disabled students may not be able to communicate their needs clearly. In such cases, it is important to be sensitive and experiment to discover how to best interact with the student.

Adapting a classroom to accommodate a special education student is somewhat akin to the kind of individualized instruction that most teachers routinely provide in order to meet all students' needs. Yet, there are some basic factors to consider in adapting instruction for special education students (Deschenes, Ebeling, and Sprague, 1994).

Some of these factors are size, time, level of support, input, difficulty, output, and participation. To briefly explain, size refers to reducing the number of items the student must learn or complete; instead of solving ten problems, the student might solve five problems. Time refers to the allotted time for learning; students with special needs often need more time to complete an assignment. Level of support refers to the ability of the student to work alone versus working with a peer; special needs students may benefit from working with a more advanced student (peer teaching). Input refers to the method of delivering instruction; students might need an audio or video tape of the lesson, for example. Difficulty describes the skill level required; for example, the student may be allowed to use a calculator or respond in other creative ways to the task. Output refers to how the student complies with or responds to instruction; for example, the student might draw a picture instead of writing a story. Finally, participation reflects the extent to which the student is required to be actively involved; the student's participation should be tailored to suit his or her intellectual and/or physical abilities. There are many resources to help teachers tailor instruction to the specific needs of special education students.

Play Development

Young children are in a period of transition between the action-based world characterized by the sensorimotor stage and the thought-based world of formal operations. For children entering school (kindergarten and the early grades), play serves to link these two worlds and to help promote more advanced cognitive and social thinking and behaviors.

Current research on play has reinforced the concept of play as a form of thinking and learning. "Pretending" or make-believe represents a critical step in passing from the sensorimotor intelligence of infancy to the symbolic thinking of adulthood. Pretend play has also been linked to creativity, problem-solving, language learning, and the development of adult social roles. Moreover, research has demonstrated that through training and the arrangement of the environment, teachers can increase the incidence of pretend-play among children. Thus, teachers have an important role to play in making sure that young children have the opportunity to engage in meaningful play times.

Although games have not always been viewed as having educational value, they have been used in school settings for recreation, physical and social development, and energy release to allow students to get back to inactive routines at their desks. But, based on what is now known about cognitive, social, and even moral development, games can be used educationally to several ends.

DeVries argues that group games can contribute to students' self-regulation or autonomy by providing a context in which they have the opportunity to choose to adopt and follow rules. A group game is one example of an activity that allows students to find out for themselves what happens when they fail to follow rules. Feelings of moral necessity can develop when students confront the basic issues of fairness, individual rights, and the reasons or rationale for rules. Games provide an opportunity to practice mutual respect (a defining characteristic of democratic principles) and cooperation. In fact, competitive games are especially conducive to moral development because opposing intentions must be coordinated within the context of cooperation; that is, competition occurs when players cooperate by agreeing on rules, enforcing rules, abiding by rules, and accepting the consequences of rules even when the rules mean they do not win the game.

Intellectually, games promote development by engaging students in opportunities to reason and become more logical as they develop strategies, understand cause-and-effect relationships, and anticipate consequences. DeVries recommends the following three criteria for selecting educational group games:

1) Is there something interesting and challenging to figure out how to do? Here the teacher must select games that are age or skill-level appropriate, not too hard and not too easy.

2) Can the players judge their success? A good group game is one in which the players are not dependent on an outside authority to tell them whether or not they are successful.

3) Do all players actively participate throughout the game? Although older students can enjoy games when they must wait for their turn, younger children must be physically active in order to be mentally active.

Some other suggestions are offered by DeVries as to how teachers can use games to an educational end. Some of these are to present rules as coming from an authority beyond the teacher (as using written rules as the guide); participate in the game as a player; when conflicts arise, support the children as they discuss the rules and negotiate how to follow the rules and play the game; when players ask what to do, avoid giving an answer but ask them to make some decisions; and encourage students to invent their own games.

Peer Pressure

Playing—interacting with others—is important in order to achieve important cognitive and psycho-social milestones (as defined by Piaget and Erikson). Therefore, peer interaction is a crucial factor in the normal and healthy development of individuals. Nonetheless, the term "peer pressure" is most often used with negative connotations, frequently defined as "when friends talk you into doing something you don't want to do and probably shouldn't do." It is important to remember, however, that peer pressure can be positive. If one's friends are trying out for the school choir, for example, the student who normally would be too shy and reserved to audition may decide also to try out for the choir. Thus, in this case, peer pressure could lead a withdrawn student to a new and rewarding activity.

On the other hand, for every example of positive peer pressure, a case of negative peer pressure can be cited. Cheating, talking during quiet time, or using illegal drugs are the negative results of peer pressure that are familiar to teachers and students alike. Because peer pressure mounts during the pre-teen and teenage years, it is important that teachers deal with the topic and provide students with tools to combat negative peer pressure. Being able to discuss ideas and feelings without fear of ridicule or criticism is important, as are opportunities to examine life values and goals. Assertiveness training and conflict resolution skills are important tools for dealing with peer pressure. Moreover, critical-thinking tools are also essential in order to foster the kind of analysis that can spot logical fallacies, question mistaken assumptions, and exercise independent thought.

Sample Question

Reuben Stein is a middle-school teacher who wants to teach his class about the classification system in the animal kingdom. He decides to introduce this unit to his class by having the students engage in general classification activities. He brings to class a paper bag filled with 30 household items. He dumps the contents of the bag onto a table and then asks the students, in groups of three or four, to put like items into piles and then to justify or explain why they placed certain items into a particular pile.

By assigning this task to his students, Mr. Stein is providing his students with a developmentally-appropriate task because

(A) middle-school students like to work in groups.

(B) the items in the bag are household items with which most students will be familiar.

(C) the assignment gives students the opportunity to practice their skills at categorizing.

(D) the assignment will give students a task to perform while the teacher finishes grading papers.

The correct response is (C). According to Piaget's theory of cognitive development, students in middle school would be at the stage of *concrete operational* thought. Students at this stage of cognitive development would be able to categorize items. (A) is a false statement. Although some students will like to work in groups, some students will prefer to work alone—at this and at any age group or cognitive stage. Preferring to learn in groups (socially) or alone (independently) is a characteristic of learning style or preference, not a characteristic of cognitive or affective development. (B) is irrelevant to the teacher's intent in assigning the task. Students could just as easily work with unfamiliar items, grouping them by observable features independent of their use or function. (D) is not a good choice under any circumstances. Teachers should assiduously avoid giving students assignments merely to keep them busy while the teacher does something else. All assignments should have an instructional purpose.

COMPETENCY 002

The teacher understands student diversity and knows how to plan learning experiences and design assessments that are responsive to differences among students and that promote all students' learning.

Effective teachers realize that students bring to the classroom a variety of characteristics, both personal and social, that create within the classroom a microcosm reflective of American society at large. Indeed, America has long held to the notion of being a "melting pot" whereby members of various racial, ethnic, religious, and national origin groups have contributed to the wealth of our culture.

Ethnocentrism is a sociological term used to describe the natural tendency of viewing one's own cultural or familial way of doing things as the right, correct, or best way. Because ethnocentrism is a natural tendency, all people are likely to engage in ethnocentric thinking and behaviors at times.

Some social critics have pointed out that ethnocentrism has played a notable role in American education. They assert that educational institutions often have been guilty of assuming a Eurocentric viewpoint, that is, solely recognizing the contributions of European writers, artists, scientists, philosophers, and so forth, at the expense of those from other cultures. These critics have also noted that the contributions of men often are disproportionately recognized over like achievements of women (Sadker & Sadker, 1994).

In fact, David and Myra Sadker (1994) have found that teachers, both male and female, at all grade levels, are more likely to call on male than female students, to give positive reinforcement to males' correct responses than to those of females, and to provide coaching or instructional help to males when their responses are incorrect. Their research has led them to conclude that teachers are usually unaware of gender bias in their teaching, but that such bias is pervasive in American schools. Their research also has persuaded them that bias can be eliminated once teachers become sensitive to its debilitating effects on students.

Another example, this time relevant to socio-economic status, can also be used to illustrate this point. One standard assessment of children's intelligence asked children to identify a picture of a small round, red fruit on a stem. Children from modest homes in South Texas were likely to identify the item as an "apple." This was not the correct answer according to the answer key, which identified the item as a "cherry." Children in South Texas were not familiar with cherries because (a) they are not a common crop in South Texas and (b) fresh cherries are very expensive in the supermarket and so are not usually purchased by families of modest means.

The point made here is that ethnocentrism or a narrow viewpoint, in any form, can be damaging because it is exclusive rather than inclusive. Eurocentric, Afrocentric, and other ethnocentric perspectives are equally limited in that they narrowly focus attention on one set of ideas to the neglect of others. Therefore, effective teachers will wisely expend a degree of effort in avoiding ethnocentric thinking and behaviors. Effective teachers will attempt to include all students in all classroom activities. The race, ethnicity, religion, national origin, and gender of learners will be viewed as strengths that enable students to learn with and from each other.

Historically speaking, educational experiments have demonstrated the importance of teachers' avoiding bias and ethnocentric thinking. The *Hawthorne effect,* or the phenomenon whereby what teachers expected became reality, was demonstrated when teachers were told that some students in their classes were extremely intelligent whereas others were extremely slow or even mentally retarded. In fact, all students had normal-range intelligence. Nonetheless, at the end of the experiment, students who had been identified to the teachers as being extremely intelligent all had made significant academic progress and were not only at the top of their class, but also performing at the top on national achievement tests. Those students who had been identified as retarded had made no progress at all; in fact, they had lost previously made gains. Thus, it was demonstrated that teachers' expectations for students often become self-fulfilling prophecies.

In today's society, there is considerable reference to multiculturalism. Multiculturalism, if it serves merely to separate and distinguish the accomplishments of select cultural and ethnic groups, has the potential to separate and alienate Americans. To view multiculturalism in a positive light is to acknowledge a kind of multiculturalism that embraces the accomplishments of all cultural and ethnic groups, thereby strengthening our country and society instead of fragmenting it.

Because multiculturalism and/or cultural diversity can be a controversial issue with many sides to consider, a reasonable approach to diversity for the classroom teacher is to distinguish between cultural diversity and learning diversity and *to focus on diversity in learning*. This approach transcends cultural boundaries and recognizes that all people have distinct learning preferences and tendencies. Furthermore, this approach acknowledges that all preferences and tendencies are equally valid and that each style of learning has strengths. The teacher who understands learning styles can validate all students in the class.

Environmental Factors

Many factors play a role in determining a student's learning style. Among those most often cited in the research literature on learning style are environmental, emotional, sociological, physiological, and psychological factors (Dunn & Dunn, 1993). Although there are several different models for understanding learning differences and many good instruments for assessing learning styles, the Dunn and Dunn (1993) model is one widely used in public schools, with versions suitable for students in elementary and secondary classrooms. It will serve as the basis for the following discussion.

Environmental factors include students' reactions to such stimuli as sound, light, temperature, and room design. Do students prefer to study and learn with or without sound, with bright or soft lights, in warm or cool rooms, with standard classroom furniture or alternative seating? Classroom teachers observe that some students are easily distracted by any noise and require absolute quiet when studying or working on assignments. On the other hand, some students seem to learn best when they can listen to music. Some researchers have found evidence that students who prefer sound learn best when classical or instrumental music is played in the background.

Light is another environmental factor, with students' preferences for light appearing to be basically inherited, as family members often exhibit the same preference. Some students prefer bright, direct illumination while others prefer dim, indirect lighting.

Temperature and design are two other environmental factors affecting learning style. Some students will prefer warmer temperatures whereas others will prefer cooler temperatures. Finally, some students will prefer to sit in straight-backed chairs at desks while others may prefer to sit on soft, comfy chairs or to sit or recline on the floor.

Although traditional classrooms are structured to provide quiet, brightly illuminated study and work areas with straight-backed chairs and desks, classroom teachers will observe that this environment meets the needs of only some of the learners in the class. An effective teacher will take into consideration the learning styles of all students and experiment with different room designs, study centers, and creating different environments in the classroom. Although classroom temperature may seem to be beyond the control of the teacher, students can be advised to dress in layers so that they can remove outer garments when they are too warm and put on more layers when they are too cool.

Emotional Factors

According to Rita and Kenneth Dunn, emotional factors include motivation, persistence, responsibility, and structure. To explain, some students are motivated intrinsically: they undertake and complete tasks because they see the value in doing so. Other students are motivated extrinsically: they undertake and complete tasks because they desire to please others or to earn good marks. In regard to persistence, some students, when they undertake assignments, become totally and completely engaged in their work; they seem to lose track of time and can work for long periods without interruption or without feeling fatigued. Other students seem to work in short spurts of energy, needing to take frequent breaks.

When it comes to responsibility, some students are nonconforming, always doing the unexpected (and sometimes unwanted), whereas other students are conforming, always following the rules. Structure refers to whether or not students need detailed and precise instructions. Some students have lots of questions about how assignments should be done, and they desire detailed, step-by-step instructions on each phase of the assignment. Other students, however, seem to work from general concepts and are usually eager to begin assignments, often beginning their work before the directions have been given.

Sociological factors include whether or not students are social learners—preferring to work in pairs or in groups—or whether they are independent learners—preferring to work alone. Another sociological factor is whether or not students work best under the close guidance and supervision of an authority figure, be it teacher or parent, or whether they work best with a minimum of adult guidance and are best left primarily on their own to do their work.

Physiological factors include students' preferences for food or drink while they study, what time of day they learn best, their mobility needs, and their perceptual strengths. Briefly, some students may need to eat or drink in order to effectively and efficiently learn. Rita Dunn says that to make sure that students do not abuse this privilege, she allows them to eat only carrot or celery sticks (cooked so that the snacks will not crunch when eaten by students) and to drink water. This way, she is certain that only students who really need intake when they are learning will take advantage of this concession.

Some students may learn best early in the morning, some later in the morning, some in early afternoon, and some later in the afternoon. Researchers have found that merely manipulating the time of day that certain students take tests can significantly affect their test performance.

Mobility needs refer to the fact that some students need to move around when they study, whereas other students can sit still for longer periods of time. Although all of these factors are important, and a growing body of literature tends to support the idea that these factors play a significant role in increasing students' performance and in increasing teachers' effectiveness with students, perhaps one of the most important elements in understanding learning style is to identify students' perceptual strengths. Perceptual strengths refer to students' learning modalities, such as whether they are visual, auditory, tactile, or kinesthetic learners. Basically, these perceptual modalities refer to whether students learn best by seeing, hearing, or doing.

Some students can be given a book or handout to read and then perform a task well based on what they have read. These students tend to have visual (iconic or semantic) perceptual strength. Other students are visual learners, too, but they tend to learn best from images. These are the students who seem to recall every event, even minor details, from films, videos, or classroom demonstrations.

Although evidence indicates that less than 15 percent of the school-age population is auditory (Dunn, 1993), much of the classroom instruction takes the form of teachers telling students information. Most students do not learn auditorially. Therefore, these students must be taught how to listen and learn from oral instructions and lecture.

Teachers who rely on telling students the information that is important would do well to remember that females are more likely to learn auditorially than males. Teachers should also keep in mind that whether or not students benefit from lectures is likely to depend on several other elements whether the students are auditory learners or not. These elements include whether or not the students like the teacher, whether or not they think the information being presented is important, or whether or not they think that listening to the teacher will help them achieve their goals (Baxter-Magolda, 1992).

On the other hand, there are students who do not seem to benefit much from lectures, textbook assignments, or visual aids. These students' perceptual strengths are tactile and kinesthetic. They learn from movement and motion, from being able to touch, handle, and manipulate objects. These students may be identified as having learning disabilities. Sometimes they are relegated to shop or cooking classes, or find their success in athletics, music, or art. Interestingly, many of the "hands on" skills that often identify a student for a career as an auto mechanic are also important skills for mechanical engineers and surgeons.

Learning Styles

The obvious benefit of knowing whether or not students are auditory, visual, tactile, or kinesthetic learners is not simply to cater to the learners' preferences or strengths. The significance is that once strengths are identified, then teachers can teach students to use those strengths in situations that are not easy or natural. For example, students who are not auditory learners (but tactile and kinesthetic) must learn responsibility for their own learning; they must learn to become involved in lecture classes. Becoming involved means that they learn to take copious notes, participate in class discussions, ask questions, and answer questions posed by the teacher.

Visual learners must sit where they can see what's going on in class, where they can see the teacher and the board. They need opportunities to draw pictures, to diagram, to take good notes, to create mind maps, and to use flashcards. They must be taught how to visualize the abstract concepts they are being taught, and they need opportunities to practice all these techniques.

For visual learners who learn best by reading, teachers can provide adequate opportunities to read in class. Students need to learn specific note-taking methods, and reading and comprehension strategies. They also can be taught to use supplemental readings, to use the library effectively, and to use workbooks.

Auditory learners need to learn attention-directing activities. They can learn to use audio cassettes as learning aids. They can learn to ask questions in class and to participate in class discussions. They must be taught how to summarize and paraphrase—especially how to state in their own words the concepts they are trying to master. They may need the teacher to repeat or to restate ideas. Students must learn to pay close attention to verbal cues such as voice tone and inflection. Reciting what they have heard (or read) is an important strategy for auditory learners as is finding someone to whom they can explain ideas they have acquired. It may be helpful for auditory learners to work on some assignments with students who are visual learners (Nolting, 1993).

Tactile, kinesthetic learners may benefit from study groups, discussion groups, role-playing situations, lab settings, computer activities, learning games, and using flashcards and other manipulatives. They must get involved in class by asking questions and participating in discussions. They learn best when they can convert what they are learning into real-life, concrete experiences; for example, they may learn fractions by cutting a pizza into slices. Often, they need to work math problems immediately after being shown examples to check their understanding. They often need to move around while they are studying, reviewing ideas while exercising or doing chores. Many times, they do their best work when they are using tools such as computers, calculators, or even their fingers.

When classroom teachers assess students' learning styles and then begin to teach to empower students to learn more effectively and perform tasks with greater proficiency, the result is that students also learn a tremendous lesson about diversity. They learn that not everyone learns in the same way, but that everyone can achieve. The products of learning can meet the same high standards although the processes for learning may be different for different students.

This is a rich lesson for students and faculty alike. It tells students that it is okay to be different; in fact, everyone is different. It tells students that it is okay to be the way they are. Apart from their race, ethnicity, religious beliefs, national origin, or gender, they are special, and they are good. They can learn. This may be one of the most important lessons that students ever learn and one that all teachers can be proud and eager to teach.

Motivational Factors

Students often say that they like teachers who motivate them. Although teachers can be highly motivated themselves and demonstrate interest in the subject-matter and in their students, in fact, teachers are not responsible for students' motivation. Motivation is a student's responsibility and must come from within the student. However, effective teachers will help students develop self-discipline, self-control, and self-motivation. These skills of self-management can be taught, yet they require a great deal of effort and practice in order for students to gain true proficiency.

When students say that they like or want teachers who motivate them, they are probably referring to some characteristics that teachers possess that are attractive and interesting to learners. So, while it is true that teachers are not responsible for students' motivation, it is also true that teachers can influence motivation, that teachers can promote and/or inhibit motivation in the classroom by their attitudes and their actions.

Three Motivational Principles

One researcher has offered three principles to guide teachers that will lead to greater effectiveness in the classroom (Baxter-Magolda, 1992). Interestingly, each of these principles leads to empowering students and, thus, is motivational in nature.

The first principle is to *validate students as knowers.* This principle is based on the idea of the active learner who brings much to the classroom (the dynamic view of human development). How can teachers validate students? Baxter-Magolda suggests that teachers display a caring attitude towards students. This means that it is appropriate for teachers to take an interest in students, to learn about their likes and dislikes and their interests and hobbies, both in school and outside school. This also means that it is okay for teachers to show enthusiasm and excitement for their classes, not only the subject-matter they teach, but the students they teach as well. It also means, as Carol Tavris (1994) noted, that it is good for teachers to show empathy for students' emotional needs.

Baxter-Magolda also recommends that teachers question authority by example and let students know that they, as teachers, can also be questioned. This means that teachers model critical thinking skills in the classroom. Teachers can question authority when they examine and evaluate readings—whether from textbooks or other sources. Teachers can question authorities when they teach propaganda techniques, exposing advertising claims and gimmicks. Teachers can question authority when they discuss the media and how so-called news sources shape and form public opinion. There are numerous opportunities for teachers in dealing with current affairs and public opinion to question authority and inculcate in their students' critical thinking and higher-ordered reasoning skills.

Also, when teachers allow students to question them, teachers are acknowledging that everyone is a learner. Everyone should participate in a lifelong process of continuous learning. It is no shame or disgrace for the teacher to admit that sometimes he or she doesn't know the answer to every question. This gives the teacher the opportunity to show students how adults think, how they have a level of awareness (metacognition) when they don't know something, and how they go about finding answers to their questions. Teachers who admit that they don't have all the answers have the opportunity to show students how answers can be found and/or to reveal to students that there are no easy answers to some of life's most difficult questions.

Third, to validate students as knowers, teachers can value students' opinions, ideas, and comments. Teachers' affirmations include smiles and nods of approval, positive comments (such as, "That's a good answer."), and encouraging cues (such as, "That may seem like a reasonable answer, but can you think of a better answer?" or "Can you explain what you mean by that answer?"). Validating students as knowers also means supporting students' voices, giving them ample opportunity to express their own ideas, to share their opinions, and to make their own contributions to the classroom. These opportunities can include times of oral discussion as well as written assignments.

Jointly Constructed Meaning

Another principle in Baxter-Magolda's guidelines for teaching effectiveness is for teachers and students to recognize that learning is *a process of jointly-constructing meaning*. To explain, Baxter-Magolda says that it is important for teachers to create a dialogue with students (also an important concept in Piagetian theory) and that teachers emphasize mutual learning. Also in agreement with Piagetian principles, Baxter-Magolda recommends that teachers reveal their own thinking processes as they approach subjects, as they analyze and understand new subjects, and as they solve problems and reach decisions. She further advises that teachers share leadership and promote collegial learning (group work), acknowledging that individual achievement is not the sole purpose or focus for learning. By allowing students to collaborate, they also will learn significant lessons directly applicable to work situations where most accomplishments are the result of team efforts, not the sole efforts of individuals.

Baxter-Magolda's final principle for teachers is to *situate learning in the students' own experiences*. She suggests that this be done by letting students know that they are wanted in class, by using inclusive language (avoiding ethnic and cultural bias and stereotyping, instead using gender-neutral and inclusive language), and focusing on activities. Activities are important for motivation because they give learners things to do, to become actively involved in, arousing their attention and interest and giving them an outlet for their physical and mental energy. Activities can have an additional positive benefit in that they can serve to connect students to each other, especially when students are given opportunities to participate in collaborative learning (the way things happen in the "real world") and to work in groups. Finally, in situating learning in students' own experiences, it is important to consider the use of personal stories in class, as appropriate (that is, without violating anyone's right to privacy and confidentiality). Moreover, teachers can share personal stories that allow them to connect with students in a deeper and more personal way.

In 1993, the child psychologist, Harvard professor, and author of numerous scholarly and popular books Robert Coles wrote of his experiences teaching in a Boston inner-city high school. He told of his disillusionment and his struggle to claim students' respect and attention so that he could teach them. Finally, there was a classroom confrontation, followed by a self-revelation (that being to show his students what he was like as a person). He shared some of his thoughts and feelings about loneliness. He told about his own boyhood experiences of visiting museums with his mother and what she taught him about art. In the end, he, too, had a revelation; he concluded that when teachers share what they have learned about themselves with their students, they often can transcend the barriers of class and race. A teacher can change a "me" and a "them" (the students) into an "us." Building camaraderie this way then becomes an optimal starting point for teaching and learning (Coles, 1993). Dr. Coles' experience was that telling his story to the class was a step towards helping his students claim some motivation of their own.

When students assume responsibility for their own motivation, they are learning a lesson of personal empowerment. Unfortunately, although personal empowerment is probably one of the most important lessons anyone ever learns, it is a lesson infrequently taught in classrooms across the country.

Empowerment has at least four components, one of which is self-esteem. A good definition of self-esteem is that it is my opinion of me, your opinion of you. It is what we think and believe to be true about ourselves, not what we think about others and not what they think about us. Self-esteem appears to be a combination of self-efficacy and self-respect as seen against a background of self-knowledge.

Self-efficacy, simply stated, is one's confidence in one's own ability to cope with life's challenges. Self-efficacy refers to having a sense of control over life or, better, over one's responses to life. Experts say that ideas about self-efficacy get established by the time children reach the age of four. Because of this early establishment of either a feeling of control or no control, classroom teachers may find that even primary grade students believe that they have no control over their life, that it makes no difference what they do or how they act. Therefore, it is all the more important that teachers attempt to help all students achieve coping skills and a sense of self-efficacy.

Control, in this definition of self-efficacy, can be examined in regard to external or internal motivators. For example, external motivators include such things as luck and the roles played by others in influencing outcomes. Internal motivators are variables within the individual. If a student does well on a test and is asked, "How did you do so well on that test," one relying on external motivators might reply, "Well, I just got lucky," or "The teacher likes me." If the student failed the test and is asked why, the student dependent on external motivators might answer, "Well, it wasn't my lucky day," "The teacher doesn't like me," or "My friends caused me to goof off and not pay attention so I didn't know the answers on the test." A student who relies on internal motivators and who does well on a test may explain, "I am smart and always do well on tests," or "I studied hard and that's why I did well." On the other hand, even the student who relies on internal motivators can do poorly on tests and then may explain, "I'm dumb and that's why I don't do well," or "I didn't think the test was important and I didn't try very hard." Even though students have similar experiences regarding issues of control, what is important is how students explain their experiences. If students have external motivators, they are likely to either dismiss their performance (success or failure) as matters of luck, or to credit or blame the influence of others. If students have internal motivators, then they are likely to attribute their performance to either their intelligence and skills (ability) or their effort.

Students who have external motivators need help understanding how their behavior contributes to and influences outcomes in school. Students need clarification as to how grades are determined and precise information about how their work is evaluated. Students who have internal motivators but low self-esteem (such as thinking, "I'm dumb") need help identifying their strengths and assets (something that can be accomplished when students are given information about learning styles). Self-efficacy can be enhanced.

Another factor in empowerment is self-respect. Self-respect is believing that one deserves happiness, achievement, and love. Self-respect is treating one's self at least as nicely as one treats other people. Many students are not aware of their internal voices (which are established at an early age). Internal voices are constantly sending messages, either positive or negative. Psychologists say that most of us have either a generally positive outlook on life, and our inner voice sends generally positive messages ("You're okay," "People like you," "Things will be all right," and so forth) or a generally negative outlook on life, and an inner voice sending negative messages ("You're not okay," "You're too fat, skinny, ugly, stupid," and so forth).

Many students need to become aware of their inner voice and how it can be setting them up for failure. They need to learn that they can tell their inner voice to stop sending negative messages, and that they can reprogram their inner voice to be kinder, gentler, and to send positive messages. However, it does require effort, practice, and time to reprogram the inner voice.

Two tools that can help students in the reprogramming process are affirmations and visualizations (Ellis, 1991). Affirmations are statements describing what students want. Affirmations must be personal, positive, and written in the present tense. What makes affirmations effective are details. For example, instead of saying, "I am stupid," students can be encouraged to say, "I am capable. I do well in school because I am organized, I study daily, I get all my work completed on time, and I take my school work seriously." Affirmations must be repeated until they can be said with total conviction.

Visualizations are images students can create whereby they see themselves the way they want to be. For example, if a student wants to improve his or her typing skills, then the student evaluates what it would look like, sound like, and feel like to be a better typist. Once the student identifies the image, then the student has to rehearse that image in her or his mind, including as many details and sensations as possible. Both visualization and affirmation can restructure attitudes and behaviors. They can be tools for students to use to increase their motivation.

Finally, the fourth component of empowerment is self-knowledge. Self-knowledge refers to an individual's strengths and weaknesses, assets and liabilities; self-knowledge comes about as a result of a realistic self-appraisal (and can be achieved by an examination of learning styles). Achieving self-knowledge also requires that students have opportunities to explore their goals and values.

Students who know what their goals and values are can more easily see how education will enable them to achieve those goals and values. Conversely, students cannot be motivated when they do not have goals and values, or when they do not know what their goals and values are. In other words, without self-knowledge, motivation is impossible. Therefore, teachers who follow Baxter-Magolda's guidelines for effective instruction and who teach their students about personal empowerment are teachers who realize the importance of motivation and who set the stage for students to claim responsibility for their own successes and failures. Such teachers help students to become motivated to make changes and accomplish more.

Sample Question

Elva Rodriguez teaches fourth grade. She has structured her class so that students can spend 30 minutes daily, after lunch, in sustained, silent reading activities with books and reading materials of their own choosing.

In order to maximize this reading opportunity and to recognize differences among learners, Ms. Rodriguez

(A)   allows some students to sit quietly at their desks while others are allowed to move to a reading area where they sit on floor cushions or recline on floor mats.

(B)   makes sure that all students have selected appropriate reading materials.

(C)   plays classical music on a tape player to enhance student learning.

(D)   dims the lights in the classroom in order to increase students' reading comprehension.

The correct response is **(A)**. Only (A) takes into account differences among learners by giving them options as to how and where they will read. (B) violates the students' freedom to select reading materials which they find interesting and wish to read. When students are allowed to choose their own reading materials, it may seem that some students select materials beyond their present reading comprehension. However, reading research indicates that students can comprehend more difficult material when their interest level is high.

Therefore, any efforts by the teacher to interfere with students' selection of their own reading material would be ill-advised. (C) and (D) are equally poor in that they both describe a concession to only one group of learners. For example, with (C), some students may prefer to read with music playing in the background, while other students will find music distracting. The best action for the teacher to take would be for her to allow some students to listen to music on earphones while others read in quiet. In regard to (D), some students will prefer bright illumination just as some students will read better with the lights dimmed. Ms. Rodriguez would do well to attempt to accommodate various learner needs by having one area of the room more brightly illuminated when lights are dimmed in another area.

COMPETENCY 003

The teacher understands procedures for designing effective and coherent instruction and assessment based on appropriate learning goals and objectives.

The curriculum in the Texas public schools is based on the Texas Essential Knowledge and Skills (TEKS). In order to teach effectively, a beginning teacher must understand these learning standards and be able to use them to set, plan, and provide appropriate instructional goals and objectives. At each grade level, the TEKS identifies the knowledge and skills that students must achieve in English language arts, mathematics, science (including biology, chemistry, and physics), social studies and citizenship, and the use of technology.

In response to national educational reforms in the late 20th century, Texas developed a testing program in the 1980s called the Texas Educational Assessment of Minimum Skills (TEAMS). However, the educational community, working with legislators and parents, soon determined that an assessment of minimal skills was not sufficient and developed the Texas Assessment of Academic Skills (TAAS), which had been the state assessment for students from 1990 until 2003. The TAAS was used to indicate that students were achieving minimum standards in identified areas (grades 3 – 8 and exit level) and making sufficient academic progress for grade promotion and/or graduation.

Since 2003, the Texas Assessment of Knowledge and Skills (TAKS) is the standard assessment. The TAKS provides better alignment with the TEKS and measure students' knowledge and skills in English language arts (including reading and writing), mathematics, science, and social studies. Writing skills are assessed at grades 4 and 7; reading is assessed at grades 3 – 9; English/language arts is assessed at grades 10 and 11; mathematics at grades 3 – 11; science at grades 5, 10, and 11; and social studies at grades 8, 10, and 11.

The TAKS replaces end-of-course exams and establishes that minimum standards have been met for high school graduation and for college readiness. When taught the knowledge and skills identified in TEKS, students are able to demonstrate their knowledge and skills by passing the statewide assessment, the TAKS.

A number of resources are available to help teachers developing materials for teaching the TEKS. A list of some of these resources appears below:

- **www.tea.state.tx.us/curriculum/index.html**

- **www.tea.state.tx.us/student.assessment/**

- **Texas Center for Reading and Language Arts**

- **Education service centers across the state**

- **Professional organizations (NCTE, IRA, TCTE, TSRA, CREST)**

- **Mathematics Center for Educator Development (CED)**

- **Social Studies Center**

- **Science Toolkit at www.tenet.edu/teks/science**

Critics of high-stakes testing programs often argue that teachers do not teach important material to students because they are forced to spend too much time "teaching to the test." Since the TAKS assessment is based on the TEKS, Texas teachers can feel confident that if they are teaching the knowledge and skills identified on the TEKS, they are teaching what students need to know to progress from grade level to grade level, and what students will need to know in order to score well on the TAKS.

To illustrate, a fifth-grade student in Texas is expected to know how to distinguish between a speaker's opinion and verifiable fact (TEKS, English Language Arts. 5.2). Therefore, a fifth-grade language arts teacher will want to be sure to provide instruction in distinguishing between fact and opinion and many opportunities for students to practice this skill and receive feedback regarding their performance. Not only is this a skill that will be assessed on the TAKS, but it is an important academic and life skill as well.

Since the standard is "to distinguish between a speaker's opinion and verifiable fact," this can be easily translated into a learning goal: "Students will be able to distinguish between a speaker's opinion and verifiable fact." The learning objective might be: "Students will identify a list of opinions and facts with 100 percent accuracy." Thus, the student who achieves the objective by scoring 100 percent on the assessment has made progress towards the educational goal.

Effective teachers know how to plan so that their curriculum guides, lesson plans, actual lessons, and tests and assessments are correlated. They plan in advance, explain the unit's goals and objectives to the students, then choose activities which will help the class reach the desired outcomes.

Criteria for Learning Goals and Objectives

Why are you teaching this? What do students need to know? How will students show or demonstrate that they do know? These are important considerations and allow teachers to set appropriate learning goals and objectives.

Learning goals and objectives must be clear; relevant; significant; age-appropriate; assessable or measurable; responsive to students' current skills and knowledge, background, needs, and interests; and aligned with campus and district goals. Frequently, educators use the terms *goals, objectives, standards,* and *outcomes* interchangeably to describe what students are supposed to know and be able to do.

Because in Texas the TEKS sets forth the curriculum, it establishes the learning outcome or goal of what the student should know and be able to do. Sometimes educators distinguish between goals and objectives by specifying that objectives are the strategies or evidence of students' progress towards broader goals. Also, educators sometimes use the term objective to refer to Bloom's Taxonomy of Educational Objectives.

Bloom's Taxonomy of Educational Objectives

Briefly stated, Bloom's Taxonomy of Educational Objectives refers to six categories, each one building on the previous level, in the cognitive domain that captures learning objectives. In ascending order the six categories are: knowledge, comprehension, application, analysis, synthesis, and evaluation. In other words, when a teacher specifies the objective of the lesson is for students to "know" the meaning of the ten vocabulary words, the teacher has used Bloom's taxonomy to require the lowest category of the cognitive domain. Specific verbs are associated with each of the categories that describe the actions required at each level of the taxonomy; for example, for the knowledge category, the verbs are *define, describe, enumerate, identify, label, list, match, name, read, record, reproduce, select, state,* and *view.* When teachers instruct students to perform assignments using these verbs, the teacher is asking students to perform at the most basic level—that of knowledge.

The **knowledge** level is similar to a closed question, with one right answer that should be obvious to students who have read or studied. Words that often elicit recall or memory answers include who, what, when, and where. Examples of knowledge-level questions include: Who developed the first microscope? What were the names of Columbus' ships? When was South Carolina first settled? Where is Tokyo?

The second level, **comprehension**, also elicits lower-level thinking and answers. The primary difference from the first level and comprehension is that students must show that they understand a concept, perhaps by explaining in their own words. The question "What does obfuscate mean?" would be answered on a knowledge level if students repeat a memorized definition from the dictionary and on a comprehension level if students explain the term in their own words. Verbs associated with this level include: *classify, cite, convert, describe, discuss, estimate, explain, generalize, give examples, make sense out of, paraphrase, restate (in one's own words), summarize, trace,* and *understand.*

The first higher-level category is **application**. Students take what they have learned and use this knowledge in a different way or in a different situation. A simple example of this level is using mathematics operations—add, subtract, multiply, and divide—to solve problems. Another example is translating an English sentence into Spanish, or applying what the students have learned about Spanish vocabulary and grammar to develop an appropriate and correct response. Another form of application is changing the format of information, e.g., create a graph from a narrative description of a survey.

The key to this level is the use or application of knowledge and skills in a similar but new situation. Verbs associated with this category are: *act, administer, articulate, assess, chart, collect, compute, construct, contribute, control, determine, develop, discover, establish, extend, implement, include, inform, instruct, operationalize, participate, predict, prepare, preserve, produce, provide, relate, report, show, solve, teach, transfer, use,* and *utilize.*

The next level is **analysis**, which involves taking something apart, looking at all the pieces, and then making a response. An example of an analytical question is, "How are these two characters alike and how are they different?" This question requires students to examine facts and characteristics of each individual, then put the information together in an understandable comparison. Another example is, "What are the advantages and disadvantages of each of these two proposals?" Another example might be, "Compare the wolves in *The Three Little Pigs* and *Little Red Riding Hood.*" Verbs describing the actions or behaviors required at this level are: *break down, correlate, diagram, differentiate, discriminate, distinguish, focus, illustrate, infer, limit, outline, recognize, separate,* and *subdivide.*

The next level is **synthesis**, which involves putting information together in a new, creative way. Developing a new way to solve problems, writing a short story, designing an experiment—these are all creative ways of synthesizing knowledge. For example, fourth-grade science students may develop and conduct research on food waste in the cafeteria and make recommendations for changes. An example of a synthesis question is, "What do you predict will happen if we combine these two chemicals?" This question assumes students will have factual knowledge. Their predictions must be reasonable and based on prior reading and/or discussion. Verbs associated with this level include: *adapt, anticipate, categorize, collaborate, combine, communicate, compare, compile, compose, contrast, create, design, devise, express, facilitate, formulate, generate, incorporate, integrate, model, modify, negotiate, plan, rearrange, reconstruct, reinforce, reorganize,* and *revise.*

The highest level is **evaluation**. This level involves making value judgments and very often involves the question "Why?" or a request to "Justify your answer." For example, students may be asked to use their analysis of two possible solutions to a problem to determine which is the better solution. Their response must be reasonable and well-supported. Verbs which can be used for activities at this level are: *appraise, compare and contrast, conclude, criticize, critique, decide, defend, interpret, judge, justify,* and *support.*

Evaluation-level activities must build on previous levels. Skipping from knowledge-level to evaluation-level questions will result in ill-conceived and poorly-supported responses. Although teachers might use an evaluation question to provoke interest in a topic, they should make sure that students have opportunities to work at other levels as they develop their responses. Much of the instruction that teachers provide is aimed at the lowest levels of knowledge and comprehension. In introducing topics, it is important that students acquire the foundation or knowledge necessary to progress to higher levels (such as application, analysis, synthesis, and evaluation). For example, students must learn basic terms and vocabulary, formulae and rubrics. This is memory work. However, the student who depends only on rote memory will be limited if comprehension (being able to restate in one's own words beyond rote memory) is not practiced and reinforced. Thus is the case at every level of the taxonomy.

This type of questioning promotes risk-taking and problem-solving, if the teacher has established a safe environment where students are encouraged and not ridiculed for creative or unusual responses. The teacher does not expect only one specific answer, but allows students to ponder several reasonable possibilities. There are educational experts who argue that only very gifted students and/or upper-grade level students can be expected to perform at the level of evaluation. However, even those students will be unable to perform if they are not given opportunities to acquire and practice this level of thinking.

Outcome-Oriented Learning

In outcome-oriented learning, teachers define outcomes, or what they want students to know, do, and be when they complete a required course of study. The teachers set high but realistic goals and objectives for their students, then plan instructional activities which will assist students in achieving these goals.

The key to effective outcome-oriented planning is to consider what outcomes must be achieved, then determine which teacher behaviors and which student behaviors will improve the probability that students will achieve the outcomes.

Outcome-based planning starts with the end product—what must be learned or accomplished in a particular course or grade level. For example, an algebra teacher may decide that the final outcome of his or her algebra course would be that students use quadratic equations to solve problems. He or she then works "backward" to determine prerequisite knowledge and skills students need to have in order to accomplish this outcome. By continuing to ask these questions about each set of prerequisites, the teacher finds a starting point for the subject or course, then develops goals and objectives. The outcomes should be important enough to be required of all students.

An outcome-oriented system means that students are given sufficient time and practice to acquire the necessary knowledge and skills. It also means that teachers take into account students' various learning styles and time required for learning, and make adaptations by providing a variety of educational opportunities.

Sources of Data

Information about what outcomes are important for students comes from several sources. Ralph Tyler has defined three basic sources of needs: students, society, and content area. Consideration of these sources leads to a draft of outcomes, which are further refined by screening them through our philosophy and through what we know about educational psychology. Society makes ever-changing demands upon the educational system. Businesses are focusing more on workers who can solve problems. Other national issues—health problems, environmental concerns, etc.—can provide data for educators.

A look at student needs determines the current level of achievement through a study of evaluation results, whether teacher-made, district-developed, or standardized. Comparing where students are with where they need to be will show teachers where to start. A consideration of student needs also involves understanding their diverse learning styles, developmental levels, achievement levels, and special adaptations for learning-disabled students. This understanding assists the effective teacher in planning a variety of activities to meet these diverse needs.

Considering content area needs involves reading current research to determine trends in the subject areas. For example, science teachers are heavily involved in providing hands-on experiences in labs. English teachers have moved in the direction of whole-language activities at all levels and an integrated approach to composition and grammar. National and state curriculum committees in mathematics have endorsed a problem-solving approach for all math classes.

Planning Processes

Madeline Hunter describes a planning model which requires teacher decisions about content, teacher behavior, and student behavior. The three parts of this model overlap and are related to each other; a decision in one category influences a decision in another. Decisions about content are often made at the state or district level. Teachers use frameworks from the state, curriculum documents developed by the district, and materials from district-chosen textbooks as bases for planning lessons.

A teacher using this model would make decisions about content, including goals and objectives for a lesson or unit, length of lesson/unit, emphasis of lesson, textbooks, and additional resource materials.

Decisions about his or her own behavior include teaching strategies, accommodations for various learning styles, types of activities, sizes of groups, uses of technology and other resources, and room arrangements.

Decisions about their students' behavior include individual or group responses, format of responses, ways students will demonstrate learning, and products of activities.

Robert Gagné delineates nine external events that are important in planning an appropriate sequence of instruction. They are: (1) gaining attention, (2) informing students of the lesson objectives, (3) stimulating recall of previous learning, (4) presenting stimuli with distinctive features, (5) guiding learning, (6) eliciting student performance, (7) providing informative feedback, (8) assessing student performance, and (9) enhancing the retention and transfer of learning.

The term *lesson cycle* has been applied to processes of lesson planning developed by a variety of people. Planning is cyclical because the process repeats itself continually. These planning processes usually include the development of objectives and a focus for attention, a design for instructional input, constant monitoring of student understanding, provision for rehearsal and practice of knowledge, and opportunities for enrichment or follow-up.

Teachers choose objectives for a lesson from a curriculum guide or develop their own from their knowledge of their subject area and the needs of students. These objectives are clearly communicated to the students in terms of what they will learn (not activities they will do) during the lesson. In a deductive lesson, these objectives are explained to students at the beginning; in an inductive lesson, objectives are clarified at the end of the lesson. Teachers develop a focus or introduction to the lesson (called anticipatory set by Hunter) which should hook the students' interest and focus attention toward the upcoming activities. A wide variety of instructional methods may be used for input, from mastery lectures or labs to cooperative learning or several different types of inductive strategies. The teacher is constantly monitoring student behavior, checking for understanding, and modifying the instruction as necessary.

After or during instructional input, the students rehearse or apply what they've learned. In guided practice, the teacher watches carefully to make sure students have grasped the material correctly. Because the teacher is on hand to assess student responses, he or she is able to provide correction or additional input if necessary. During independent practice, students work independently. At the end of each lesson (or at the end of the class), the teacher or students summarize or review what has been learned. An additional feature is enrichment, which should be for all students, not just the ones who learn quickly. Enrichment means that students either delve deeper into a subject they have been studying or broaden their understanding of the general topic. For example, students who have been studying the stock market could research the history of its development, or they could study the market in other countries.

Lesson cycles are repeated for additional blocks of content. A "lesson" may last anywhere from a few minutes to several days; it isn't limited by the period or the bell.

Thematic Curriculum

The effective teacher knows how to collaborate with peers to plan instruction. Collaboration may be as simple as planning and sharing ideas, or as complex as developing a multidisciplinary thematic unit in which teachers of several subject areas teach around a common theme.

Planning thematic curriculum often involves teachers from several areas—such as math, English, history, science, and health—although individual teachers could plan thematic units for their own classes. Based on a system developed by Sandra Kaplan, the team of teachers develops a one-word universal theme which is applied in all areas, e.g., survival, conflict, traditions, frontiers, or changes. The team lists a series of key words associated with universal themes, e.g., significance, relationships, types, functions, origins, value, or causes. They develop a generalization for the unit, then each teacher plans outcomes for his/her subject area and class. For example, for the theme "Conflict," the team may choose as the generalization, "Conflict is an inherent part of life." The English teacher then develops a literature and composition unit which encourages students to describe conflicts and how they are solved in literature.

The history teacher might focus on conditions which tend to lead to conflict or the effects of conflict. A science unit could explore conflicts between people and the environment. The math teacher might focus on research methods that attempt to resolve conflicts. The health teacher could address constructive ways of solving conflicts between good health practices and unhealthy life-styles.

All teachers would plan learning experiences to lead students to understand the generalization as it applies to their particular subject and to the students' personal lives. These experiences may be carried out using a wide variety of instructional strategies and resources.

Sample Question

Mrs. Rodriguez, a tenth-grade English teacher, has five classes of 25 to 28 students who will begin studying *Julius Caesar* in two weeks. She realizes that today's students may find it difficult to relate to events which took place a long time ago. In previous years, she has asked students to read the play in class, with each student taking different roles. This year she wants to encourage greater student excitement in this unit.

Which of the following instructional approaches would be most appropriate for Mrs. Rodriguez to use to encourage students to be self-directed learners?

(A) Writing a study guide with questions about each act for students to answer in a booklet

(B) Showing a video of the play and then asking students to role play several scenes

(C) Developing a list of activities related to the play and having the class vote on which ones they want to do

(D) Providing a list of objectives and having students develop and carry out two activities to help them meet the objectives

The correct response is (**D**). The question asks how Mrs. Rodriguez can encourage her students to take control of their own learning. (D) is the best answer because the students are being asked to develop their own learning strategies matching goals of the class. This process requires higher-level thinking by the students. The teacher is determining the basic outcomes, but the students will help determine the methods of achieving these outcomes. (A) is a very structured plan, which students may complete at their own pace, but it does not allow for choices or innovations by the students. Viewing a video (B) would be an excellent visual activity to help students understand the play, but the students aren't asked to plan or make decisions. Their role-playing may not be creative because they may tend to imitate the actions from the video. (C) allows students to choose among several activities, which is a good strategy, but all the planning and goal-setting have been done by the teacher.

COMPETENCY 004

The teacher understands learning processes and factors that impact student learning and demonstrates this knowledge by planning effective, engaging instruction and appropriate assessments.

It is one thing for teachers to have command of their subject matter, for English teachers to write well, for math teachers to compute and calculate, for science teachers to know and understand science; however, it is something else—and something at least as important—that teachers know how to teach.

When teachers understand learners, that is, when teachers understand developmental processes common to all learners, and how environmental features and learning styles, varied and diverse, affect learning, then teachers are better able to design and deliver effective instruction. Although there may be some intuitive aspects to teaching (and it seems that some people were born to teach), teaching skills can be acquired through processes of introspection, observation, direct instruction, self-evaluation, and experimentation.

How teachers teach should be directly related to how learners learn. Theories of cognitive development describe how learners learn new information and acquire new skills. There are many theories of cognitive development, two of which will be included in this review; they are (a) the Piagetian (or Neo-Piagetian) theory, and (b) information processing theories.

Piagetian theory (including Neo-Piagetian theory), introduced in some detail in the review for Competency 001, describes learning in discrete and predictable stages. Therefore, teachers who understand this theory can provide students with developmentally-appropriate instruction. This theory also describes learners moving from simpler ways of thinking to more complex ways of problem-solving and thinking. For teachers, there are many important implications of this theoretical perspective. For example, teachers must create enriched environments that present learners with multiple opportunities to encounter new and unfamiliar stimuli—be they objects or ideas. Teachers must also provide learners with opportunities to engage in extended dialogue with adults; according to Piaget's theory, conversational interactions with adults are a key component in cognitive development, especially the acquisition of formal operations (or higher-ordered thinking skills). Moreover, it is important that adults (and teachers in particular) model desired behaviors; teachers must reveal their own complex ways of thinking and solving problems to students.

On the other hand, information processing theories of human development take a different approach to describing and understanding how learners learn. Based on a computer metaphor and borrowing computer imagery to describe how people learn, information processing theories begin by determining the processing demands of a particular cognitive challenge (or problem to solve) necessitating a detailed task-analysis of how the human mind changes external objects or events into a useful form according to certain, precisely specified rules or strategies, similar to the way a computer programmer programs a computer to perform a function. Thus, information processing theories focus on the process, how the learner arrives at a response or answer.

A brief analysis of one information processing theory will serve to illustrate this point. Robert Sternberg's (1985) triarchic theory of intelligence is a theory taking into account three features of learning. Those three features are (a) the mechanics or components of intelligence (including both higher-ordered thinking processes, such as planning, decision-making, and problem-solving, and lower-ordered processes, such as making inferences, mapping, selectively encoding information, retaining information in memory, transferring new information in memory, and so forth); (b) the learner's experiences; and (c) the learner's context (including the adaptation to and the shaping and selecting of environments).

According to Sternberg, learners' use of the mechanics of intelligence is influenced by learners' experiences. To illustrate, some cognitive processes (such as those required in reading) become automatized as a result of continued exposure to and practice of those skills. Learners who come from homes where parents read and where there are lots of different reading materials tend to be more proficient readers; certainly, learners who read a lot become more proficient readers. Those learners who are exposed to reading activities and who have ample opportunities to practice reading have greater skill and expertise in reading; and in a cyclical manner, students who have skills in reading like to read. Conversely, those who lack reading skills don't like to read. Students who don't like to read, don't read; thus, their reading skills, lacking practice, fail to improve.

An information processing approach acknowledges that not only are individuals influenced by their environments and adapt to those environments, individuals also are active in shaping their own environments. In other words, a child who wants to read but who has no books at home may ask parents to buy books, or may go to the library to read, or check out books to read at home.

Information processing theory is of interest to educators because of its insistence on the idea that intelligent performance can be facilitated through instruction and direct training. In sum, intelligent thinking can be taught. Sternberg has urged teachers to identify the mental processes that academic tasks require and to teach learners those processes; he challenges teachers to teach learners what processes to use, when and how to use them, and how to combine them into strategies for solving problems and accomplishing assignments.

Teachers who wish to follow Sternberg's advice might choose to begin teaching by identifying *instructional objectives*; that is, what should students be able to do as a result of instruction. Second, teachers would analyze the objectives in terms of identifying the *instructional outcomes*, those being the tasks or assignments that students can perform as a result of achieving the instructional objectives. Third, teachers would analyze instructional outcomes in terms of the *cognitive skills* or mental processes required to perform those tasks or assignments. After following these three steps and identifying instructional objectives, instructional outcomes, and cognitive skills involved, the teacher is ready to conduct a *preassessment* (or pretest) to determine what students already know.

Instruction is then based on the results of the preassessment with teachers focusing on teaching directly the cognitive skills needed in order for students to perform the task(s). Following instruction, teachers would conduct a *post-assessment* (or post-test) to evaluate the results of instruction. Further instruction would be based on the results of the post-assessment, that is, whether or not students had achieved expected outcomes and whether or not teachers had achieved instructional objectives.

Regardless of which theoretical perspective is adopted by teachers (at times, teachers may find themselves taking a rather eclectic approach and borrowing elements from several theoretical bases), it is helpful for teachers to consider if they are structuring their classrooms to satisfy learners' needs or merely their own. Furthermore, if the teachers' goal is to increase teaching effectiveness by facilitating learners' knowledge and skill acquisition, then teachers will engage continuously in a process of self-examination and self-evaluation.

Metacognition

Self-examination and self-evaluation are both types of *metacognitive* thinking. *Metacognition* is a term used to describe what, how, and why people know what they know when they know it. In short, it is thinking about thinking and knowing about knowing. Cognitive psychologists describe metacognition as a characteristic of higher-ordered, mature, and sophisticated thinking. Generally speaking, as learners achieve higher levels of cognitive skills, they also increase their metacognitive skills. Therefore, not only should teachers engage in metacognitive thinking, they should model that thinking for their students, and encourage their students to develop metacognitive skills.

Metacognition can be understood in terms of (a) metacognitive knowledge and (b) metacognitive control (Flavell, 1987). Basically, metacognitive knowledge is what learners need to know and metacognitive control is what learners need to do. Metacognitive control, therefore, is in the hands of the learner. Teachers cannot control learners' behavior although they can encourage and admonish. The best that teachers can do is help learners expand their metacognitive awareness and knowledge.

Awareness can be increased by talking about metacognition. John Flavell has explained that there are three kinds of metacognitive knowledge, those three kinds being (a) person knowledge, (b) task knowledge, and (c) strategy knowledge.

Person knowledge falls into one of three categories: (a) intraindividual knowledge, (b) interindividual knowledge, and (c) universal knowledge. First, intraindividual knowledge is what the learner knows or understands about him- or herself. Therefore, it is important that learners have opportunities to learn about themselves, about their interests, abilities, propensities, and so forth. For this reason (among others), it is important that learners have opportunities to learn about their own learning style and their perceptual strengths. It is also helpful for them to have opportunities to examine their personalities, values, and goals.

Furthermore, in a model that recognizes the dynamic nature of instruction, that is, one which recognizes that the learner also knows certain things and can contribute to the classroom, teachers realize that they are learners, too. This notion, in fact, is entirely consistent with systems theory, which posits that a change in any part of a whole will, in turn, affect the other parts of the whole. For example, in application to the family, a change (the birth or adoption of a new family member) affects every other member of the family. In application to the educational setting, a change in principals affects all the teachers and students, a change in teachers affects the students, principal, and other teachers.

Teachers, then, can benefit from examining their own learning style, perceptual strengths, personalities, values, and goals. Moreover, it can be extremely beneficial for teachers to consider their own instructional style.

Instructional Style Assessment

One instrument that assesses instructional style, the Instructional Style Inventory (Canfield & Canfield, 1988), identifies instructional styles in four general categories (although there also can be combinations of different styles). The four categories are *social, independent, applied,* and *conceptual.* Briefly stated, the social style is one that describes the teacher who values classroom interactions, who stresses teamwork and group work; the independent style describes the teacher who emphasizes working alone and is likely to rely on self-paced, individualized, and programmed instruction; the applied style is one that stresses real-world experiences, avoids lecture and preparatory reading, but focuses on practicums and site visits; and finally, the conceptual style is one describing the teacher who is language-oriented and likes highly organized materials and tends to depend on lectures and readings.

Teacher and Student Roles

An effective teacher plays many roles in the classroom in addition to the traditional instructor role. In one lesson, teachers may play several roles as they use several different strategies. Teachers who use lecture are in the role of an instructor who provides information. Students who listen to lectures are usually in a passive, often inattentive, role of listener. Teachers who use cooperative strategies take on the roles of a coach, who encourages his students to work together, and a facilitator who helps activities proceed smoothly and provides resources. Students in a collaborative role must learn social and group roles, as well as content, in order to accomplish learning tasks. Teachers who use inquiry strategies take the role of a facilitator who plans outcomes and provides resources for students as they work. Students in an inquirer role must take more responsibility for their own learning by planning, carrying out, and presenting research and projects. Teachers who listen to student discussions and presentations and evaluate student papers and projects take on the role of an audience that provides constructive feedback. Students in a discussion role must prepare carefully and think seriously about the topic under discussion.

The most natural role for teachers is that of instructor, since that is the role that they have seen modeled most often. The usual role for students is that of passive listener, since that is the role they have practiced most often. Taking on other roles requires commitment to learning new methods and procedures, as well as practice for perfecting them. Both teachers and students may feel uncomfortable in new roles until they are practiced enough to become familiar.

It is vital that teachers realize that even though their comfort level is probably higher when they function in one particular capacity (as facilitator, lecturer, or co-learner, for example), in order to provide effective instruction for all students, there will be occasions when they will be required to function outside that comfort level. For example, the teacher whose highest comfort and satisfaction is in lecturing may discover that in some situation with certain content, lecture is less effective than discussion or hands-on exploration. In those situations, effective teachers are those who are willing to take risks and experiment with different modes of instruction. It is also important to keep in mind that instruction that works well in one situation at one point in time may be less effective in another situation at another point in time. Thus, the role of the effective teacher is to constantly experiment and explore modes of delivering effective instruction.

Individual, Task, and Strategy Knowledge (*Metacognition continued*)

Returning to the discussion on metacognitive knowledge, the second kind of person knowledge is interindividual knowledge, how learners are alike and how they are different. This is another reason why the recognition of diversity, brought about by studying learning styles, can inform learners and improve their cognitive performance. As they become aware of their own learning style, learners also observe that their classmates have some similarities and some differences when it comes to the various elements or factors in determining learning style. Interindividual knowledge is increased as students realize that there are many different ways to learn.

Finally, the third kind of person knowledge is universal knowledge, the knowledge that there are degrees of understanding. Examples include the realization that short-term memory is fallible and has limited capacity, that people can make mistakes, that it is easier to remember things if they are written down, and that memory work requires repetition. To examine students' understanding of universal knowledge, teachers might ask students to identify what they know about learning, possibly by asking students to write what they know about how people learn on notecards or by brainstorming the question in class.

The second broad category of metacognitive knowledge, according to Flavell, is task knowledge. Task knowledge includes several different variables, such as whether information is interesting or boring, new or familiar, easy or difficult. Task knowledge enables learners to plan appropriately for undertaking tasks (for example, if something is hard to learn, then it may take more time, more concentration, and more effort), and tells them how to go about accomplishing the task (for example, if the task requires memory, then a memory strategy is needed).

Specific tasks relevant to academic disciplines can be identified by classroom teachers; however, there are academic tasks that are generally applicable to all content-areas. These academic tasks include what are broadly referred to as study skills, but are foundational skills for all learning. They include such tasks as time management, directing attention, processing information, finding main ideas, studying, and taking tests, among others (Weinstein, Schulte, & Palmer, 1988).

Flavell's final category of metacognitive knowledge is strategy knowledge, which takes into account how learners can best accomplish particular tasks and how they can be reasonably certain that they have reached their cognitive goals. Strategy knowledge also equips learners to monitor their cognitive activities and to gain confidence in their abilities. To illustrate, if the task is to find main ideas, then learners need strategies for finding main ideas. Strategies for this task include learning (a) to preview or survey reading assignments (reading headings and words in bold print, looking at illustrations and graphic aids); (b) to ask questions (What is this about? Who is this about? When did it happen? Where did it happen? How did it happen? Why did it happen?); and (c) to read the first and last sentences in each paragraph (knowing that the first and last sentences in paragraphs are most likely to be topic sentences).

Study Strategies

If the task is to study, then learners need specific strategies for studying. These strategies can include (a) outlining, mapping, or summarizing text (from books or notes); (b) marking text (using margins for notetaking and summarizing); (c) participating in group review sessions; (d) comparing notes with a friend, tutor, or teacher; (e) getting extra help (from a tutor, teacher, or parent); and (f) going to the library (to get additional information from alternative sources). Of course, strategies such as outlining can be further delineated into specific steps for various kinds of outlines.

Obviously, there is an interaction between person, task, and strategy knowledge. For example, if the task is studying, then a visual learner who learns well by reading (individual characteristic) might choose to go to the library to find an alternative source of information (strategy characteristic); in this example, there is a three-way interaction involving task, individual, and strategy.

Although teachers willingly expend considerable energy teaching students about tasks, they often erroneously assume that students will automatically or tacitly acquire learning strategies. However, the fact is that many students do not acquire these strategies and that even those who may learn some strategies would benefit from direct instruction in the use of specific learning strategies. The research literature indicates that the use of think-aloud protocols, spontaneous private speech, skimming, rereading, context clues, error-detection, grouping skills, and examination/evaluation skills (distinguishing between conceptual versus superficial features, between major themes and minor details, between decoding and comprehension, between verbatim recall and recall for gist) can significantly enhance learners' performance.

Teachers who incorporate an understanding of the role played by metacognition (especially in teaching middle-school and older students) into their instruction will find that they are preparing their students well for a lifetime of learning. Flavell (1979) explained that metacognition is necessary for the oral communication of information, oral persuasion, oral comprehension, reading comprehension, writing, language acquisition, attention, memory, problem-solving, social cognition, self-control, and self-instruction. It is hard to imagine a task that one might do that wouldn't require metacognition.

A recent critique of education in America includes the observation that the movement to teach basic academic skills in America's schools may have resulted in more students performing well on tests of basic skills; however, thinking skills, not just basic skills, are needed in the real world of jobs, families, and citizenship. To better prepare students for the real world, teachers need to focus on the **process** of learning, teaching students **how to think and learn**. Teaching metacognitive awareness and fostering the development of metacognitive knowledge are steps in the right direction.

Self-Directed Learning

Effective teachers not only set goals for their students, but also teach students to set and accomplish their own goals, both individually and in groups. Students need to learn how to plan for their individual learning as well as for learning in a group of students. If students are unaccustomed to setting goals, the effective teacher begins by modeling the process. The teacher explains how he or she develops goals and objectives for the class. One way of encouraging students to set goals is to ask them to set a performance standard for themselves regarding time needed to complete a project. For example, students might determine they will need 15 minutes to answer five questions, writing one paragraph of at least five sentences for each question. In order to accomplish this goal, the students must focus their attention very carefully and limit themselves to about three minutes per question. The teacher should then ask questions to help students determine whether their goal was realistic, and if not, what adjustments they need to make.

Other steps could be to ask students to develop their own questions about material to be learned or to plan activities to accomplish the goals of the lesson. The highest level is to have students determine the goals for their own learning. For example, a science teacher might introduce the topic of earthquakes, then help students determine what they need to know about earthquakes and the activities and resources that will help them learn. Students also need to develop plans for products which will show that they have met their goals.

Another way to encourage self-directed thinking and learning is to use higher-level questioning strategies and to teach students to use them as well.

Sample Question

Karla Dixon is a second-grade teacher who has selected a book to read to her class after lunch. She shows the students the picture on the cover of the book and reads the title of the book to them. She then asks, "What do you think this book is about?"

By asking this question, Ms. Dixon is

(A)   learning which students are interested in reading strategies.

(B)   trying to keep the students awake since she knows they usually get sleepy after lunch.

(C)   encouraging students to make a prediction, a precursor of hypothetical thinking.

(D)   finding out which students are good readers.

The correct response is (C). The teacher is encouraging students to become actively engaged in the learning process by making a prediction based on limited information given in the book title and cover illustration. When students can generate their own predictions or formulate hypotheses about possible outcomes on the basis of available (although limited) data, they are gaining preparatory skills for formal operations (or abstract thinking). Although second-grade students would not be expected to be at the level of cognitive development characterized by formal operations, Piagetian theory would indicate that teachers who model appropriate behaviors and who give students opportunities to reach or stretch for new cognitive skills are fostering students' cognitive growth. (A) is a poor choice because students' responses to this one question posed by the teacher cannot be used to assess adequately their interest in reading activities. (B), likewise, is a poor choice in that it implies no instructional intent for asking the question. (D) is incorrect because students' responses to a single question cannot allow the instructor to determine which students are good readers and which are not.

TExES

Texas Examinations of Educator Standards

Chapter 2

Domain II:
Creating a Positive, Productive Classroom Environment

Chapter 2

DOMAIN II:
Creating a Positive, Productive Classroom Environment

Teachers are responsible for creating a classroom environment that is conducive to learning. Although students must make their own commitment to learning, professional educators must make the commitment to do everything in their power to ensure that all students learn what they need to learn. The teacher is responsible for making classes interesting instead of dull, appropriate instead of irrelevant, and challenging instead of boring. Students will learn more if the class is interesting, appropriate, and challenging. If students aren't learning, then no teaching has occurred, no matter how many lectures and activities are provided.

The professional educator is responsible for careful planning, alone or with others, so that the class has purpose and direction. The educator also teaches students how to make their own goals and objectives so that they can become self-directed learners. Although students may provide suggestions and make plans for classroom activities, the teacher is ultimately responsible for what goes on in the classroom. The teacher must be an effective communicator, using both spoken and written language to convey ideas and serve as a model for student communication. Knowing how to ask questions and what questions to ask is essential. The word educate comes from root words that mean to *draw out*. Skillful questioning can draw out from students more ideas and work than they ever thought possible.

Professional educators must use a variety of teaching methods, choosing different methods for different goals. They must expand their repertoire from lecture (with which the new teacher is most familiar) to a wide variety of methods, including cooperative learning, inquiry or discovery, discussion, synectics, and other deductive and inductive methods. Today's educator must use all available resources in order to meet a variety of learning styles. The teacher must be able to use computers to enhance instruction in a variety of ways.

Assessment must be authentic, appropriate to the learning task and reflective of what the student has actually learned or accomplished. Essay questions, portfolios, projects, and peer and self-assessment are usually more authentic measures than true/false or multiple-choice tests.

The professional educator must also master the art of organizing a classroom so that maximum use is made of available time and resources. The teacher must use classroom rules, consequences, and procedures that enforce consistency. Although students may be allowed input as to suggestions about rules, the educator is responsible for seeing that no one interferes with another's learning.

In short, in order to enhance each student's achievement to its full potential, the professional educator must be a master planner, communicator, teacher, facilitator, organizer, guide, and role model. The two competencies that are required to fulfill this task are as follows:

005. The teacher knows how to establish a classroom climate that fosters learning, equity, and excellence and uses this knowledge to create a physical and emotional environment that is safe and productive.

006. The teacher understands strategies for creating an organized and productive learning environment and for managing student behavior.

Competency 005

The teacher knows how to establish a classroom climate that fosters learning, equity, and excellence and uses this knowledge to create a physical and emotional environment that is safe and productive.

This competency addresses the need for teachers to be able to recognize and identify both external and internal factors that affect student learning. The preceding discussion on human development emphasized primarily the characteristics of learners or what may be considered internal factors. Internal factors, beyond the general characteristics that humans share as they grow and mature, also include factors such as students' personality characteristics, their self-concept and sense of self-esteem, their self-discipline and self-control, their ability to cope with stress, and their general outlook on life.

External factors are those things outside the student that have an impact on the student. They include the home environment, family relationships, peer relationships, community situations, and the school environment. In other words, external factors constitute the context in which the student lives and learns.

Maslow's Hierarchy of Needs

Abraham Maslow's hierarchy of human needs is a model applicable to many diverse fields, including education, business and industry, health and medical professions, and more. Maslow identifies different levels of individuals' needs in a hierarchical sequence, meaning that lower level needs must be satisfied before individuals could ascend to higher levels of achievement. He identifies the fulfillment of basic physiological needs as fundamental to individuals' sense of well-being and their ability to engage in any meaningful activity. Simply stated, students' physiological needs (to have hunger and thirst satisfied, to have sleep needs met, to be adequately warm, and so forth) must be met before students can perform school tasks. Today's schools provide students with breakfast and lunch when needed, and great effort and expense is often directed towards heating and cooling school buildings.

Maslow's second level of need concerns safety. Students must feel safe from harm and danger before they are ready to learn. Today, schools often are equipped with metal detectors to increase students' sense of safety. In some schools, guards and security officers patrol the halls.

The third level of need, according to Maslow's theory, is the need for affiliation, or the need to belong and to be accepted by others. Although this need may, at first glance, seem less related to the student's environment, it does, indeed, refer to the student's social environment. Students need the opportunity to develop social relationships and to establish friendships among their peers. In essence, Maslow determined that environmental factors are important in education.

Another significant principle of human development arises from a long debate between those experts who believed that innate characteristics (those the individual is born with) play the most important role in determining who the individual will become and what he or she will do versus those who believed that environmental characteristics are most important. This argument is referred to as the **nature** versus **nurture** debate.

Nature and Nurture

After experts on both sides of the argument state their positions, the conclusion seems to be that both *nature* (the internal variables) and *nurture* (the environment) play equally important roles in determining the outcome of individuals' growth and maturation. Again, it is important to remember the interaction of the individual with her or his environment, recalling that this view is the *dynamic* view of human development.

Before proceeding, teachers would do well to understand that perception plays an important role for learners to the extent that perception creates our individual reality. The world as we know it is a result of our selective perception. We cannot attend to all events and variables in our environment. We select certain events and variables to notice, to attend to. The phenomena we observe form our perceptions; thus, we create our own reality.

Thus, it is one thing for teachers to be aware of and sensitive to the students' environment; it is, however, impossible for teachers to see, feel, and understand the individual's environment in exactly the same way that it is seen, felt, and understood by the student.

Carol Tavris, a social psychologist and author of the book *Anger: the Misunderstood Emotion*, notes that emotion plays a significant role in students' perceptions. For example, guilt is an emotion aroused by thoughts such as, "I should study or my parents will kill (be disappointed in) me." This is easily contrasted with the emotion of fear generated by the thought, "I should study or I will be a failure in life." Furthermore, guilt and fear can be compared to the emotion of anger which is prompted by thoughts such as, "Why should I study when my teacher is out to get me?" Today's student often sees the teacher as an enemy, not as an authority figure or a friend. Tavris identifies anger as a primary emotion experienced by many students today and one that plays a significant role in shaping their academic perceptions which, in turn, forms their reality of classroom experiences.

Explaining further, Tavris observes that unfulfilled expectations lead to anger. For example, if a student is led to believe (by teachers, school administrators, peers, or by parents and siblings) that attending class is somehow irrelevant to academic achievement, then the student who is frequently absent still has the expectation of being successful. The student's perception is that absenteeism is compatible with academic achievement. If, because of absenteeism, the student fails to master essential elements of the curriculum and does not succeed, then the student will feel anger, the appropriate and anticipated emotion.

Anger, however, can be diffused by addressing perceptions, correcting false impressions, and establishing appropriate and realistic expectations. To illustrate, if all those individuals significant to the student emphasize the importance of class attendance, then the student acquires the (in this case correct) perception that attendance is important for academic achievement and that absenteeism leads to academic failure.

For the sake of illustration only, consider what might happen if the teacher stresses attendance and the parents do not. In this case, the best route for the teacher to take is to show empathy for the student's dilemma. The teacher can acknowledge how difficult it is for the student to attend class when the parents are not supporting attendance, but the teacher also must seek to empower the student to make choices and to take responsibility for her or his own behavior.

In the situation described here, the student undergoes stress because of conflicting messages, and stress is faced by students and faculty alike. In fact, in the above example, the teacher is stressed too in that the teacher faces the conflict between supporting the parents of the student and supporting that which is in the best educational interests of the student.

Stress is the product of any change; both negative and positive changes produce stress. Environmental, physiological, and psychological factors cause stress. For example, environmental factors such as noise, air pollution, and crowding (among others) create stress; physiological factors such as sickness and physical injuries create stress; and, finally, psychological factors such as self-deprecating thoughts and negative self-image cause stress. In addition to the normal stressors that everyone experiences, some students are living in dysfunctional families; some students are dealing with substance abuse and addictions; some are experiencing sexual abuse. There are numerous sources of stress in the lives of students.

Since life is a stressful process, it is important that students and faculty learn acceptable ways to cope with stress. The first step in coping with stress is to recognize the role that stress plays in our lives. A teacher might lead a class through a brainstorming activity to help the students become aware of the various sources of stress affecting them. Next, the teacher could identify positive ways of coping with stress such as positive self-talk, physical exercise, proper nutrition, adequate sleep, balanced activities, time-management techniques, good study habits, and relaxation exercises.

Students who are stressed often become angry rather easily; however, students are not just angry. They experience a wide range of emotions, and may be sad, depressed, frustrated, afraid, or, on the positive side, happy and surprised. Effective teachers realize that students' emotions, as explained in this section and the preceding section on human development, play a significant role in students' classroom performance and achievement. Thus, effective teachers seek to create a classroom environment supportive of students' emotional needs. They have appropriate empathy and compassion for the emotional conflicts facing students, yet their concern is tempered by a realistic awareness of the importance of students attaining crucial academic and social skills that will grant them some control over their environment as they become increasingly independent and, eventually, prepare to be productive citizens.

Effective teachers recognize the effects of students' perceptions on the learning process and the effects of many environmental factors; as a result, they plan instruction to enhance students' self-esteem and to promote realistic expectations. It is important that teachers be able to differentiate positive and negative environmental factors, maximizing the positive variables and minimizing the negative ones. The teacher has the primary responsibility of creating a classroom environment that recognizes the different environmental factors affecting each student and that encourages each learner to excel, to achieve her or his personal best. Effective teachers work hard at creating learning environments in which all students are ready to learn—where students feel safe, accepted, competent, and productive.

Physical Setting

The effective teacher creates a physical setting conducive to achieving the goals of the school, the classroom, the teacher, and the students. While there are certain physical aspects of the classroom that cannot be changed (size, shape, number of windows, type of lighting, etc.), there are others that can be. Windows can have shades or blinds that distribute light correctly and allow for the room to be darkened for video or computer viewing. If the light switches do not allow part of the lights to remain on, sometimes schools will change the wiring system. If not, teachers can use a lamp to provide minimum lighting for monitoring students during videos or films.

Schools often schedule maintenance such as painting and floor cleaning during the summer. Often, school administrators will accede to requests for a specific color of paint, given sufficient time for planning.

All secondary school classrooms should have a bulletin board used by the teacher and by the students. The effective teacher has plans for changing the board according to units of study. Space should be reserved for display of student work and projects, either on the bulletin board, the wall, or in the hallway. (Secondary teachers who need creative ideas can visit elementary classrooms.)

Bare walls can be depressing; however, covering the wall with too many posters can be visually distracting. Posters that promote cooperation, study skills, and content ideas should be displayed, but the same ones should not stay up all year because they become invisible when too familiar.

Most classrooms have movable desks, which allows for varied seating arrangements. If students are accustomed to sitting in rows, this is sometimes a good way to start the year. Harry K. Wong has described his method of assigning seats on the first day of school, which is to assign each desk a column and row number, then give students assignment cards as they come into the room. Another method is to put seating assignments on an overhead, visible when students enter the room. Once students are comfortable with classroom rules and procedures, the teacher can explain to students how to quickly move their desks into different formations for special activities, then return them to their original positions in the last 60 seconds of class.

The best place for the teacher's desk is often at the back of a room, so there are few barriers between the teacher and the students and between the students and the chalkboards. This encourages the teacher to walk around the classroom for better monitoring of students.

Social and Emotional Climate

The effective teacher maintains a climate that promotes the lifelong pursuit of learning. One way to do this is to practice research skills that will be helpful throughout life. All subject areas can promote the skills of searching for information to answer a question, filtering it to determine what is appropriate, and using what is helpful to solve a problem.

Most English teachers require some type of research project, from middle school through the senior year. Ken Macrorie's books on meaningful research can guide English teachers as they develop a project that can answer a real-life issue for students. For example, a student who is trying to decide which school to attend could engage in database and print research on schools that have the major characteristics he is interested in. He could compile and review telephone or written interviews with school officials and current students, review school catalogs and other school documents, and magazine or journal articles that deal with the school. At the end of the process, students will have engaged in primary, as well as secondary research, plus they will have an answer to a personal question.

The English teacher can team up with any other subject area teacher to collaborate on a joint research project. The resulting product satisfies both the need of the English teacher to teach research skills and the need of the subject area teacher to teach content knowledge as well as research skills. Primary research can be done through local or regional resources such as business owners, lawyers, physicians, and the general public. Research questions could include: What effects do artificial sweeteners have on the human body's functioning (biology)? What process is used to develop the platform of a political party (history)? What happens when a business is accused of Title IX violations (business)? What effects have higher medical costs had on family budgets (economics)? How has the popularity of music CDs affected the music industry and businesses that sell records and tapes (music and business)?

Effective teachers also facilitate a positive social and emotional atmosphere and promote a risk-taking environment for students. They set up classroom rules and guidelines for how they will treat students, how students will treat them, and how students will treat each other. In part, this means that they don't allow ridicule or put-downs, issued either from themselves or among the students. It also means that they have an accepting attitude toward student ideas, especially when the idea is not what they expected to hear. Sometimes, students can invent excellent ideas that are not always clear until they are asked to explain how they arrived at them.

Students should feel free to answer and ask any questions that are relevant to the class, without fear of sarcasm or ridicule. Teachers should always avoid sarcasm. Sometimes teachers consider sarcasm to be mere teasing, but because some students often interpret it negatively, effective teachers avoid all types and levels of sarcasm.

Routines and Transitions

The effective teacher manages routines and transitions with a minimum of disturbance to students and to learning. Procedures are planned before students come to the first class. A routine is a procedure that has been practiced so that it works automatically. A transition is moving from one activity to another or from one desk arrangement to another.

Teachers need to consider how they want students to behave in the classroom: how students will ask questions, how they will sharpen pencils, how they will pass in papers, how they will put headings on papers, how they will move to get into groups. Teachers also need to determine their own behaviors: how to start class, how to take roll, how to call students to attention, how to handle tardiness, how to distribute materials, how to handle materials that can be checked out, and how to deal with late papers or projects.

Some procedures should be taught the first day, such as tornado and/or emergency drills. Teachers might also teach students how they will call them to attention, how they will start class, and how they will ask questions. It is better not to teach all procedures at once; they can be taught as needed. For example, the best time to teach students how to pass in papers is the first time they need to do so. If students are sitting in groups of four, the teacher may teach the students that the group leader should collect papers from each group member, then bring them to the teacher. This means that only one-fourth of the class is moving around. If students are sitting in rows, the teacher may decide to have students pass papers across instead of up the rows. This allows the teacher to monitor students while he or she walks down one aisle to collect the papers. This method also prevents some forms of student misbehavior.

Effective teachers have the students start class immediately, often by putting instructions for a short activity on the board or the overhead as the class enters the room. He or she teaches the students that they should start work on the activity immediately. Math teachers often put up two or three problems for students to work. English teachers often use several sentences that students must write correctly. Any content area teacher can list several content words that students must define, a few questions to review previous work, a brain-teaser, or a puzzle. While students are completing this activity, the teacher can quickly check roll with a seating chart. The activity can be checked before moving into new activities for the day.

Teachers may decide that all students must raise their hands to be recognized before speaking in the large group. They should teach this procedure the first day, then make sure they enforce it constantly and consistently, reminding students of the procedure and verbally reinforcing the class for following it. ("I appreciate your remembering to raise your hands to ask a question or make a contribution. That makes the class run more smoothly.")

Teachers who want students to work collaboratively will also teach procedures for group work. They may decide that before a student in a group can ask the teacher a question, everyone else in the group must first be asked. If no one has an answer, then the group leader for the day can raise a hand for teacher assistance. This way, only one-fourth of the class is asking for attention. One member of the group can be assigned the role of materials clerk; only one-fourth of the class is moving around the room.

One method of calling a group back to attention, especially during group work, is for the teacher to raise a hand, indicating that all students should raise their own hands, stop talking, and focus attention on the teacher. The reason students raise their hands is that some will have their backs to the teacher, but they will be able to see other students raise hands. This procedure can be taught and practiced in three or four minutes and is effective in a classroom or in a large auditorium. Students should have several opportunities for practice, then the teacher should periodically reinforce the group for following the procedure quickly.

The effective teacher plans all transitions ahead of time, then gives clear instructions and a time limit for students to make the move. A teacher who wants students to move themselves or their desks should give all instructions before allowing students to move. It is easier to maintain student attention while they are still in the large group, plus they can start work as soon as they are in the new arrangement. Instructions for what students will do in the group should come before making membership assignments, so that student attention will be focused on the task. The best way to make group assignments is by giving students a list of group members or by putting the list on the overhead or wall. After checking for questions, the teacher should give the students a reasonable time limit for moving into groups— five to eight seconds—then count off the seconds for the first transition and praise students for making the quick transition. ("Thank you for moving so quickly. This gives you more time to accomplish your task.")

Sample Question

Maria Smith is a high school English teacher who is concerned about a student who is failing her junior English class. The student has not turned in any outside assignments, and Ms. Smith has noticed a definite decline in the quality of work the student completes in class. Ms. Smith also has observed that the student has great difficulty staying awake in class and that she seems irritable and distracted most of the time.

In her efforts to help the student, Ms. Smith decides to ask the student

(A)   if she has been having family problems.

(B)   if she realizes that the quality of her classwork is suffering and if she knows of any reasons for the decline.

(C)   to work on better time-management skills.

(D)   to start coming in early or to stay after class to receive extra help with her work.

The correct response is (**B**). This question opens the door for dialogue with the student about a range of possible problems. This response shows that the teacher is concerned about the student and her welfare without making assumptions, jumping to conclusions, and/or intruding into the private affairs of the student. (A) presumes that the source of all problems lies with the family. Although the student may be having family-related difficulties, there are other possibilities to consider as well. The student may have taken a job that is taking too much of her time away from her studies or the student may be having health problems. It is unwise for the teacher to conclude that the student is having family problems. (C) is inappropriate because it too narrowly identifies one possible coping mechanism as the solution to the student's problem. Although the student may benefit from acquiring better time-management skills, it also is possible that the student's present problems have little or nothing to do with time-management. (D) is equally inappropriate in that it demands that the student devote even more time to school although she currently is having trouble with present demands. If the student is unwell, then certainly spending more time at school is not the solution to her problem. Clearly, (B) is the best alternative to helping the student identify her problem(s) and find a solution.

COMPETENCY 006

The teacher understands strategies for creating an organized and productive environment and for managing student behavior.

Academic Learning Time

The effective teacher maximizes the amount of time spent for instruction. A teacher who loses five minutes at the beginning of class and five minutes at the end of class wastes ten minutes a day that could have been spent in educational activities. This is equivalent to a whole period a week, four classes a month, and 25 periods a year.

Academic learning time is the amount of allocated time that students spend in an activity at the appropriate level of difficulty with the appropriate level of success. The appropriate level of difficulty is one that challenges students without frustrating them. Students who have typically been low achievers need a higher rate of success than those who have typically been higher achievers.

One way to increase academic learning time is to teach students procedures so they will make transitions quickly. Another is to have materials and resources ready for quick distribution and use. Another is to give students a time limit for a transition or an activity. In general, time limits for group work should be slightly shorter than students need, in order to encourage time on task and to prevent off-task behavior and discipline problems. It is essential for the teacher to have additional activities planned should the class finish activities sooner than anticipated. As students complete group work, they should have other group or individual activities so they can work up until the last minute before the end of class.

Collaborative Learning

Collaborative or cooperative learning strategies provide important ways students learn to work and plan together. David and Roger Johnson and Robert Slavin are three of several educators who have researched cooperative learning and have developed strategies, materials, and resources to assist teachers and students in learning how to work together.

Cooperative groups are formed heterogeneously, with differences in mind. These differences can be general (such as age, intelligence, developmental level, school performance) or task-specific. The purpose is to provide an opportunity or vehicle for students of various groups or levels to learn from each other. Often, lower-achieving and higher-achieving studies are grouped together. In such instances, lower-achieving students are challenged to keep up with and contribute to their groups; advanced students gain a deeper understanding when they discuss concepts with others. Research has shown that there is a level of "optimal heterogeneity" that requires a balance between enough difference among members of the group or team to trigger conflict and yet enough mutual interest and intelligibility to allow dialogue and cooperation.

The groups vary in size from three to five members; typically, the groups work together with each other for several months in order to develop profitable relationships.

There are five basic elements associated with collaborative learning. The first is *face-to-face interaction.* Group members should be sitting very close to each other so they can look each other in the eye while they discuss. It is important that students begin to form working relationships with their peers. This closeness also helps reduce the noise level of talking.

Another element is *positive interdependence,* which means that students must learn to depend on each other to complete a project or achieve a goal. This is often achieved by providing only one set of resources or one answer sheet. Students must work together in order to perform the task. Another is to provide incentives, such as five extra points on individual tests if everyone in the group makes at least 80 percent. This encourages students to help each other learn so that all will do well on the assessment.

The third element is *individual accountability.* This means that each student in the group is held accountable for everything that is to be learned. One way of encouraging this is to give individual tests. Although students work and study together, each must pass a test for himself. Another method is to give the same grade to each person in the group. This encourages interdependence because students hold each other accountable for learning and performing the assigned part. It encourages individual accountability because the group is successful only if all members perform well. A common error teachers make with this element is neglecting to make sure that all students do their part. Success of the group should not depend on one diligent student or be undermined because of one lazy student.

The next element is *social skills.* The effective teacher has two types of objectives for collaborative learning: cognitive and affective. The cognitive objectives relate to the content that students must understand and master; the affective objectives relate to social skills that are necessary for students to be able to function in their groups. Examples of social skills include listening actively to others, listening without interrupting, encouraging each other, and using polite language and manners. In addition, teachers assign roles to each member of the group. For example, one student may have the role of group recorder, responsible for writing and turning in any papers or products. Another may have the role of resource clerk, responsible for obtaining and returning materials. Each group member should have a different role; the effective teacher rotates role assignments so that each member has an opportunity to become proficient in each role.

The final element is very important, but it is often omitted. During *group processing,* students reflect on how well their group worked together. They also determine what they can do to function more effectively during the next group assignment. Students learn to set goals for their collaborative groups, in terms of achievement and products. They learn to evaluate their own performance so they can improve it during future projects. The effective teacher helps students set their goals, then monitors to make sure they are making progress. If they are, the teacher will positively reinforce their goal-oriented behavior; if they are not, the teacher will steer them back on course, usually by asking questions which lead students to decide what they need to do next.

Research studies have shown that cooperative learning results in an atmosphere of achievement, the development and use of critical-thinking skills, positive relations among different ethnic groups, the implementation of peer coaching, the establishment of an environment where academic achievement is valued, and better-managed schools. More than 70 major studies (including federally-funded research centers, field investigations, and local school districts) have shown that cooperative learning is effective in improving student achievement (especially when group goals and individual accountability are used together), that students of very different groups learn to like one another when they work together, and that students with learning disabilities benefit when teamed with other students in their class (Office of Education Research, 1992).

Classroom Discipline

The effective teacher realizes that having an interesting, carefully planned curriculum is one of the best ways to prevent most discipline problems. Another way is to have a discipline system of classroom rules, consequences, and rewards, which are applied consistently to every student. All classroom rules, consequences, and rewards must be in compliance with campus requirements. The goals of a classroom system of discipline are that students become self-disciplined and that all but the most serious misbehavior is handled in the classroom by the teacher.

The effective teacher limits rules to four or five essential behaviors by determining the conditions that have to be in order for learning to take place. One might be that students must respect each other by not engaging in sarcasm or cutting remarks. Another might be that students must come to class on time with textbooks, paper, and pencil. Another teacher might insist that students raise their hands to be recognized before speaking. A teacher might have as a general principle that students will not hinder the teaching, their own learning, or the learning of other students. (Class rules should not be confused with classroom procedures, such as how to pass in papers.)

The effective teacher knows what the rules will be before students come to the first class, or develops them with the students during the first couple of days. Many teachers choose to have two or three rules, then ask students for input on two more rules for classroom behavior. Others ask for student input for all four or five rules. Most classes will come up with rules that are acceptable to the teacher and to the class. Often, teachers will ask students to come up with one or two rules for the teacher (returning tests within two days, making at least one helpful comment on each paper, etc.).

Once the rules have been determined, the teacher makes sure that each student understands each rule, the consequences for breaking a rule, and the rewards for keeping the rules. Consequences should be spelled out in advance, before rules are broken. Some teachers prefer a system of increasingly serious consequences, such as: (1) name on the board, (2) detention after school, (3) call home to parents, (4) visit to the principal. If being sent to the office is a consequence for repeated misbehavior, then the principal must be aware of and approve the consequence. Most principals also have a system of consequences, once students are sent to their office. In general, additional homework should not be assigned as a consequence, because negative feelings transfer to the idea of learning.

Rewards also help maintain discipline. The goal of a discipline system is that students become self-disciplined; however, external rewards can help the classroom run more smoothly. The reward should not be perceived as a bribe, but as a reward for appropriate behavior. Teachers often ask students for a list of possible rewards. They can include verbal praise, stickers, and positive notes home. They can also include class rewards such as ten minutes of free time on Friday or listening to a radio while doing class work, if no more than five misbehaviors have occurred during the week. Classes can accumulate points to "win" a class reward at the end of the six weeks.

After the system of rules, consequences, and rewards has been determined, the teacher should put them on a poster in the room and give students copies for their notebooks. Often, a teacher asks students and a parent or guardian to sign a copy and return it for his or her files, to ensure that both the student and parents understand what type of behavior is expected.

One key to effective discipline is consistency. A teacher who has a rule that students must raise their hands to be called on, but who lets students call out questions or answers, will soon find that no one raises his hand. The rule must also be applied to every student. This is one reason that rules must be carefully chosen. A teacher with a rule that states, "Any student who does not turn in homework at the beginning of the period will get a zero," has no room to make allowances for reasonable excuses for not having homework. The rule might be better stated, "Students should turn in homework at the beginning of each class," with a range of consequences that can be chosen by the teacher, based on whether it is a first or repeated infraction.

Correcting Students

The best way to correct students is usually privately. A teacher who reprimands or criticizes a student in front of the rest of the class will often provoke negative or hostile responses from the student. Harry K. Wong and others have described various methods of confronting students privately. The teacher moves close to the student, calls him or her by name, looks the student in the eye, makes a statement of what behavior needs to stop and what behavior needs to begin, thanks him or her, then moves away. If students are accustomed to having the teacher move around the room to monitor achievement, they often will not even know that a student has been corrected.

The effective teacher also perfects "the look," which can be an unobtrusive way to let a student know he or she needs to change their behavior. Effective teachers also avoid falling into the trap of arguing with students. A student who wants to argue with a teacher can be defused if the teacher doesn't respond to the challenge, but restates the expected change and moves on. No one wins in a struggle to defend his or her own position or authority.

Student Ownership

One way of promoting student ownership in the classroom is to provide multiple opportunities for their input. Many teachers do this through allowing students to determine two or three rules for the classroom. Sometimes they also have class meetings where students discuss issues or problems that have arisen in an attempt to solve or alleviate them.

Effective teachers also give students choices in what they will study or research, within the parameters of the outcomes for the course. Often, this can be accomplished by giving a list of options for assignments, or asking students to brainstorm questions about a topic, then letting them choose from among the ones that are feasible, based on the curriculum and on the available resources. Teachers first determine the overall outcome for the unit, then brainstorm possibilities that would be acceptable.

A history teacher may determine that outcomes of a study of a South American country would be that students could explain how climate affects the development of agriculture and industry, how the form of government affects economic development, how sanitary conditions affect health and population growth, and how religion affects customs and traditions. The teacher could allow students to choose what country to learn about and pick either one country for the entire class or different countries for groups of students. Students can brainstorm questions about the country, then determine which questions they will answer in their research. The teacher, as facilitator, can guide the questions or add some of his own to ensure that the research will address the general areas of business and industry, economic development, health conditions, and religion.

The effective teacher promotes student ownership of and membership in a smoothly functioning learning community first by modeling positive, cooperative behavior, then by requiring students to exhibit positive behavior to each other. Cooperative learning strategies also promote an environment in which members are responsible, cooperative, purposeful, and mutually supportive. Collaborative activities provide practice in working together and developing social skills necessary to be successful in future classes, vocational or technical school or college, and careers. They allow students to develop leadership ability through the group roles they are assigned.

Sample Question

Mr. Deavers, a high school physical education teacher, usually has from 50 to 60 students in each class. He often has difficulty in checking roll and sometimes doesn't know who is present and who is absent from class. He realizes that he needs to institute a new plan.

What would be the best procedure for him to institute?

(A)   Have students gather on the bleachers, call each student's name and have each student respond, then put a check on the roll sheet.

(B)   Divide students into ten groups of five or six, appoint a leader, and have the leaders report absences.

(C)   Design a chart with ten rows, assign each student a specific place to stand or sit at the beginning of class, then check roll visually using the chart.

(D)   Have students start an activity, then visually identify each student and put checks on the roll sheet.

The correct response is (C). The question asks for an effective method of taking roll that doesn't detract from class. (C) is the best option. By assigning each student a specific place to stand, Mr. Deavers can quickly check attendance, in a method similar to the one he would use in assigning seats in a classroom. If teachers use seating charts in the classroom, this method would be familiar to the students. By requiring students to take this position immediately, he can also assign students to lead warmup exercises while he checks roll, thus making good use of the time. (A) is a poor choice. Although it might increase his awareness of who is absent and who is present, this method wastes instructional time. Also, without organization, one student may answer for another. (B) may be effective, but it assumes that all student leaders will be present each day and that they will all be responsible. A teacher who wants to teach responsibility may use a similar system, but would need to teach responsibility to the student leaders and to have assistant leaders as a backup. (D) is almost impossible if the students are engaged in an activity that requires movement. It would be very time-consuming as well, distracting the teacher's attention from the activity itself.

TExES

Texas Examinations of Educator Standards

Chapter 3

Domain III: Implementing Effective, Responsive Instruction & Assessment

Chapter 3

DOMAIN III:
Implementing Effective, Responsive Instruction and Assessment

Teachers provide instruction, and they assess learning so they can improve the process: teach, assess to measure learning, re-teach. This is the common cycle of instruction. However, providing instruction and assessment may accurately be viewed as an art rather than a simple series of skills. Parker Palmer, in his noted book *The Courage to Teach,* reminds the reader that "Good teaching cannot be reduced to technique; good teaching comes from the identity and integrity of the teacher" (p. 10). In this remark, Palmer underscores the importance of teaching as a journey of self-discovery and a profession with talents and skills that develop and become refined over time. Yet, the beginning teacher must possess certain skills in order to undertake the task of teaching others. With these precepts in mind, the following competencies are discussed:

007: The teacher understands and applies principles and strategies for communicating effectively in varied teaching and learning contexts.

008: The teacher provides appropriate instruction that actively engages students in the learning process.

009: The teacher incorporates the effective use of technology to plan, organize, deliver, and evaluate instruction for all students.

010: The teacher monitors student performance and achievement; provides students with timely, high-quality feedback; and responds flexibly to promote learning for all students.

COMPETENCY 007

The teacher understands and applies principles and strategies for communicating effectively in varied teaching and learning contexts.

Effective communication is an obvious mark of an effective teacher. Communication occurs only when someone sends a message and another person receives it. Teachers may "teach" and think they are sending a message, but if students aren't listening, there has been no communication because the receivers are not tuned in.

Principles of Verbal Communication

There are several principles which apply to written and oral messages in the classroom.

The message must be accurate. As Mark Twain said, "The difference between the right word and the almost right word is the difference between lightning and the lightning bug." Teachers in particular must be careful to use very specific words that carry the appropriate denotation (literal meaning), as well as connotation (feelings, associations, and emotions associated with the word). Content teachers must carefully teach vocabulary related to the subject area.

It is possible to be completely accurate, however, without being clear. At times a teacher may use an excessive amount of jargon from his or her subject area. While students must learn vocabulary related to the subject area, the teacher must ensure that the words are taught and then reviewed so the students have practice using them. At other times, a teacher may assume that students understand difficult words. Many students are hesitant to ask what a word means; teachers must be alert to nonverbal signs that students don't understand a word (confused looks, pauses in writing a word down, failure to answer a question containing the word, etc.). Taking a couple of seconds to ask students to define a word will help them understand the larger content area concepts.

Words should also be specific or concrete. The more abstract a word, the more ambiguous it will be. For example, "physical activity" is very general; "Little League baseball" is much more specific. Although students need to learn abstract words, explaining them in a concrete manner will increase their understanding. Saying that a war causes economic difficulties is general; being more specific would be to say that it reduces the amount of tax money available to cities because of money spent on munitions.

A teacher's communications must also be organized. Students will not be able to follow directions that are given in jumbled order, interrupted with, "Oh, I forgot to tell you." Effective teachers plan their directions carefully, writing them down for the students or making notes for themselves so they will give directions or explain concepts in appropriate order.

Other communication strategies include monitoring the effects of a message or making sure that the audience actually received and understood the message. A teacher may encourage students to be active and reflective listeners by having each student summarize what another has said before making his or her own contribution. A teacher may ask students to record instructions in a notebook and then check each student's notation for accuracy to be sure that assignments are correctly recorded.

Nonverbal Communication

Even when the verbal or written message is accurate, clear, specific, and organized, nonverbal communication can confuse the message. Sometimes, the nonverbal aspect of communication can carry more weight than the verbal. Nonverbal messages can be sent by the way teachers dress, the way they use their facial expressions, and the way they use their voice. Experienced educators realize that students respond better when teachers dress professionally. Most people find it easier to take seriously someone dressed in neat, clean clothes than someone in wrinkled, ill-fitting clothing. Also, students behave better when they themselves are dressed neatly and comfortably.

Eye Contact and Body Language

Facial expressions communicate a world of emotions and ideas. Teachers use many voluntary facial expressions. All students have seen "the look" from a teacher, usually when a student does something out of order. A frown or raised eyebrows can also be very effective. Although positive involuntary expressions such as smiles and laughter are appropriate, teachers should guard against involuntary negative facial expressions that convey contempt, anger, or dislike to a student.

Eye contact can be used to control interactions. Teachers often look directly at students to encourage them to speak or look away to discourage them from speaking. "The stare" can be part of "the look" that teachers use for discipline reasons. Making eye contact with students is important when the teacher is giving instructions, sharing information, or answering questions. Many people make a habit of scanning the room with their eyes, pausing briefly to meet the gaze of many members of an audience. However, eye contact should last about four seconds to assure the person in the audience (or classroom) that the speaker has actually made contact.

Students also use their eyes, making contact with the teacher when they want to answer a question, but often looking at the floor or ceiling when they want to avoid being called on. However, teachers must be careful in making assumptions about eye contact. Research has revealed that students who are visually oriented tend to look upward while they are thinking about a response; kinesthetic learners tend to look down while they are thinking; auditory learners may look to the side. The teacher who says to a student, "The answer's not written on the floor!" may not understand the student's mode of thinking. Effective teachers who are encouraging higher-level thinking may find a classroom filled with eyes that look in various directions.

Cultural factors may also contribute to confusion about eye contact. Many cultures teach children that it is very disrespectful to look an adult in the eye; therefore, these students may stand or sit with downcast eyes as a gesture of respect. Forcing the issue only makes the students and teacher uncomfortable and actually hinders communication.

Body language can also convey feelings and emotions to students. A teacher can emphasize points and generalizations by gesturing or tapping something on the chalkboard. If a teacher gestures too often or too wildly, students find it difficult to determine what the teacher is trying to emphasize. Too many gestures can also cause the students to watch the gestures instead of attending to the information.

Beginning teachers especially need to convey a relaxed but formal body posture, which denotes strength, openness, and friendliness. Hiding behind the desk or crossing the arms indicate timidity or even fear. A teacher who meets students at the door with a smile and even a handshake shows confidence and control.

The way a teacher uses the voice conveys prejudices, feelings, and emotions. When a teacher's words convey one meaning and the tone of voice conveys another, the students will believe the tone rather than the meaning. Students immediately know the difference between, "That's a great idea," said in a low voice with a shrug, and, "That's a great idea!" said with energy and a smile. A teacher's tone of voice can tell a student, "I'm asking you, but I don't think you can answer this." Messages can be modified by varying the loudness or softness, by varying the tone, by using high or low pitch, and by changing the quality of speech.

A teacher's expectations for student behavior can be revealed through a combination of verbal and nonverbal communication. Jere Brophy and others have researched the relationship between teacher expectations and student behavior. This research shows that teachers often communicate differently when dealing with high-achievers and low-achievers. This behavior is not always deliberate or conscious on the part of the teacher, but it can communicate negative expectations. When dealing with high-achievers as opposed to low-achievers, teachers tend to listen more carefully, give them more time to answer, prompt or assist them more, call on them more often, give more feedback, and look more interested. The effective communicator will be careful not to differentiate communication based on a student's achievement level.

Media communication has become a vital part of the classroom process. Effective teachers use a variety of audio-visuals in every class, including posters, graphs, overhead transparencies, films, videos, CD-ROMs, and laser disks. (See Competency 009.)

Questioning

There are many ways that teachers can ask questions that elicit different levels of thinking, although studies of teachers' skills in questioning often reveal frequent use of lower-level questions and infrequent use of higher-level ones.

A simple method is to divide questions into two types: closed and open. An example of a closed question is, "What was the main character's name?" There is usually only one right answer to a closed question. Often students can point to a phrase or sentence in a book to answer a closed question.

An open-ended question requires students to think carefully about the answer. There may be more than one appropriate answer to an open-ended question. An example is, "What do you think was the most important contribution of Pascal to the field of mathematics?" Teachers who ask open-ended questions are not looking for one specific answer, rather they are looking for well-supported responses. Asking an open-ended question but requiring one specific answer will discourage rather than encourage thinking.

An example of a closed math question is, "What is 5 times 5?" An example of an open-ended math question is, "What is the best way to solve this problem?" The open-ended question assumes that the teacher will accept all reasonable methods of solving the problem, provided the students can explain why their method is best.

There are other ways to categorize questions. Benjamin Bloom (whose Taxonomy of Educational Objectives was described in some detail in the section of this book dealing with Competency 003) developed a taxonomy that teachers have used for a variety of purposes in addition to writing objectives, including categorizing questions and activities. Refer to the table below for a recap of the information about Bloom's Taxonomy.

Bloom's Taxonomy of Educational Objectives

Level of Question	Description	Questioning Verbs
Level 1: Knowledge	Remembers, recalls learned (or memorized) information	*defines; describes; enumerates; identifies; labels; lists; matches; names; reads; records; reproduces; selects; states; views*
Level 2: Comprehension	Understands the meaning of information and is able to restate in own words	*classifies; cites; converts; describes; discusses; estimates; explains; generalizes; gives examples; makes sense out of; paraphrases; restates (in own words); summarizes; traces; understands*
Level 3: Application	Uses the information in new situations	*acts; administers; articulates; assesses; charts; collects; computes; constructs; contributes; controls; determines; develops; discovers; establishes; extends; implements; includes; informs; instructs; oper-*

Level of Question	Description	Questioning Verbs
		ationalizes; participates; predicts; prepares; preserves; produces; projects; provides; relates; reports; shows; solves; teaches; transfers; uses; utilizes
Level 4: Analysis	Breaks down information into component parts; examines parts for divergent thinking and inferences	*breaks down; correlates; diagrams; differentiates; discriminates; distinguishes; focuses; illustrates; infers; limits; outlines; points out; prioritizes; recognizes; separates; subdivides*
Level 5: Synthesis	Creates something new by divergently or creatively using information	*adapts; anticipates; categorizes; collaborates; combines; communicates; compares; compiles; composes; contrasts; creates; designs; devises; expresses; facilitates; formulates; generates; incorporates; individualizes; initiates; integrates; intervenes; models; modifies; negotiates; plans; progresses; rearranges; reconstructs; reinforces; reorganizes; revises; structures; substitutes; validates*
Level 6: Evaluation	Judges on the basis of informed criteria	*appraises; compares and contrasts; concludes; criticizes; critiques; decides; defends; interprets; judges; justifies; reframes; supports*

Effective teachers also appreciate cultural dimensions of communication and are aware that some cultures teach their children not to question adults. These teachers explain to students that they expect questions, encourage students to ask them, but do not force the issue if students are very uncomfortable. Sometimes students may be willing to write down and turn in questions for the teacher. Teacher attitude can promote or deter questions, even by so simple a tactic as changing, "Does anybody have any questions?" to, "What questions do you have?" The first question implies that no one should have questions; the second assumes that there will be questions.

Classroom Climate

All of the elements of effective communication can be used to promote an atmosphere of active inquiry in the classroom. Teachers can present an idea to students, ask a real question that they are interested in, then guide exploration, using effective communication skills to encourage and lead the students.

Effective teachers also teach students to use the elements of communication so they can work together to explore concepts and then make effective presentations to the rest of the class (or other classrooms). Structured cooperative learning activities can promote collaborative learning and effective communication. The elements of communication are social skills that can be addressed during cooperative activities.

Sample Question

Miss Bailey teaches fifth-grade social studies in a self-contained classroom with 25 students of various achievement levels. She is starting a unit on the history of their local community and wants to stimulate the students' thinking. She also wants to encourage students to develop a project as a result of their study.

Which type of project would encourage the higher-level thinking by the students?

(A) Give students a list of questions about people, dates, and events, then have them put the answers on a poster with appropriate pictures to display in the class.

(B) Give students questions to use to interview older members of the community, then ask students to write articles based on the interviews and publish them in a booklet.

(C) Discuss the influence of the past on the present community, then ask students to project what the community might be like in 100 years.

(D) Use archived newspapers to collect data, then draw a timeline that includes the major events of the community from its beginning to the current date.

The correct response is (C). The question asks for work on the analysis, synthesis, or evaluation level. (C) is the best choice because it asks the students to analyze how past causes have produced current effects, then to predict what future effects might be, based on what they have learned about cause-effect relationships. It requires students to put information together in a new way. (A) may involve some creativity in putting the information on a poster, but in general, answering factual questions calls for lower-level (knowledge or comprehension) thinking. (B) may involve some degree of creativity, but giving students prepared questions requires thinking at a lower level than having students develop their own questions, and then determine which answers to write about. (D) is a lower-level activity, although there may be a great deal of research for factual information. All options may be good learning activities, but (A), (B), and (D) do not require as much deep thinking as (C). Depending on the depth of the study, a teacher may want to include several of these activities.

COMPETENCY 008

The teacher provides appropriate instruction that actively engages students in the learning process.

Effective teachers use not one but many methods and strategies to enhance student learning. Furthermore, in order to actively engage students it is imperative that teachers understand the developmental characteristics of their students, cognitively, physically, socially, and psychologically. For example, knowing that younger children have shorter attention spans, teachers should create a greater variety of activities and opportunities for younger students to physically move and act at regular intervals. In teaching all ages and levels, it is necessary for teachers to take into account students' attention span and other cognitive and noncognitive variables.

Teachers choose different strategies to meet different purposes and the needs of the content and the students. If the purpose is to provide a foundation for future investigations, the teacher might choose to use a short mastery lecture with questions. If the purpose is to encourage creative thinking, the teacher might choose a synectic strategy. If the purpose is to encourage expression of a variety of viewpoints about a topic, the teacher might choose structured discussion. If the purpose is to investigate current problems without specific answers, the teacher might choose an inquiry lesson.

Moreover, there is an adage that in teaching, "the one who does the talking is the one who learns the most." For this reason, it is important that teachers interact with students and give them the opportunity to practice important learning strategies, such as paraphrasing, rehearsing/practicing, questioning, and summarizing ideas. This idea is the same as that previously discussed as the role of the teacher as a guide rather than the "sage on the stage." It is also akin to the previously discussed importance of learning strategies.

We know that approximately ten percent of learners can learn best and most effectively by listening (auditory learners) whereas about 40 percent or more learn best by seeing (visual learners). Yet, that means that the remaining students learn best and most effectively when they are involved in hands-on activities and doing something (tactile-kinesthetic learners). These factors are closely related to this competency.

Deductive Strategies

Methods can be divided into two categories: deductive and inductive. Deductive methods are those in which teachers present material through mastery lecture, or students teach each other through presentations. In deductive lessons, the generalizations or rules are taught from the beginning, then examples and elaboration are developed which support the generalizations or rules. Deductive thinking often requires students to make assessments based on specific criteria that they or others develop. Inductive methods are those in which teachers encourage students to study, research, and analyze data they collect, then develop generalizations and rules based on their findings.

During inductive lessons, a hypothesis or concept is introduced at the beginning, but generalizations are developed later in the lesson and are based on inferences from data.

The lecture is a deductive method, whereby information is presented to students by the teacher. New teachers are especially attuned to lecture because that is the usual mode of instruction in college classes. An advantage of lecture is that large amounts of information can be presented in an efficient manner; however, effective teachers avoid dumping loads of information through lectures. Mastery lectures should be short, usually no more than 10 or 15 minutes at a time, and constantly interrupted with questions to and from students. Questions during a lecture tend to be lower-level ones, when the teacher is building a foundation of knowledge for students to use in later activities. The effective teacher, however, uses higher-level questions even during lectures.

Information sessions must also be supplemented with an array of visual materials that will appeal to visual learners as well as auditory ones. Putting words or outlines on the board or a transparency is very helpful; however, this is still basically a verbal strategy. Drawings, diagrams, cartoons, pictures, caricatures, and graphs are visual aids for lectures. Teacher drawings need not be highly artistic, merely memorable. Often a rough or humorous sketch will be more firmly etched in students' minds than elaborate drawings. Using a very simple sketch provides a better means of teaching the critical attributes than a complicated one. The major points stand out in a simple sketch; details can be added once students understand the basic concepts. For example, a very simple sketch of the shapes of the snouts of alligators and crocodiles can fix the difference in students' memory; identification from pictures then becomes easier.

Teachers should also be careful to include instruction on how to take notes while listening to a speaker, a skill that will be useful during every student's career, whether listening to instructions from a supervisor or a speaker at meetings and conferences. One way a teacher can do this is to show students notes or an outline from the mini-lecture he or she is about to present or to write notes or an outline on the board or overhead while she is presenting the information. This activity requires careful planning by the teacher and will result in a more organized lecture. This type of structure is especially helpful for sequential learners, who like organization. It will also help random learners develop organizational skills. A web or map or cluster is a more right-brained method of connecting important points in a lecture or a chapter. The effective teacher will use both systems and teach both to students, so they have a choice of strategies.

Inductive Strategies

Inquiry or discovery lessons are inductive in nature. Inquiry lessons start with a thought-provoking question for which students are interested in finding an explanation. The question can be followed by brainstorming a list of what the students already know about the topic, then categorizing the information. The categories can then be used as topics for group or individual research. Deductive presentations by students of their research can follow.

Some advantages of inductive lessons are that they generally require higher-level thinking by both teacher and students, and they usually result in higher student motivation, interest, and retention. They are also more interesting to the teacher, who deals with the same concepts year after year. Disadvantages include the need for additional preparation by the teacher, the need for access to a large number of resources, and additional time for students to research the concepts. The teacher spends a great amount of time in planning the lessons, then acts as facilitator during classes.

Generally, the greater the amount of planning and prediction by the teacher, the greater the success of the students. This does not mean that the activity must be tightly structured or set in concrete, but the effective teacher tries to predict student responses and potential reactions to them. The need for purchasing additional resources has been moderated by computerized bibliographic services, interlibrary loan, and CD-ROMs with all types of information. Because inductive, research-oriented units require more class time, subject-area teachers must work together to determine what concepts are essential for students to understand; other nonessential concepts are omitted.

An English teacher wishing to introduce an inductive study of *Julius Caesar* might ask students what would happen if a group of United States senators and representatives banded together to kill the current president and take control of the government. After brainstorming ideas about causes and effects of the assassination, students could categorize the ideas (political, irrational, economic, etc.), then work in cooperative groups to develop their predictions about each area. Groups could also research the assassinations of Lincoln, McKinley, and Kennedy, then study *Julius Caesar* for comparison of motives and effects. A culminating activity could be to write a scenario of what might happen in an assassination of the current president. English and history teachers who want to team teach could develop this project together.

A computer science teacher could ask students if they think there will ever be a computer that is smarter than a human being. This would lead to a definition of terms, then investigation into human intelligence, artificial intelligence, computer languages, films such as *2001: A Space Odyssey*, along with demonstrations of computer programs related to artificial intelligence.

Books such as *The Timetables of History* or *The People's Chronology* can be used as a reference for history, English, science, business, and the arts. Students can analyze ten-year periods to discover what was happening in Western Europe and the Americas in several of the seven topics, then look for connections. Is literature connected to political events? Do art and music reflect current events? What effects do scientific discoveries have on economics? Does the U.S. "Black Friday" of October 28, 1929, have any relationship to the "Black Friday" in Germany in 1927? What predictions does William Beveridge make in his 1942 "Report on Social Security"? A major class project could be to extend a section of the timetables to include African and Asian events through research into each of the seven topics. Over a period of several years, this could become a valuable resource for the school.

Science teachers have numerous opportunities for inductive approaches; in fact, they could develop a complete curriculum around problems to solve. This teacher could ask students to brainstorm a list of everything they can think of that runs by electrical power, then to predict what the world might be like today if electricity had not yet been discovered, or if it hadn't been discovered until 1950. Would there have been world wars? atomic weapons? movies? pollution? Their study could include effects of this discovery on the people in the time it was discovered (including violent reactions), resulting devices that use electricity, ecological issues, possible future uses of electrical power, etc.

Science teachers could also lead discussions of ethical issues in science during a study of cell biology. What would happen if biochemists discover how to clone people, and a dangerous criminal steals the formula and clones himself or warlike leaders of nations? What effects might this have on law and order, peace and war? Should there be laws to stop scientific experiments of certain types?

Teachers of mathematics could introduce a lesson on place value or number systems by asking students how mathematics might be different if people had eight or twelve fingers instead of ten. Students could then investigate number systems and even invent one of their own.

Art or music teachers could show a selection of paintings or play several recordings and ask students in what decade they were painted or written. Students must explain their reasons for giving a particular date. Research could lead to discussion on what paintings or music of a particular decade had in common, their countries of origin, the influence of religion on art or music, and whether political events influence art and music. They could also be asked to predict what art will look like or how music will sound in the year 2050. Students could do projects based on how someone in the year 2050 might write about current art or music. Content area teachers can team with an art teacher to discuss mathematics in art and music, the influence of historical events on the arts, poems or plays related to the art or music world, or the science of sound. Art or music students could develop original projects as part of subject area class assignments.

Business teachers might ask students what kind of business they would like to own, if money were no object. Students would need to explain their reasons, then research the business they choose. The class could brainstorm questions for study, then categorize them to determine general areas of research. Students who choose the same business could work together; resource people from the business community could visit the class to explain business concepts, answer questions, and predict what business will be like in 10 or 20 or 50 years.

Cooperative learning lessons may be developed as deductive or inductive. Deductive activities include practice and review of information through games or tournaments and presentations made by the teacher or by students. Inductive activities include research, analysis, and synthesis of information.

Discussion Strategies

Discussions are often thought of as unstructured talk by students sitting around in a circle, answering the basic question, "What do you think about _____?" However, profitable discussions are carefully planned, with specific objectives leading to the understanding of specific concepts.

Discussion lessons may be deductive or inductive, depending on the emphasis. Deductive lessons will be more structured, often with clear answers which the teacher expects and leads the students to provide. Inductive lessons will be less structured, but very well planned. Teachers ask open-ended questions and accept a variety of answers that are well supported by information or inferences from the text. The effective teacher plans a variety of questions, with learner outcomes in mind, and leads the discussion without dominating it. The teacher also makes certain that all students participate and have an opportunity to contribute. Students may also plan and lead discussions, with careful assistance from the teacher.

An English teacher may plan a discussion of *Our Town*. All students write a variety of questions, e.g., based on levels of Bloom's taxonomy. Half the class discusses among themselves the questions presented by the other half of the class; roles change for the last half of the period or the next class period. The teacher's main role is to facilitate and make sure students follow the guidelines.

An important advantage, which is also a disadvantage, is the amount of time required by genuine discussion. The advantage is that all students have opportunities to contribute to learning and therefore feel a greater sense of ownership; the disadvantage is that productive discussion takes a great deal of time.

Comparison/Contrast

An important higher-order thinking skill is the ability to compare and contrast two things or concepts that are dissimilar on the surface. Thomas Gordon has described a process of synectics, whereby students are forced to make an analogy between something that is familiar and something that is new; the concepts seem to be completely different, but through a series of steps, students discover underlying similarities. For example, a biology teacher might plan an analogy between a cell (new concept) and a city government (familiar concept). Although they seem impossibly different, they both have systems for transportation, disposal of unwanted materials, and parts that govern these systems. By comparing something new with something familiar, students have a "hook" for the new information, which will help them remember it as well as better understand it. For example, students trying to remember functions of a cell would be assisted by remembering parts of the city government.

Wait Time / Think Time

Wait time as an important instructional variable was identified by Mary Budd Rowe. In her research, she found that teachers rarely waited more than one or one and half seconds for an answer after posing a question. However, she discovered that if teachers waited three seconds, the following improvements were found:

- The length of students' responses and the correctness of their responses increased.

- The number of "I don't know" responses decreased.

- The number of volunteered, appropriate answers by students increased.

- The scores of students on tests increased.

Not only did Rowe's research uncover these positive findings for students' responses, she also learned that increasing wait time improved teacher performance in several ways; namely, teachers increased the variety and flexibility of their questioning strategies; they decreased the quantity, but increased the quality of their questions; and they asked questions requiring more complex information processing and higher-level thinking skills (Stahl, 1994).

In addition to wait time, Stahl (1994) identified think time as an important instructional variable. Defining think time as "a distinct period of uninterrupted silence by the teacher and all students so that they both can complete appropriate information processing tasks, feelings, oral responses, and actions," he found that by allowing three seconds of think time contributed significantly to improved teaching and learning.

Monitoring Instruction

Successful teachers constantly monitor students' understanding and adjust instruction to meet students' needs. K. Patricia Cross and Tom Angelo (1994) describe a number of ways to assess students' thinking and learning and teachers' effectiveness through the tools of classroom assessment. They describe their approach as having the following characteristics: learner-centered, teacher-directed, mutually beneficial, formative, context-specific, ongoing, and rooted in good teaching practice.

To explain, the focus is on the student as the learner and requires that students be active participants in the process. Moreover, the individual teacher decides what to assess, when to assess, and how to respond to the assessment so the process is teacher-directed. Because it requires students' participation, classroom assessment allows students to reinforce their understanding of course content and skills and, when they know that teachers are interested, student motivation is increased. Faculty also continue to increase their teaching effectiveness because their attention is focused on the knowledge and skills and what students are learning. This kind of assessment is usually anonymous and usually ungraded; it is used to improve the quality of learning, not for evaluating or grading students. By using quick and simple assessment techniques, teachers get feedback from students and are able to give students feedback with suggestions for improving learning. Finally, it is rooted in good practice because it makes student feedback systematic, immediate, more flexible, and more effective.

For example, after ten minutes of instruction, the teacher may ask the class to write a one-sentence summary, answering the questions Who, What, When, Where, How and Why? The teacher then immediately collects the responses and reads them to the class to determine exactly what the students have understood or what has been misunderstood.

Another example is the Minute Paper. Students are given one minute to write a summary of what they have learned. The papers are immediately collected and the teacher responds to each one.

Teachers can give students tables or grids with blanks to fill in to find out what students did or did not understand. Teachers can ask students to give examples. They can ask students to complete the sentence, "How I feel about this . . ." or "What I think about this . . ." or "What I will remember about . . ." By collecting these responses and then immediately responding to them, the teacher is giving immediate feedback to help shape students' learning. These student responses also serve to reinforce what the teacher is doing well and what needs more or clearer explanation or description.

Tacit Knowledge or the Product of Direct Instruction

Tacit knowledge is a term used to describe that kind of information and knowledge that is acquired or understood without direct instruction and/or awareness. Sometimes it is described as the kind of knowledge that one unconsciously learns or understands. To simplify, tacit knowledge is sometimes called "knowing how" and explicit knowledge is sometimes referred to as "knowing that." For example, an expert plans, acts, and makes decisions without specifically thinking about rules or principles involved. To illustrate, a professional writer composes sentences without consciously thinking about the subject and predicate or nouns and adjectives, simply understanding how syntax operates and what is required for clear and correct written communication.

On the other hand, explicit knowledge is that which is directly taught. To explain, the novice or beginning writer may need explicit instruction in crafting a sentence or may have to recite spelling rules in order to spell words correctly or think about hand position when starting to use a keyboard.

Teachers often erroneously assume that students have the same kind or level of tacit knowledge when, in fact, there are widely varying kinds and levels of tacit knowledge among students just as there are among teachers. For example, the calculus teacher may have such a thorough understanding of the quadratic equation that he or she no longer has to think about the process but solves the equation as if it were an eye-hand coordination exercise. By keeping in mind that various cultural, socio-economic factors and even personality types can result in different kinds and levels of tacit knowledge, teachers will avoid making assumptions that everyone knows or understands, and unfairly penalizing those students who do not.

In math class for example, if the goal is for students to memorize the multiplication tables, there will be some students who immediately understand that memorizing $2 \times 2 = 4$ has a meaning beyond simple memorization. They will immediately understand that 2 times 2 equals four means two objects twice or the same as 2 plus 2 and will have a conceptual understanding of $2 \times 2 = 4$. Other students, however, will simply memorize the phrase "$2 \times 2 = 4$" without thinking about what it means. For this reason, teachers are wise to use concrete examples and provide direct instruction.

Teachers might be tempted to believe that older students know how to annotate text to improve comprehension or how to paraphrase from a source when, in reality, even older students have not been taught these skills. The fewer assumptions made, the fewer mistakes will be made by teachers.

Sample Question

Mr. Swenson teaches mathematics in high school. He is planning a unit on fractal geometry, using the computer lab for demonstrations and for exploration for his advanced math students. The students have used various computer programs to solve algebra and calculus problems. As Mr. Swenson plans a unit of study, he determines that a cognitive outcome will be that students will design and produce fractals using a computer program. An effective outcome is that students will become excited about investigating a new field of mathematics and will show this interest by choosing to develop a math project relating to fractals.

The most appropriate strategy to use *first* would be

(A)   lecturing to explain the exciting development of fractal geometry over the past 10 to 15 years.

(B)   demonstrating on the computer the way to input values into formulas to produce fractal designs.

(C)   giving students a few simple fractal designs and asking them to figure out the formulas for producing them.

(D)   showing students color pictures of complex fractals and asking them for ideas about how they could be drawn mathematically.

The correct response is **(D)**. The question relates to appropriate sequencing of activities. (D) is the best introductory activity in order to generate student interest in this new field of mathematics and to get students thinking about how to produce fractals. It would stimulate students to use higher-level thinking skills to make predictions by drawing on their knowledge of how to solve problems mathematically. (A) would be the least appropriate to begin the study. Students who want to learn more could research this topic after they have developed an interest in fractals. (B) would be appropriate as a later step, after students are interested in the process and are ready to learn how to produce fractals. (C) would be appropriate as a subsequent step in the process of learning how to produce fractals. (B) requires students to use preplanned formulas; (C) allows them to develop their own formulas, a very high-level activity.

COMPETENCY 009

The teacher incorporates the effective use of technology to plan, organize, deliver, and evaluate instruction for all students.

The effective teacher includes resources of all types in the curriculum planning process. The educator should be very familiar with the school library, city/county library, education service center resources, and the library of any college or university in the area. The teacher should have a list of all audiovisual aids that may be borrowed, e.g., kits, films, filmstrips, videos, laser disks, and computer software. All audiovisual aids should be related to curricular objectives. Many librarians have keyed their resources to objectives in related subject areas, so the teacher can incorporate them with ease into the lessons. However, resources should never be used with a class unless they have been previewed and approved by the teacher. The list of resources to be used in a lesson or unit should be included in the curriculum guide or the lesson plan for ease of use.

Planning for Resources

The effective teacher determines the appropriate place in the lesson for audiovisual aids. If the material is especially interesting and thought-provoking, he or she may use it to introduce a unit. For example, a travel video on coral reefs or snorkeling might be an excellent introduction to the study of tropical fish and plants. The same video could be used at the end of the study to see how many fish and plants the students can recognize and name. Computer software that "dissects" frogs or worms may be used after a discussion of what students already know about the animals and how their internal organs compare with those of humans. A video of a Shakespearean play could be intermixed with discussion and class reading of scenes from the play.

Videos, films, and filmstrips may be stopped for discussion. Research reveals that students comprehend better and remember longer if the teacher introduces a video or film appropriately, then stops it frequently to discuss what the students have just seen and heard. This method also helps keep students' attention focused and assists them in learning note-taking skills.

Print Resources

The most common print material is the textbook, which has been selected by teachers on the campus from a list of books approved by the state. Textbooks are readily available, economical, and written to match state curriculum requirements. However, the adoption process is a long one, and textbooks (particularly science and history) can become out-of-date quickly; therefore, the teacher must use additional resources with recent dates.

Local, state, and national newspapers and magazines should not be overlooked.

Some newspapers and magazines have special programs to help teachers use their products in the classroom for reading and writing opportunities as well as for sources of information. Local newspapers may be willing to send specialists to work with students or act as special resource persons.

A limitation of textbooks is their tendency to provide sketchy or minimal treatment of topics, partly because publishers are required to include such a broad range of topics. An ineffective teacher may use the "chapter a week" theory of "covering" a textbook. This method pays no consideration to the importance of information in each chapter or its relevance to the overall district curriculum. Neither does it promote critical thinking on the part of the teacher or the student. Students tend to believe the textbook is something to be endured and not employed as a tool for learning. The effective teacher chooses sections from the textbook that are relevant to his or her learning goals and omits the rest. He or she also supplements the sketchy treatments by using an abundance of other resources.

Visual Materials

The most available tools in classrooms are the chalkboard and the overhead projector. There are several principles which apply to both. The teacher must write clearly and in large letters. Overhead transparencies should never be typed on a regular typewriter, because the print is too small. Computers allow type sizes of at least 18 points, which is the minimum readable size. Also, both boards and transparencies should be free of clutter. Old information should be removed before new information is added. These tools work more effectively if the teacher plans ahead of time what she will write or draw on them. Using different colors will emphasize relationships or differences.

Posters and charts can complement lessons, but the walls should not be so cluttered that students are unable to focus on what's important for the current lesson. Posters and charts can be displayed on a rotating basis. Filmstrips, films, and videos are appealing to students because they are surrounded by visual images on television, computers, and video games. Films and filmstrips have the advantage of being projected on a large screen, so all students can see clearly. Videos and computers can be connected to large displays or projected on large screens, but these projection devices are rather expensive. If the available screen is too small for large-group viewing, then the teacher might break the class into groups and have several different projects for them to do on a rotating basis.

Some of the best graphic aids will be those developed by individual students or by groups of students. Along with learning about subject area concepts, students will be learning about design and presentation of information. Students can take pictures of their products to put in a portfolio or scrapbook.

Videodisc and Interactive Video

Videodiscs provide a sturdy, compact system of storage for pictures and sound. They can store more than 50,000 separate frames of still images, up to 50 hours of digitized stereo music, or about 325 minutes of motion pictures with sound. An advantage of videodisc over videotape is that each frame can be accessed separately and quickly. The simplest level of use involves commands to play, pause, skip forward, or skip back. Individual frames can be accessed by inputting their number.

These programs can become interactive by linking them to a computer. The teacher can then individually access, sequence, and pace the information from the interactive system. An art teacher with a collection of pictures of the world's art treasures can choose which pictures to use and the order in which to show them, then design custom-made lessons that can be used repeatedly or easily revised. He or she might decide to develop a program on landscapes as portrayed in art during a certain period of time. By using the videodisc's reference guide, the teacher determines which pictures to use and the length of time he wants each displayed. He or she can develop numerous lessons from one videodisc.

More comprehensive interactive programs can use the computer to present information, access a videodisc to illustrate main points, then ask for responses from the student. A multimedia production run by the computer can include images, text, and sound from a videodisc, CD-ROM, graphics software, word processing software, and a sound effects program. Teachers can develop classroom presentations, but students can also develop learning units as part of a research or inquiry project.

The cost of a multimedia system remains relatively high, but students can use it to develop high-level thought processes, collaborative work, and research skills, as well as content knowledge and understanding.

Computer Software Tools

There are several software tools that are extremely useful for teachers and students. Word processing allows teachers and students to write, edit, and polish assignments and reports. Most programs have a spelling-checker or even a grammar-checker to enhance written products. Students in all subjects can use word processors to write term papers or reports of their research. Many word processors allow writers to put the text into columns, so that students can produce newsletters with headlines of varying sizes. For example, an English class could write a series of reviews of Shakespeare's plays or sonnets, add information about Shakespeare and his times, then collect everything into a newsletter as a class project. There are also desktop publishing programs that allow text and graphics to be integrated to produce publications, such as a class newsletter and school newspapers and yearbooks.

Databases are like electronic file cards; they allow students to input data, then retrieve it in various ways and arrangements. History students can input data about various countries, e.g., population, population growth rate, infant mortality rate, average income, and average education level. They then manipulate the database to call out information in a variety of ways. The more important step in learning about databases is dealing with huge quantities of information. Students need to learn how to analyze and interpret the data that they see to discover connections between isolated facts and figures and how to eliminate inappropriate information.

On-line databases are essential tools for research. Students can access databases related to English, history, science—any number of subject areas. Most programs allow electronic mail, so that students can communicate over the computer with people from around the world. There are also massive bibliographic databases which help students and teachers find resources they need. Many of the print materials can then be borrowed through interlibrary loan. The use of electronic systems can exponentially increase the materials available to students.

Spreadsheets are similar to teacher gradebooks. Rows and columns of numbers can be linked to produce totals and averages. Formulas can connect information in one cell (the intersection of a row and column) to another cell. Teachers often keep gradebooks on a spreadsheet, because of the ease in updating information. Once formulas are in place, teachers can enter grades and have completely up-to-date averages for all students. Students can use spreadsheets to collect and analyze numerical data, which can be sorted in various orders. Some spreadsheet programs also include a chart function, so that teachers could display class averages on a bar chart to provide a visual comparison of the classes' performance. Students can enter population figures from various countries, then draw various types of graphs—bars, columns, scatters, histograms, pies—to convey information. This type of graphic information can also be used in multimedia presentations. There are also various stand-alone graph and chart software packages.

Graphics or paint programs allow users to draw freehand to produce any type of picture or use tools to produce boxes, circles, or other shapes. These programs can illustrate classroom presentations or individual research projects. Many word processing programs have some graphic elements. With the use of these relatively simple tools, teachers can create handouts and instructional materials with a very professional and polished appearance.

Today's teachers also need to acquire and demonstrate skill in using presentation software (such as Microsoft PowerPoint) to prepare instructional lessons. In many classrooms, the use of presentation software makes the traditional use of transparencies on an overhead projector obsolete. Presentation software also makes it possible to provide students with instructional handouts and outlines to complement classroom instruction. In some situations and in some schools, web authoring experience and skills will also prove useful.

Design Issues

Although it is very likely that prospective teachers have had some background in instructional design, some basic guidelines are offered (Truehaft, 1995). To begin, it is important that teachers consider the purpose of the presentation: What is the message? Teachers should avoid the temptation to include "bells and whistles" (or any super-duper technology) that are too dazzling and detract from the message.

Second, it is important for the presentation to be consistent; that is, the transitions from slide to slide should, in general, be the same. The backgrounds (or templates) should be remain the same. Type/font and sizes should be consistent. The use of color to highlight or separate text should also be consistent.

Third, your audience (students) must be able to see clearly. Make sure the type size is large enough—if you are projecting on a television screen, the image will be smaller than if you are using an LCD projector. Be sure to limit the amount of text on a slide—your presentation must be clearly readable. More than six or eight lines of type on a single slide will be hard to read. Use lots of "white space" to give your presentation a clean and easily read appearance.

Stick to one or two kinds of font. If you have only a small amount of text (a title or label), sans serif type may be best (such as Arial or Helvetica); however, if you have a passage of text, serif type (such as Times New Roman or Bookman) is easier to read.

Just as it is recommended to limit the amount of text on a slide and the fonts used, it is also important to limit the number of graphic elements used. Use only one or two per slide and remember—you want one message or main point on each slide.

Think about visibility. Whether or not the text is readable will depend on the contrast between the text color and the background. It is best to use dark text on a light background or vice versa (such as black on white, or white on black). You can use an accent color (such as red) to add emphasis.

Before your presentation, check your equipment. If you are using sound, check the volume. Make sure you know how to use the computer and the projection device controls. You want to be fully in charge of the presentation.

Computer-Assisted Instruction

Many early uses of computers tended to be drill-and-practice, where students practiced simple skills such as mathematics operations. Many elaborate systems of practice and testing were developed, with management systems so that teachers could keep track of how well the students were achieving. This type of software is useful for skills that students need to practice. An advantage is immediate feedback so students know if they chose the correct answer. Many of these programs have a game format to make the practice more interesting. A disadvantage is their generally low-level nature.

Tutorials are a step above drill-and-practice programs, because they also include explanations and information. Students are asked to make a response, then the program branches to the most appropriate section, based on the students' answer. Tutorials are often used for remedial work, but are also useful for instruction in English as a second language. Improved graphics and sound allow non-native speakers of English to listen to correct pronunciation while viewing pictures of words. Tutorials are used to supplement, not supplant, teacher instruction.

Simulations or problem-solving programs provide opportunities for students to have experiences that would take too long to experience in real-time, would be too costly or difficult to experience, or would be impossible to experience. For example, one of the most popular simulations allows students to see if they could survive the Oregon Trail. Users made several choices about food, ammunition, supplies, etc., and then the computer moved them along the trail until they reached their goal or died along the way. There are several simulations that allow students to "dissect" animals. This saves time and materials, is less messy, and allows students who might be reluctant to dissect real animals to learn about them. Other software explores the effects of weightlessness on plant growth, an impossible situation to set up in the classroom lab. There are several social studies simulations that allow students to do things like invent a country and then see the effects of their political and economic decisions on the country.

Manipulatives and Labs

Other types of materials that can be used effectively are manipulatives. Manipulatives are touchable, movable materials that enhance students' understanding of a concept. They are used particularly in mathematics and science to give students a concrete way of dealing with concepts, but tangible materials are appropriate and helpful in all subject areas. Math teachers use plastic shapes in studying geometry. Number lines, place value cubes, and tessellation blocks are used to help students understand math, not only in elementary classes but also in algebra, trigonometry, and calculus. Elementary language arts teachers use wooden letters or cut-outs to help students learn the alphabet; secondary English teachers can make parts-of-speech cards for sentence structure, frames for structured poetry, and blocks for essay structure. Science teachers are required to use many manipulatives during hands-on lab activities. Social studies and history teachers can use a wealth of cultural artifacts from countries they are studying.

The Internet

The Internet and the World Wide Web are having a profound effect on students and teachers alike. This very powerful learning tool is best viewed as a source of information.

By linking computers around the world, the Internet serves as a network of networks. From 500 hosts in 1983, the Internet has rapidly grown to about 30 million hosts in

1998 and the number continued to mount at a dramatic rate. At the start of the 21st century some 360 million people were believed to have access to the Internet.

Oscar Wilde once argued that there is no such thing as a good or bad book, that a work of literature exists apart from issues of morality. The same logic could be applied to the Internet. As any source of information, the Internet can be used well or badly. Because the amount of information available is so enormous, it is often difficult to find the exact information one is seeking. Also, with such large amounts of information and no quality control, a good deal of inaccurate and false information is available. For these reasons, the Internet makes it necessary that teachers address critical thinking skills and how to judge the accuracy of information, to look for evidence and substantiation of claims, and to separate facts from opinions. Educators, just as parents, must also be concerned about the appropriateness of the information accessed by students, since a wide range of material is available and some of it is unsuitable for children.

To safeguard children and provide some kind of quality control, many public schools use Internet filters. These tools are designed to limit access to unsuitable material; however, some of the filters do not discriminate adequately, so that questionable material may still be accessed while some acceptable material may be denied. For this reason, it is necessary that teachers carefully supervise the use of this powerful resource.

While it is assumed that teachers today will have acquired experience and expertise in using the Internet while completing their educational training, there are many tools that classroom teachers will find valuable. Basically, teachers should be familiar with common Internet browsers (such as Microsoft Explorer and Netscape) and popular search engines (such as Yahoo, Excite, Lycos, and Google) that make it possible to research any topic. Many Web sites offer teaching tips and tools, so teachers will want to investigate these and bookmark the ones that are most pertinent and reliable. Communicating with colleagues, parents, and even students is made convenient through email.

The Internet, then, is a common tool of the twenty-first century, used by both teachers and students. Internet sites are constantly being developed and renovated, so sites that are popular today may be gone tomorrow. However, a few popular sites for teachers are listed below:

http://www.ed.gov

http://www.tea.state.tx.us

http://www.education-world.com

http://www.nea.org

http://school.discovery.com/teachingtools/teachingtools.html

http://www.teachersfirst.com

Children's Internet Protection

As they find ways to use the Internet as a teaching tool, it is also important that teachers be mindful of the Children's Internet Protection Act (CIPA) and the Neighborhood Children's Internet Protection Act (N-CIPA), which passed Congress in December of 2000. Both were part of a large federal appropriations measure (PL 106-554).

There are three basic requirements in the legislation that applicants must meet, or be "undertaking actions" to meet. The requirements are:

1. The school or library must use blocking or filtering technology on all computers with Internet access. The blocking or filtering must protect against access to certain visual depictions, including obscenity, child pornography, and materials harmful to minors. The law does not require the filtering of text.

2. The school or library must adopt and implement an Internet safety policy that addresses the key criteria, including

   a) access by minors to inappropriate matter on the Internet and the Web;

   b) the safety and security of minors when using electronic mail, chat rooms, and other forms of direct electronic communications;

   c) unauthorized access, including so-called "hacking," and other unlawful activities by minors online;

   d) unauthorized disclosure, use, and dissemination of personal identification information regarding minors; and

   e) measures designed to restrict minors' access to materials harmful to minors.

3. The school or library must hold a public meeting to discuss the Internet safety policy; specifically, the law requires that the school or library "provide reasonable public notice and hold at least one public hearing or meeting to address the proposed Internet safety policy."

Technology and Copyright Issues

Copyright is a form of protection provided by the laws of the United States (title 17, U.S. Code) to the authors of "original works of authorship," including literary, dramatic, musical, artistic, and certain other intellectual works. This protection is available to both published and unpublished works.

It is illegal for anyone to violate any of the rights provided by copyright law to the owner of the copyright. These rights, however, are not unlimited. Sections 107 through 121 of the 1976 Copyright Act establish limitations on these rights. In some cases, these limitations are specified exemptions from copyright liability. One major limitation is the doctrine of "fair use," which is given a statutory basis in section 107 of the 1976 Copyright Act.

The "fair use" doctrine allows limited reproduction of copyrighted works for educational and research purposes. In general, a teacher can copy a chapter from a book; an article from a periodical or newspaper; a short story, short essay, or short poem, whether or not from a collective work; and/or a chart, graph, diagram, drawing, cartoon, or picture from a book, periodical, or newspaper. For a classroom, a teacher can make multiple copies (not to exceed the number of students in the class) as long as the copying meets the following tests of brevity and spontaneity, meets the cumulative effect test, and each copy includes a notice of copyright.

Brevity generally refers to a poem of 250 words or less or a prose passage less than 2,500 words. *Spontaneity* refers to the need for a teacher to use a work without undertaking the normal time to obtain copyright permission. Finally, the *cumulative effect test* refers to copying material for only one class, from a single author and no more than nine times during a term. Suggested guidelines for *fair use* can be found at the University of Texas System web site:

http://www.utsystem.edu/ogc/intellectualproperty/clasguid.html

In regard to fair use of multimedia materials, in general, it is acceptable for faculty and students to incorporate others' work into a multimedia presentation and display or perform the multimedia work as long as it is for a class assignment. It is suggested that educators be prudent in the use of such materials by being conservative (using only small amounts of others' work) and not making unnecessary copies of such works.

Complete information about copyright can be found at the official web site of the United States Library of Congress Copyright Office:

http://www.loc.gov/copyright

Technology and Thinking Skills

Technology experts, such as Ian Jukes, argue that tools such as the Internet make available such a wide-range and substantial amount of content that today's teachers have a greater role than ever teaching students process skills (such as critical and creative thinking) rather than teaching mere content skills. Content will change and expand; however, thinking processes remain salient and necessary, regardless of the content.

Richard Paul, Director of the Center for Critical Thinking at Sonoma State University and Chair of the National Council for Excellence in Critical Thinking, has written and spoken widely about how teachers can improve the thinking skills of their students. He provides eight elements of reasoning that can help teachers address and assess critical thinking:

1) Purpose, goal, or end in view (What is the objective of thinking? The teacher's role is to provide feedback to students: Is the purpose clear, significant, realistic, achievable, and consistent?)

2) Question or problem (Is the question or problem clear, significant, relevant, and answerable?)

3) Point of view or frame of reference (Is the view too narrow, based on false or misleading information, analogies, or metaphors; does it contain contradictions or is it restricted and unfair? On the other hand, is it broad, flexible, fair, clearly stated, and consistent?)

4) The empirical dimension (Are there experiences, data, evidence, or raw material that can be gathered and reported clearly, fairly, and accurately? Are the data relevant, adequate, and consistent?)

5) The conceptual dimension (Are theories, principles, rules and/or axioms relevant to the problem?)

6) Assumptions (Are assumptions clear or unclear, justified or unjustified, crucial or extraneous, consistent or contradictory?)

7) Implications and consequences (Are outcomes significant and realistic or unimportant and unrealistic? Are consequences valid?)

8) Inferences (Are inferences sound, clear, justified, and deep or trivial and superficial?)

Paul argues that a teacher's role in providing feedback regarding these elements is of paramount importance if students are to acquire critical and valid creative thinking skills.

Human Resources

Parents and other members of the community can be excellent local experts from which students can learn about any subject—mathematics from bankers, art and music from artists, English from public relations persons, history from club or church historians or librarians, business from owners of companies. The list can be endless. Effective teachers make sure that any guest who is invited to speak or perform understands the purpose of the visit and the goals or objectives the teacher is trying to accomplish. Preparation can make the class period more focused and meaningful.

Field trips are excellent sources of information, especially about careers and current issues such as pollution control. One field trip can yield assignments in mathematics, history, science, and English, and often art, architecture, music, or health. Teachers can collaborate with each other to produce thematic assignments for the field trip or simply to coordinate the students' assignments. Often, a history report can serve as an English paper as well. Data can be analyzed in math classes and presented with the aid of computers.

Selection and Evaluation Criteria

The effective teacher uses criteria to evaluate audiovisual, multimedia, computer resources, and human resources. The first thing to look for is congruence with lesson goals. If the software doesn't reinforce student outcomes, then it shouldn't be used, no matter how flashy or well-done. A checklist for instructional computer software could include appropriate sequence of instruction, meaningful student interaction with the software, learner control of screens and pacing, and motivation. Other factors should be considered, such as ability to control sound and save progress, effective use of color, clarity of text and graphics on the screen, and potential as an individual or group assignment.

In addition to congruence with curriculum goals, the teacher considers students' strengths and needs, their learning styles or preferred modalities, and their interests. Students' needs can be determined through formal or informal assessment. Most standardized tests include an indication of which objectives the student did not master. Mastering these objectives can be assisted with computer or multimedia aids.

Learning styles can be assessed with a variety of instruments and models, including those developed by Rita Dunn and Anthony Gregorc. Students with highly visual learning modes will benefit from audiovisuals. Student interests may be revealed by a questionnaire, either purchased or developed by the district or teacher. A knowledge of student interests will help the teacher provide resources to suit individual needs. The effective teacher can design activity choices that relate to class goals but also to student interests.

Evaluation of resources should be accomplished in advance by the teacher, before purchase whenever possible. Evaluation is also conducted during student use of materials. Assessment after student use may be by considering achievement level of the students and/or by surveys that ask for students' responses.

Sample Question

Mr. Roberts' sixth-grade social studies class has developed a research project to survey student use of various types of video games. They designed a questionnaire and then administered it to all fourth-, fifth-, and sixth-grade students on their campus. The students plan to analyze their data and then develop a presentation to show at the next parent-teacher meeting.

What type of computer software would *not* be helpful during this class project?

(A)   Word processing

(B)   Database

(C)   Simulation

(D)   Graph/chart

The correct response is **(C)**. This question asks for an evaluation of software programs that might help students achieve their goals of analyzing data and presenting the results. A simulation **(C)** would *not* be appropriate here, because the students' basic purpose is to collect data and analyze it. The project does not call for a program to simulate a situation or event. Word processing **(A)** would be used in developing and printing the questionnaire, as well as writing a report on the results. A database **(B)** would be used to sort and print out information in various categories so students could organize and analyze their data. A graph or chart **(D)** would be very useful in analyzing information and in presenting it to others.

COMPETENCY 010

The teacher monitors student performance and achievement; provides students with timely, high-quality feedback; and responds flexibly to promote learning for all students.

The basic goals of assessment are to enhance the teachers' knowledge of learners and their needs, to monitor students' progress toward goals and outcomes, and to modify instruction when progress is not sufficient.

Purposes of Assessment

The effective teacher understands the importance of ongoing assessment as an instructional tool for the classroom and uses both informal and formal assessment measures. Informal measures can include observation, journals, written drafts, and conversations. More formal measures can include teacher-made tests, district exams, and standardized tests. Effective teachers use both formative and summative evaluation. Formative evaluation occurs during the process of learning, when the teacher or the students monitor progress in obtaining outcomes, while it is still possible to modify instruction. Summative evaluation occurs at the end of a specific time period or course, usually by a single grade used to represent a student's performance.

Teacher-Made Tests

The effective teacher uses a variety of assessment techniques. Teacher-made instruments are ideally developed at the same time as the goals and outcomes are planned, rather than at the last minute after all the lessons have been taught. Carefully planned objectives and assessment instruments serve as lesson development guides for the teacher.

Paper and pencil tests are the most common method for evaluation of student progress. There are a number of different types of questions: multiple-choice, true/false, matching, fill-in-the-blank, short answer, and longer essay. The first five tend to test the knowledge or comprehension levels. Essays often test at the lower levels, but are suitable for assessing learning at higher levels. Projects, papers, and portfolios can provide assessment of higher-level thinking skills.

If the purpose is to test student recall of factual information, a short objective test (multiple-choice, true/false, matching, fill-in-the blank) would be most effective and efficient. The first three types of questions can be answered on machine-scorable scan sheets to provide quick and accurate scoring. Disadvantages are that they generally test lower levels of knowledge and don't provide an opportunity for an explanation of answers.

If the purpose is to test student ability to analyze an event, compare and contrast two concepts, make predictions about an experiment, or evaluate a character's actions, then an essay question would provide the best paper/pencil opportunity for the student to show what he can do. Teachers should make the question explicit enough for students to know exactly what is expected. For example, "Explain the results of World War II" is too broad; students won't really understand what the teacher expects. It would be more explicit to say, "Explain three results of World War II that you feel had the most impact on participating nations. Explain the criteria you used in selecting these results."

Advantages of an essay include the possibility for students to be creative in their answers, the opportunity for students to explain their responses, and the potential to test for higher-level thinking skills. Disadvantages of essay questions include the time needed for students to formulate meaningful responses, language difficulties of some students, and the time needed to evaluate the essays. Consistency in evaluation is also a problem for the teacher, but this can be alleviated by using an outline of the acceptable answers. Teachers who write specific questions and who know what they are looking for will be more consistent in grading. Also, if there are several essay questions, the effective teacher grades all student responses to the first question, then moves on to all responses to the second, and so on.

Authentic Assessments

Paper and pencil tests or essays are only one method of assessment. Others include projects, observation, checklists, anecdotal records, portfolios, self-assessment, and peer assessment. Although these types of assessment often take more time and effort to plan and administer, they can often provide a more authentic assessment of student progress.

Projects are common in almost all subject areas. They promote student control of learning experiences and provide opportunities for research into a variety of topics, as well as the chance to use visuals, graphics, videos, or multimedia presentations in place of, or in addition to, written reports. Projects also promote student self-assessment because students must evaluate their progress along each step of the project. Many schools have science or history fairs for which students plan, develop, and display their projects. Projects can also be part of business, English, music, art, mathematics, social sciences, health, or physical education courses.

Effective teachers must make clear the requirements and the criteria for evaluation of projects before students begin working on them. They must also assist students in selecting projects that are feasible, for which the school has learning resources, and that can be completed in a reasonable amount of time with little or no expense to students.

Advantages of projects are that students can use visual, graphic, art, or music abilities; students can be creative in their topic or research; and the projects can appeal to various learning styles. Disadvantages include difficulty with grading, although this can be overcome by devising a checklist for required elements and a rating scale for quality.

Observations may be made for individual or group work. This method is very suitable for skills or for effective learning. Teachers usually make a list of competencies, skills, or requirements, then check off the ones that are observed in the student or group. An office skills teacher wishing to emphasize interviewing skills may devise a checklist that includes personal appearance, mannerisms, confidence, and addressing the questions that are asked. A teacher who wants to emphasize careful listening may observe a discussion with a checklist that includes paying attention, not interrupting, summarizing another person's ideas, and asking questions of other students.

Anecdotal records may be helpful in some instances, such as capturing the process a group of students uses to solve a problem. This formative data can be useful during feedback to the group. Students can also be taught to write an explanation of the procedures they use for a project or a science experiment. An advantage of an anecdotal record is that it can include all relevant information. Disadvantages include the amount of time necessary to complete the record and difficulty in assigning a grade. If used for feedback, then no grade is necessary.

Advantages of checklists include the potential for capturing behavior that can't be accurately measured with a paper and pencil test, i.e., shooting free throws on the basketball court, following the correct sequence of steps in a science experiment, or including all important elements in a speech in class. One characteristic of a checklist that is both an advantage and a disadvantage is its structure, which provides consistency but inflexibility. An open-ended comment section at the end of a checklist can overcome this disadvantage.

Portfolios are collections of students' best work. They can be used in any subject area where the teacher wants students to take more responsibility for planning, carrying out, and organizing their own learning. They may be used in the same way that artists, models, or performers use them to provide a succinct picture of their best work. Portfolios may be essays or articles written on paper, video tapes, multimedia presentations on computer disks, or a combination. English teachers often use portfolios as a means of collecting the best samples of student writing over the whole year. Sometimes they pass on the work to the next year's teacher to help her assess the needs of her new students. Any subject area can use portfolios, since they contain documentation that reflects growth and learning over a period of time.

Teachers should provide or assist students in developing guidelines for what materials should be placed in portfolios, since it would be unrealistic to include every piece of work. The use of portfolios requires the students to devise a means of evaluating their own work. A portfolio should be a collection of the student's own best work, not a scrapbook for collecting handouts or work done by other individuals, although it can certainly include work by a group in which the student was a participant.

Some advantages of portfolios over testing are that they provide a clearer picture of a student's progress, they are not affected by one inferior test grade, and they help develop self-assessment skills in students. One disadvantage is the amount of time required to teach students how to develop meaningful portfolios. However, this time can be well spent if students learn valuable skills. Another concern is the amount of time teachers must spend to assess portfolios. However, as students become more proficient at self-assessment, the teacher can spend more time in coaching and advising students throughout the development of their portfolios. Another concern is that parents may not understand how portfolios will be graded. The effective teacher devises a system that the students and parents understand before work on the portfolio begins.

Self and Peer Assessment

One goal of an assessment system is to promote student self-assessment. Since most careers require employees or managers to evaluate their own productivity as well as that of others, self-assessment and peer assessment are important lifelong skills.

Effective teachers use a structured approach to teach self-assessment, helping students set standards at first by making recommendations about standards, then gradually moving toward student development of their own criteria and application of the criteria to their work.

One method of developing self-assessment is to ask students to apply the teacher's own standards to a product. For example, an English teacher who uses a rating scale for essays might have students use that scale on their own papers, then compare their evaluations with those of the teacher. A science teacher who uses a checklist while observing an experiment might ask students to use the checklist, then compare theirs with the teacher's.

The class can set standards for evaluating group work as well as individual work. Collaborative groups are effective vehicles for practicing the skills involved in assessment.

Standardized Testing

In *criterion-referenced* tests, each student is measured against uniform objectives or criteria. CRTs allow the possibility that all students can score 100 percent because they understand the concepts being tested. Teacher-made tests should be criterion-referenced, because the teacher should develop them to measure the achievement of predetermined outcomes for the course. If teachers have properly prepared lessons based on the outcomes, and if students have mastered the outcomes, then scores should be high. This type of test may be called noncompetitive, because students are not in competition with each other for a high score, and there is no limit to the number of students who can score well. Some commercially developed tests are criterion-referenced; however, the majority are norm-referenced.

The purpose of a *norm-referenced* test is to provide a way to compare the performance of groups of students. This type of test may be called competitive, because a limited number of students can score well. A plot of large numbers of NRT scores will resemble a bell-shaped curve, with most scores clustering around the center and a few scores at each end. The midpoint is an average of data; therefore, by definition, half of the population will score above average and half below average.

The bell-shaped curve was developed as a mathematical description of the results of tossing coins. As such, it represents the chance or normal distribution of skills, knowledge, or events across the general population. A survey of the height of sixth-grade boys will result in an average height, with half the boys above average and half below. There will be a very small number with heights way above average and a very small number with heights way below average, with most heights clustering around the average.

NRT scores are usually reported in percentile scores (not to be confused with percentages), which indicate the percent of the population whose scores fall at or below the score. For example, a group score at the 80th percentile means that the group scored as well as or better than 80 percent of the students who took the test. A student with a score at the 50th percentile has an average score.

Percentile scores rank students from highest to lowest. By themselves, the percentile scores do not indicate how well the student has mastered the content objectives. Raw scores indicate how many questions the student answered correctly and are therefore useful in computing the percentage of questions a student answered correctly.

A national test for biology is designed to include objectives for the widest possible biology curriculum, for the broadest use of the test. Normed scores are reported so that schools can compare the performance of their students with the performance of students used as a norm group by test developers. The test will likely include more objectives than are included in a particular school's curriculum; therefore, that school's students may score low in comparison to the norm group. Teachers must be very careful in selecting a norm-referenced test, and should look for a test that includes objectives that are the most congruent with the school's curriculum.

Schools must also consider the reliability of a test, or whether the instrument will give consistent results when the measurement is repeated. A reliable bathroom scale, for example, will give identical weights for the same person measured three times in a morning. An unreliable scale, however, may give weights that differ by six pounds. Teachers evaluate test reliability over time when they give the same, or almost the same, test to different groups of students. Because there are many factors that affect reliability, teachers must be careful in evaluating this factor.

Schools must also be careful to assess the validity of a test, or whether the test actually measures what it is supposed to measure. If students score low on a test because they can't understand the questions, then the test is not valid because it measures reading ability instead of content knowledge. If students score low because the test covers material that was not studied, the test is not valid for that situation. A teacher assesses the validity of his or her own tests by examining the questions to see if they measure what was planned and taught in her classroom.

A test must be reliable before it can be valid. However, measurements can be consistent without being valid. A scale can indicate identical weights for three weigh-ins of the same person during one morning, but actually be 15 pounds in error. A history test may produce similar results each time it is given, but not be a valid measure of what was taught and learned. Tests should be both reliable and valid. If the test doesn't measure consistently, then it can't be accurate. If it doesn't measure what it's supposed to measure, then its reliability doesn't matter.

Commercial test producers perform various statistical measures of the reliability and validity of their tests and provide the results in the test administrator's booklet.

Performance-Based Assessment

Some states and districts are moving toward performance-based testing, which means that students are assessed on how well they perform certain tasks. This allows students to use higher-level thinking skills to apply, analyze, synthesize, and evaluate ideas and data. For example, a biology performance-based assessment may require students to read a problem, design and carry out a laboratory experiment, then write a summary of their findings. Students would be evaluated both on the process they used and the output they produced. A history performance-based assessment may require students to research a specific topic over a period of several days, make presentations of their findings to the rest of the class, then write a response that uses what they have learned from their own research and that of their classmates. Students are then evaluated on the process and the product of their research. An English performance-based test may require students to read a selection of literature, then write a critical analysis. A mathematics test may state a general problem to be solved, then require the student to invent one or more methods of solving the problem, use one of the methods to arrive at a solution, then write the solution and an explanation of the processes used.

Performance-based assessment allows students to be creative in solutions to problems or questions, and it requires them to use higher-level skills. This type of assessment can be time-consuming; however, students are working on content-related problems, using skills that are useful in a variety of contexts. This type of assessment also requires multiple resources, which can be expensive. It also requires teachers to be trained in how to use this type of assessment. However, many schools consider performance-based testing to be a more authentic measure of student achievement than traditional tests.

Sample Question

Mrs. Johnson teaches middle school reading. She teaches reading skills and comprehension through workbooks, reading, and class discussion of specific plays, short stories, and novels. She also allows students to make some selections according to their own interests. Because she believes there is a strong connection between reading and writing, her students are required to write their responses to literature in a variety of ways. Some of her students have heard their high school brothers and sisters discuss portfolios, and they have asked Mrs. Johnson if they can use them, also.

Which of the following statements is appropriate for Mrs. Johnson to consider in deciding whether to agree to the students' request?

(A)   Portfolios may help her students develop new skills.

(B)   Portfolios will make Mrs. Johnson's students feel more mature because they would be making the same product as their older brothers and sisters.

(C)   Portfolios will assist her students in meeting course outcomes relating to reading and writing.

(D)   Portfolios will make grading easier because there will be fewer papers and projects to evaluate.

The correct response is (**C**). The question asks for an appropriate question for Mrs. Johnson to consider in making an instructional decision. (C) is the most appropriate reason to decide whether to use portfolios. Most activities and projects that promote achievement of course outcomes would be considered appropriate strategies. (A) is a good reason for teaching students how to develop portfolios. Teachers should teach students the skills that will be useful in school and in their careers. However, here it is not the most important reason. Although (B) may produce positive results, feeling mature because students are imitating older siblings is not a sufficient reason to choose portfolios. (D) is not necessarily true; portfolio assessment can result in more written work, which can be more time consuming. Even if it were true, emphasizing student achievement is more important than easing the workload of teachers.

TExES

Texas Examinations of Educator Standards

Chapter 4

Domain IV:
Fulfilling Professional Roles and Responsibilities

Chapter 4

DOMAIN IV:
Fulfilling Professional
Roles and Responsibilities

The preparation of the teacher—in the respective content field as well as in the understanding of youth, the personal experiences that the teacher brings to the classroom, and the attitude toward the teaching assignment—affects the quality of instruction a teacher is able to deliver. Equally critical to the success of the teacher, however, is the ability to fit into the school environment, to be able to relate to the parents and community, and to interpret and support the regulations governing Texas teachers as well as the ethical concerns associated with the procedures involved in educating youth. The teacher's growth as a professional is nurtured by all of these contacts and experiences.

Often, individuals are reminded that "no man is an island." Teachers must be especially sensitive to the vital role they play by interacting positively and successfully with others. The students in the classroom, the teacher across the hall, the principal of the building, the fellow teachers on special assignment committees and teams, the campus technology expert—these are just a few of the immediate continuing contacts the teacher must deal with on a regular basis. Equally important to the teacher's success are the interactions with parents and community members. In addition to the teacher's awareness of his or her own personal strengths and needs, varied professional contacts, as well as communications with people in the community, can assist the teacher in selecting the best professional growth opportunities and experiences to reinforce, enrich, and expand his or her skills and knowledge.

This knowledge, expressed as an understanding of the teaching environment, is summarized in the following competencies:

011. The teacher understands the importance of family involvement in children's education and knows how to interact and communicate effectively with families.

012. The teacher enhances professional knowledge and skills by effectively interacting with other members of the educational community and participating in various types of professional activities.

013. The teacher understands and adheres to legal and ethical requirements for educators and is knowledgeable of the structure of education in Texas.

COMPETENCY 011

The teacher understands the importance of family involvement in children's education and knows how to interact and communicate effectively with families.

Even in the days of the one-room school in Texas, teachers had to be sensitive to the expectations of parents and community members. Often these expectations focused upon the social behavior of the teacher as much as the effectiveness of the teacher in the classroom. Since teachers often roomed with a family in the community, close observation of personal behavior was a simple matter. Community members generally agreed upon the rather rigid code of behavior deemed suitable for someone to whom the community entrusted its children each day.

Today, such agreement is not as clearly defined. The teacher's role is still one often considered a model of what should be, no matter how unrealistic the role model may be. For this reason, the teacher's skill in communicating with the parents and leaders of the community is vitally important. The success of conducting conferences with parents, of sending response-seeking notes or telephone messages to parents, and of assisting parents in working out positive study support techniques or behavior modification programs for students are all based upon the parents' trust in the teacher and, therefore, in the teacher's recommendations and referrals.

In addition to this concept of the teacher's personal responsibility and effectiveness in working with parents, the teacher needs to understand the environment students experience when they are not at school. In the home, with friends at neighborhood parks or recreation centers, or "hanging out" at the mall—wherever the student is outside of school hours will affect the student when he or she returns to school. Perhaps no other factor can affect the role of the students more than what goes on in their lives during the hours spent with peers, especially when the students are congregating without parents or other adult supervision.

This competency focuses upon the teacher's understanding and skill in working with the parent(s) or guardian of each of the students in a class. Strategies to establish a positive relationship with parents early in the school year provide the basis for better interpersonal communication when an educational or disciplinary problem does necessitate a meeting with parents later. If a feeling of trust and mutual respect has been cultivated, the subsequent parent-conferencing will not be as difficult. Ways to continue open communications with parents include techniques for pursuing a working relationship with nonresponsive parents.

Developing a Positive Relationship with Parents Early

The teacher will often have a more difficult time getting to know parents today than one or two generations ago. Often parents' attitudes toward becoming involved with the school have changed. This change is not necessarily due to disinterest but to different conditions in life-style. Many parents work outside the community and have less time and energy to develop an interest in the school than formerly. Also, often, a single parent is the sole responsibility for the child's immediate welfare. The single parent, working to provide the necessities for the family, has little free time. Gone also are the days when many parents themselves attended their child's school and even studied under some of the same teachers. Greater mobility in the population and the resulting community instability in both population and shared values have taken their toll. What can the teacher do to establish not only a friendly relationship with the parents but a relationship that has developed a degree of mutual trust and respect?

At the beginning of the school year, before an educational or behavioral problem arises with a student, the teacher can make positive contact with all parents. This contact may be by a written note, telephone call, or even a home visit in the late afternoon if the building administrator is not opposed to such visits. During the visit, the teacher can mention several of the immediate content and skill areas that will be studied during the next five or six weeks. He can ask the parent to describe the student's general attitude toward school, the successes of previous years of study, and special interests of the student, and the child's comments about the beginning of the new year. Finally, the teacher can ask the parents about their goals for their children during the coming year.

Parent/Teacher Communication

One of the most helpful resources for the teacher to establish continuing dialogue with the parents is to maintain an informal journal for all parental communications. Recording what the teacher brings to the meeting as well as ideas and attitudes the teacher leaves with can assist the teacher in making each contact non-repetitive and highly personalized.

If the teaching load of the teacher is too great for the one-on-one approach described, the teacher can try to set up meetings of small groups of parents immediately after school or at another convenient time. Working parents sometimes like to come in early before school in the morning; others can come during a lunch break where teacher and parents "brownbag" in the teacher's room at noon if no other place to meet is available. The group of four or five parents, although not as individualized in focus, is still small enough for the teacher to begin building a sense of cooperation and respect with each, essential in problem intervention or solution that may be required later in the school year. The initial attitude of the parents' role is one of a partnership, focused upon the child's well-being and awareness of the classroom objectives and strategies. Any step that avoids future adversarial parental response, almost always a negative base of communication, can only serve as a benefit for the teacher.

One concern of most parents is the quality of instruction occurring in the classroom. When the teacher can share his or her goals and indicate a continuity of study from day to day and week to week, parents respond positively. After the initial parental contact, teachers can begin a pattern of sending home papers for parents to see. A variety of papers—those showing strengths as well as weaknesses of students—should be selected for this step. If a student begins to show repeated weaknesses in work or attitude toward work, calling the parent for a conference is indicated.

Before the conference, the teacher needs to gather all of the materials needed— examples of the student's work to indicate the problem(s) under focus, the record of the student's daily effort if failure to accomplish assignments is the problem or part of it, anecdotes of misbehavior if the problem is one related to discipline, attempts made to change the negative performance of a student, and certainly suggestions for solving the problem. The teacher should always allow time for the parent to present his or her perspective of the situation as well as the child's attitude about the problem. Sometimes, having the student present becomes a useful strategy, especially if the student has been omitting part of the story when talking about it at home.

The end of any conference should include writing down the actions each participant—teacher, parent, and student—will take to help improve the situation. A tentative date for meeting again, or at least communicating between teacher and parent, should also be set before the participants leave. Within a few days, the teacher should try to find opportunity to provide feedback to both the parent and the student about the matter discussed, especially if improvement of a negative situation can be noted.

As students progress through school, their parents generally tend to have less interest in pursuing conferences with teachers. The parent of an elementary child is much more responsive to the teacher's initial overture to meet than the parent of a secondary student. Sometimes the parent has been to countless meetings with educators over the years, and the student is still exhibiting the same undesirable traits. The parent in this case tends to give up on helping the child. The secondary teachers, too, are often not as enthusiastic about contacting and arranging meetings with all students' parents. The secondary teacher, with well over 100 students, has a real scheduling dilemma compared to the elementary teacher. Often limiting meetings to parents of students with difficulty becomes the major effort of the secondary teacher. Whatever effort the teacher makes, however, is to his or her credit.

Responding to Nonresponsive Parents

Parents of some students, invited repeatedly to meet with a teacher, never seem to be able to arrange a time when they can come. The scheduling problem may be a genuine one, since many parents work long hours some distance from the home or hold more than one job. Sometimes when parents do attend a meeting, they are tired or distracted by even more stressful personal problems than the school situation.

When the teacher receives no response to an invitation for parent conferencing, a notation of the effort to make contact on a specific date should be made in the teacher's journal. Another attempt can be made six or eight weeks later. If a parent in this group does come to a school visitation program or is met informally in the community, the teacher should make every effort to show his or her pleasure at meeting the student's parent. Ideally, the teacher will have a recent anecdote about the child or some specific positive learning comment to make to the parent.

Certainly, these parents should also be included in any note sent to parents about projects or other classroom activities. Since these notes will usually be photocopied, a handwritten line or two is easily added to the nonresponding parents' notes. As always, the assurance to the parent that the child's educational welfare and personal well-being are continuing major concerns of the teacher will reinforce the goal of this competency.

Sample Question

John Kelly, a fifth-grade teacher, has been having many behavioral problems with a new student in his class, Bryan Underwood. During the four weeks Bryan has been enrolled, he has been unable to stay in his seat during class activities. He repeatedly speaks out during the middle of class to ask questions unrelated to the work underway. He disturbs other students with his aggressive behavior, often pushing or punching them. Mr. Kelly has called Bryan's mother and talked to her about his behavior. Mrs. Underwood, a single parent, has agreed to come before school to a meeting with Mr. Kelly about her son's behavior.

When Mrs. Underwood arrives for the conference, Mr. Kelly should greet her with which words?

(A) "I just don't know what I'm going to do with your son!"

(B) "Can you tell me why Bryan is so aggressive in my classroom? Has he exhibited these traits before?"

(C) "Mrs. Underwood, I think you have a real problem with your son."

(D) "Mrs. Underwood, let's see what we can come up with to help your son feel happier about his move to a new school."

The correct response is (D). Mr. Kelly's response is an opening that establishes the shared responsibility of the teacher and the parent to help Bryan. Recognition of a possible cause of Bryan's behavior is given—his recent move from another school. The basic cause of his aggressive behavior is indicated as a factor not related to the parent's handling of her son. A positive tone has been used and, even though Mr. Kelly may not feel as optimistic about Bryan's change in behavior as his words sound, he is making no promises but is seeking support from Bryan's mother to help bring about the desired change. Mr. Kelly is inviting Mrs. Underwood to enter into a collaborative working relationship with him, having Bryan's welfare as the focus.

Answers (A), (B), and (C) are incorrect. (A) expresses a negative tone about Bryan and the chance of changing Bryan's aggressive behavior. Mr. Kelly's words do not show the professional confidence that would be expected of an educator truly "in charge" of the situation. Mrs. Underwood, who may well be in need of help in managing her son, cannot be inspired to turn to Mr. Kelly for assistance. (B) immediately places the responsibility upon Mrs. Underwood to explain her son's behavior. Before hearing from the professional educator about the classroom situation, she is asked to tell about previous aggressive traits Bryan has exhibited. (C) also initiates the conference with a negative tone. All of the blame is placed upon Mrs. Underwood. Little hope for a positive solution to the problem is indicated by Mr. Underwood's first words. The major purpose of the conference, to work together for the child's benefit, is prevented by Mr. Kelly's direct assault. All of the wrong answers demonstrate how the lack of communication skills can get a parent conference off to a bad start and possibly doom the session to little positive outcome.

COMPETENCY 012

The teacher enhances professional knowledge and skills by effectively interacting with other members of the educational community and participating in various types of professional activities.

This competency focuses upon the teacher's understanding that he or she is one member of a team—professional educators, support staff, and others assigned to assist on a specific campus, all of whom must work together in varied ways to accomplish educational goals. The teacher has a continuing responsibility to maintain a positive attitude in attempting to find solutions affecting the success of all learners, in exploring new ideas, and in trying to reduce stress within himself or herself and within others. The teacher will be examining his or her own personal growth needs—both the psychological factors that determine the teacher's success in interacting with others, as well as the training opportunities that enhance the teacher's continuing growth in professional knowledge and skill. Three major aspects of this competency are the teacher's personal traits, the teacher's skills as a team member, and the teacher's planning for professional growth.

The Teacher's Personal Traits

Knowing one's self is an essential characteristic of a successful person in any area of life. The qualities enabling the teacher to work well in a work situation that is often described by others as stressful or boring are the same qualities that make a businessperson or salesperson successful. The teacher, like the banker or clerk, will never be isolated from others and must use a variety of personal interactive skills on a daily basis. Working with students in the classroom, sharing curriculum ideas in a grade-level meeting, projecting a positive image as a well-trained professional who is planning successfully for his or her assignment, or responding maturely to constructive evaluative comments from a supervisor—in every scenario, the excelling teacher demonstrates certain personal traits that project a strong self image: confidence, competence, dedication, enthusiasm, and a sense of humor. These are all traits that cannot be taught through a teacher education program. They are the result of the experiences of the individual during the developmental stages of his or her life and prepare the individual for a successful career in the area chosen.

Teachers are aware of their personal traits. They feel confident of the skills and content acquired during the years of training to become a teacher. Knowing various ways to modify classwork for a student with special needs or how to bring a highly excited class back to a calmer mode of operation instills a feeling of security in the teacher, a sense of being in control that communicates itself to the students without repetitious reprimand or threat.

The teacher's competence in handling the unexpected as well as the routine is clearly observable, as a professional efficiency of being in control of the situation is demonstrated. Enjoying work with both students and fellow professionals, the self-confident teacher is positive about what is going on in the classroom and meeting with staff members. Enthusiasm is often contagious. When the teacher is excited about the students' work, both younger and older students will respond similarly. Finally, finding laughter a healthy outlet, the teacher shares a sense of humor with the students. Even though students may groan at a teacher's puns, their acceptance of the educator's enjoyment of language will be a further linkage in building a positive working environment in the classroom.

In addition to the personal traits that denote a strong self-image, other traits of the individual identify the person who will have the greatest chance for success in a teaching career. A high energy level is most valuable. The apparently tireless teacher can match, perhaps even surpass, the energy level of the students. A well-organized teacher can achieve equally as much, however, since a plan of accomplishing the endless amount of work also brings about successful outcomes. Teachers described as successful are also understanding. Instead of always doing the talking, they find time to listen to students. In the fine art of communicating, too frequently the vital role of being a good listener is sometimes overlooked. When students have problems, an open attitude and a warmth of response can help the student to work out the solution needed.

Of course, sometimes students misbehave and do not respond to the initial efforts of the teacher to bring the student back into acceptable behavioral patterns. Consistency in disciplining students assists the teacher in promoting students' positive behavior. When students who have dropped out of the class focus know a teacher's warning will be followed by action, the students are much more likely to join the classwork as requested.

One trait that serves as a valuable adjunct to all other traits listed may elude many teachers. This is the trait of creativity. Although some teacher preparation programs promote training in innovative methodology, many teachers either lack time or the type of thinking skill that brings about fresh ideas for the classroom. Good interpersonal skills can come to the rescue as the less original teacher can observe and in various ways emulate ideas from other teachers who tend to be more innovative.

The preceding discussion has mentioned traits and skills to develop if they are not apparent in a teacher's personality. One other group of traits remains—behaviors to avoid. The negative traits of griping, carelessness, belittling others, or giving up on a student or the job assignment are the special afflictions released from Pandora's Box just to plague teachers. These energy-draining traits can also be contagious; therefore, stay away from anyone who exhibits signs of infection. Examine your behaviors and attitudes occasionally, working toward ever greater success in your teaching assignment.

Team Responsibilities in Teaching

A second aspect of this competency concerns the teacher's role in serving as a member of a team. Increasingly, teachers find their work affected by the need to coordinate with other teachers—in planning, in delivering the lessons, and in evaluating students and curriculum. Many of the personal traits that make a successful classroom teacher will also enable a teacher to work well with other professionals on various assignments and in self-developed team projects.

Perhaps the strongest team of teachers is one made up of two or more teachers or support staff members, all of whom possess the five basic traits of successful individuals discussed: confidence, competence, dedication, enthusiasm, and a sense of humor. The team members complement one another, sharing the responsibility and fully enjoying their work. Humor responds to humor; therefore, each team member especially appreciates his or her teammates' lack of griping and working toward the final goal—the improved learning of the students.

A successful team often allows the teachers to be more innovative. The immediate feedback of positive, respected peers ensures teachers of their decision-making wisdom. Bringing about change—perhaps the primary charge of a team—can be constantly monitored through more than one perspective.

Even if the team members are not equally strong in the personal traits that create a masterful educator, the teachers can learn to share their strengths for the benefit of the students. When a new teacher is assigned to work with a clearly outstanding professional, the opportunity for the less experienced teacher to move along more rapidly in developing successful strategies and polishing skills of instructing occurs.

Teaming Assignments

Frequently, the team-teaching activities are described as being either vertical or horizontal. Vertical teaming refers to forming groups across grade levels according to content or discipline.

Vertical teaming, thus, encourages communication and cooperation among elementary, middle, and high school teachers, allowing professionals to collaborate and achieve the Texas goal of a seamless curriculum, beginning in kindergarten and continuing through high school. This is an inclusive approach that helps teachers coordinate and integrate curriculum, share best professional practices, provide instructional cohesion and sequential skills development, and discuss common areas of curriculum and pedagogy.

Horizontal teaming, on the other hand, is the forming of groups based on a course of study (for example, all social studies teachers in grade seven) or across all subjects at a grade level (all grade seven teachers, for example). The purpose of horizontal teaming is to coordinate activities so that all children in all courses (regardless of the teacher) have exposure to the same content and the same approximate learning experiences.

Teaming assignments may be for a variety of purposes. Among the more frequently occurring patterns are the following:

1. Classroom instruction—Teachers may be teaching together for the entire day or for specified periods of time. Usually the class section is larger than the class of a single teacher. The teachers may have the same certification or compatible areas of specialization such as social studies, reading, and language arts.

2. Special needs adaptation for the classroom—Since the students who once were placed in special education classes are now integrated into regular classes of study, the classroom teacher becomes a working partner with the specialist. Ways to modify instruction for specific students are discussed and assistance provided by the expert.

3. Curriculum-related committees—Teachers and curriculum specialists work together to evaluate the existing curriculum and plan the changes needed. Often, the teacher tries new materials in the classroom and reports to the team about the effectiveness of the new ideas or resources. One annual committee of this nature is the textbook selection committee. Different teachers review and recommend for adoption a specific textbook each year. Teachers may work on a committee for the new textbook in their own subject area or on the district committee, making the final recommendations for all textbook areas to be selected during a single year.

4. Site-based management planning—One of the newer strategies used in Texas schools, committees to assist in making decisions about the management of the school are made up of a variety of staff members. Curriculum, discipline, school regulations, and other concerns affecting the total campus environment become the focus of each meeting, and the teacher's role is often representative of many other teachers on the staff. Meeting time each month may easily total several hours.

5. Special committees—From the calendar committee for the next school year to the cheer committee concerned with providing appropriate contact with ill or bereaved peers, various concerns necessitate that groups of staff members work together. Most of these assignments require only several hours of meeting time, but a demanding issue can extend that time estimate.

In each of the assignments for working together, teachers have the opportunity to demonstrate their positive skills in communicating with others. Often, as in teaching, listening becomes a vital key to the successful outcome of a team meeting.

The Teacher as a Resource Evaluator

In Texas, textbooks are selected by teachers, along with other professional staff members and patrons of the district, on a regular basis scheduled every few years. Textbooks being considered in a specific yearly adoption period are reviewed for several months by individual teachers. Often the teacher will use the trial textbooks to teach one or more concepts in a class. The teachers within a department will agree upon the textbook preferred and make a recommendation to the Central Textbook Committee, which in turn makes its recommendations to the School Board about all textbook areas being considered. At some point in many teachers' careers, each may receive an appointment to serve on the Central Textbook Committee. As with many committee appointments, a certain degree of prestige accompanies the appointment, and the work of the teacher becomes part of his or her professional record.

Publishers and producers of teaching resources will often request a teacher to preview a certain film, tape, or other resource, evaluating its pertinence and effectiveness for instruction. Usually, school administrators like to know about such activities in the classroom prior to their occurrence.

At budget preparation time, each teacher will be asked to submit a list of resources deemed worthy of purchasing. Having reviewed materials available is a much more meaningful way of making wise choices than catalog shopping.

The Teacher as a Curriculum Worker

One job that seems never to be completed is the preparation of curriculum guides for grade level and/or content areas of instruction. Evaluation of the existing curriculum is an on-going process by teachers, and the major revision of curriculum is usually a major focus every four or five years, especially as new textbooks are adopted and other resources purchased or made available. Special concepts often become fashionable trends in education. During the last 20 years, all grade levels and content areas have had major revision in curricula to include such matters as writing across the content area, reading in the content area, career education, holistic scoring of writing, inquiry study, multicultural concerns, strands of instruction for gifted and talented students, portfolio assessment, and the ever-popular basic skills instruction. One buzz phrase in the mid-1990s, for instance, is values training, not to be confused with the values clarification emphasis of the 1970s. Since the home and community may have lost effectiveness as a strong values support system, the school has been automatically selected as the agent to maintain the values for the society. Whatever the reason for curriculum revision, the individual teacher will be affected.

Of course, since the teachers are the ones who use the curriculum, developing it should be a welcomed assignment. Sometimes districts do allocate in-service time for this purpose; other districts pay teachers for working on curriculum during the summer. With the recent financial crunch, however, some teachers are having to work on the curriculum development assignment whenever they can on their own time. (In reality, no amount of time provided, or budget allocated, has ever been sufficient to provide adequate compensation for the time and effort dedicated teachers will spend in rewriting curriculum.)

Associated with the curriculum work will be the teacher's public presenting of the newly revised curriculum to groups of interested adults. Often an overview of the work is expected by the school board of the district. An active curriculum committee of the local Parent-Teacher Association, a group that may have been involved in earlier stages of revision work, will want to hear about the end product. When a school district has developed innovative, exciting ideas, professional groups will often request a presentation at area or state conferences. The dedicated teacher, again, is the one most familiar with the development and specific working ideas of the new curriculum.

The Teacher as a Specialist

Each teacher has specific certification that defines the areas of assignment he or she expects to receive. This area of specialization will not be addressed at this time. The concern of the teacher as a specialist relates to the teacher's assignment to areas for which he or she is not trained and has little or no interest or skill.

Two generations ago, teachers were often assigned out of their field and frequently stayed in such a teaching assignment for extended periods of time. The current trend is to make teachers' assignments within their certification specialties but to require of every teacher the ability to handle instructional focus for special areas that cross all disciplines. Over the last several years, instructional concepts that overlay subject areas have included drug education, career awareness, reading and writing in the content areas, and values reinforcement. Staff development sessions will focus upon these special expectations of every teacher.

Another specialist area affecting the regular teacher in the mid-1990s concerns students formerly designated as special education students. Currently, many such previously segregated students are being re-entered into mainstream classes. The regular classroom teacher has students, therefore, who have previously been taught primarily by special education teachers. The regular teacher must learn to offer modifications of instruction for these students and maintain a record of the various techniques used to meet the students' special needs. Modification may be as simple as allowing more time on a timed activity or accepting oral testing in place of written assessment. However, the teacher must have several strategies for teaching each unit of work and make available to students the method by which the student best learns.

Other areas of specialization expected of the teacher may concern special responsibilities to accompany the regular teaching assignment. Being offered a job may be contingent on the teacher's acceptance of a coaching assignment, although the teacher had not been seeking a coaching position. Serving as a sponsor of a school organization or activity group may also be expected of many teachers. As sponsor of the cheerleaders, the teacher will have hours outside of the regular school day to direct and supervise the practice of the cheerleaders and to attend school functions requiring the cheerleaders' performance. As sponsor of the National Honor Society, directing the process of selecting new members and planning the induction ceremony may be pleasant experiences. Of course, responding to angry parents whose sons and daughters were not selected for the prestigious group can be less satisfying.

Teacher education programs attempt to keep up with the reality of assignments met by new teachers, trying to prepare the teachers for whatever they meet. The diversity of schools and school districts, however, account for sometimes surprising job descriptions facing the teacher with a contract offer.

The Role of the Community

Other members of the community can become strong allies of the effective teacher. The school today, as a center of activity in the community and increasingly as an unpopular factor since it determines the increased tax base on homes within the community, is a focal point of interest to all members of the community—not just those with children or grandchildren attending the school. Patrons of the school district want their "money's worth," be it a school with competitive test scores (equating to a good "product" in the business world), a seat on the school board or at least a voice at the next school board meeting, or a positive contact with a member of the teaching staff—you. This more visible interaction today is two-fold, however, and can bring many benefits to the teacher. The education specialist at the computer store can assist the teacher in understanding the working of established programs and in locating and using software for the classroom. The librarian, always an active friend of the classroom teacher, can share which authors are the popular ones for the summer readers of any age group. Likewise, the video rental clerks will know the hot movies for the various ages. Community workers in specialized fields, such as involvement with drugs or gangs, provide much information for the teacher who has just moved into the community as a workplace.

The teacher, united with the various members of the community, becomes a stronger figure, one who is not only providing classroom instruction but also providing assistance to the students in other ways to be better equipped to meet the demands of life.

Finally, in order to fulfill the role delegated to today's educator, the teacher needs to be aware of the many roles to be enacted while under contract to teach. The local campus and district will have specific expectations for each employee. These expectations will involve matters of legal responsibility as well as ethical considerations. Often, the expectations are clearly delineated in a teacher's handbook at the beginning of the school year; however, some expectations are more traditional and can only be learned by observing experienced teachers' behavior. Finding a person who is open and well-informed about the practices and attitudes expected of the professional staff members on the campus is a wise step for a beginner. Such a person may be the teacher across the hall, a counselor, or a secretary.

State rules and regulations associated with education often relate to information that a teacher becomes aware of—matters concerning the privacy of student records, the responsibility to report signs of child abuse, student depression, and self-destructive attitudes, special needs of some student populations, and equal rights of all children regardless of race, religion, or sexual orientation. The teacher needs to know how to help and how to get help; also, the teacher must be aware of occasions when he or she cannot help but must make referrals for specialized assistance for the student.

Within the work environment, the teacher will constantly be facing decision-making situations that extend well beyond the lesson plans for the day or week. Knowing potential roles, utilizing the various sources of available support services, and exercising communication skills effectively to bring the greatest benefits to the students, the teacher clearly demonstrates an in-depth understanding of the teaching environment.

Mentoring

Over the last ten or fifteen years, mentoring as a formal process or program has gained popularity in the workplace, including schools. However, it is not a new development for more experienced teachers to share their knowledge and best practices with new or beginning teachers.

The idea of mentoring can be traced to Greek mythology. In Homer's *Odyssey*, Mentor was a teacher and a symbol for wisdom because he was half god, half human, half male, and half female.

In some schools, mentoring is an informal process while in others, there may be more structured mentoring programs and/or activities in place. Some school districts use mentoring to support curriculum development or staff development programs. Still, in other cases, mentoring is used to refer to individualized support and guidance.

Basically, a mentor is a friend, advisor, guide, and coach. The mentor possesses greater knowledge and advanced or expert skills and is expected to nurture a less experienced and skilled individual.

Mentoring has been used successfully to help new teachers gain perspective and understanding of both broad and specific issues by giving the beginning professional the opportunity to develop a relationship with a more experienced teacher. Frequently, mentoring activities include such things as looking at the academic calendar for the year and discussing important milestones, sharing teaching resources, discussing semester or year goals and objectives, reviewing state or district curriculum guides (TEKS), sharing ideas about time management and classroom organization, sharing ideas for managing student behavior and implementing rules and guidelines, and collaborating on projects—to name just a few of the possibilities.

The rewards of the mentoring relationship are many, but there are some risks. In most cases, mentoring is more effective when both parties (the mentor and the mentee) have open minds and discuss mutual goals at the onset of working together. Many schools have established training processes for mentors and provide guidelines for establishing, monitoring, and evaluating the mentor-mentee relationship.

Professional Growth

As a skilled educator, leader, mediator, and listener, the self-aware teacher can identify shaky or worn traits in order to bring about more effective results in work assignments. Some teachers need to develop new traits to provide greater potential for success in certain work-related encounters. Educational practice in Texas allows for this improvement in skills through the staff development programs required for all teachers throughout the year. More and more teachers are able to help design these in-service training sessions so that their specific needs are more adequately met. One major committee assignment of teachers is the planning of staff development within a district on specified days. Sessions that enhance the individual's knowledge in a content field are balanced with other opportunities, such as those that work to improve individuals' interpersonal skills, better understanding of technology, or wider knowledge of the available resources within the community.

In addition to required in-service meetings, many teachers continue advanced study at nearby universities. Many of these courses specialize in the needs expressed by the teachers on a campus. For instance, if several teachers are pursuing gifted and talented certification, a university may bring the required courses to a district campus for the teachers' convenience. Individual teachers often belong to the national organizations of their certified area. The reading of the professional magazines and/or journals of such organizations and the attendance at state and/or national conferences also provide a chance for gaining new content knowledge and strategies of instruction. Many times, teachers will find it professional and personally rewarding to join organizations that promote teaching in general as well as association or organizations of their content specialty.

The teacher's growth as a professional is never ending. New ideas, new technology, changing roles—all demand continual renewal. The resulting educator, the fully actualized teacher, leads the way.

Sample Question

Jana Davis's eleventh-grade English classes will participate for the first time in a team research project with the American History classes in her high school. Two teachers in social studies will be working on the project with Mrs. Davis, teaching the same students that she has in her English classes. The project indicates that the students' pre-writing activities will include reading a novel by an American author, researching the historical accuracy and/or relevance of the setting of the novel (time and place), and planning the paper.

After the paper has been written, each student's social studies teacher will evaluate the content accuracy, focusing upon the historical research. Mrs. Davis will focus her evaluation of the paper upon the analytical aspects of the novel as well as the written expression—style, mechanics, sentence structure, and usage.

During staff development time prior to the implementation of the research project, Mrs. Davis has asked the two American History teachers to meet with her. None of the teachers have ever worked on a team project like this one. Mrs. Davis has prepared a list of questions to initiate the meeting of the teachers on the team.

"I'd like us to plan the calendar for our research project so that we won't run into problems or be rushed in grading the final product. I know the students will need at least two weeks to read their novels. I have some other questions though before the project begins. What are some of the main points we should use to check progress during the pre-writing and planning stages? Should we both approve the thesis statement of the paper? How will our joint grading be reflected in the evaluation rubric? I know you must have some questions, too. I look forward to our getting together as soon as possible. Will our joint planning period next Tuesday be a good day for us to meet?"

Jane Davis's questions are intended to

(A)   show her interest in the team research project.

(B)   indicate to the other two teachers her control of the project.

(C)   demonstrate her willingness to accomplish the team project successfully.

(D)   clarify the problems in the proposed team project.

The correct response is **(C)**. Jana Davis has asked questions about concerns and decisions that will have a direct impact upon the success of the proposed project. By seeking clarification of these aspects of teaming with two of her teaching colleagues and inviting them to express their ideas and concerns, she will avoid problems and reduce stress associated with working across disciplines. Her pleasant, clearly worded note indicates confidence in working on this team project and a respect for the other two teachers. Her concern about the timing of various stages of the project indicates a good organizational sense and an awareness of the involved nature of the team project.

Incorrect answers for this question are (A), (B), and (D). (A) expresses Mrs. Davis's interest in the project. Her note, however, indicates much more professional forethought than merely expressing an interest. She is ready to get to work in organizing the project and establishing vital points of agreement for the teaming teachers before the students become involved in their research. When she refers to an evaluation rubric, she demonstrates her professional knowledge of creative and meaningful ways to evaluate, especially a way that may be used by more than one evaluator working on the same product. (B) expresses an attitude that is missing in the communication sent by Mrs. Davis. Her message to the teaming teachers is warm and open to input in determining the answers to considerations she mentions. Her capacity to lead is evident, but no strong overtone of seeking control has been expressed in her note. She speaks as an enthusiastic team member, one ready to contribute her time and talent to the joint venture. (D) centers on clarifying problems with the proposed project. Mrs. Davis's questions and her positive tone indicate a willingness to solve potential problems before they actually appear, not accentuate them at this early stage of planning.

COMPETENCY 013

The teacher understands and adheres to legal and ethical requirements for educators and is knowledgeable of the structure of education in Texas.

Teaching in Texas requires that practitioners be thoroughly familiar with expectations placed upon them by professional educators and concerned members of the community, while at the same time abiding by the legal and ethical principles that currently are used to design, direct, and monitor the total educational process within the state.

Other teachers, administrators of the school and of the district, and patrons of the community who serve on the school board work in a support organization of the campus, or take an active role because they have children enrolled at the school—all of these people have specific expectations regarding the teacher's fulfillment of the teaching assignment and its related responsibilities. Teacher education programs, as well as continuing staff development programs, inform and, when necessary, prepare each educator to respond appropriately to specific directives from the Texas Education Agency. Equally important is the teacher's comprehension of legal and ethical concerns related to the educational process.

Legal Issues

A fundamental expectation of the school board hiring a teacher is that this individual will be well-informed of the legal issues affecting teaching and always work in compliance with them. Staff development sessions based upon legal requirements for educators will be offered to teachers, and the teacher's district or campus handbook will itemize these concerns.

One of the major concerns of all teachers should be the safety and welfare of their students. Thus, students are not left without supervision while on the campus during the school day. The daily appearance of a student should be noted. Any indication of child neglect or physical abuse must be reported promptly to law enforcement authorities. More subtle is the alarm revealed by a child's written or oral language. Such evidence of a disturbed state of mind, especially one that could represent suicidal tendencies, should be reported at once.

In working with students in a class, the teacher must be sure to work with each in a manner that shows respect. Certainly, prejudicial treatment due to a student's religious beliefs, race, or sexual orientation is never acceptable in the classroom. The teacher is responsible as well for the unbiased atmosphere within the classroom during class discussion and study. Sexist language or harassment by the teacher or by students is intolerable.

The confidentiality of a student's records, including his or her current performance in a teacher's classroom, is also a protected right by law. The Family Educational Right to Privacy Act (known as the Buckley Amendment) specifies the conditions under which information about students can and cannot be dispensed. Since teachers have access to the permanent records of each student, they must be careful to whom they talk about these records. Idle chatter in the teachers' lounge or over lunch with fellow professionals is never appropriate or legal. Likewise, a teacher cannot discuss a student's performance record with adults other than the student's own parents or guardians.

Some important legal issues, such as copyright law and fair use policy and the Children Internet Protection laws, have already been addressed in other sections of this book. However, another important law with implications for teaching is the Americans with Disabilities Act of 1990 (ADA).

The ADA is intended to break down barriers to employment, transportation, public accommodations, public services, and telecommunications by extending to individuals with disabilities the same civil rights protection afforded to individuals on the basis of race, color, sex, national origin, age, and religion. Basically, ADA guarantees equal opportunity for individuals with disabilities.

Of course, ADA does include students with learning disabilities, including students with dyslexia (reading disability), dysgraphia (writing disability), dyscalculia (math disability), dyspraxia (or apraxia, a difficulty with motor planning and coordination), auditory discrimination problems, visual perception difficulties, and attention deficit disorder (ADD) or attention deficit hyperactivity disorder (ADHD). In sum, a learning disability is a neurological disorder that interferes with an individual's ability to store, process, or produce information, resulting in a gap between one's ability (intelligence) and performance. Individuals with learning disabilities, therefore, are usually average or above average in intelligence.

Learning disabilities are not the same as mental retardation, autism, deafness, blindness, or behavioral disorders. Learning disabilities are not the result of economic disadvantage, environmental factors, or cultural differences. In fact, most learning disabilities are the result of heredity, problems during pregnancy and childbirth (including illness or injury during or before birth, such as drug or alcohol use by the mother), and incidents after birth (such as head injury, nutritional deprivation, or exposure to poisonous substances).

Another more recent law important to teachers, which goes beyond the ADA in providing special education, is the Individuals with Disabilities Education Act of 1997 (IDEA). The purpose of this law is to ensure that all children with disabilities have available to them a free appropriate public education that emphasizes special education and related services. This law is designed to meet the unique needs of these students and to prepare them for future employment and independent living. The regulations for complying with this law were not released until 1999 so many schools are still developing guidelines and procedures for full compliance with the law.

IDEA defines disability as "mental retardation, a hearing impairment including deafness, a speech or language impairment, a vision impairment including blindness, a serious emotional disturbance, an orthopedic impairment, autism, traumatic brain injury, and other health impairment, a specific learning disability, deaf-blindness, or multiple disabilities."

The teacher is often referred to as a professional, a person who has completed advanced study and is deemed worthy of the highest standards of performance. Continually displaying the integrity associated with the teaching of young people, the new teacher can and will easily earn the respect of co-workers, parents, and teachers.

Ethical Guidelines

The Texas State Board for Educator Certification provides an Educators' Code of Ethics that describes the professional responsibility of Texas educators, as follows:

The Texas educator should strive to create an atmosphere that will nurture to fulfillment the potential of each student. The educator shall comply with standard practices and ethical conduct toward students, professional colleagues, school officials, parents, and members of the community. In conscientiously conducting his or her affairs, the educator shall exemplify the highest standards of professional commitment (Texas Administrative Code, Title 19, Part 7, § 247.2).

The Code of Standard Practices then outlines and details five principles for teachers. Those principles include:

I. Professional ethical conduct: respecting and obeying the law, demonstrating integrity, and exemplifying honesty;

II. Professional practices and performance: adhering to terms of a contract, organizing instruction, continuing professional growth, and complying with school policies and laws;

III. Ethical conduct towards professional colleagues: keeping confidential information, respecting political and citizenship rights and responsibilities, respecting colleagues' rights and privileges, eschewing coercion or special treatment to curry favor, and practicing academic freedom;

IV. Ethical conduct towards students: resolving problems according to school policy and law; protecting students from disparagement; keeping confidential information about students; exercising reasonable efforts to keep students from detriments to learning, health, or safety; including students without regard to race, color, sex, disability, national origin, religion, or family status; and respecting students' independent action and points of view;

V. Ethical conduct toward parents and community: communicating to parents, understanding community cultures, and manifesting a positive role in school-public relations.

A National Perspective

Not only are there ethics and standard practices in Texas governing the actions and behaviors of teachers, there are also established national standards and guidelines. One such example is found in the publications of the National Educational Association (NEA).

Emphasizing the educator's belief in the worth and dignity of each individual, NEA stresses the importance of the pursuit of truth, devotion to excellence, and the nurture of democratic principles. NEA's Code of Ethics of the Education Profession states that "essential to these goals is the protection of the freedom to learn and to teach and the guarantee of equal educational opportunity for all." The NEA code of ethics is promulgated on two principles: (a) Commitment to the student, and (b) Commitment to the profession. These principles are based on the values of honesty, truthfulness, and integrity.

Other Professional Responsibilities

Teachers also have responsibilities to keep accurate records (such as attendance records, testing information, routine school forms, parental permission slips, and documentation on parent conferences). Teachers must abide by all the rules and regulations to ensure the confidentiality and maintain the security of testing instruments, following legal guidelines and company directives.

Teachers must monitor student performance to ensure that the highest standards of academic integrity are upheld and that cheating is not allowed. Teachers should make students aware of the consequences and penalties for academic dishonesty (including plagiarism).

In many cases, teachers are expected to perform a number of professional duties, as assigned. This refers to special assignments from the department chair, the principal, and/or other members of the school administration. As long as teachers' fundamental civil rights are not violated and they are not asked to do anything illegal or unethical, they will be expected to perform many other duties, including supervising student activities, attending extracurricular events, and sponsoring students clubs and organizations, just to name a few.

Structure of the State Education System

Texas public education has a strong support network. The Texas Education Agency (TEA), headed by the Commissioner for Public Education (appointed by the Governor), provides school management assistance and oversight through the direction of the State Board of Education, individuals elected by citizens across the state to represent local and state interests and needs. Major policy decisions are made by the State Board. Members of the State Board are advised and assisted by the staff of the TEA (who investigate, examine, and report on various issues). The Commissioner is charged with managing the TEA staff and implementing the policies of the State Board.

The state model is reflected in school districts across the state, where superintendents of local school districts provide management and oversight through the direction and governance of locally elected individuals who serve on individual school boards. Again, these individuals set policies that are implemented by superintendents who manage teams of principals and other school administrators. In local districts, there may be many or a few administrators, depending on the size of the district.

The State Board of Educator Certification sets the guidelines and implements the policies for (a) preparing teachers, (b) assessing and accounting for teacher preparation, (c) certifying teachers, and (d) investigating complaints and enforcing standards of conduct for teachers. The TExES test is one of the functions of the State Board of Educator Certification.

In addition, Texas is divided into 20 geographic regions and each is served by a Regional Education Service Center (ESC). These regional centers provide management, curricular and professional development, and technical support, among other services. Each center employs a staff of professionals who are able to assist teachers, administrators, and parents in a number of ways. [For more information about each of the centers in Texas, visit the TEA Web site at http://www.tea.state.tx.us/ESC/.]

Teaching and Community Values

As important issues have been discussed in this text, emphasis has been placed on the teacher as a member of a team. Whether the teachers are team-teaching or serving on a school district team, working with colleagues in an informal way or interacting with parents, teachers are valued members of any community. As such, teachers must be prepared to support the philosophy of their school district in regard to its educational mission. Furthermore, teachers must be prepared to interact appropriately with the students, parents, and community members when topics such as censorship or sex education become matters of concern.

Each campus will have an approved approach to values education. The teacher should work within these guidelines. Texas school boards are showing an increased acceptance of character building strategies and expect teachers to promote the human qualities deemed admirable. Generally these qualities, once strongly supported by all facets of communities across the state, especially the home and the church, concern the traits of a good, law-abiding citizen and decent human being. The model of self-discipline and hard work, once traits identified with the head of a family, now may be exhibited as a worthy model for some students only by the teacher.

The teaching of values may be best achieved as students and teachers discuss pertinent events in their everyday lives or in their reading for school. The media's tendency to provide sensational coverage of well-known sports figures, politicians, and business leaders in the news brings the ugliest of human motives and behavior to everyone's attention. Appropriate class discussion, carefully moderated and directed toward a greater depth of understanding human nature, can help students struggle with a public hero or heroine's fall from grace. The stories read in class, or the events recounted from history, offer equally valid opportunities for discussion.

The whole concept of censorship is another aspect of values interchange that a teacher may meet. Even if a teacher limits reading to the state-adopted textbooks, some materials or ideas within these textbooks may be challenged by some parents or community members. A district committee for dealing with problems of censorship may be in effect, and the teacher's responsibility will end once the problem is submitted to the committee. Complaints from parents are generally sincere, directed by their concerns for their own children. Sometimes, however, organized groups exert pressure to remove certain reading from the classroom. In recent years, censorship hearings in Texas have reviewed complaints ranging from Shirley Jackson's short story "The Lottery" to the children's fairy tale "Rumpelstiltskin," from Bram Stoker's *Dracula* to the study of classical Greek mythology. Whenever a matter of censorship arises, the teacher should inform the school administrator promptly and follow the district guidelines for such matters.

Although the problems that are related to sex education are generally limited to teachers of health education or biology, all teachers need to be informed of the district policies regarding this potentially controversial issue. Even very young students are now exposed to early sexual information and even actual experience. Surveys indicate that many middle school students have had intimate relationships of a sexual nature. Each teacher's situation will be different; therefore, teachers need to determine before a situation arises (1) how to handle essays or poems making direct reference to sexual matters, (2) how to help students who have earnest questions of a sexual nature, and (3) how much discussion to allow in the classroom on the subject when it relates to the current study.

The Teacher as Advocate

The major Texas pattern of decision-making on school campuses since the mid-1990s has been based upon site-based management. The individual teacher may, therefore, have a leadership role early in his or her career. In site-based management, a team of professionals on the campus discusses the needs of the campus, makes recommendations to accomplish these needs, and evaluates the resulting actions taken. As a member of the team, the teacher may lead an inquiry or information-gathering committee, reporting the findings to the other team members—fellow teachers, a school administrator, support staff members, parents, and students. As with many other responsibilities undertaken by the teacher, this leadership role often requires after-hours attendance at meetings and offers no remuneration. The days of the "moonlighting" teacher seem to belong to the past.

Larger campuses are usually departmentalized. Teachers work together for various purposes, organized under a chairperson. Sometimes the role of chairperson may extend over many years; other patterns limit the role to a two- or three-year term of duty. The major budget responsibility for the department is the chairperson's. Each grade level on larger campuses may also have a grade-level chairperson. A new teacher can surprisingly find himself or herself named as the grade-level chairperson, serving as a spokesperson for this grade level.

A completely different area of leadership expected of the teacher is as a participant in the professional organizations of the teacher's certification and assignment areas. Area, regional, state, and national organizations service their teachers in various ways, offering displays of new books and other resources for the instructional area as well as workshops and conferences for teachers of the same discipline or teaching interest. Many of these meetings are held on weekends so that teaching responsibilities will not be interrupted.

Sample Question

Kate Tillerson is an art teacher at McGregor High School, where she has taught for several years successfully. She is respected by her students as well as her fellow teachers. This year, the new Director of Instruction for her school district has introduced several curriculum ideas, one of which is the concept of authentic assessment. All curriculum areas have had one or more staff development sessions on this concept. The idea will be incorporated into the curriculum as one of the strategies for assessment in each discipline and at each grade level.

Ms. Tillerson has just received a request from the Fine Arts Department chairperson to submit an example of a lesson involving authentic assessment. A central office form to complete the example accompanies the request along with a review of the authentic assessment concept, a model of a completed example, and a deadline for submitting teachers' samples.

Ms. Tillerson's general response to the entire focus on authentic assessment has been that all she does in her classroom is based upon authentic assessment philosophy. She really sees no need for making any changes in the curriculum guide or for preparing the assignment sent to her. On the other hand, Ms. Tillerson is an excellent teacher and generally cooperates in the various curriculum tasks requested of her. She has been a leader of staff development sessions within the district and has shared her innovative ideas with fellow professionals at both regional and state meetings of art educators.

Which of the following responses should Ms. Tillerson make to her departmental chairperson's request?

(A)   She files the request under things to do and forgets about it.

(B)   She writes a passionate letter in response to the Fine Arts Department chairperson's request, explaining how she feels about the proposed example of an authentic assessment in art. She sends a copy of this letter to her chairperson and also to the Director of Curriculum and takes no further action.

(C)   She writes a passionate letter in response to the Fine Arts Department chairperson's request, explaining how she feels about the proposed example of an authentic assessment in art. Attached to the letter is a model unit of study she has used in her classes, including an authentic assessment project described in detail but not submitted on the form provided by the Director of Curriculum. She sends copies of these items to both her chairperson and the Director of Instruction.

(D)   She completes an authentic assessment project idea on the form provided by her chairperson. She submits this idea with supplementary examples of students' projects photographed and a copy of the grading rubric returned to the students for each project photographed. She also sends a videotape of a student discussing the project he has submitted for the unit of study.

The correct response is **(D)**. Ms. Tillerson, as an effective teacher and respected professional in her school as well as beyond her district, realizes that the intent of central office curriculum efforts is to raise the standards of instruction throughout the district. While Ms. Tillerson, as a team player in the educational process, may be performing at the highest level, other teachers need boosting. The work that she submits will probably be used as a model for other teachers throughout the district. The thoroughness of her response indicates that she will be invited to make other presentations at area and state professional meetings, perhaps on the topic of authentic assessment.

(A) is an unprofessional action by Ms. Tillerson. Perhaps she is forgetful or lazy; she is certainly expressing rudeness and lack of cooperation by ignoring the request made of her and all teachers in the district. None of these characteristics represent a teacher who is effective in the classroom and highly respected by her students and peers. (B) indicates that Ms. Tillerson, not forgetful or lazy, is unaware or resentful of the role she plays as a curriculum developer within her teaching assignment. Her decision to write a "passionate letter in response" to the request is somewhat immature. The professional teacher who seriously questions a curricular approach from central office would discuss the situation reasonably, calmly, and privately with the new Director of Instruction.

(C) is incorrect because Ms. Tillerson, although showing support for the concept of authentic assessment, is still blocking the central office efforts to get some degree of uniformity in preparation of curriculum material. Again, her "passionate letter in response" to the request for an authentic assessment sample indicates poor judgment on her part. Does the strong expression of her feelings indicate an independent nature or a rebel in regards to teamwork? Is her refusal to rewrite her model unit of study to conform to the district format laziness, a rejection of authority, or some other indicator of malcontent? The effective professional would find some other way to communicate her concerns if the provided format for the model of authentic assessment could be improved. Skill in communications is an essential quality in the educational process, and the action described in (C) demonstrates a lack of understanding of vital components in effective communicating.

TExES

Texas Examinations of Educator Standards

Practice Test 1: PPR EC–4

This test is also on CD-ROM in our special interactive TExES TEST*ware*®. It is highly recommended that you first take this exam on computer. You will then have the additional study features and benefits of enforced timed conditions, individual diagnostic analysis, and instant scoring. See page 3 for guidance on how to get the most out of our TExES book and software.

PRACTICE TEST 1:
TExES PPR EC–4

(Answer sheets begin on page 392.)

TIME: 5 hours
90 questions

DIRECTIONS: Read each stimulus carefully, and answer the questions that follow. Mark your responses on the answer sheet provided.

The fourth-grade students in Mrs. Alvarez's class are studying Native Americans. Mrs. Alvarez wants to strengthen her students' ability to work independently. She also wants to provide opportunities for the students to use a variety of print and media resources during this unit of study. Mrs. Alvarez plans to begin the unit by leading the class in a brainstorming session to formulate questions to guide their research about Native Americans.

1. Which of the following criteria should guide Mrs. Alvarez as she leads the brainstorming session?

    (A) The questions should emphasize the factual content presented in the available print materials.

    (B) The questions should emphasize higher-order thinking skills, such as comparison, analysis, and evaluation.

    (C) The questions should reflect the interest of the students.

    (D) The questions should include all of the fourth-grade objectives for this unit.

Mrs. Alvarez has collected a variety of print and media resources for the students to use in their research.

2. Which of the following will probably be the best way to motivate students to research the questions they have prepared?

    (A) Mrs. Alvarez should assign two to three questions to each student so that all the questions are covered.

    (B)   Mrs. Alvarez should allow each individual student to select three questions he/she would like to research.

    (C)   Mrs. Alvarez should select three key questions and assign them to all the students.

    (D)   Mrs. Alvarez should assign one topic to each student, then provide each student with additional information.

3.   Mrs. Alvarez is using which of the following instructional delivery systems?

    (A)   Direct instruction

    (B)   Role-playing and simulation

    (C)   Exposition and discussion

    (D)   Inquiry and problem solving

Mrs. Alvarez plans to use contemporary assessment techniques at the conclusion of the unit. She is also concerned about providing sufficient feedback to the students.

4.   Which of the following is most likely to meet these assessment goals?

    (A)   A teacher-made objective test with questions that match the unit's content

    (B)   A variety of formal and informal assessments

    (C)   A standardized test with established reliability and validity

    (D)   Individual tests for each student that allow for individual differences.

At the conclusion of the unit, Mrs. Alvarez plans to ask her students to present the projects and activities that were prepared for the unit to the other fourth-grade classes in the building.

5.   Allowing time for students to prepare their presentation indicates that Mrs. Alvarez

    (A)   is concerned about bringing appropriate closure to the unit.

    (B)   wants to work collaboratively with other teachers.

    (C)   hopes to be appointed grade-level chairperson.

    (D)   wants to promote a feeling of student ownership and membership in the class.

As part of the presentation of projects and activities, Mrs. Alvarez asks her students to write a narrative explanation of their projects. Then she arranges presentations for the class that are to be videotaped as students read their prepared explanations. A student is appointed "filming director" for each project, and another student is appointed "reporter." All other students who participate are "writers" and contribute to the written script.

6.   This activity is an example of

   (A)   using a variety of instructional resources to motivate students and support individual and group learning.

   (B)   inappropriate use of school video equipment.

   (C)   providing "directors," "reporters," and "writers" with information about those careers.

   (D)   a homogeneously grouped cooperative learning exercise.

A museum of Native Americans who lived in what is now Texas is located about 45 miles from school. Mrs. Alvarez is considering a field trip to the museum.

7.   Which of the following elements should most influence her decision?

   (A)   The relevance of the current exhibits to the topics her students researched

   (B)   The cost of admission, the distance from the school, and the availability of transportation

   (C)   The difficulty in obtaining permission slips from each student

   (D)   The loss of class time in other subject areas

Ms. Hanley is a second-grade teacher in an urban school district in central Texas. Her campus is a Pre-K – Grade 5 school with almost 800 students. 70 percent of the students receive free- or reduced-price lunch and 41 percent participate in classes for English as a Second Language (ESL). Her class of 19 includes 10 boys and 9 girls. 4 of the students attend special education and 5 receive ESL services. Ms. Hanley has just reorganized her class schedule to accommodate the changes made for lunch, recess, specials (art, music, and PE), and various pull-out programs reflected in the campus master schedule. Her morning block allows for almost 2 hours of reading and language arts instruction. At the end of this block, her special needs students leave the classroom to work in the resource room. Ms. Hanley generally allows her more able learners to spend this time silently reading self-selected books from the classroom library while she works with the 5 ESL students. This schedule will continue to work well unless new special education or ESL students are added to the class.

The five ESL students in Ms. Hanley's class are from Spanish-speaking homes. Three of the students rarely speak in school, one uses one-word English phrases and points at things to communicate, and the fifth speaks in Spanish almost constantly.

8.   In order to build their literacy abilities, the most appropriate instructional tasks for these students would be to

   (A)   use flashcards of high-frequency English words in a small group mini-lesson.

   (B)   prepare lessons that regularly include read-alouds, discussions of picture books, and classroom experiences that encourage students to converse in English.

   (C)   practice the letter/sound associations for the English alphabet.

   (D)   have the students write word lists in English to match categories of study (i.e., weather – cloud, rain, snow, temperature).

A new student is added to Ms. Hanley's class. His records indicate that he has been receiving content mastery services for spelling and composition. Based on Ms. Hanley's reading inventory screening, the student reads just below grade level. A writing sample reveals that while his story includes many good ideas, he does not apply the conventions of spelling and mechanics. Ms. Hanley does not want to send the student for special services because it will require a major scheduling revision and she will likely lose the time with her ESL students for individual instruction.

9.   Which of the following criteria should guide her decision-making in this dilemma?

   (A)   Wait until someone in the special education department initiates an Individual Education Plan (IEP) review.

   (B)   Consult with the principal and special education personnel regarding options for scheduling so that the needs of all the students are best met.

   (C)   Work on the student's specific needs to build evidence that there is really no need for special services.

   (D)   Resign herself to the realities of conflicting schedules and adjust to the new situation.

One night while grocery shopping, Ms. Hanley meets Mrs. Ramirez, the parent of Juan, one of her students. After a cordial conversation about the family and how Juan is doing in school, Mrs. Ramirez inquires about an incident on the playground involving her son and a classmate Joey. She is unhappy about the "unfair" treatment that Juan received, while Joey "got off without any punishment." She is concerned about this unequal treatment and wants to know why Joey received an "easier punishment."

10.   What should Ms. Hanley say?

   (A)   "That's not true. Joey received the same punishment as Juan."

   (B)   "I make it a point to treat students fairly. That does not always mean that I treat them the same way. While Juan was on his third warning, Joey was only on his first. Therefore, the punishments were appropriate even though they were different."

   (C)   "I can see that you are upset about this. But it is inappropriate for me to discuss decisions concerning another student with you."

   (D)   "What Joey does and how I discipline him is none of your business."

Ms. White, Ms. Marks, and Ms. Ross are in their first year of teaching after having gone to college together for four years. The night after the TAKS administration they all go out to dinner. Ms. Marks starts talking about Mrs. Martinez, a veteran teacher on her team. In the classroom they are using, there are four bulletin boards that are supposed to be covered up during testing. Each board is designed to help students learn the different styles of writing. Instead of covering up the boards before the test, Mrs. Martinez started taking them down after the test had already started. She told the students that the board she would take down last would show the style of writing they were supposed to use when answering the writing prompt on the test.

11.   What should Ms. White and her colleagues do?

   (A)   Agree to say nothing to anyone regarding the incident

   (B)   Approach the veteran teacher and ask her to inform the principal about her actions

   (C)   Report the testing irregularity immediately to the principal and the campus testing coordinator

   (D)   Ask other veteran teachers what they should do in this situation

Mr. Garcia, a third-grade teacher, believes that the best way for children to learn to write is to write everyday for authentic purposes. His Language Arts block includes a thirty-minute composition time. During this block, students work independently on the pieces they have started in their journals. When they are finished with their drafts, students put their journals in the editing box for Mr. Garcia to review. He wants to develop his students' abilities to assess their own work for edits and revisions.

12.   The best way to accomplish this goal is to

   (A)   encourage students to read through their work before they turn it in.

   (B)   post a TAAS rubric for holistic scoring.

   (C)   post a simple checklist that includes the major points for editing and revision.

   (D)   pair students into teams to proofread each other's work.

Mrs. Gerig, a second-grade teacher, is worried about a new student, Roseanna Jimenez, who will probably be tested for Limited English Proficiency (LEP) soon. Roseanna does not speak in class. She watches what the other children do and follows suit. She nods yes and no. She laughs at silly things she sees, but she rarely utters a word at school. When she is asked to read with Mrs. Gerig, she hunches over and cries. When she is asked to write, she copies words from the word wall or writes her ABC's. After a few days, Mrs. Gerig checks the student records and sees that the parents have listed English as the home language.

13.   What should Mrs. Gerig do?

   (A)   Demand that Roseanne speak, read, and write in English

   (B)   Request a meeting with the parents, the campus designee for LEP, and a campus administrator as soon as possible to discuss Roseanne's academic progress and the benefits of the LEP program

   (C)   File a concern with the district office regarding the likelihood of the inaccuracy of the parent information reported on the home language survey

   (D)   Say nothing and do the best she can to teach Roseanne to read and write in English.

Lisa, a new student in Mr. Elva's fourth-grade class, has not done well on several assignments over the past two weeks. Mr. Elva is concerned that repeated failure will result in behavior problems and further academic problems.

14. His course of action might include

    (A)   using formal and informal assessments to determine what Lisa knows in order to focus instruction more appropriately while closely monitoring and recording observations regarding Lisa's progress.

    (B)   having Lisa miss recess and snack break to complete and correct failed assignments.

    (C)   requesting a parent conference to discuss possible retention in the grade.

    (D)   requesting that Lisa be tested for special programs.

Mr. Elva is concerned that Lisa's current achievement level will have negative effects on her behavior and future academic success. He understands how important it is that his expectations for learning and instructional strategies match Lisa's development and ability.

15. This awareness demonstrates Mr. Elva's knowledge of

    (A)   teaching strategies.

    (B)   learning styles.

    (C)   metacognition.

    (D)   cognitive/psycho-social theory.

◆◆◆◆◆◆◆◆

Ms. Borders, a second-year, third-grade teacher, is preparing a theme study on water and the related concepts of conservation, ecology, and human needs. One of her instructional outcomes deals with students' abilities to demonstrate their new learning in a variety of ways.

16. As she plans her unit of study, Ms. Borders first needs to consider

    (A)   the strengths and needs of the diverse learners in her classroom.

    (B)   the amount of reading material she assigns.

    (C)   how the theme connects to other academic disciplines.

    (D)   inviting guest speakers to the classroom.

Mrs. Gettler teaches 26 third-graders in a large inner city school. About one-third of her students participate in the ESL program at the school. Mrs. Gettler suspects that some of the students' parents are unable to read or write in English. Four of the students receive services from the learning resource teacher. At the beginning of the year, none of the students read above 2.0 grade level, and some of the students did not know all the letters of the alphabet.

17. Which of the following describes the instructional strategy that is most likely to improve the reading levels of Mrs. Gettler's students?

   (A) An intensive phonics program that includes drills and practice work on basic sight words

   (B) An intensive literacy program emphasizing pattern books and journal writing

   (C) An instructional program that closely follows the third-grade basal reader

   (D) All the students should participate in the school's ESL program and receive services from the learning resource center.

Mrs. Gettler is selecting books for the classroom library.

18. In addition to stimulating student interest, which of the following would be the most important considerations?

   (A) The books should have a reading level that matches the students' reading ability.

   (B) The books should only have a reading level that is challenging to the students.

   (C) The books should include separate word lists for student practice.

   (D) A classroom library is not appropriate for students at such a low reading level.

19. Which of the following instructional approaches is most suitable for Mrs. Gettler's class?

   (A) Tests for reading rate on a regular basis to determine fluency

   (B) A restaurant center where students create and read menus, write food orders, and pay the bill with play money

   (C) A daily read-aloud with the teacher in the grade-level basal

   (D) A science center where students record the results of experiments with combining liquids such as bleach, vinegar, cooking oil, food coloring, and rubbing alcohol

Mrs. Gettler realizes that a student's preferred learning style contributes to his or her success as a student. Mrs. Gettler wants to accommodate as many of her students' individual learning styles as possible.

20. Which of the following describes the way to identify baseline information about the students' learning styles?

   (A) Mrs. Gettler should record her observations of individual student's behaviors over a period of several weeks.

   (B) Each of the students should be tested by the school psychologist.

   (C) Mrs. Gettler should administer a group screening test for identifying learning styles.

   (D) Mrs. Gettler should review the permanent file of each student and compare the individual's previous test scores with classroom performance.

21. During the first parent-teacher conference of the year, Mrs. Gettler should

   (A) stress that it is unlikely that each student in her class will be promoted to the fourth grade.

   (B) determine the educational background of each parent and recommend the district GED program as needed.

   (C) emphasize her willingness to work with each student to enable each student to be successful.

   (D) recommend that parents secure an individual tutor for each student who is reading below grade level.

As the school year progresses, Mrs. Gettler includes discussions of holidays of many cultures. She introduces the holiday prior to the actual day of celebration. The children prepare decorations, learn songs, and read stories about children in the countries where the holiday is celebrated.

22. Which of the following best describes the most likely purpose of this activity?

   (A) Celebrating holidays of many cultures is one way to teach appreciation of human diversity.

   (B) Celebrating holidays of many cultures is one way to satisfy the demands of political action groups.

   (C) Celebrating holidays is one way to encourage students to read aloud to one another.

(D)   Celebrating holidays is one way to encourage students to participate in class activities.

Bob Whitrock, a third-year teacher, works in a large urban district in north central Texas heading a class of 24 fourth-graders. His campus is deep in the inner city, surrounded by dilapidated buildings, vacated warehouses, and low-income housing projects, and sits virtually under the mix-master of a major interstate highway. His students are almost evenly divided between three ethnic groups: Hispanic, African American, and Caucasian. There are 13 boys and 11 girls ranging in age from 9 to 12. Eight of the students have been retained once and two more have been retained twice. All of his students read a minimum of one year below grade level. Only 27% passed the Grade 3 state-level reading test, while 44% passed the math section. His students are lively learners but lack perseverance. They give up on tasks that require real work on their part. Parent-teacher conferences are scheduled for next month. Teachers are expected to make appointments with each parent for a 20-30 minute visit to discuss the student's progress and educational program. Mr. Whitrock has learned from his experience the past two years that these conferences are generally not well attended by the parents for a variety of reasons. When the principal calls a faculty meeting to review the expectations and procedures for parent conferences, Mr. Whitrock considers how to handle the issue of low parent attendance.

23.   After careful consideration, Mr. Whitrock should

(A)   schedule conferences for all parents as required by district policy and send letters or postcards regarding student progress to parents who do not confirm a scheduled appointment and/or do not attend their conference.

(B)   discuss the problem of low attendance with colleagues.

(C)   complain to the campus administration that the work required to prepare for conferences is disproportionate with the outcomes since so few parents attend.

(D)   schedule appointments for the parents he believes will attend and leave open slots for others if they choose to come on the conference days.

Marcus, an over-aged third-grader in Mr. Nedham's class, has begun to exhibit some negative behaviors during math class. His guided and independent practice indicates that he can repeat the steps of the algorithm, but has not yet mastered the mathematical concepts underlying the word problems. He is not completing the homework. During parent conferences, Marcus' parents ask Mr. Nedham to let them know what they can do to help Marcus during the year. Mr. Nedham believes that close monitoring during classroom practice and appropriate independent practice in the form of homework generally results in increased understanding and retention.

24. In order to support Marcus's learning, Mr. Nedham should

    (A) make an initial phone call to Marcus's parents and establish a daily dialogue journal to communicate expectations and directions for the homework assignment and report on the day's work.

    (B) allow Marcus to complete homework assignments during recess.

    (C) initiate a phone conference to alert Marcus's parents that homework has not been returned completed.

    (D) send Marcus to in-school suspension for repeated failure to complete assignments.

After two weeks, Mr. Nedham begins to see that Marcus is more engaged not only in his math work but also in his reading and social studies. In a one-on-one conference, Mr. Nedham discusses with Marcus his improvement across these areas.

25. In discussing his improvements, Mr. Nedham wants to emphasize

    (A) how pleased and surprised he is at the change in Marcus's progress.

    (B) how making better grades will pay off later in life.

    (C) how Marcus's finally buckling down and doing the work will make things in the classroom go a lot smoother.

    (D) how Marcus's attention to and engagement in the learning task results in improved achievement and how good it feels to learn new things and contribute to the classroom learning.

Mr. Bell is very conscious of the age and maturity differences among his fourth-grade students. He knows that the older students are pre-adolescent and are increasingly interested in the issues of young adolescents while the younger students are still in childhood. He has already had to address the behavior of one or two of the older students. He is concerned about providing appropriate support, both socially and academically, for the various needs of his learners.

26. Which of the following describes an appropriate strategy for addressing the students' diverse needs?

    (A) Group students in same-age groups for academic tasks

    (B) Volunteer to participate in the student support program involving community mentors, students from the middle school, and across-grade level book buddies

(C)   Stay after school twice a week to play chess with the two students he is concerned with

(D)   Ask the counselor to speak to the class regarding issues of appropriate behavior

Several students in Mrs. Hannity's fourth-grade class have asked to lengthen the silent reading time from fifteen minutes to twenty minutes per day. Mrs. Hannity is already concerned that some students are not using the full fifteen minutes for reading.

27.   Which of the following describes an appropriate strategy for dealing with this student request?

(A)   Tell the students that some of their peers are not reading for the full fifteen minutes and that it would be a waste of time to extend it

(B)   Tell the students that fifteen minutes is all the time she has to let them read

(C)   Agree to add a five-minute 'share time' at the end of the fifteen minute reading period

(D)   Agree to extend the reading period for a trial period making clear expectations for behavior and consequences for failure to use the time for reading

Mr. Kyle, a second-year, third-grade teacher, has planned a nine-week unit based on the historic missions of Texas including the various ethnicities, religions, and cultural factors involved in their establishment. His plan includes the development of small group or individual multi-media presentations based on the content of the unit.

28.   Which of the following strategies might facilitate his evaluation of these multi-media projects?

(A)   Accept all projects with a grade of 'B' since it is the first attempt at technology presentations

(B)   Create rubrics or checklists with point values based on the criteria of the assignment

(C)   Look at each project holistically and grade on a descriptive scale (Excellent, Satisfactory, Needs Improvement, Unsatisfactory)

(D)   Let students self-assess

In the unit on missions in Texas, Mr. Kyle has allowed two opportunities for students to make decisions about their work. First, he has allowed them to choose the mission they will research. This research is done in pairs. Each pair has to conduct research on the establishment of the mission in its locale. Second, each pair of students will decide who researches the "before" and the "after" of the land and its people in relation to the establishment of the mission.

29. Allowing for this decision-making on the part of his students indicates that Mr. Kyle

    (A) understands the importance of teaching decision-making through class-room tasks and the relationship between interest and motivation.

    (B) is not concerned about cooperative learning.

    (C) does not worry about covering all the related TEKS for this unit.

    (D) has attended training in learning styles.

Rubrics designed to evaluate the multi-media project for the missions of Texas study are based on four achievement levels: Accomplished (A work), Proficient (B work), Basic (C work – meets minimum expectations), and Developing (D or F work). There are four grading criteria: Quality of Written Communication, Quality of Research Resources, Quality Application of Technology, and Quality of Overall Presentation. At each achievement level, a point value is determined, and descriptors for each criteria are listed so students can self-assess their work as they complete it.

30. This practice indicates that Mr. Kyle

    (A) understands that writing rubrics serves to protect him from parents who complain about student grades.

    (B) knows how to evaluate fairly.

    (C) understands that clearly communicating expectations is important to student success.

    (D) understands that using rubrics allows him to grade students against one another so as to be completely fair.

The students in Mr. Connor's fourth-grade class come from diverse backgrounds. Even though they are all from lower socio-economic homes, there is considerable disparity in their accessibility to technology, books, and other resources to support academic tasks.

31. Which of the following strategies appropriately addresses the discrepancies noted by Mr. Connor?

    (A) Establishing routines for students to arrange for additional computer time, library visits on an as-needed basis, and the check-out of classroom magazines and periodicals.

    (B) Each student has a scheduled time to use the classroom computer during the week.

    (C) Students are allowed to visit the library each week.

    (D) Students are encouraged to come to the computer lab before and after school for additional time.

A traditional elementary school reading program for grades EC–4 has been evaluated. The results show that a majority of students are not reading at grade level. Library records reveal the students' lack of interest in reading. The reading coordinator, Mrs. Sivart, has been assigned to coordinate efforts to improve the reading skills for all grades. The improvement of reading skills to at least near grade level is the school objective.

Mrs. Sivart's first action is to form a committee of the school psychometrist, the media specialist, and one teacher from each of the five grades. The psychometrist is to study the test results and determine which of the reading skills are lacking in the students. She reports that only 30 percent of the students are deficient in specific reading skills. The remainder of the students is deficient in no particular area but has an overall deficiency. She explains that there are developmental progressions and ranges of individual variation in each domain that account for about 10 percent of the students.

Mrs. Sivart asks the teachers to design a plan of study for those students who fall within the 10 percent.

32. The rationale for her request is based upon

    (A) lessening the work load for the teachers.

    (B) obtaining a framework for remediating the other 20 percent of the students.

    (C) facilitating the development of a project plan best suited to address the academic needs of individual students.

    (D) recognizing the benefits of working cooperatively to achieve goals.

Mrs. Sivart begins to design a plan of study for those students who are deficient in one or more areas of reading skills. She chooses a plan that allows the student to rotate from one teacher to another, remediating one reading skill with each teacher. This will allow teachers to work closely with each student and set up individual study plans depending on students' previous knowledge. When students have mastered all deficient skills, they won't need to attend the sessions any longer.

33. A principle for developing this plan is that

    (A)   students learn faster when they perceive they are learning less.

    (B)   teachers are more receptive to teaching one reading skill instead of all of them.

    (C)   parents are less likely to perceive the remediation as a negative activity.

    (D)   assimilation occurs more rapidly for the student when new information is linked to old information.

The media specialist suggests a library reading program that will correlate highly with the teaching program and reward the students as they read. The rewards will be provided by the business community. A pencil carrier will be the reward for having read 25 books, a baseball cap the reward for having read 30 books, a tee shirt for 50 books, and a backpack for having read 100 books.

34. The media specialist's suggestion is based on her knowledge that

    (A)   students enjoy doing those things they do well.

    (B)   students will read to receive the reward.

    (C)   instruction that is planned to enhance students' self-esteem will create an environment where the student feels accepted, competent, and productive.

    (D)   library materials that correlate with teaching strategies are more meaningful and help to create an atmosphere that motivates students to continue to read additional books.

Mrs. Sivart requests that computers be made available in the small group area of the library. Software containing comprehension questions for 500 books will be provided. As students complete a book, they are free to come to the library and take the comprehension quiz. The computer keeps a record of those books read and comprehended. If comprehension falls below 80 percent, only the students know if they need to reread the book and retake the exam.

35. This is a good instructional plan because it demonstrates that

    (A) students' motivation is easily lowered if others are aware of their failures.

    (B) the teacher is not needed to inform students if they need to reread and retake the test.

    (C) the use of the computers prevents the media specialist from having an increased workload.

    (D) the combination of appropriate instructional materials and resources helps students to understand the role of technology as a learning tool.

After yet another brainstorming session with all members of the school action committee, the group decides to post by the name of the student the title of each book each time it is read and comprehended.

36. Publicly displaying the titles of the books is based upon

    (A) understanding that students need frequent and concrete feedback in order to reach their goals.

    (B) facilitating motivation for all students.

    (C) helping the students become independent thinkers and problem-solvers.

    (D) varying the role of the teachers in the instructional process.

37. An essential learning principle emphasized by the action committee is to

    (A) maximize the amount of classroom time.

    (B) preserve a positive atmosphere in the classroom.

    (C) manage routines and transitions.

    (D) structure a learning environment that not only maintains a positive classroom environment, but also promotes the lifelong pursuit of learning.

Ms. Sanchez is a second-year teacher of a multi-age kindergarten and first-grade class made up of 18 five-, six-, and seven-year-olds in south Texas. She has just completed her Grade 1 Reading Academy training and is interested in implementing many of the strategies presented in the training. However, she is concerned about classroom management issues. Her team members, all veteran teachers, seem to understand how to make decisions regarding grouping and resource selection. Her principal, Mr. Smith, has made it clear that teachers are to "follow the guidelines of the state-mandated training."

Ms. Sanchez is arranging her room to facilitate the reading and writing strategies she learned in the summer training.

38.   What criteria might guide her decision-making?

    (A)   Her routines and procedures for accessing materials

    (B)   Areas for quiet and noisy work

    (C)   Her own path of vision to all areas of the room from her desk and/or other primary work areas in regard to the location of water, electrical outlets, and general safety features.

    (D)   Her classroom rules, rewards, and consequences

Ms. Sanchez has completed the Texas Primary Reading Inventory for students in her classroom.

39.   The assessment results can serve to inform her instructional decision-making if she

    (A)   divides the students into three or four groups based on reading levels.

    (B)   matches her lesson plan objective to the TEKS.

    (C)   identifies the strengths and approximations of each learner prior to determining reading materials, teaching strategy, and students for each group.

    (D)   follows the curriculum guide provided by the central office.

Ms. Sanchez has noticed that some students in her class are off-task while she is working in reading groups or writing conferences.

40.   Which of the following is the most appropriate remedy for this dilemma?

    (A)   Establish and maintain routines and procedures for student behavior during times when she is engaged in small group instruction

    (B)   Take names of students who don't stay busy and deduct time from their recess

    (C)   Use whole-group, direct instruction for all reading and writing lessons to ensure student engagement

(D) Talk to her veteran colleagues about how to deal with these discipline problems

41. In order to help her students learn the expectations for behavior and the procedures for walking down the school hallways, Ms. Sanchez might consider which of the following measures when she gives these instructions?

(A) Tell students that the principal expects them to be quiet because other students are trying to learn

(B) Tell students in clear, simple terms what is expected, model the desired behavior, and allow students the opportunity to practice the behavior

(C) Tell students they are to be silent in the hallway, with their hands and feet to themselves, or they will lose playtime

(D) Wait to see how they do as they pass through the halls and then correct their behavior

Ms. Sanchez provides time each day for her students to plan and draft stories in their journals. As students complete their drafts, she reviews them for revision and editing, then conferences with individual students communicating strengths and approximations evident in their work.

42. This practice indicates that Ms. Sanchez understands

(A) that writing is important.

(B) the importance of monitoring student performance and providing timely, high-quality feedback.

(C) that journals are more effective than worksheets in teaching writing.

(D) that routines and procedures facilitate classroom management.

As Ms. Sanchez reviews her students' writing journals, she notes specific teaching points and plans future instruction based on identified needs.

43. This practice indicates that Ms. Sanchez understands

(A) the importance of having high expectations for all students.

(B) the importance of student interactions in the learning community.

(C) how to schedule activities and manage time.

(D) the importance of planning learning experiences that are responsive to diverse students' needs and that promote learning for all students.

The students in the class have written stories following the "Brown Bear, Brown Bear" format. The stories have been revised and edited by Ms. Sanchez. For the next several days, students will enter their stories into the computer using a special software package that allows the addition of graphics and animation. Based on student need, Ms. Sanchez scaffolds each student's work on an as-needed basis.

44. Which of the following criteria should guide her decision-making as she designs an evaluation rubric for the publishing task?

    (A) The Technology Applications TEKS and the prior experience of her students regarding technology use

    (B) Information from the parent survey regarding student interests

    (C) Roles and responsibilities of support staff in the building

    (D) The stages of play development in young children and the correlation to computer readiness

Ms. Sanchez wants to keep parents informed about topics of instruction, special projects, and calendar events. She has decided to prepare a weekly newsletter.

45. Which of the following criteria should she keep in mind as she prepares the newsletter?

    (A) It is best to conform to the practice of one's grade level team.

    (B) Supportive and interactive classroom climates are the most productive criteria.

    (C) Students come from diverse backgrounds and therefore may differ in language, customs, beliefs, and values.

    (D) All communications should be delivered in English and Spanish.

Ms. Sanchez and other new teachers meet with the instructional specialist (IS) twice a month to discuss issues related to teaching and learning. The IS makes observations and discusses teacher and student interactions taking place during the observation in a conference at the end of the day. When the teachers come together to dialogue, they think about their instruction and attempt to clarify their understanding of teaching and learning with the help of research texts.

46. This practice demonstrates that the faculty and campus leadership understands

    (A) the importance of faculty relationships.

    (B) the importance of teacher observations.

  (C) the importance of student-teacher interactions.

  (D) the importance of self-reflection and continuous professional development.

The home-room mother wants to create a phone list of all the students in the class. She distributes the list to the parents to facilitate communication while planning and preparing for parties, field-trips, and other special projects during the year.

47. Ms. Sanchez must

  (A) make sure that all students are included on the list so that no one is left out.

  (B) determine that only students whose parents have approved the release of this information are included on the list.

  (C) prepare the list herself to ensure accuracy.

  (D) tell the home-room mother that the campus leadership must approve the idea and the release of this information.

The home economics teacher, Mrs. Green, is planning a unit on nutrition. Her first task is to identify performance objectives. She concludes that she wants students to master the content of her lecture, but she also wants them to be capable of independent research in the library on the topic of nutrition. Her second task is to prepare an evaluative tool to be used at the completion of the unit. She decides to have a paper-and-pencil test, as well as a performance exam. Step three consists of choosing resources for the class presentation. She chooses a beginning text on foods, the nutrition unit from the curriculum materials, two Measure Up games from the media center, teacher-made worksheets covering the appropriate content, a computer program for enhancing the classroom presentation, and the required tools and ingredients for the performance aspect of the unit. The unit will be concluded with a field trip.

48. The presentation of the unit is designed to

  (A) communicate through verbal and nonverbal presentation and media, thus imparting the expectations and ideas to create a climate of inquiry.

  (B) present the material in a variety of mediums using several techniques.

  (C) give the students a choice of what they are to learn.

  (D) integrate with other subjects in the school.

49. The strength of requiring a cognitive objective and a performance objective is that

   (A) some students are not test-takers and do poorly on paper and pencil tests.

   (B) the score for one objective could offset the score for the other objective.

   (C) comprehension and application are both desired learning outcomes for the instruction planned.

   (D) the teacher is matching the students' learning styles to her teaching style.

50. The multiple resources Mrs. Green has planned provide for

   (A) enhancing student achievement.

   (B) engaging the students in meaningful inquiry.

   (C) eliciting different levels of thinking from the students.

   (D) promoting problem-solving.

To begin the unit, Mrs. Green presents the information through lecture. She instructs the students to add notes to the lecture outline that she has provided for them. After the information is presented, the students complete the supplementary activities and plan the activities that will be carried out in the labs. The labs contain the ingredients for various recipes. Mrs. Green instructs some of the students to deliberately mismeasure one of the key ingredients in the recipe. Later, the recipe is analyzed to determine why the result was a failure. A discussion follows with various students reporting that while watching their parents cook, they often use a "dab," a "dash," or a "pinch" of ingredients, and do not actually measure.

51. The demonstration of not accurately measuring the ingredients in a recipe is used to

   (A) show the students what happens when directions are not followed and stimulate curiosity in the students.

   (B) evaluate the observation techniques used by the students.

   (C) determine whether groups are actively engaged and working cooperatively.

   (D) illustrate how waste can occur in the kitchen.

The culminating field trip is scheduled at the cafeteria, where the students are familiarized with special measuring tools: e.g., scales, gallons, and pounds. As the students observe the use of these special tools and amounts, Mrs. Green asks them to try to imagine the quantity that a particular recipe produces and how many servings it provides.

52.   The field trip is planned as a culminating experience to

(A)   bring closure to the unit.

(B)   promote responsibility for one's own learning.

(C)   confine the students' learning to the classroom, keeping it in an academic setting.

(D)   allow the students to make the connection between their current skills and those that are new to them.

Bill Drayton is a first-year teacher. He teaches in a town in the desert of west Texas. Late in the fall semester, Mr. Drayton arrives home just as a rental moving truck pulls up in front of the house across the street. The "For Sale" sign on the house has recently been taken down, and Mr. Drayton is eager to meet his new neighbors. While he is introducing himself, a van pulls up into the driveway and a woman comes around the side of the van in order to help a young girl in a wheelchair. "Come and meet my wife, Rachel, and our daughter, Myra," says the new neighbor, who has introduced himself as Harry Jacobsen. "Myra is in fourth grade," says her mother. "Then you'll be in one of my classes," says Mr. Drayton. "We have two fourth-grade classes. Each one spends half the day in Ms. Wade's room, and the other half of the day in mine. I teach language arts and math, while she teaches social studies, science, and art. We have a lot of fun, because we teach around themes. For example, Ms. Wade's social studies classes are learning about how Texas history was influenced by geography, so in my language arts class, we're reading stories about Texas history and discussing how the geography contributed to the things that happened in those stories. We also pretend that we are early Texans and write journals and newspapers about the events that shaped our history as those events relate to geography. In my math classes, we're using math to better understand Texas geography: things such as lengths of rivers, miles between cities located on the waterways, and so forth." Myra is excited. "Can I be in his room, Mama?" she asks. Rachel shakes her head. "No, honey, I'm sorry." Then she explains to Mr. Drayton that Myra has to go to a private school because the local schools are not wheelchair accessible. "Myra can't get through the outer doors, the inner doors, up the stairs to the classroom, the cafeteria, the gym, or anywhere else. In fact, she can't even get into the toilet stalls," she explains. "These changes would be very expensive, and the district can't spend that kind of money on Myra."

53.   What should Mr. Drayton say?

(A)   "I'm sorry. But maybe I can bring home some fun materials from school to share with Myra."

(B)   "It is illegal for the school not to make itself accessible to all people with handicaps, regardless of the cost. Have you talked to the principal?"

(C)   "I'm sorry. If the costs were reasonable, perhaps the district could make changes. But you're right. We can't make changes that expensive for only one student."

(D)   "You should sue the school district and make them do the changes."

That evening, Mr. Drayton and his wife go out to dinner. They decide to go for a drive before they go home. As they round a corner not far from their home, Mr. Drayton sees one of his students, Cade Evans, running down the street. Cade is with a group of boys, one of whom throws something down as they run. Although Mr. Drayton does not see the faces of any of the boys except for Cade, judging from their size, he thinks that they are probably also fourth-graders. He stops his car and looks around. He discovers newly painted graffiti on the side of the building by the corner.

54.   What is Mr. Drayton's best course of action?

(A)   Chase down the boys with his car and make a citizen's arrest

(B)   Call the police and report what he saw

(C)   Call the superintendent and report what he saw

(D)   Refer Cade to Big Brothers as a child in need of a special friend

Troubled by what seems to be an increase in gang-type activity among younger and younger children, Mr. Drayton wants to find out what his students think and know about gangs. He wants to learn the most he can about the students' thinking in the least amount of time. While he wants all students to have the chance to share what they think and know, he also wants to maximize interaction among students. The students will spend the entire morning reading, talking, and writing a group report about this subject.

55.   Which of the following seating arrangements would best help Mr. Drayton meet his objectives?

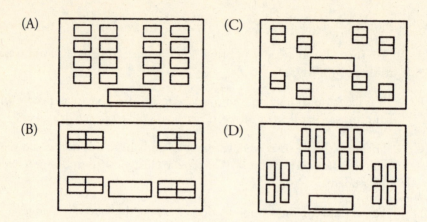

Mr. Drayton spends the next day on his regularly scheduled language arts activities. The students are learning how the desert affected early settlers.

56. Since his hidden curriculum is to help students prepare for positions of leadership in the community, what would be the best classroom organization for the day's activity?

    (A)   Cooperative activities   (C)   Independent activities

    (B)   Competitive activities   (D)   Whole group activities

57. Since the class is studying how the desert impacted the early settlement of Texas, which of the following would be the best choices of instructional materials and resources?

    (A)   A video of desert plants and animals

    (B)   A sand table and a variety of desert plants

    (C)   The archives of the local newspaper and local senior citizens

    (D)   A collection of books on the deserts of the world

In his language arts class, Mr. Drayton is currently teaching the thematic study of the impact of geographic features on the history of Texas. One of the activities that he decides to employ during this segment is storytelling; he has studied the art of storytelling and aspires to one day be a master storyteller.

58. What would be the most important reason for Mr. Drayton to learn to be a master storyteller?

    (A)   Everyone loves a good story.

    (B)   Storytelling is a highly cost-effective method of teaching.

(C)   According to Witkin, storytelling is one of the most effective ways of teaching social learners.

(D)   According to Witkin, storytelling is one of the most effective ways of teaching field-independent students.

Following two days of activities that include Mr. Drayton's storytelling sessions, he tells the children that they are to each write a story to tell to the class. He will then compile all the students' stories into a journal and distribute a copy to each student's parents or caretakers.

59.   What is the most likely instructional reason to have students write a story with the intent of first telling it to the class and then making it accessible to the parents, as opposed to merely telling a story?

(A)   Publication is a highly effective tool in motivating people to do their best work.

(B)   Being able to speak in public is a crucial skill for success in a democratic society.

(C)   The students will learn to critique their own work.

(D)   Students' prior exposure to stories is important to their ability to write a story.

That afternoon, Mr. Drayton and Ms. Wade meet after school to begin planning for the next thematic unit of study. Ms. Wade, who is also a first-year teacher, is ready to move on to the unit on people who made contributions to the development of Texas.

60.   Which strategy for planning for outcome-oriented learning experiences would be the best to start with?

(A)   Select desired learning activities

(B)   Determine time and space constraints

(C)   Determine desired learner outcomes

(D)   Solicit input from students

Mr. Drayton comes to the planning session with a notecard on which he has listed the essential elements that he plans to address during the new unit of study.

LISTENING	*Distinguish between fact and opinion*
SPEAKING	*Adapt content and formality of oral language to fit the purpose and audience*
READING	*Identify multiple causes of characters' actions; Understand the feelings of characters*
WRITING	*Use ideas/sources other than personal opinion/experiences*

61.   Which of the following resources are most likely to be of use to Mr. Drayton?

(A)   Computer with word processing program

(B)   Laserdisk player with laserdisk of influential Texans and primary sources

(C)   Local expert on desert ecology

(D)   A field trip to a museum

◆◆◆◆◆◆◆◆

Mr. Owen, a third-grade teacher in west Texas, has been teaching in a small rural district for three years. He enjoys the slow pace of the community and the fact that he knows most of his students' families relatively well. He is a member of the Evening Lion's Club, plays on the church basketball team, and volunteers at the animal shelter.

His class this year is made up of 21 eight- and nine-year-olds. Most of the students are of average ability, two receive special services for learning disabilities, and one receives speech therapy. Mr. Owen works hard at making his classroom an exciting place to learn with lots of hands-on, problem-based cooperative group projects. In the past, students have had difficulty grasping relationships between math concepts and economics. Mr. Owen has decided to offer a savings program with the help of local banks. Once a week, students will make deposits into their savings accounts. Periodically, they will use their accounts to figure interest at different rates, class totals saved, etc. As part of the Social Studies TEKS, he encourages them to do chores at home and in their neighborhoods to earn the money for their savings.

62.   This approach is evidence that Mr. Owen understands the importance of

(A)   the relevance and authenticity in planning instructional activities for students.

(B)   integrating curriculum concepts across disciplines that support learning.

(C) saving money.

(D) all of the above.

The campus hosts a Meet-the-Teacher Night early in the Fall semester. Mr. Owen introduces himself, shares the grade three curriculum, and communicates his goals for the year. He encourages parents to volunteer for special projects and invites them to share their expertise as speakers during the various units of study throughout the year. He provides a sign-up list for parents to leave their names, e-mail addresses, phone numbers, and notes about their hobbies or work.

63. This practice is evidence that Mr. Owen understands the importance of

(A) having Meet-the-Teacher Night.

(B) participating in school and community activities.

(C) family involvement in a child's education.

(D) his role as an advocate for children in the community.

The students have started studying heroes. The study begins with a word study investigating the definitions and various concepts of the word. Mr. Owen presents character studies of people from a variety of cultures and walks of life who might serve as examples. He asks students to identify heroes from the past and present based on the criteria they develop in class. Students research their heroes and, after extensive reading and discussion, the class prepares a program that includes oral narratives, music, and multi-media visual elements. In addition to performing their program for the school assembly, Mr. Owen has arranged for the students to perform at the local Memorial Day Celebration and at a luncheon honoring the veterans of foreign wars.

64. This teaching activity and culminating experience indicate that Mr. Owen

(A) has analyzed the cognitive abilities of his learners and matched them in cooperative groups.

(B) has established a learning environment that emphasizes collaboration and supportive interactions grounded in active engagement by all students.

(C) does not use the direct instruction model.

(D) does not believe that ownership or student responsibility has an impact on student interest or motivation.

Ms. Carter is a second-grade social studies teacher at a small rural school in southern Texas. Several times during the semester, she has found herself in conversations with colleagues in the school and various community members regarding concerns about a program initiated by the school librarian who is active in the wildlife refuge program in the county. The librarian often brings hurt or orphaned animals to the library to care for them during the day. Several parents are concerned about issues of hygiene and students with allergies.

65. As a member of the site-based decision-making (SBDM) committee, Ms. Carter's best course of action is to

   (A) tell the librarian to remove the animals at once.

   (B) submit an agenda item to the principal to discuss the concerns at the next meeting.

   (C) call the Health Department for a surprise inspection.

   (D) take up for the librarian and praise her efforts to expose students to the issues of wildlife preservation.

Mr. Keller is concerned about the off-task behavior of two students in his fourth-grade class.

66. In addition to ensuring that the instructional objectives and lesson cycles are appropriate for these students, which of the following is the best first step in addressing the problem?

   (A) Call the parents and request a conference

   (B) Establish and communicate clear expectations and logical consequences for classroom behavior

   (C) Refer the students to the principal for disciplinary action

   (D) Refer the students to the counselor

Many of the students in Mr. Tellman's third-grade class have failed the first TAAS/ TAKS practice test. In reviewing the questions missed, he discovers that several of the problems use vocabulary with which students are unfamiliar.

67. Which of the following describes the best course of action to address the problem?

   (A) Post math vocabulary terms on the word wall

(B)   Increase the number of practice problems students are required to do daily

(C)   Require all students scoring below 75% on practice tests to attend tutorials.

(D)   When teaching math lessons, first use vocabulary students are familiar with and then introduce questions using the vocabulary of the test.

Ms. Fisher wants to emphasize appreciation of diverse cultures in a social studies unit she is preparing for her second-grade class.

68.   Which of the following describes the best approach for meeting this goal?

(A)   Have students read about different cultures' customs

(B)   Have students list customs common among Americans

(C)   Have students interview their parents and grandparents regarding their cultural traditions, arts, and customs

(D)   Read folktales from different cultures

Gerene Thompson is a first-year teacher who has accepted a position as a first-grade teacher in an inner city school. In college, Ms. Thompson's elementary teaching field was science. She is eager to begin working with her first-graders so that in addition to teaching them literacy skills, she can teach them to enjoy science and mathematics.

During the last week before school starts, Ms. Thompson has much to do in order to get ready for the first day of school.

69.   Of the many tasks that she must perform, which is likely to have the most significant impact on her students' success in first grade?

(A)   Having a wide variety of teaching material ready and available

(B)   Making the room look inviting by creating bulletin boards depicting students of many nations

(C)   Personally contacting the parents or caretakers of each child

(D)   Coordinating her science activities with her reading activities

70. Of all of the students who do not have documented handicaps, which students are most likely to be poor readers?

(A) Those whose parents or caretakers seldom read aloud to them

(B) Those whose parents or caretakers place them in daycare for more than three hours per day

(C) Those whose parents or caretakers allow them to watch more than two hours of television daily

(D) Those who are being raised by a grandparent

71. In planning her first week's activities, what factors should Ms. Thompson consider?

(A) The interests and prior knowledge of her first-graders

(B) Her students' kindergarten grade reports

(C) The material from the grade one basal reader series

(D) The expectations of her first-grade team

On the first day, Ms. Thompson plans to introduce her students to the phoneme/grapheme relationship of the letter M.

72. Which of the following would be the best set of strategies for this objective?

(A) She should tell her students what sound the letter M makes. She should then provide them with a wide variety of fun paper/pencil and coloring activities as independent work to help them internalize the letter name with its sound. She should schedule the students throughout the day to take turns on the class computer's phonics program.

(B) She should engage the students in a repetitive, rhythmic oral activity using the letter M phoneme/grapheme relationship. She should use a picture as a cue card and display it where the students can see it at all times. She should not place students at the computer without direct supervision for the first several times.

(C) She should not engage the students in repetitive activity, as repetition will quickly bore them and act as an aversive reinforcer to the reading activity. She should employ paper/pencil activities supplemented with coloring and making M's out of clay, papier-mache, and other manipulative materials. She should also use large-muscle movement activities that reinforce the letter-sound relationship. She should use the interactive laser disk with the entire group to show the students many objects that start with the M sound, but she should not allow students to use the equipment individually.

(D)   She should engage the students in repetitive, rhythmic activities using the letter M in its phoneme/grapheme relationship. She should read at least one picture book aloud to the students in a story-circle and discuss it at length with them as she reads it. She should display a picture cue card for the letter M in a prominent place. She should use a wide variety of paper/pencil and art activities employing the letter M.

Ms. Thompson wants to teach her students about methods of collecting data in science. This is a skill required by the Texas State Curriculum for first-graders.

73.   Which of the following describes the most appropriate method of teaching students about collecting data in science?

(A)   Ms. Thompson should arrange the students into groups of four. She should then have each group observe, while she gently touches the class's pet mouse with a feather. The students should record how many times out of ten the pet mouse moves away from the feather. Then, she should gently touch the class's philodendron ten times with a feather. The students should record how many out of ten times the philodendron moves away from the feather.

(B)   Ms. Thompson should arrange the students into groups of four. She should give each group five solid balls made of materials that will float and five solid balls made of materials that will not float. She should have the students drop the balls into a bowl of water and record how many float and how many do not.

(C)   Ms. Thompson should show the students a video about scientific methods of gathering data.

(D)   Ms. Thompson should have a scientist come and talk to the class about methods of collecting data. If she cannot get a scientist, she should have a science teacher from the high school come and speak about scientific methods of data collection.

Ms. Thompson wants to reinforce the notion of data collection by assigning a homework project that will involve the students' families.

74.   Which of the following would be the most appropriate assignment?

(A)   Have the students and their families watch a program on data collection on the Discovery channel

    (B)   Have the parents take their students to the exhibit on data collection at the local museum

    (C)   Have the students ask their parents to help them count the number of times that their heart beats per minute at rest and after five minutes of exercise

    (D)   Have the students ask their parents to read to them about a famous scientist

75.   How can Ms. Thompson best teach her students to be lifelong learners and lovers of science?

    (A)   Give them examples of famous people who were/are lifelong learners.

    (B)   Talk and read about famous scientists.

    (C)   Enthusiastically employ many hands-on activities that are difficult enough to challenge the students, yet direct enough that the students will succeed.

    (D)   Reward students who work hard and punish students who do not perform.

76.   In general, how can Ms. Thompson best address the learning styles of her female students in science activities?

    (A)   Employ cooperative, noncompetitive teaching strategies that utilize many experiences with hands-on activities

    (B)   Employ competitive teaching strategies that utilize many experiences with hands-on activities

    (C)   Employ teaching strategies that require students to work independently with hands-on activities

    (D)   Employ teaching strategies utilizing computer-assisted, programmed instruction

77.   In general, how should Ms. Thompson respond when Molly Carter, a student of African-American heritage, makes statements such as "My mama, she works at the store down the block"?

    (A)   She should tell Molly that it is important that she learn to speak standard English.

    (B)   She should not reinforce Molly's speech patterns by interacting with her when she does not speak standard English.

(C)   She should say, "Molly dear, it is not correct to say 'My mama, she works.' You should say 'My mama works' if you want people to understand you."

(D)   She should ask, "Tell me, what kinds of things does your mama do at work?"

Sally Banks is a first-year, early childhood teacher in a suburban school district. Her students are three- and four-year-olds who qualify for the program as students with special needs, English language deficits, or low socio-economic status. Only two of twelve are from homes that can afford to pay tuition to attend. After the first week of school, Ms. Banks is astounded by the differences among her students.

78.   Which of the following criteria should guide her thinking as she plans her whole group and center activities?

(A)   Young children's need of clear guidelines for behavior and logical consequences for misbehavior

(B)   The stages of cognitive, social, physical, and emotional development of the young child

(C)   The time it takes for children to all function at the same academic level

(D)   Consistent reinforcement of her routines and procedures to manage student behavior

Ms. Banks has a Spanish-speaking aide working with her in the class. The aide works with all the students, but carefully monitors the work of those with English language deficits. Ms. Banks worries about communicating the progress and goals of the students to the parents.

79.   Which option most effectively addresses this issue?

(A)   Ms. Banks needs a crash course in Spanish.

(B)   Ms. Banks presents the students' portfolio of work for the parents to see.

(C)   Ms. Banks and the aide hold joint conferences with these parents.

(D)   The aide should hold the conferences with these parents, while Ms. Banks holds conferences with the English-speaking parents.

Mrs. Tyler and her class of four-year-olds go on a nature walk around the school looking for examples of living things. After the walk, Mrs. Tyler intends to read a book on butterflies and moths. While on the walk, the students discover two horned toads by the concrete foundation of the building. They begin asking questions and telling what they know about these creatures.

80. Which of the following best describes the most appropriate response to this unexpected event?

    (A) Return to the classroom and read about butterflies and moths and promise to find a book about horned toads for tomorrow

    (B) Tell students they will study desert animals of Texas in first-grade Science

    (C) Have students draw pictures of the horned toads and dictate their stories to Mrs. Tyler so that she can write them on their papers

    (D) Find a book about horned toads to read the next day

Mrs. Tyler has observed that two children are regularly excluding others from their group of playmates on the playground. On numerous occasions, she has overheard name calling and taunting of these two children by the group.

81. What criteria should guide her decision-making as she determines how to respond?

    (A) Children are resilient and will find playmates they get along with on their own.

    (B) There is no place in a classroom for disrespectful or hurtful behavior since it is known to negatively impact the learning environment.

    (C) Some people just don't like other people.

    (D) It is the parents' job to teach children to accept others.

Mr. Bates is a second-year early childhood teacher in an urban school. Because so many of his students have language deficits, he uses songs and gestures to call them together, line them up, and accomplish other organizational procedures.

82. This practice indicates that Mr. Bates understands the

    (A) importance of continuous monitoring of instructional effectiveness.

    (B) developmental characteristics of young children.

(C)   importance of communicating enthusiasm for learning.

(D)   importance of adjusting communication to ensure that directions and explanations are understood.

Ms. Axtel has two years of experience teaching sixth-grade students. However, this school year, she has been asked to teach a group of 25 second-graders. She wants to prepare several units before school begins.

83.   Which of the following principles is the most important to consider as she prepares her units?

(A)   The major difference between sixth-grade students and second-grade students is their physical size.

(B)   Second-grade students are developmentally very different from sixth-grade students.

(C)   Some second-grade students read as well as sixth-grade students.

(D)   Sixth-grade students like to read books on topics that are very different from the topics that second-grade students prefer.

In January, a new student, Jerry Rodriguez, joins Ms. Axtel's class. Neither Jerry nor his parents speak much English.

84.   It is most important that Ms. Axtel

(A)   give Jerry a non-verbal intelligence test.

(B)   be certain that Jerry receives the services of the school's ESL instructor.

(C)   keep Jerry isolated from the other students until he feels more comfortable.

(D)   be certain that Jerry's parents are learning English.

Ms. Axtel's knowledge of Spanish is limited. She is concerned about communicating with Jerry during class activities.

85.   Which of the following is the best approach?

(A)   Appoint another student to be Jerry's "buddy."

(B)   Ask Jerry to do math worksheets until he learns basic English.

(C)   Give Jerry picture books, paper, and markers.

(D)   Allow Jerry to look and listen for as long as he likes.

At the end of each week, Ms. Axtel takes a few minutes to write in her journal. She makes written comments about the lessons she taught that week, as well as the students' response to those lessons. She also includes comments about how to change or revise the lessons in the future.

86.   This practice indicates that Ms. Axtel is

(A)   concerned about process writing.

(B)   a reflective practitioner.

(C)   keeping notes for her formal evaluation.

(D)   is a habitual journal writer.

Ms. Axtel is concerned that Jerry is not making much progress in learning English. She borrows a series of Spanish language computer programs in a variety of content areas from the local Education Service Center. She uses the programs to set up a special learning center with several computers in the classroom. A computer is available to Jerry at any time during the day, and all of the other students can use the center if they choose.

87.   This indicates that Ms. Axtel is

(A)   concerned that Jerry can learn material best only if it is presented in a visual manner.

(B)   concerned that Jerry will not meet state-mandated requirements.

(C)   concerned that Jerry has special needs that can only be met by using a wide variety of learning materials.

(D)   concerned that Jerry may need the assistance of a resource teacher.

Ms. Axtel realizes that she has much to learn about the second-grade curriculum.

88.   Which of the following would probably be the best way to quickly acquaint herself with the curriculum and materials used in her school?

(A)   She should consult with the other second-grade teachers in her school.

(B)   She should call the local textbook representative and arrange a time to meet.

(C)   She should study the scope and sequence provided by each publisher for the text used in second grade.

(D)   She realizes that the best way to become acquainted with a curriculum is over time and not to be in a hurry to learn it.

One Monday morning, Ms. Axtel arrives early for school. She notices that Angela, a second-grade student in her class, is waiting outside the front door even though it is at least an hour before the earliest bus should arrive. When Ms. Axtel stops to ask Angela if she is all right, Angela begins to cry. Ms. Axtel notices several large bruises on her legs and arms.

89.   It is Ms. Axtel's responsibility to

(A)   notify law enforcement authorities as soon as possible that she suspects that Angela may have been beaten or abused.

(B)   comfort Angela and call her mother later in the day to learn what happened.

(C)   recognize that Angela must have misbehaved and was punished by her parents.

(D)   learn more about Angela's family before making any other decisions.

Ms. Axtel's school district requires teachers to attend one in-service session per month. The in-service workshop this month is about the special needs of emotionally disturbed children. None of the children in Ms. Axtel's class have been identified as emotionally disturbed. There are no other in-service workshops offered this month.

90.   What should Ms. Axtel do?

(A)   Skip the in-service, stay home, and prepare for future lessons

(B)   Complain to the principal about the lack of choices and stay home in protest

(C)   Attend the in-service because she might have an emotionally disturbed student in the future

(D)   Attend the in-service but plan to leave early

ANSWER KEY

1.	(C)	24.	(A)	46.	(D)	68.	(C)
2.	(B)	25.	(D)	47.	(B)	69.	(C)
3.	(D)	26.	(B)	48.	(A)	70.	(A)
4.	(B)	27.	(D)	49.	(C)	71.	(A)
5.	(D)	28.	(B)	50.	(A)	72.	(D)
6.	(A)	29.	(A)	51.	(A)	73.	(B)
7.	(A)	30.	(C)	52.	(D)	74.	(C)
8.	(B)	31.	(A)	53.	(B)	75.	(C)
9.	(B)	32.	(C)	54.	(B)	76.	(A)
10.	(C)	33.	(D)	55.	(B)	77.	(D)
11.	(C)	34.	(C)	56.	(A)	78.	(B)
12.	(C)	35.	(D)	57.	(C)	79.	(C)
13.	(B)	36.	(A)	58.	(C)	80.	(C)
14.	(A)	37.	(D)	59.	(A)	81.	(B)
15.	(D)	38.	(C)	60.	(C)	82.	(D)
16.	(A)	39.	(C)	61.	(B)	83.	(B)
17.	(B)	40.	(A)	62.	(D)	84.	(B)
18.	(A)	41.	(B)	63.	(C)	85.	(A)
19.	(B)	42.	(B)	64.	(B)	86.	(B)
20.	(A)	43.	(D)	65.	(B)	87.	(C)
21.	(C)	44.	(A)	66.	(B)	88.	(A)
22.	(A)	45.	(C)	67.	(D)	89.	(A)
23.	(A)					90.	(C)

To determine in which domains your strengths and weaknesses lie, use the table on page 208.

TExES PPR EC–4

DETAILED EXPLANATIONS
OF ANSWERS

1. **(C)** The correct response is (C). The use of instructional strategies that make learning relevant to individual student interests is a powerful motivating force that facilitates learning and independent thinking. (A) and (B) are both important factors to consider during a brainstorming session of this type, but both of these factors should influence the teacher only after the student interests have been included. (D) indicates a misunderstanding of the situation described. The students are setting the objectives for the unit as they brainstorm questions.
    Competency 008

2. **(B)** The correct response is (B). Choice is an important element in motivating students to learn. (A) is contradictory with the stated purpose of the activity. The students proposed the questions, so covering all the questions should not be a problem. (C) is incorrect because the students have chosen what they consider to be key questions; the teacher should select different or additional key questions. (D) is a possibility, but only if there is a specific reason why all the students should not research all the questions.
    Competency 005

3. **(D)** The correct response is (D). The instructional strategy described is one technique used in inquiry and problem-solving. (A) is incorrect because direct instruction requires the teacher to present the content to be learned, asking students frequent questions to monitor comprehension. (B) is incorrect because role-playing and simulation are not part of a brainstorming session. (C) is incorrect because exposition and discussion are teacher-led activities that use previously established objectives and content.
    Competency 008

4. **(B)** The correct response is (B). Ongoing assessment and evaluation using a variety of formal and informal assessment techniques is essential for quality instruction. (A) is incorrect because although the teacher may want to use an objective test as part of the overall assessment and evaluation of the unit, this kind of test is insufficient assessment without additional instruments. (C) is incorrect because a standardized test is rarely an appropriate tool for an individual unit of instruction. Standardized tests are best used as an end-of-the-year evaluation. (D) is incorrect

because every assessment should provide for individual differences. Individual assessments might be part of a total assessment program, but would be inappropriate if used in isolation.
 Competency 010

5. **(D)** The correct response is (D). Providing an opportunity to share class projects and activities with other classes will promote a feeling of student ownership and reinforce a feeling of membership in the class as a group. (A) is incorrect because closure refers to that part of a lesson plan that reminds the teacher to conclude the lesson by restating the purpose of or by summarizing the content of the lesson. (B) is incorrect because although teachers are expected to work collaboratively with other teachers, sharing a class project involves little actual collaboration. (C) is incorrect because although a teacher may be interested in being appointed grade level chairperson, sharing class projects is a valuable instructional strategy that is not related to a promotion in a school.
 Competency 008

6. **(A)** The correct response is (A). Asking students to videotape their project explanations could be highly motivating to the entire class and is an additional way to focus attention and reinforce the significance of the content. (B) is incorrect because this is an appropriate use of video equipment. The value of the equipment and the fact that it is school property is not an issue. (C) is incorrect because the purpose of this activity is not to provide students with information about different careers. In addition, fourth-grade students are not likely to think about their future career goals already. (D) is incorrect because the activity is aimed at both individual and group learning.
 Competency 009

7. **(A)** The correct response is (A). The relevance of the current exhibits to the unit the students are studying is the most important factor in determining whether a field trip should be planned. (B) is incorrect because the school should be able to afford the cost of admission for each student or at least for those students who are not able to pay for their own admission. The distance from the school is simply an element that must be considered when planning the field trip; it should not be considered a deciding factor in whether or not the trip should be planned. School buses are generally available for field trips, but must be reserved in advance. (C) is incorrect because although obtaining permission slips for each student can be difficult, it should not prevent a teacher from planning a field trip. (D) is incorrect because adjusting the scheduled time for each subject in the following weeks can compensate for any time lost for a particular subject during the field trip.
 Competency 008

8. **(B)** The correct answer is (B). Building oral language through authentic experience and usage as well as hearing storybook language through repeated readings of quality literature will help to build literary ability. (A) is incorrect because while the use of flashcards may be beneficial at some point in language development, it is

not the top learning objective at this point in the students' learning. (C) is incorrect because at this stage of development it is not the priority that children learn the letter/sound associations of English. (D) is incorrect because copying English words does not support language development until the word has meaning in the child's oral usage.
  Competency 007

9.   **(B)**   The correct answer is (B). The teacher is responsible to see that the student's IEP is activated and met while the logistics of schedules are considered. It is always the responsibility of the classroom teacher to focus the instruction of each child based on his/her identified need. (A) is incorrect because, until modified, the IEP is the instructional plan for the child. The teacher is responsible for immediate implementation. (C) is incorrect because it negates the evaluation that established the need for services without further assessment and evaluation. This is not in compliance with the federal mandate and procedures. (D) is incorrect because it is the teacher's responsibility to maximize the learning for all students.
  Competency 013

10.   **(C)**   The correct answer is (C). Teachers are not at liberty to discuss students with anyone other than the parents and case-related school personnel. (A) and (B) share information about Joey, which is not permissible. (D) is abrupt and rude; this is never appropriate for a professional educator.
  Competency 013

11.   **(C)**   The correct answer is (C). It is the responsibility of teachers to maintain the integrity of the testing administration and report any irregularities to the principal and/or test coordinator. (A) is incorrect because it ignores this responsibility. (B) and (D) are incorrect because they unnecessarily spread information across the campus and district. It is most appropriate to inform the responsible leadership and say nothing about the matter to anyone else.
  Competency 013

12.   **(C)**   The correct answer is (C). The objective is to develop revision and editing skills in these third-graders. Checklists with simple reminders to check spelling of familiar words, to check for capitals and punctuation, and to make sure that the piece makes sense guide the students through the process. (A), (B), and (D) may help students internalize the process of editing, but here they are not the best answers. (A) is incorrect because students may read through a composition without attending to the issues of comprehension and mechanics if a posted prompt is not available. (B) is incorrect because the holistic scoring rubric for TAAS is more general than the revision and editing ability Mr. Garcia is targeting at this time. (D) is incorrect because just having students read each other's work does not ensure that they know what to edit and revise for. Without a posted checklist, it may be a case of the blind leading the blind.
  Competency 013

13. **(B)** The correct answer is (B). This response is respectful of the learner and her parents while providing an opportunity to discuss the student's needs and the teacher's instructional goals. Parents who do not speak English often opt out of the LEP services because they want their children to speak English. They may not understand that the foundation of reading and writing is oral language and therefore, the LEP program would offer the strongest academic program for learning to read and write as well as learn to speak English. (A) is incorrect because it is not centered around the student and would force inappropriate instructional cycles for this student. (C) is incorrect because it dismisses the option of a campus-level solution with the parents and moves it to a policy-level issue. (D) is wrong because it is not student-centered and very likely is out of compliance with district policy and procedure.
Competency 013

14. **(A)** The correct answer is (A). By assessing Lisa's knowledge base through a variety of methods, Mr. Elva can determine how to modify and focus his instruction so that Lisa's progress continues. This strategy helps Mr. Elva make informed decisions regarding Lisa's learning needs. (B) is incorrect because it inappropriately assumes that Lisa is able to do the work and needs more time. In addition, it is important that Lisa interacts with her classmates in social settings while she is still new to the class. Making her miss recess would be an inappropriate strategy. (C) is inappropriate because there has not been sufficient time to provide focused instruction that may result in the necessary achievement gains. (D) is incorrect because classroom assessments have not been completed, and those would be expected prior to a referral for further formal testing.
Competency 003

15. **(D)** The correct answer is (D). The teacher understands that Lisa must experience success if she is to develop a sense of industry and avoid feelings of inferiority, which contribute to negative cycles of learning, referring to Erikson's theories of pyschosocial development. (A), (B), and (C) are all critical areas of knowledge for the teacher, but are not specifically related to the issue described here.
Competency 001

16. **(A)** The correct answer is (A). Ms. Borders must consider the learning preferences and emotional factors of her learners as she constructs learning activities for the study. To consider cooperative group projects versus independent work is one aspect of her preparation. Another would be the range of products deemed acceptable as demonstrations of knowledge (written or spoken, visual or performed art, technology-based, etc.). (A), (B), and (C) might be considered once she plans the study, but they are unrelated to the issue of preparing for the stated instructional outcomes.
Competency 002

17.   **(B)**   The correct response is (B). The best way to teach children to read, regardless of grade level, is to use a program of emergent literacy that includes pattern books and journal writing. (A) and (C) are incorrect because although an intensive phonics program that includes drill and practice seat work on basic sight words or an instructional program that follows the third-grade basal reader may be effective with some students, they are not the most effective way to teach all students to read. (D) is incorrect because an ESL program is intended to provide assistance only to those students who are learning English as a second language. Additionally, the learning resource teacher should provide assistance only to those students who have been identified as having a learning disability that qualifies them to receive services.
      Competency 004

18.   **(A)**   The correct response is (A). By selecting books for the classroom library that correspond to students' independent reading abilities, the teacher is recognizing that students must improve their reading ability by beginning at their own level and progressing to more difficult materials. (B) is incorrect because books that are so challenging that they are too difficult will most likely be frustrating to many students. (C) is incorrect because the presence or absence of separate word lists should not be a determining factor in selecting books for a classroom library. (D) is incorrect because all children need access to a classroom library, regardless of their reading abilities.
      Competency 004

19.   **(B)**   The correct response is (B). A center approach encourages a variety of reading and writing activities that address the students' current needs. (A) is incorrect because while checking for fluency is important, the priority for these Second Language Learners is English usage. (C) is incorrect because reading daily in the grade-level basal would be frustrating for readers of a 2.0 level. (D) is incorrect because combining the chemicals in the science center poses an obvious danger to young children.
      Competency 004

20.   **(A)**   The correct response is (A). One of the most reliable ways to identify individual learning styles is to observe students over a period of time and to make informal notes about their work habits and their choices within the classroom. (B) is incorrect because although a school psychologist could provide information about each student's learning style, teachers can identify this information on their own. (C) is incorrect because although administering a group screening test will identify learning styles, such a test may be difficult to obtain, and the teacher could gain the same knowledge through simple observation. (D) is incorrect because a student's permanent file may not contain this information. An individual student's learning style may have changed over the years, and there is no guarantee that this change will be noted in the permanent record.
      Competency 010

21. (C) The correct response is (C). Teachers must make clear that they are willing to work with each child, and that they believe that each child can be successful. (A) is incorrect because emphasizing failure early in the year is not appropriate in establishing a feeling of trust with parents. (B) is incorrect because the teacher should emphasize the child during a parent/teacher conference and not discuss the parent's education unless specifically asked for advice. (D) is incorrect because asking parents to secure an individual tutor may be an unrealistic financial burden. In addition, not all children reading below grade level do necessarily need a tutor.
    Competency 013

22. (A) The correct response is (A). Celebrating holidays of different cultures teaches appreciation for human diversity. (B) is incorrect because while celebrating different cultures has become a political issue, this should not influence a teacher when planning such a lesson. (C) is incorrect because although celebrating holidays is one way to encourage students to read, this may or may not be related to encouraging students to read aloud. (D) is incorrect because celebrating holidays may encourage all students to participate in class activities, but teaching an appreciation for human diversity is a more accurate statement of the most significant reason for the activity.
    Competency 003

23. (A) The correct answer is (A). It not only meets the requirements of the policy, but also its spirit. The goal of the policy is to provide opportunities for parents to be informed about the academic and behavioral progress of their children. By scheduling a conference time for every family, Mr. Whitrock has done what was required. By sending a brief note to each parent sharing the strengths and needs of the child's progress along with the goals for future instruction, he shows an "above and beyond" willingness to support each student. (B) is incorrect because it does not address the issue of teacher-parent communication. (C) is incorrect because it focuses on changing policy and not on the issue of communication with parents. (D) is incorrect because the response addresses policy change while subverting the intent of the policy.
    Competency 011

24. (A) The correct answer is (A). This response focuses on defining a joint plan for helping the student learn the content of the math curriculum. (B) is incorrect because it only addresses completing an assignment and not mastering the concept. (C) is incorrect because while it attempts to communicate a situation with the parents, it does not focus on a plan for student mastery of the content. (D) is incorrect because it is punitive and not instructionally focused.
    Competency 011

25. (D) The correct answer is (D). By emphasizing Marcus's own hard work, the results, and how good that feels, Mr. Nedham is building a sense of self-efficacy, an internal locus of control, and intrinsic motivation within Marcus. Students who

exhibit these characteristics generally are life-long learners and enjoy learning for the sake of learning. (A) is incorrect because communicating surprise at student achievement sends a message of low expectations. (B) and (C) are incorrect because they place the emphasis on external factors rather than on building the desirable internal strategies for the learner.

Competency 004

26. **(B)** The correct answer is (B). By choosing to participate in the new mentoring program, Mr. Bell may be able to match the supports for each student most appropriately. He can then be assured that all students have role models and an outlet to share their developing selves through conversation and experience. However, while teachers acting as mentors show a wonderful commitment, it is recommended that the mentee not be a student of the teacher. (A) is incorrect because static grouping cannot address the needs for differentiation of diverse learners. (C) is incorrect because it only addresses the needs of some of the students. This practice might also raise concerns of favoritism among the rest of the class or their parents. (D) does not address the issue of supporting the diverse needs of the students.

Competency 005

27. **(D)** The correct answer is (D). Students are allowed to demonstrate their ability to accept responsibility for their own behavior and use this independent learning time wisely. The teacher has reserved the right to change the plan based on the students' behavior. (A) is inappropriate because it places blame on students, and this might result in harming the overall learning environment within the classroom. (B) is inappropriate because it communicates that reading is not important enough to allocate time to in the school schedule. (C) is incorrect because it does not address the student request of more reading time.

Competency 006

28. **(B)** The correct answer is (B). By letting students know at the beginning of the assignment what the expectations are, they know how to proceed with their planning and time management. Over time, the point values might be adjusted to reflect importance of various aspects of the task. (A), (C), and (D) do not provide constructive feedback regarding the intended learning or competencies of the task.

Competency 009

29. **(A)** The correct answer is (A). Mr. Kyle's decision to allow students the opportunity to make choices of their own regarding their work demonstrates his awareness that choice and responsibility are key factors in learning success. (B) and (D) are incorrect because the question of student choice and responsibility is broader than the issues of cooperative learning or learning styles. (C) is incorrect because it cannot be assumed that Mr. Kyle's plan does not include strategies for addressing content not selected by student pairs.

Competency 001

30. **(C)** The correct answer is (C). Rubrics can be used to assess a student's level of achievement based on objective criteria. This enables the teacher to be clear about minimum expectations, set high expectations that exceed the minimums, and communicate to individual students their next learning steps. (A) is incorrect because even though rubrics are based on stated criteria, evaluation is still subjective, which is what most parents object to with regard to grades. (B) is incorrect because we cannot assume that just because a rubric is in place, Mr. Kyle consistently evaluates student work objectively. (D) is incorrect because rubrics are criteria-based assessments and, therefore, students are not compared to one another, but to the standard criteria.

Competency 010

31. **(A)** The correct answer is (A). The students' home environments are diverse in terms of accessibility to technology and books. Mr. Connor's procedures attempt to diversify access based on the students' needs. While weekly routines address the issue of access for all students, his additional procedures address equity issues. (A), (B) and (C) are only partially correct; none addresses all the areas of concern.

Competency 002

32. **(C)** The correct response is (C). The teacher uses an understanding of human developmental processes to nurture student growth through developmentally appropriate instruction. (A) is not relevant to the scenario. It is correct that the framework used in the plan of study designed for the 10 percent could also be used for the other 20 percent (B), however, the framework is a result of the plan of study, not the criteria for a plan. There are intrinsic benefits derived from cooperatively working to achieve goals (D), however, in this case, the cooperative work is supposed to develop a plan of study, not achieve benefits for the teachers.

Competency 001

33. **(D)** The correct response is (D). The teacher understands how learning occurs, and can apply this understanding to design and implement effective instruction. (A) is a false statement. (B) may or may not be false, but this is an attitude distinctive to each teacher. (C) is a subjective statement; it is an opinion and is dependent upon individual parents.

Competency 004

34. **(C)** The correct response is (C). The teacher understands factors inside and outside the classroom that influence students' perceptions of their own potential and worth. (A) is a true statement; however, it is encompassed within response (C). Some students are extrinsically motivated (B), but some are intrinsically motivated. The basic foundation for motivation lies in self-esteem. (D) is a true statement; library materials that are highly correlated to instruction are more meaningful. However, this statement is implied in the correct response (C).

Competency 002

35.   **(D)**   The correct response is (D). The combination of appropriate instructional materials helps students to understand the role of technology as a learning tool. Students' motivation might or might not be lowered if others knew of their need to re-read a book and re-take an exam (A); the statement is subjective. The strategy suggested in (B) would remove the teacher from the role of informing the student; however, teachers fill many roles each day. Filling the role is not the key; the teacher's attitude and communication with the student will be the critical element. (C) is a true statement, but the workload of the media specialist is not the issue. The issue is student privacy.
    Competency 009

36.   **(A)**   The correct response is (A). EC–4 students are at the concrete operations level and benefit from frequent feedback with concrete examples. (B) is a true statement, but it is incorporated in (A), the correct response. Becoming independent thinkers and problem solvers (C) is a result of higher-level reading skills and an interest/curiosity in books. Publicly displaying the titles of the books would vary the teacher's role (D) and would not emphasize it as much at this phase of the instructional strategy. The issue, however, is not the teacher's role, but the effectiveness of instruction and techniques for monitoring it.
    Competency 010

37.   **(D)**   The correct response is (D). The goal of the instructional design is to structure a positive classroom environment that promotes lifelong learning. (A) is a true statement: classroom time is maximized. Yet it is a component of a positive classroom environment that is encompassed in the correct answer choice (D). (B) and (C) are both true statements as well, but they are also encompassed within the correct response (D).
    Competency 011

38.   **(C)**   The correct answer is (C). When contemplating the set-up of the classroom, the primary consideration must be for the safety and comfort of all classroom participants, thereby facilitating the highest level of learning for all. (A), (B), and (D) are important considerations but are incorrect because they are secondary to the issue of a safe learning environment.
    Competency 005

39.   **(C)**   The correct answer is (C). This state-mandated assessment is most helpful when the teacher analyzes the individual student data and uses it to pinpoint instructional needs. Flexible groupings, varied texts for reading, and diverse strategies can be selected to focus instruction to accelerate achievement. (A) is incorrect because using reading levels alone to form student reading groups does not ensure that the needs of individual students are being addressed. (B) and (D) are incorrect because while all lessons should be TEKS-based and most curriculum guides are aligned with the TEKS, this fact alone does not ensure that the lesson is appropriate to the learning needs of all students.
    Competency 003

40. (A)   The correct answer is (A). When establishing a productive learning environment, it is the teacher's responsibility to set clear expectations for student behavior during instructional time while providing routines and procedures for what to do when the current assignment has been completed. (B) and (D) are incorrect because they assume that the situation is a discipline problem and not a teacher management issue. (C) is incorrect because whole-group direct instruction will not always be the most appropriate instructional approach. Therefore, this solution inappropriately limits the variety of strategies available to the teacher.
   Competency 006

41. (B)   The correct answer is (B). Clearly stating the expectations and procedures in simple terms followed by a demonstration and guided practice is the most effective and efficient solution to this dilemma. It is also desirable to stop and practice when students fail to demonstrate ability to meet the behavioral expectations. (A) is incorrect because it does not communicate how to achieve the desired behavior. (C) is incorrect because it acts as a threat for failure to achieve the desired behavior without instruction or practice. (D) is incorrect because it sets students up for failure, creating a discipline situation and "unlearning" negative behavior patterns.
   Competency 007

42. (B)   The correct answer is (B). Ms. Sanchez emphasizes the journal activity because it provides informal teaching conferences with individual students, allowing feedback on different aspects of the writing process and mechanics. (A) is incorrect because while writing is important, this practice focuses on the monitoring of student work and giving prompt feedback. (C) is incorrect because both journals and worksheets can be used effectively when based on student need and instructional objective. (D) is incorrect because the emphasis of Ms. Sanchez's practice is not on management, but on instructional feedback.
   Competency 010

43. (D)   The correct answer is (D). This response acknowledges the importance of planning differentiated instruction based on identified student needs. By recording observations and reviewing student work samples from the journals, the teacher is able to plan focused instructional cycles to meet the students' needs. (A) is incorrect because while having high expectations is clearly important, it is not indicated in Ms. Sanchez's practice. (B) is incorrect because her practice does not indicate that student interactions are planned for. (C) is incorrect because even though scheduling and managing time are important, this is not the focus of Ms. Sanchez's practice.
   Competency 002

44. (A)   The correct answer is (A). The evaluation rubric should be based on the technology standards as represented in the TEKS. Since this is a multi-aged classroom, the rubric should include competencies from both grade levels. (B) is

incorrect because a parent survey will not provide the information needed to design a rubric. (C) is incorrect because knowing the job expectations for colleagues is not relevant to this problem. (D) is incorrect because stages of play development and computer readiness do not relate to the issue of rubric design.

Competency 009

45.　(C)　The correct answer is (C). In preparing a newsletter, the teacher must consider the diverse nature of her class and plan for cultural and language barriers. (A) is incorrect because doing what everyone else does is not an acceptable response when one's needs are different. (B) is incorrect because the newsletter is unrelated to the classroom climate. (D) is incorrect because it is arbitrary; it may not be necessary to translate the newsletter into Spanish (or any other language) if the need is not there.

Competency 011

46.　(D)　The correct answer is (D). The practice of observation, conference, and instructional dialogue values reflective practice and supportive, relational professional development. Because the professional development model involves many teachers from the campus and is based on observed teacher behaviors, it not only builds teacher competence but serves as a mechanism for culture-building on the campus. (A), (B), and (C) are incorrect because although faculty relationships, teacher observations, and student/teacher interactions are all important aspects of quality professional development models, the purpose here is to build reflective practice in teachers.

Competency 012

47.　(B)　The correct answer is (B). Regulations regarding privacy must be followed at all times. To this end, most districts have adopted policies and procedures that facilitate getting approval from parents to release this information. Teachers must ensure that only the approved information is released. (A) is incorrect because in this case, privacy trumps inclusion. (C) is incorrect because it is not necessary for Ms. Sanchez to prepare the list herself. It would be enough if she checked it for approved release status as well as accuracy. (D) is incorrect because campuses and districts adopt procedures to facilitate and make uniform the release of this information.

Competency 013

48.　(A)　The correct response is (A). (B), (C), and (D) are all a part of communicating expectations and ideas, thereby creating a climate of inquiry. Even if a variety of materials is presented using several techniques (B), the goal for the class is to impart teacher expectations to the students and to create a climate of inquiry. In this case, the students are not given a choice of what they are to learn (C). The unit can be integrated across campus into other curricula (D), but this is not the goal in this case.

Competency 007

49. **(C)** The correct response is (C). By requiring both a comprehension and an application objective, students are required to show that they have acquired knowledge at two levels. Although (A) is true, it is not the foundation for developing specific objectives. (B) is an assumption and not relevant to the setting of certain objectives. Teaching style and learning styles are not relevant to the behavioral objectives (D).

Competency 001

50. **(A)** The correct response is (A). (B), (C), and (D) are components of (A). Enhancing student achievement (B), eliciting different levels of thinking from the students (C), and problem-solving (D) are all included in student achievement.

Competency 006

51. **(A)** The correct response is (A). The demonstration is intended to show what happens when directions are not followed. The expected behavioral outcome is curiosity. The terminal goal for the activity is not assessment (B), but the acquisition of knowledge of the importance of correct measurement. (C) is incorrect because, like (B), the purpose of the task is not the evaluation of group functions. (D) is only partially correct. Even though waste can occur in the kitchen, this is not what the demonstration is intended to show.

Competency 007

52. **(D)** The correct response is (D). The purpose of the field trip is to extend an academic environment into the community. The students are expected to see the relationship between what they are taught in the classroom and its practical application in the community. The final activity for the unit will be an evaluation; therefore, (A) is incorrect. The field trip does not promote responsibility for one's own learning (B), because the students are given no instructions prior to arriving in the cafeteria. The purpose of the field trip is to extend the students' learning beyond the classroom and into the community (C).

Competency 001

53. **(B)** The correct response is (B). Both federal and state law require that schools be accessible to persons who use wheelchairs. Mr. Drayton should make the principal aware that Myra resides in the district, and that the building is not accessible to her. Disregarding the school's noncompliance with the law by simply offering to share materials with Myra (A) is in no way sufficient. The expense to the school posed by making the necessary accommodations does not excuse the school from compliance with the law (C). There is no reason to believe, however, that the school has intentionally failed to comply with the law. Thus, proposing a lawsuit is not called for. The school may be eager to comply once the noncompliance is called to their attention (D).

Competency 013

54.   **(B)**   The correct response is (B). As a responsible member of the community, Mr. Drayton should notify the police of the vandalism. Chasing the boys down himself (A) may place him in great danger, and is therefore not a good solution. Calling the superintendent (C) is not an appropriate response. This is a legal issue; therefore, it is the responsibility of the police force to make contact with school personnel as necessary. (D) reaches for a strategy to rehabilitate the student's behavior. It is more appropriate to confer with the school counselor and determine how to proceed with additional student support.
   Competency 012

55.   **(B)**   The correct response is (B). Placing the students in small groups in which they meet face to face will allow Mr. Drayton to maximize the students' interaction while giving each student the maximum opportunity to speak. Placing students in the traditional rows facing the front (A) discourages student interaction and minimizes each student's opportunities to speak. While placing students in pairs (C) maximizes each student's opportunity to speak, it limits the sources of interaction; each student may share thoughts with only one other student. In contrast, a group of four (B) allows the student to interact as part of three dyads, two triads, and a quadrant. When placing the students in cooperative groups, it is wise to arrange the desks within the physical space of the classroom in such a way that each group's talking does not distract the members of other groups.
   Competency 005

56.   **(A)**   The correct response is (A). Community leaders must be able to work cooperatively in order to achieve community goals, so the cooperative activities will best help Mr. Drayton meet his goals. While it may be important to learn to work competitively (B), a competitive atmosphere within the classroom will not help Mr. Drayton's students learn to work toward group goals. While it may be important to learn to work independently (C), this will not help students learn to work toward group goals. Whole group activities (D) provide few students with opportunities to develop leadership and are not a strong method of allowing students to work cooperatively toward group goals.
   Competency 011

57.   **(C)**   The correct response is (C). Articles in the archives that discuss such phenomena as drought, flash floods, dry wells, and tornadoes will help students begin to understand the impact of the desert on early settlement. Senior citizens will be able to elaborate and personalize the information, helping students to develop a greater appreciation of how the desert affected settlers. While it is useful to know about desert plants and animals, neither a video about plants and animals (A), nor a sand table (B) helps students understand how the desert impacted human settlement. Reading books about the deserts of the world (D) will give students an idea of deserts' impact on people's lives, but this is missing the local aspect and is not as effective a resource as local archives and senior citizens.
   Competency 009

58. **(C)** The correct response is (C). Storytelling and other narrative approaches are highly effective ways of teaching social learners. While most people do enjoy a good story, this is not the most important reason why teachers should be good storytellers (A). While storytelling is also a highly cost-effective teaching technique, its cost-effectiveness is only a secondary advantage to its utility in teaching social learners (B). Storytelling is not one of the most effective ways of teaching field-independent students (D).
Competency 004

59. **(A)** The correct response is (A). People seldom perform to the best of their ability. Knowing that their work will receive public attention, however, is an important motivation for people to do their best. While being able to speak in public is undoubtedly a crucial skill for success in a democratic society (B), this answer is not worded in such a way that it would be an instructional reason for having students tell their stories. Having students tell their stories to the class does focus on having students learn to critique their own work (C), but in this case it is not the most important reason. Prior exposure has nothing to do with Mr. Drayton's instructional reason to have students tell the stories that they write (D).
Competency 005

60. **(C)** The correct response is (C). The first task in developing a unit of study is to determine learner outcomes. Learning activities (A) are contingent on desired learner outcomes. While time and space constraints (B) affect activities, Mr. Drayton and Ms. Wade must determine desired learner outcomes before they proceed to consider other planning factors. Soliciting input from students (D) helps assure student ownership; however, this step in planning a unit comes after determining learner outcomes.
Competency 004

61. **(B)** The correct response is (B). The laser disk and player comprise a superb supplement to primary sources written by the influential Texans themselves. While a computer and word processing program are valuable tools (A), they are not the most valuable tools for this activity because students must know something about content before they can write. A local expert on desert ecology (B) is not relevant to a study of persons who make contributions to the development of Texas. Answer (D) is incorrect because while museums provide interesting information and may include facts about influential Texans, this is not the most effective or efficient method described for achieving the learning.
Competency 009

62. **(D)** The correct answer is (D). The integrated, real-life nature of this project builds deeper understandings of the economic concept of work and wages, saving vs. spending, and banking. While providing the authentic experience of working and saving, the project also builds children's capacity to complete mathematical functions like figuring interest rates and compounding interest. In addition, the idea of saving money has been communicated.
Competency 003

63. **(C)** The correct answer is (C). By inviting parents to share their expertise in the classroom, Mr. Owen strengthens the school-family ties that are essential to positive learning experiences. He is also valuing the expertise of others. This communicates to his students the importance of appreciating the gifts and strengths of others. (A), (B), and (C) are important in his role as teacher, but do not specifically address the practice of family involvement in the instructional program.
   Competency 011

64. **(B)** The correct answer is (B). The task, as well as the planned performances, are evidence that the teacher emphasizes clarifying values in the social context of the collaborative work of schooling and strives for active engagement of all learners. (A) is incorrect because there is no indication of how the group work is structured. (C) is incorrect because the fact that this learning experience is collaborative and interactive does not mean that the teacher does not use the direct instruction model when it is the best approach for the learning objective. (D) is incorrect because the task described allows for student choice and a high level of student responsibility resulting in high student engagement and interest.
   Competency 005

65. **(B)** The correct answer is (B). This is the procedure in place at the campus level to deal with this type of issue. It respects the processes and oversight authority of the SBDM while addressing the concern of faculty and community. (A) is incorrect because Ms. Carter does not have the authority to enforce the removal of the animals. (C) is incorrect because the issue should remain at the campus until the SBDM and the principal have an opportunity to consider the concerns. (D) is incorrect because even though Ms. Carter may appreciate the librarian's efforts, the health concerns are legitimate. Ms. Carter should remain neutral until the campus can act on the issue.
   Competency 012

66. **(B)** The correct answer is (B). After addressing the issue of appropriate instruction, clear communication of the expectations and consequences is the first course of action. The teacher must be certain that students understand the expectations before they move on to the consequences. (A), (C), and (D) are incorrect because they are consequences for misbehavior. Consequences must follow clear statements of expectations.
   Competency 006

67. **(D)** The correct answer is (D). If students are unfamiliar with the vocabulary of the test, only instruction that connects the known terms with the unknown will make a difference. (A) is incorrect because just recognizing the new terms is insufficient to the task of creating meaning when reading a word problem. (B) is incorrect because completing more practice problems will not develop vocabulary. (C) is incorrect because attending tutorials alone will not address the problem. Only

tutorials focused on vocabulary understanding in word problems will have the desired results.
    Competency 007

68.   **(C)**   The correct answer is (C). This approach builds on the lives of the students and their families making the task relevant and authentic. Students from common cultures can compare their information for similarities and differences, as well as comparing with peers from other cultures. (A), (B), and (D) are incorrect because although these answer choices address the learning objective generally, they are not as engaging as the task involving students' own family stories and traditions.
    Competency 002

69.   **(C)**   The correct response is (C). Making a personal contact with each child's parents or caretakers is the most crucial task that Ms. Thompson can perform in order to assure the success of her students. Having a variety of teaching materials ready and available (A) is helpful, but would not have the most important impact on the students' success. Using bulletin boards to make the room look inviting and using materials representing the students of many nations (B) will assist in making the new students feel at home; however, the effects of this task are secondary to that of establishing a strong home-school relationship. Coordinating science activities with reading activities would not have a significant impact on ensuring the success of first-graders (D).
    Competency 011

70.   **(A)**   The correct response is (A). The most important predictor variable of reading success is whether or not the children's parents or caretakers immerse them in print (read to them) before they start school. An enriched daycare environment can be beneficial to a child's development (B), especially if shared reading and story activities are stressed. While research suggests that excessive television watching by young students may have deleterious effects, the amount of time spent watching television (C) is not as important a predictor of reading success as being read to by a parent. Being raised by a grandparent is not a predictor of poor reading ability (D).
    Competency 002

71.   **(A)**   The correct response is (A). When planning a unit of study it is essential to consider the interests of the students and their level of prior knowledge. (B) is incorrect because while the grade reports from the previous year will provide valuable information, the first week's activities should not be driven by this data. (C) is incorrect because a teaching manual should never be the fundamental source for planning instruction. (D) is incorrect because while working with the team is important, the needs of the students should be the primary factor in planning instruction.
    Competency 006

72.   (D)   The correct response is (D). Ms. Thompson should employ a wide variety of instructional strategies and materials in order to teach to the phoneme/grapheme relationship. This is a bottom-up approach for teaching someone to read. Ms. Thompson should also use a top-down approach by reading a story to the students and discussing it at length. (A) does not include a wide variety of learning activities. In addition, the answer omits the important book-reading activity. (B) fails to employ a wide variety of learning activities and fails to employ the book-reading activity. Whether or not to place students at the computer without direct supervision depends on the students involved and the software employed. (C) encompasses a wide variety of learning activities; however, it includes the false statement that students dislike repetitive activities and that repetition serves as an aversive reinforcer to reading. Although adults become bored with repetition, young students enjoy repetitive activity, as it gives them a sense of mastery.
   Competency 008

73.   (B)   The correct response is (B). The hands-on activity will best help the students learn about data collection. Since (B) is the only one that employs a hands-on activity, this is the best answer. The students would learn about direct observation by watching Ms. Thompson tickle the mouse and the philodendron (A); however, this method would not be as effective as allowing the students to conduct their own data collection. Research suggests that viewing a video is an inefficient method of learning (C). Having a guest speaker tell the students about data collection (D) is not a good choice for first-graders.
   Competency 004

74.   (C)   The correct response is (C). As in the previous question, the hands-on activity is the best choice; however, another issue should be considered in this question: the child's econiche. Many families cannot afford cable television's premium channels, and therefore do not have access to the Discovery channel (A). Parents may lack transportation, time, or money to take their child to a museum (B). Parents may not have access to books, or they may work schedules that prevent them from reading to their students. In addition, some parents may be unable to read themselves (D).
   Competency 002

75.   (C)   The correct response is (C). By modeling enthusiasm for learning, Ms. Thompson will help her students become lifelong learners. By employing developmentally appropriate hands-on activities, Ms. Thompson will help her students become enthusiastic learners. Giving students examples of famous people who were lifelong learners is not a strong instructional technique for helping the students become lifelong learners (A). Talking and reading about famous scientists will create background knowledge and possibly interest a few students, but it is not the strongest approach described for creating lifelong learners in science (B). Punishing students who do not perform will not help students to become lifelong learners (C).
   Competency 008

76.   **(A)**   The correct response is (A). Research suggests that girls learn science best in cooperative groups with activities that employ many hands-on experiences. In contrast, competitive teaching strategies (B) are contraindicated for the purposes of helping girls learn science. Independent activities (C) are also not good choices for the purpose of helping girls learn science. Although computer-assisted instruction (D) may be helpful, the key ingredients in developing a successful science program for girls are cooperative learning and frequent hands-on experiences.
   Competency 003

77.   **(D)**   The correct response is (D). Research suggests that the best teachers of African-American students are those who themselves are competent speakers of Ebonics (Black English). However, even teachers who do not speak Ebonics should respect Ebonics as a legitimate language, rather than considering it a substandard form of English. By respecting Molly's mother tongue, Ms. Thompson encourages her to engage in literacy activities and promotes her self-esteem. By criticizing Molly's use of Ebonics (A), Ms. Thompson will negatively impact Molly's self-esteem and will discourage her from engaging in literacy activities. By refusing to speak to Molly (B), Ms. Thompson will also negatively affect both her self-esteem and her desire to engage in speaking, reading, and writing activities. Since Molly knows that people understand her when she says, "My mama, she works," the statement that people won't understand her (C) will be confusing to Molly. It is appropriate to encourage Molly to use standard English when engaging in formal language and literacy instruction; however, it is inappropriate to discourage her from using her mother tongue in casual interaction.
   Competency 003

78.   **(B)**   The correct answer is (B). While basing her instruction (whether in whole group or centers) on the Texas Pre-Kindergarten Curriculum Guidelines, Ms. Banks must make it a priority to differentiate the range of activity so that all students benefit from the experiences offered. (A) is incorrect because it addresses only the behavioral aspects of instruction. (C) is incorrect because although time is a factor in mastery of learning, it will not make instruction developmentally appropriate. (D) is incorrect because the response fails to address the variety of needs of the young learner, even though Ms. Banks' routines and procedures are important to the management of student behavior.
   Competency 001

79.   **(C)**   The correct answer is (C). As the teacher, Ms. Banks must conference with all parents. The aide can interpret her remarks, as well as the questions or comments of the parents. Since the aide works so closely with these students, she might also contribute observations that are important to the goal-setting process. (A) is incorrect because Sally needs more Spanish than a crash course can provide, given the technical aspect of much of the educational and cognitive vocabulary. (B) is incorrect because viewing the portfolio (while being a powerful tool in communicating student progress) would be insufficient to clarify the student's current knowledge,

progress, and future learning goals. (D) is incorrect because as the teacher, Sally must make contact with each parent.
> *Competency 011*

80.　**(C)**　The correct answer is (C). Seize the day! When the unexpected happens and the teachable moment presents itself, go with it. Using the language experience approach is a method that will capture students' vocabulary and conceptual knowledge about the topic. (A) and (D) are incorrect because they ignore the needs of the learners. Young children will not hold this excitement and inquisitiveness until the next day. (B) is incorrect because for a four-year-old, first grade is too far in the distant future to care about.
> *Competency 010*

81.　**(B)**　The correct answer is (B). Teachers must be vigilant in establishing and maintaining a safe, nurturing, and respectful learning environment. It must be made clear from the beginning that cruelty and disrespect will not be tolerated. (A) is incorrect because even though children are resilient, their early social experiences impact their future learning both positively and negatively. (C) is incorrect because children must be taught that they must be kind to everyone in the class, even if they are not close friends. (D) is incorrect; while it is the parent's responsibility to model this behavior, unfortunately it is often not the case and therefore must be explicitly taught in schools.
> *Competency 005*

82.　**(D)**　The correct answer is (D). Songs, rhymes, and hand and arm signals resonate with young children as play. When procedural instructions are prompted in this way, young children have connections on cognitive, emotional, and physical levels. (A), (B), and (C) are incorrect because they do not focus on communicating directions for organizational procedures.
> *Competency 007*

83.　**(B)**　The correct response is (B). There are many significant developmental differences between second- and sixth-graders. These differences must be considered when planning instructions. (A) is incorrect because physical size is only one of the ways in which the students differ. (C) is incorrect because reading ability is an issue to consider, but developmental differences include more than just reading ability. (D) is incorrect because preferred topics for reading reflect overall development.
> *Competency 001*

84.　**(B)**　The correct response is (B). All non-native speakers of English are eligible for the services of an ESL teacher. It is the responsibility of the classroom teacher to be certain that the ESL teacher is aware of the student's needs. (A) is incorrect because if Jerry speaks little English, such a non-verbal intelligence test would be useless. Additionally, Jerry's intelligence is not the issue. The teacher's attention should be focused on helping Jerry learn English rather than determining his IQ. (C) is incorrect because isolation from other students would only slow Jerry's progress. (D) is incorrect because while it might help Jerry to learn English along with his parents, this is certainly not the most important thing for Ms. Axtel to do.

Competency 013

85.　**(A)**　The correct response is (A). One of the best ways to assist students who are learning English is to appoint a classroom "buddy" who is willing to explain directions using non-verbal examples and sign language. (B) is incorrect because asking Jerry to concentrate on math will only extend the time it takes for him to learn English. (C) is incorrect because although picture books might help him learn English, he must have the opportunity to discuss these books with English speakers. (D) is incorrect because Jerry must be actively encouraged to participate in class activities so that he can learn English quickly.

Competency 007

86.　**(B)**　The correct response is (B). Maintaining a written journal about both events in the classroom and student responses is a technique used by reflective practitioners in order to review and evaluate their personal growth as professionals. (A) is incorrect because journal writing may or may not indicate a concern about process writing. Additionally, journal writing alone is not the same as process writing. (C) is incorrect because the purpose of the journal is much broader, even though the instructor may use some of her journal entries in her formal evaluation. (D) is incorrect because it is too simplistic. If Ms. Axtel were a habitual journal writer, she would be writing about a variety of topics, not just emphasizing those related to teaching.

Competency 012

87.　**(C)**　The correct response is (C). The instructor has made special provisions for Jerry to learn content material by using the Spanish language computer programs as he develops fluency in English. (A) is incorrect because it is too early to determine Jerry's learning style. (B) is incorrect because the instructor's main concern should be that Jerry learns English and content material. In addition, testing requirements make special provisions for students not yet fluent in English. (D) is incorrect because there is no evidence to suggest that Jerry needs the services of a resource teacher.

Competency 009

88.　**(A)**　The correct response is (A). The best source of information about a school's curriculum is through the teachers themselves. (B) is incorrect because a textbook company representative could provide information about the publisher's intended curriculum, but not that of the school. (C) is incorrect for the same reason as response (B). (D) is incorrect because an instructor cannot wait for time to fix a problem, but should seek out solutions on his or her own.

Competency 012

89. **(A)** The correct response is (A). Teachers are responsible to report any suspected cases of child abuse to the appropriate authorities. (B) is incorrect because regardless of the parent's explanations, if the instructor feels that the child may have been abused, it must be reported. (C) is incorrect because the bruises described would not be consistent with an ordinary spanking for misbehavior. (D) is incorrect because while further information might be helpful, the instructor must still report the incident.

Competency 012

90. **(C)** The correct response is (C). It is a teacher's responsibility to be prepared to work with a child with learning or emotional problems. Even though Ms. Axtel may not have a child with these problems this year, she should still attend the workshop. (A) is incorrect because the teacher is required to attend the in-service provided by the district. (B) is incorrect because to stay home in protest would be childish and serve no purpose. (D) is incorrect because all teachers are expected to attend the entire in-service session.

Competency 012

Practice Test 1: PPR EC–4

Answers, Sorted by Competency

Question	Domain	Competency	Answer	Did You Answer Correctly?	Question	Domain	Competency	Answer	Did You Answer Correctly?
15	I	1	D		82	III	7	D	
29	I	1	A		85	III	7	A	
32	I	1	C		1	III	8	C	
49	I	1	C		3	III	8	D	
52	I	1	D		5	III	8	D	
78	I	1	B		7	III	8	A	
83	I	1	B		72	III	8	D	
16	I	2	A		75	III	8	C	
31	I	2	A		6	III	9	A	
34	I	2	C		28	III	9	B	
43	I	2	D		35	III	9	D	
68	I	2	C		44	III	9	A	
70	I	2	A		57	III	9	C	
74	I	2	C		61	III	9	B	
14	I	3	A		87	III	9	C	
22	I	3	A		4	III	10	B	
39	I	3	C		20	III	10	A	
62	I	3	D		30	III	10	C	
76	I	3	A		36	III	10	A	
77	I	3	D		42	III	10	B	
17	I	4	B		80	III	10	C	
18	I	4	A		23	III	11	A	
19	I	4	B		24	III	11	A	
25	I	4	D		37	III	11	D	
33	I	4	D		45	III	11	C	
58	I	4	C		56	III	11	A	
60	I	4	C		63	III	11	C	
73	I	4	B		69	III	11	C	
2	II	5	B		79	III	11	C	
26	II	5	B		46	IV	12	D	
38	II	5	C		54	IV	12	B	
55	II	5	B		65	IV	12	B	
59	II	5	A		86	IV	12	B	
64	II	5	B		88	IV	12	A	
81	II	5	B		89	IV	12	A	
27	II	6	D		90	IV	12	C	
40	II	6	A		9	IV	13	B	
50	II	6	A		10	IV	13	C	
66	II	6	B		11	IV	13	C	
71	II	6	A		12	IV	13	C	
8	III	7	B		13	IV	13	B	
41	III	7	B		21	IV	13	C	
48	III	7	A		47	IV	13	B	
51	III	7	A		53	IV	13	B	
67	III	7	D		84	IV	13	B	

TExES

Texas Examinations of Educator Standards

Practice Test 2: PPR 4–8

This test is also on CD-ROM in our special interactive TExES TESTware®. It is highly recommended that you first take this exam on computer. You will then have the additional study features and benefits of enforced timed conditions, individual diagnostic analysis, and instant scoring. See page 3 for guidance on how to get the most out of our TExES book and software.

PRACTICE TEST 2:
TExES PPR 4–8

(Answer sheets begin on page 392.)

TIME: 5 hours
90 questions

DIRECTIONS: Read each stimulus carefully, and answer the questions that follow. Mark your responses on the answer sheet provided.

Mr. Lambert is a sixth-grade math teacher of a diverse class of 28 students. The first day of math activity, he places five math problems on the board and has the students work them as seatwork as soon as they enter the classroom. Mr. Lambert has posted objectives on the board, showing how to work the problems. He collects the answers and grades them. Most of the students earn either an "A" or a "B" on this assignment. At night, he phones each parent to introduce himself and tell the parent about the assignment and the student's grade. The next day many of the students tell Mr. Lambert, "You called my parents last night and said I did really well on the assignment. Wow, that's great."

1. Mr. Lambert calls the students' parents the first night of school because he wants

    (A) the parents to like him.

    (B) to get a sense of what each student's parents are like.

    (C) to open positive lines of communication with the parents as soon as possible.

    (D) to let the students know he will call their parents if they disrupt class.

Ms. Radetski teaches a diverse group of 22 fourth-graders in a large urban school. There are several different ethnic groups in the class, along with several students identified as needing special education services, and five English as a Second Language (ESL) students. It is evident to Ms. Radetski that these students come from a wide range of economic backgrounds. Because she wishes to ensure that all her students appreciate diversity and learn to include everyone in class activities, she utilizes various means to determine the learning style of each student and identifies each student's strong and weak multiple intelligences in order to incorporate multiple intelligences into daily lesson plans.

2. In order to ensure that the students in her class appreciate and celebrate their diversity, Ms. Radetski should

    (A) keep the students separated by ethnic group and special condition to prevent conflict as much as possible.

    (B) give the students in her class free time to socialize, so they are able to get to know each other better.

    (C) place the students in heterogeneous groups and use cooperative learning techniques for part of every class period.

    (D) spend at least fifteen minutes of every class period talking to the class about why it is important to get along with each other.

3. Knowing the diversity that exists in her classroom, what other type of instructional technique can Ms. Radetski use to teach effectively in this class?

    (A) Be sure the classroom is a learner-friendly environment.

    (B) Use the direct instruction model as much as possible.

    (C) Send troublemakers directly to the office so that disruptions are minimal.

    (D) Lecture on the history of various ethnic groups.

Ms. Radetski realizes that assessment is a vital part of the teaching-learning cycle. She sets up her lessons so that student peers assess performance tasks and she uses informal observations and discussions to assess students' work on performance tasks.

4. What other assessment tool would be effective to ensure she is adequately assessing diversity in her classroom?

    (A) She administers at least five quizzes and four essay type exams per subject every grading period.

    (B) She gives two spelling tests each week.

    (C) She places students in cooperative groups in order to complete several performance tasks related to the stated objectives of the lessons.

    (D) She sends a note home when her students do not seem to understand.

Ms. Felder's sixth-grade class is studying the world of work. She discusses a new idea related to this study with a more experienced teacher. Ms. Felder is planning to invite all parents to visit the class, talk about their own work, and respond to students' questions. She hopes to have three or four parents a day for this activity over a period of two weeks or so. The fellow teacher encourages Ms. Felder to go ahead and make plans for this activity, after receiving approval of the project from the principal.

5. Which of the following reasons is the major benefit pointed out by the experienced teacher?

   (A) Ms. Felder will have the opportunity to further her career awareness goals of the curriculum and the relationship she is trying to establish with the families of her students.

   (B) The project will be a free way to have guest speakers for the class.

   (C) The project will introduce students to a variety of careers and help them select the careers they want to follow some day.

   (D) Ms. Felder will be able to see which parents will cooperate with her when she has a need for their help.

Mrs. Kresmeier teaches sixth-grade language arts classes. One of her curriculum goals is to help students improve their spelling. As one of her techniques, she has developed a number of special mnemonic devices that she uses with the students, getting the idea from the old teaching rhymes like "I before E except after C or when sounding like A as in neighbor or weigh." Her own memory tricks—"The moose can't get loose from the noose" or "Spell rhyme? Why me?"—have caught the interest of her students. Now, besides Mrs. Kresmeier's memory tricks for better spelling, her students are developing and sharing their own creative ways to memorize more effectively.

6. To improve her students' spelling, Mrs. Kresmeier's method has been successful primarily because of which of the following factors related to student achievement?

   (A) The students are not relying on phonics or sight words to spell difficult words.

   (B) Mrs. Kresmeier has impressed her students with the need to learn to spell.

   (C) The ideas are effective with many students and help to create a learning environment that is open to student interaction.

   (D) Mrs. Kresmeier teaches spelling using only words that can be adapted to mnemonic clues.

Mr. Freeman is preparing a year-long unit on process writing for his fifth-grade class. He plans for each student to write about a series of topics over each six-week grading period. At the end of each grading period, students will select three completed writing assignments that reflect their best work. Mr. Freeman will review the assignments and conference with each student. During the conference, Mr. Freeman will assist the students with preparing a list of writing goals for the next grading term.

7. Which of the following best describes Mr. Freeman's plan for reviewing student writing assignments, conferencing with each student, and helping each student set specific goals for writing to be accomplished during the next grading period?

    (A) Summative evaluation

    (B) Summative assessment

    (C) Formative assessment

    (D) Peer evaluation

8. Mr. Freeman's goal in planning to conference with each student about his/her writing could be described as

    (A) creating a climate of trust and encouraging a positive attitude toward writing.

    (B) an efficient process for grading student writing assignments.

    (C) an opportunity to stress the importance of careful editing of completed writing assignments.

    (D) an opportunity to stress the value of prewriting in producing a final product.

Philip is a student in Mr. Freeman's class who receives services from a resource teacher for a learning disability that affects his reading and writing.

9. Which of the following is the most appropriate request that Mr. Freeman should make of the resource teacher to help Philip complete the writing unit?

    (A) Mr. Freeman should ask the resource teacher to provide writing instruction for Philip.

    (B) Mr. Freeman should excuse Philip from writing assignments.

    (C) Mr. Freeman should ask the resource teacher for help in modifying the writing unit to match Philip's needs.

(D)   Mr. Freeman should ask the resource teacher to schedule extra tutoring sessions to help Philip with the writing assignments.

Mr. Banks, an eighth-grade math teacher, uses several techniques to ensure that his students maximize their chances of learning important math concepts. First, he has his students practice key concepts using rap or poetry. For example, his students learn the quadratic equation by putting it in story form. The students break into teams and present the equation story using a rap or poem they have created. Another technique Mr. Banks uses is to take his students on a short field trip once a month. He takes them to different places around town, like the bank or the park, where he has them look for patterns or measure different objects. He attempts to relate things seen on the trips to mathematics.

10.   Mr. Banks has his students practice the math concepts with rap and poetry as part of the learning process because he

(A)   wants to prevent boredom in his classroom.

(B)   believes that if he keeps the students busy, there will be a smaller chance of disruptive activity in the classroom.

(C)   wants to have student presentations in his class.

(D)   knows that the neural pathways in the brain will become more efficient if students repeat an earlier learning.

11.   Mr. Banks takes his students on field trips

(A)   to provide appropriate learning stimuli.

(B)   to keep the pace in the classroom moving rapidly.

(C)   to vary his daily routine.

(D)   as a classroom management tool.

Ms. Pearson is a first-year, sixth-grade Texas history teacher. She has five computer terminals with access to the World Wide Web in her classroom of 25 students. Ms. Pearson begins each class period with student seatwork. While the students are working, she takes attendance. She usually starts the class with a direct-teach, in which, after dimming the lights, she uses transparencies with an overhead projector. Several times she has paused and turned up the lights, only to find several students off-task. While in the lounge, Ms. Pearson mentions this problem to her department chair, Mr. Lopez. He reminds her that the school has a grant that provides PowerPoint software and projectors for use in the classroom. She can use PowerPoint for her direct-teaches and teach her students how to use the software for their reports, stories, and projects. Ms. Pearson thanks Mr. Lopez for his advice and agrees to begin using PowerPoint for herself and her students.

12. The most important reason for incorporating the use of PowerPoint in Ms. Pearson's class is the fact that

   (A) she can show her students that she has mastered the computer.

   (B) PowerPoint can allow students to become more involved in the learning process.

   (C) PowerPoint is easy to learn.

   (D) she can save her presentations and use them again next year.

Ms. Garcia is a first-year, fifth-grade teacher in a large school district in San Antonio, Texas. She wants to make sure her students develop good note-taking skills. The first week of school, after teaching her students the classroom rules and procedures, she decides to teach her students the note-taking technique known as mind-mapping. The students view a short video about mind-mapping. Ms. Garcia tells them that she is going to give a short lecture on Mexico. She places the students in groups of four and gives each group a set of colored markers. She asks the students to turn their papers sideways and begin by placing the topic, "Mexico," in the center of the paper and drawing a circle around it. As Ms. Garcia talks about Mexico, each subtopic is drawn as a branch from the main topic, using a different colored marker. Further subtopics are put on lines drawn from the main branches. After the lecture is completed, students are given time to embellish their mind maps with small drawings or figures in various colors. The students are encouraged to practice mind-mapping whenever possible to get familiar with this technique. When the students are finished, Ms. Garcia notices that the students seem pleased with their mind maps.

13. Ms. Garcia uses the mind-mapping technique because she

   (A) feels that working in groups with the markers would be a change of pace.

   (B) wants to give her students an opportunity to work with colored markers.

   (C) does not like to use direct instruction.

   (D) knows that many students process information best when it is in mind-mapping form.

Ms. Garcia tries to plan a variety of instructional activities for each class period such as videos, music, hands-on activities, and physical movement. After each activity, Ms. Garcia allows the students time to process the information covered in the activity.

14. She uses these different activities to

   (A) provide variety in her teaching.

(B)   reach as many students in her class as possible through their different learning styles.

(C)   show the parents how much she cares about the students.

(D)   provide variety so she will not become bored with her teaching.

To teach all students in the class, a teacher should strive to reduce student stress.

15.   The teacher can best accomplish this by

(A)   inducing stress on the students and teaching them what to do about it.

(B)   ignoring threats from outside the class and from other students.

(C)   reducing threats from other students by setting up clear classroom expectations for student behavior.

(D)   not getting involved in students' problems.

Mr. Dobson teaches fifth-grade mathematics at Valverde Elementary. He encourages students to work in groups of two or three as they begin homework assignments so that they can answer questions for each other. Mr. Dobson notices immediately that some of his students chose to work alone even though they had been asked to work in groups. He also notices that some students are easily distracted even though the other members of their group are working on the assignment as directed.

16.   Which of the following is the most likely explanation for the students' behavior?

(A)   Fifth-grade students are not physically or mentally capable of working in small groups; small groups are more suitable for older students.

(B)   Fifth-grade students vary greatly in their physical development and maturity; this variance influences the students' interests and attitudes.

(C)   Fifth-grade students lack the ability for internal control and, therefore, learn best in structured settings. It is usually best to seat fifth-graders in single rows.

(D)   Mr. Dobson needs to be more specific in his expectations for student behavior.

Mr. Dobson wants to encourage all of his students to participate in discussions related to the use of math in the real world. Five students in his math class are very shy and introverted.

17.   Which of the following would most likely be the best way to encourage these students to participate in the discussion?

    (A)   Mr. Dobson should call on these students by name at least once each day and give participation grades.

    (B)   Mr. Dobson should not be concerned about these students because they will become less shy and introverted as they mature during the year.

    (C)   Mr. Dobson should divide the class into small groups for discussion so these students will not be overwhelmed by speaking in front of the whole class.

    (D)   Mr. Dobson should speak with these students individually and encourage them to participate more in class discussions.

In the same class, Mr. Dobson has two students who are overly talkative. These two students volunteer to answer every question.

18.   Which of the following is the best way to deal with these students?

    (A)   Mr. Dobson should call on the overly talkative students only once during each class.

    (B)   Mr. Dobson should ask these students to be the observers in small group discussions and take notes about participation and topics discussed.

    (C)   Mr. Dobson should place these students in a group by themselves so that they can discuss all they want and not disturb the other students.

    (D)   Mr. Dobson should recognize that overly talkative students need lots of attention and should be called on to participate throughout the class period.

Mr. Dobson wants his fifth-grade students to serve as tutors for the first-graders who are learning addition and subtraction.

19.   The main advantage for the fifth-graders who participate is that

    (A)   they will develop proficiency and self-esteem.

    (B)   they will be encouraged to view teaching as a possible career.

    (C)   they will learn specific tutoring techniques.

    (D)   they will have an opportunity to become friends with younger children.

Mr. Dobson plans mathematics lessons so that all students will experience at least 70 percent success during independent practice.

20. Considering student success during independent practice reflects Mr. Dobson's understanding that

   (A) a student's academic success influences overall achievements and contributes to positive self-esteem.

   (B) students who are academically successful have happy parents.

   (C) if students are successful when working alone they can finish their homework independently.

   (D) if students are successful they will ask fewer questions, giving Mr. Dobson more time to plan future lessons.

Mr. Dobson has just explained a new procedure for solving a particular kind of mathematics problem. He has solved several demonstration problems on the board. Several students raise their hands to ask questions.

21. If a student's question requires more than two or three minutes to answer, then Mr. Dobson suspects that the

   (A) original explanation was faulty.

   (B) students were not paying attention.

   (C) students are below average in listening skills.

   (D) students have a very poor background in mathematics.

Mr. Dobson and Mr. Lowery (a science teacher) are planning a celebration of Galileo's birthday. The students will research Galileo's discoveries, draw posters of those discoveries, and prepare short plays depicting important events in his life. They will present the plays and display the posters to students in grades 1 to 4.

22. This is an example of

   (A) an end-of-the-year project.

   (B) problem-solving and inquiry teaching.

   (C) horizontal learning to plan instructions.

   (D) teachers preparing to ask the PTA for science lab equipment.

Mr. Dobson wants to use a variety of grouping strategies during the year. Sometimes he groups students with similar ability, or he groups students with varying ability. Once in a while he permits students to choose their own groupings. At times he suggests that students work with a particular partner, or he allows them to work individually. Sometimes he assigns a partner.

23.   This flexibility in grouping strategies indicates that Mr. Dobson recognizes that

    (A)   fifth-graders like surprises and unpredictable teacher behavior.

    (B)   grouping patterns affect students perceptions of self-esteem and competence.

    (C)   frequent changes in the classroom keep students alert and interested.

    (D)   it is not fair to place the worst students in the same group consistently.

The principal asks Mr. Dobson and Ms. Gonzalez, another fifth-grade math teacher in the school, to visit the math classes and the computer lab in the middle school that most of the students at Valverde will attend.

24.   By asking Mr. Dobson and Ms. Gonzalez to visit the middle school, the principal is most likely encouraging

    (A)   collaboration and vertical teaming among math teachers at Valverde and the middle school.

    (B)   Mr. Dobson and Ms. Gonzalez to consider applying for a job at the middle school.

    (C)   the use of computers in math classes at Valverde.

    (D)   the use of the middle school math curriculum in the fifth-grade classes.

Mr. Hawkins recently implemented cooperative learning in his fourth-grade classroom in a medium-sized school district in south Texas. Shortly after he began using this instructional method, Mr. Johnson, another fourth-grade teacher, came by and questioned Mr. Hawkins about his use of this technique. Mr. Johnson asked, "Why should I use cooperative learning in my classroom? What possible benefits could it give my students? When students are supposedly working together, some students will do all of the work, while others do nothing." Mr. Hawkins replied, "There are many benefits to cooperative learning. Once you try it you will see the benefits. Why don't you come to my class on your off-period and observe it in action?"

25. Mr. Hawkins should further inform Mr. Johnson that cooperative learning is

    (A) not backed by a large body of research but works in his classroom.

    (B) teaching socialization skills and how to work collaboratively, much the same as on a job.

    (C) teaching students how to be competitive in the real world.

    (D) promoting higher achievement by using competitive and individualistic learning structures.

Mr. Hawkins' fourth-grade class is very diverse. There are five black students, seven Hispanic students, and twelve Anglo students in his class. At the beginning of the semester, Mr. Hawkins notices many awkward moments when students of different groups have difficulty communicating or sometimes make negative comments towards each other. Once the cooperative learning activities are put in place and the students feel comfortable with it, Mr. Hawkins notices more constructive interactions between students of different ethnic groups.

26. He attributes this to

    (A) the positive effects of cooperative learning.

    (B) his punishment of those who acted negatively toward members of other ethnic groups.

    (C) the fact that the principal sent a note home to parents warning of the negative consequences of inappropriate behavior.

    (D) an assembly with a speaker who talked about people of different ethnic backgrounds and how they should try to get along with each other.

Jan Rodgers is a seventh-grade teacher in Dallas, Texas. When students walk into her class, they sit down immediately and begin working on an assignment she has prepared for them. While they are working, Ms. Rodgers takes attendance by looking at a hand-held seating chart. The attendance documentation process takes seconds. One morning, another teacher, Ms. Simpson, is in her class to distribute some papers and notices how Ms. Rodgers takes attendance. She asks: "Why do you take attendance this way? I have my students sign a roll sheet."

27. Ms. Rodgers uses her procedure for taking attendance to

    (A) allow her more time to prepare for daily activities.

    (B) show the students and administrators how much control she has over her classroom.

(C) maximize students' time on task and to perform the task accurately, with as little disruption as possible.

(D) comply with the principal's order to get the roll sheets to the office as quickly as possible.

Mr. Brand teaches eighth-grade language arts. He begins to notice that he is spending a large amount of his time entering and keeping track of grades. This is especially true at the end of the nine-week grading period. One afternoon, as he is working on grades, Mr. Rodriquez, a neighboring teacher, enters his room. After hearing Mr. Brand complain about how long it takes to enter grades, Mr. Rodriquez recommends the use of available software to keep track of all the grades. He suggests that Mr. Brand put his grade book on computer.

28. Why should Mr. Brand consider using a computer program to keep up with grading?

(A) He could impress the principal with technical expertise.

(B) Other teachers would be impressed by what he is doing.

(C) He would be able to leave school earlier.

(D) He could use technology to save time for other work.

Ms. Parker, a first-year, sixth-grade teacher in San Marcos, Texas, wants to create a learner-friendly classroom for her students. She is concerned about the problem of student tension and would like to reduce high stress in her classroom. In addition, Ms. Parker wants to ensure that each of her students is provided with an enriched learning environment. As she is preparing her classroom, Ms. Stinson, the teacher in the classroom next door, notices the many interesting educational posters and pictures Ms. Parker has placed on the walls of her classroom. She remarks to Ms. Parker, "I love all of the things you have on your walls. These things provide a very enriched classroom." Ms. Parker replies, "Actually, these things on the wall do not necessarily mean that this is an enriched classroom. I provide appropriate challenges and make sure feedback is specific, timely, and learner-controlled."

29. Ms. Parker adds that in order to have an enriched classroom, a teacher must also

(A) provide adequate instruction to each student on a daily basis.

(B) provide activities that include problem-solving, critical thinking, relevant projects, and complex activities.

(C) make sure the walls and bulletin boards are filled with pictures and posters.

(D)   be certain to hug each child every day to build their self-esteem.

Mr. Heaney teaches seventh-grade social studies. At the beginning of each school year, he gives his students a pre-test and ranks their scores from highest to lowest. He places students in groups of four by taking one student from the top of the list, one from the bottom, and two from the middle. This results in five heterogeneous groups: four groups of four students and one group of three students. He then implements cooperative learning structures designed to distribute a task to every member of the group. Mr. Heaney facilitates activities by continually moving from group to group. He begins most lessons with 10 to 15 minutes of direct instruction, and then gives the groups a cooperative learning structure to process the information. Mr. Heaney is always careful to keep close watch on the time taken for each activity.

30.   Mr. Heaney closely monitors the cooperative learning activities because he wants to make sure students are working together productively and

   (A)   ensure that the students do not step out of line and misbehave.

   (B)   knows cooperative learning activities require careful facilitation and that successful cooperative learning is, in part, a function of effective time management.

   (C)   realizes that he is responsible to ensure that the gifted and talented students take the leadership roles in each group.

   (D)   wants his presence known to each group in case the campus administrator decides to do a walk-through observation during the activity.

Mrs. Doe starts planning a two-week unit involving the study of Native Americans of Texas for her fifth-grade class. To begin the unit, she presents a movie on today's Texas Native American. The movie sparks a lively debate led by Mrs. Doe. All students participate and most of them describe a Native American with which they are personally acquainted. As Mrs. Doe reflectively listens, key questions are asked. "From where do our ancestors come?" "How did people get food before grocery stores were built?" and "How did they travel before cars?"

The following day Mrs. Doe reviews the use of encyclopedias, indexes, and atlases. The students are divided into groups and taken to the library. Each group is responsible for locating information on assigned topics of expressed interests. The topics include topography of the land; the changing climate, plants and animals; migration routes; and the location of general areas where Native Americans settled.

31. The students' involvement in this unit of study is primarily a result of

    (A) the teacher's reflective listening during the discussion because she directed them into the desired areas of study.

    (B) the students' personal acquaintances with some Native Americans because this "brings the study close to home."

    (C) the students' natural abilities to perform research in these topics.

    (D) the use of available resources and materials along with careful planning.

Days 3 and 4 are spent with each group being involved in library research. Information is written on index cards. Each group prepares a class presentation that includes a written explanation of an assigned topic, a shadowbox, and a sawdust map or models of Native American clothing. Additionally, a pictograph is to be used in the telling of a legend or folk story. The presentation concludes with a collage depicting the Native American way of life.

32. Mrs. Doe utilizes multiple strategies and techniques to allow each student to participate in the project, regardless of ability, and to

    (A) develop a foundation for teaching American history.

    (B) create the illusion that she is an easy teacher so that students will clamor to enroll in her class next year.

    (C) motivate the group to have positive effects on individual learning while integrating several subjects into the project.

    (D) show that her students are learning those skills required by the TEKS.

On day 8, Mrs. Doe arranges a display of Native American artifacts and crafts in the hallway. At the onset of her planning, she collaborated with the music teacher to arrange a general assembly of the entire student body. Thus, she takes her students to the auditorium for a general assembly consisting of Native American poetry read by Fawn Lonewolf with Native American music and dance by the school chorus. At the conclusion of the assembly, the class is invited to view the video *The Trail of Tears*. Native American refreshments, including fried bread, are served to the students. As the students eat, *Knots on a Counting Rope* is read by the reading teacher. Following the reading, the physical education teacher teaches the students several games that have been played by Native American children.

33. The planning of these activities requires the stimulation of the curiosity of the student body, the recognition of individual talents among the students, and

    (A) the taking of risks by both the teacher and the students.

    (B) the approval of the school board.

    (C) the utilization of the collaborative process of working with other teachers.

    (D) the written approval of all parents/caretakers.

Day 10 of the unit is Field Trip Day. The students are given a choice of visiting the Omniplex for more Native American archeological experiences, visiting Anadarko, Indian City, USA, or visiting Tallequah, the capital of the Cherokee Nation. Whatever the student's choice, he or she is to take notes of what is seen, heard, and experienced. These will be shared with the other members of the class on the following school day.

34. Of the following choices, what is the best reason for utilizing the Field Trip Day for learning?

    (A) A sense of community will be nurtured.

    (B) Internal factors create a learning environment that takes advantage of positive factors.

    (C) Students will be able to make connections between their current skills and those that are new to them.

    (D) Students will take responsibility for their own learning.

35. The fact that students are allowed to choose the location of their field trip is designed to

    (A) enhance the students' ability to make decisions.

    (B) respect differences and enhance the students' understandings of the society in which they live.

    (C) limit the view of learning as a purposeful pursuit.

    (D) be an example of direct instruction strategies.

Mr. Warren teaches sixth-grade language arts. At the beginning of every school year, he spends the first five days of school setting up rules and procedures. Before school begins, Mr. Warren prepares a list of rules and procedures he wants the students to learn and follow. The first day of class he passes out the list and gives students time to read it. He goes over each rule and procedure with the students and asks for their comments about the fairness of each. Many students do comment, and when Mr. Warren feels the comments are justified, he changes or modifies the rule or procedure. When he and the students are satisfied, he begins practicing the procedures with the students. When the students demonstrate knowledge of the classroom procedures, Mr. Warren begins to teach course content.

36. Why does Mr. Warren involve the students in the creation of the classroom rules and procedures?

    (A) He wants them to know that he can overrule them at any time.

    (B) He believes that this action will reduce his problems with parents.

    (C) He knows that involving students in developing rules and procedures is an effective method of managing student behavior.

    (D) He feels the students will respect him more.

Ms. Pope is a fifth-grade history teacher in a Texas town with a population of 20,000. Since the beginning of the school year, her students have worked in cooperative groups. Today, she is conducting a discussion about why pioneers settled the West. Each group then imagines that they are travelers in their own Conestoga wagon and lists the items they will take on their journey west. The discussion stalls as Ms. Pope has difficulty getting all students to respond to her questions. Some students want to answer all the questions and others do not want to respond at all. Ms. Pope senses that she is going too fast, but she isn't sure what she should do about the problem. After school, she sees Ms. Perez, an experienced teacher, in the teacher workroom and tells her what happened. Ms. Perez advises Ms. Pope to slow down the pace of her discussions and allow "wait time" between her questions and student responses.

37. What further advice should Ms. Perez give Ms. Pope to improve the situation?

    (A) She should suggest Ms. Pope encourage the reticent students during the discussion.

    (B) She should advise Ms. Pope to broaden participation by utilizing strategies that allow more students to participate at one time, such as "think-pair-share" or "buzz groups."

    (C) She should suggest Ms. Pope offer candy or other rewards for students who participate in the discussions.

    (D) She should advise Ms. Pope to "continue on" as there is nothing she can do to improve the situation.

Julie Harris is a first-year, fifth-grade teacher in a medium-sized Texas city. Whenever she tries to give her students directions, there seems to be confusion. This particular day, her mentor teacher, Ms. Avila, is observing her. Ms. Harris wants her students to open their books to page 36 and begin reading out loud in turns. She says, "Alright students, please take out your books and turn to page 36." She waits about 30 seconds and says, "Jeremy, will you read the first paragraph?" As Jeremy begins reading, Ms. Harris notices that several students do not have their textbooks out and are still looking for them. Several other students have their books on their desks, but have not found the right page. Ms. Harris instructs Jeremy to stop reading and wait for all students to get their books and open to the correct page. After class, Ms. Harris asks Ms. Avila what she should do to eliminate the problems she is having concerning giving directions.

38.   What should Ms. Avila tell her?

(A)   Give all directions one at a time and wait until everyone has followed each step before giving another direction

(B)   Prepare a copy of the directions and pass them out to the students at the beginning of class

(C)   Read the entire set of directions to determine if all students are paying attention

(D)   Tell the class at the beginning of the school year that all students who correctly follow directions will get a prize at the end of each week

Ms. Randal, a first-year teacher, teaches seventh-grade history in an East Texas town of 40,000 people. The school is on a block schedule with four ninety-minute classes and a thirty-minute lunch each day. Today, Ms. Dawson, Ms. Randal's mentor, is in her class observing her lesson on the 1860s. Ms. Randal gives an effective direct-teach for about ten minutes. The students seem interested and are taking notes. When she finishes, she immediately starts a class discussion by asking, "Any questions?" She waits ten or fifteen seconds and then says, "Come on. You're not trying? Show me you care. This material is important! It'll be on the test." Finally, someone raises a hand and sheepishly asks a question. After several other students ask questions, the students form groups and discuss various points of the 1860s. Ms. Randal begins the next part of the lesson. She asks, "How many of you have been to Promontory Point, Utah?" Several students halfway raise their hands; other students just look at each other. Ms. Randal is puzzled, but she goes on with her lesson.

39.   Did Ms. Randal correctly begin the class discussion?

(A)   Yes, the question she asked is just what was needed to get the discussion going.

(B)   Yes, challenging students by accusation is an intrinsic motivator.

(C)   No, it would be useful to give students a chance to verbally prepare their thoughts before beginning the discussion.

(D)   Yes, students at this stage of development need these kinds of prompts to begin a class discussion.

40.   Ms. Randal's question about Promontory Point, Utah,

(A)   is a straightforward question, requiring a simple answer.

(B)   could elicit the desired response by slightly changing the wording.

(C)   is the kind of motivational question needed to generate a lively discussion.

(D)   is a good question because it focuses on the topic of the 1860s.

There are six Internet-connected computers in Ms. Randal's classroom that she controls with one password. She allows her students to use the computers for extension activities. When students complete their work early, they search the World Wide Web for information on the topic the class is studying. Quite often, Ms. Randal is using the computer when the students enter the classroom for help before school starts. They always seem interested in what she is doing. While eating lunch one day, Ms. Randal speaks to Mr. Sampras, a more experienced teacher, about student computer use in her classroom. Ms. Randal tells him that her students are in cooperative groups and the extension activities are a perfect complement to this instructional method.

41.   Mr. Sampras could best respond to Ms. Randal by stating that

(A)   the computer activities are adequate for the students.

(B)   because students have to be able to use technology, experts agree they should spend half their classroom time on the computer.

(C)   students should not be allowed to use the World Wide Web because of access to controversial information.

(D)   she should assign small-group projects that allow her cooperative groups to work together on the computers.

◆◆◆◆◆◆◆◆

Ms. Hay is a first-year, fourth-grade teacher in Waco, Texas. She has a wide range of students in her class representing several ethnic groups. One day, while eating lunch in the cafeteria, Ms. Jinkins tells Ms. Hay about a set of spelling software that she purchased on sale at a computer software store. She is using it in her class with great success. She offers to let Ms. Hay copy the software for use in her class.

42. Should Ms. Hay take the software package?

   (A) No, because all software has a copyright, and copying it can result in very large fines, unless the school possesses a license to copy it.

   (B) Yes, because schools are exempt from most copyright laws.

   (C) Yes, she should take the software. When a teacher buys software for his or her class, the law allows use by five other teachers.

   (D) No, because software sold for schools cannot physically be copied.

Several average classes of fifth-graders are found to be inadequately prepared for fifth-grade work. It is important that their problem-solving skills and motivation improve in order to meet the pre-entry criteria for a new middle school. Most of the students cannot comprehend fifth-grade textual material. They lack enthusiasm for projects and problems. Many of the students have become frightened by their academic failure and are withdrawing in confusion.

Mrs. Sivart is retained to help the classes improve their problem-solving skills and to facilitate motivation and enthusiasm. After reviewing test scores and evaluating daily work, she calls for a conference with the concerned teachers. Mrs. Sivart asks them what they perceive to be the problem, and all teachers agree that the students did not learn the appropriate skills in the lower grades. They feel that their first responsibility is to make sure each student meets the objectives required by the state each year and that they don't have time to remediate the failing students. Mrs. Sivart reflects for a moment, then gently asks which text teachers currently use. After hearing that standard fifth-grade social studies text from Blank Publishing Company are used, she asks for another meeting at the same time the next day.

The following day Mrs. Sivart appears in the meeting with readability charts, texts, paper, and pencils. Each teacher agrees to do a readability on the text. As they complete the readability, a stunned silence follows. The teachers realize that they are expecting students to read materials that are three years above their grade level. They ask Mrs. Sivart what they can do to remedy this situation.

43. At this point in the solving of the problem, Mrs. Sivart has

   (A) caused each teacher to focus upon reflection and self-evaluation and to recognize their bias.

   (B) allowed the teachers to shift part of the blame to the publisher from the elementary teachers.

(C)   allowed the teachers to seek out opportunities to grow professionally by using different sources of support and guidance to enhance their own professional skills.

(D)   used informal assessment to understand the learners.

44.   The teachers' statement that they are expected to meet the state objectives each year reveals that they

(A)   are refusing to reflect upon their responsibility to the students and are unwilling to change teaching strategies.

(B)   understand the requirements and expectations of teaching in Texas.

(C)   are inflexible in their strategies and the use of collaborative processes.

(D)   probably have a deficiency in using a variety of instructional materials.

At the following planning meeting, Mrs. Sivart agrees to demonstrate a strategy that can be used in each class to make the adopted text appropriate for that class. Following her demonstration, she asks the teachers to develop an exam that covers the material they have just modified. Each teacher is then to do a readability on the exam. As Mrs. Sivart circulates among the teachers, she sees puzzled expressions and overhears "I have just written a ninth-grade exam for fifth-grade students. I can't believe I did that. What do I do now?" With a smile, Mrs. Sivart responds that the exam can be rewritten until it is on the fifth-grade level. By using the readability chart and checking each item on the exam, items can be modified until they are written on the correct level. She continues, "What you have done is very common among teachers, but with practice, you will soon be writing exams on grade level. By combining modification of the text with writing your exams on grade level and using a few techniques for increasing comprehension, you should see a great change in your students. Nothing breeds success like success."

45.   Through the demonstration, the in-service training of writing exams, and the extra techniques for improving comprehension, Mrs. Sivart has demonstrated that

(A)   the teacher is to constantly monitor and adjust strategies in response to student feedback.

(B)   the teacher can promote student learning by designing instruction for different situations.

(C)   the teacher should be able to recognize factors and situations that will either promote or diminish motivation.

(D)   external factors may affect students' performance in school.

46. The concept that Mrs. Sivart has caused the teachers to focus upon is that

    (A) most of the time when students fail, it is not their fault.

    (B) individualizing instruction does not have to be tedious and time-consuming, but is seldom necessary.

    (C) external factors may affect students' performance in class.

    (D) diversity in the classroom may affect learning.

Mr. Harris is a first-year, seventh-grade math teacher in a small town near Waco, Texas. He has a class of 20 students who are organized into five teams of four students. Mr. Harris has five computers in his classroom. Before becoming a teacher, Mr. Harris was a professional land surveyor. He wants his math class to experience some surveying activities, so he installs a package of surveyor training software on the classroom computers. He previously secured permission from the software developers to use the package in his class. Each team is assigned a computer; the students practice surveying imaginary tracts of land and are required to solve a surveying project. While in the teacher's lounge, Mr. Daniels, another math teacher, says to Mr. Harris, "I hear you are having your students work on surveying projects. Is that the proper way to use the computers in your class?"

47. Mr. Harris should reply,

    (A) "Good point, please don't say anything about this."

    (B) "Yes it is. Computers are interactive and constructivist and work best when students are working on small-group projects."

    (C) "You're right. For financial purposes we should use the software provided to us by the school district."

    (D) "Yes it is. This is a good method of reducing boredom in my classroom."

Ms. Dudly, a first-year teacher in a north Texas city of 50,000, teaches 24 fourth-grade students. She spends at least two hours every night developing lesson plans. She feels disorganized at school. She feels that a great deal of her time is spent working on various kinds of paperwork. Although Ms. Dudly is computer-literate, she continues most of her planning by hand or on the word processor. She observes other teachers, including two other first-year teachers, who seem to be less bogged down with paperwork and appear to have more free time. Finally, she can't stand it any longer. She sees one of the other new teachers, Ms. Fisk, on the way to the parking lot after school and asks her how she handles her preparation and planning. Ms. Fisk replies that she sometimes feels overwhelmed as well, but that she saves a lot of time by using software programs to assist her with much of the work.

48. What kinds of programs could Ms. Fisk be using to save time in organizing her classroom?

    (A) Lesson planning software, worksheet and puzzle tools, and grade keeping software

    (B) Tutorials or drill-and-practice software, which create student exercises

    (C) Software that automatically composes original essays

    (D) Software designed for students to learn new skills by manipulating the computer

Ms. Woods, a fifth-grade language arts/social studies teacher in a large urban school, teaches a class of 22 ethnically diverse students. She wants her students to begin thinking about college now. So, she decides to have her students create a poster and write an essay entitled "Why I want to go to college." She plans to allow groups of four students to search the World Wide Web for information about colleges. Several college students will come to her class to talk with the fifth-graders about their post-high school experiences. After all of the students complete their work, Ms. Woods plans a Family Night where all of the students will explain their posters and read their essays in front of the parents.

49. What kind of an assessment is the Family Night?

    (A) Portfolio assessment

    (B) Holistic assessment

    (C) Performance assessment

    (D) Authentic assessment

Buzz Huerta is a first-year, sixth-grade teacher in a town of 30,000 in south Texas. He has organized his classroom into a self-governing body that is conceptualized as "The Family." Each student has a "twin" of the same gender who serves as his/her thinking and working partner. Each pair of twins has a second pair of twins (either the same or opposite gender) with whom they make up a sib-group. Dividing "The Family" into sib-groups allows Mr. Huerta to have stable heterogeneous cooperative groups of four, yet maintain the sense of class unity that the family metaphor provides.

While the class is largely self-governing, Mr. Huerta retains final authority over all classroom life. He seldom feels the need to exert his authority, but when he does, he does not hesitate, and the students take appropriate note.

Elena Monteverde runs up to Mr. Huerta as he is finishing grading a math assignment before school. "Mr. H.," says Elena. "Look at this." Elena hands Mr. Huerta a news clipping about a pen pal program that matches a North American class with a South American class. "Can we do this?" He reads the clipping and struggles to keep from smiling. "Sounds interesting," he says. "What do you think?" "I think it would be neat. We could learn a lot." "You might be right. What should we do first?" Elena furrows her brow for a moment. "I know. Maybe we should ask the class to vote on it." "Good idea," says Mr. Huerta. "Tomorrow is class meeting day. Ask Freeman to put it on the agenda for new business."

50. Mr. Huerta has planned to begin a unit on South America the following week. Why doesn't he tell Elena that when she approaches him with the idea of South American pen pals?

    (A) Mr. Huerta wants to give Elena and the class a delightful surprise when he announces the study unit on South America following the class's vote on the pen pal project; he knows that the surprise will provide a strong motivational basis for the unit.

    (B) Mr. Huerta wants Elena and the class to feel ownership of the pen pal activity and subsequently of the South American unit of study. He knows that it will appear to the students that the South American unit has grown out of the pen pal project, and that this sense of ownership of the South American unit will provide a strong motivational base.

    (C) Mr. Huerta doesn't want Elena and the class to start thinking about the South American unit before they finish with the current unit; he knows that the quality of the present unit will suffer if Elena and the class become distracted thinking about the next unit of study.

    (D) Mr. Huerta wants Elena to assess her own understanding of the pen pal activity; he does not want to complicate the issue by introducing new information related to the unit of study.

Instead of praising Elena for her suggestion, Mr. Huerta tells her that her idea "sounds interesting," and he asks her what she thinks about the idea.

51. Evaluate this strategy.

    (A) This is a poor strategy. Mr. Huerta should have reinforced Elena for bringing her idea to him, therefore assuring that she would continue to share her ideas with him.

    (B) This is a good strategy. Mr. Huerta's response probes Elena to evaluate her own thinking, thus promoting a climate of active inquiry.

(C)   This is a good strategy. Mr. Huerta understands cognitive child development and uses this opportunity to assess Elena's cognitive development.

(D)   This is a poor strategy. Mr. Huerta understands the outside factors that affect a child's learning. Since the clipping about the pen pals results from an outside factor, he is assessing the impact of this outside influence. However, that is not an appropriate strategy, since he should have reinforced her instead.

52.   Mr. Huerta then asks Elena, "What should we do first?" What is his purpose in asking this particular question in this way?

(A)   He wants her to use a problem-solving strategy called "scaffolding."

(B)   He wants to encourage her to make her own decision about the project.

(C)   He wants her to consider all of the alternatives available to her.

(D)   He wants to reinforce her initiative by prolonging the conversation.

53.   Near the end of their encounter, Mr. Huerta says, "Good idea." Why?

(A)   He is trying to increase Elena's self-esteem.

(B)   He is signaling Elena that the conversational transaction has been completed.

(C)   He is attempting to reinforce Elena for her self-evaluative behavior.

(D)   He is attempting to reinforce Elena for suggesting that the idea be put to a vote.

At noon, Mr. Huerta goes to the cafeteria for lunch. He knows that the cafeteria is serving Sloppy Joes today, which he does not like, but he nevertheless takes a tray and joins his colleagues at the faculty table. "How's the Family Man?" asks Mr. Reynolds as he motions to the empty seat beside him. Mr. Huerta grins. He is growing accustomed to the teasing of the older teachers who do not understand his use of the family metaphor as a classroom organizational framework. "The Family Man is rolling along," he says.

As they eat, Mr. Huerta tells Ms. Wilson, the choir teacher, that he is beginning a unit on South America soon. He asks her whether she might be able to incorporate some South American music into her curriculum during the next month. She tells him that she usually teaches several Latin American songs later in the year, but that she can move them up to accommodate him. Although music is not an interest of his, Mr. Huerta asks her to tell him what makes Hispanic music sound so different from the traditional American forms of music. Ms. Wilson enters into a rather complicated discussion of Latin music. Mr. Huerta nods and listens carefully. When he leaves, Ms. Wilson asks him if he could tell her more about his classroom organization the next time they have lunch together.

54.   Why does Mr. Huerta choose to eat lunch in the cafeteria?

   (A)   He knows that first-year teachers are at increased risk of illness and understands the importance of maintaining good nutrition during this crucial year.

   (B)   He wants to set a good example for his students by eating in the cafeteria.

   (C)   He wants to know more about South American music and hopes to find Ms. Wilson in the cafeteria so that he can ask her to explain its elements to him.

   (D)   He is trying to promote collegiality, thereby creating a school culture that enhances learning and encourages positive change.

55.   Mr. Huerta is pleased that Ms. Wilson has asked about his classroom organization. What is the most likely reason for using the "Family" concept?

   (A)   Since he does not have a family of his own, he feels as though the children belong to him.

   (B)   Mr. Huerta has found the family metaphor to be the best organizational framework to help him cover the most amount of material in the least amount of time.

   (C)   Since his class is heavily Hispanic and African-American, Mr. Huerta employs the family metaphor because this appears to be a culturally appropriate structure for teaching his social learners.

   (D)   Mr. Huerta has found that the family-centered setup allows the students to infer the rules of the classroom based on their own experiences.

On Class Meeting Day, Freeman Morgan asks Elena to present her pen pal idea to "The Family." After discussion of the proposal, Elena's classroom twin moves that The Family write for pen pals; another sib in her sib group seconds the motion. The motion carries 14-2. The two votes against the motion are cast by Dave Botts and Norman Rogers. Both boys are students who are diagnosed as having special needs and who attend the resource room for literacy help and social skills instruction for one hour each day. Before this year, the boys attended a self-contained class for five hours daily. This year, however, the district has implemented an inclusion program, and the boys' Admission, Review, and Dismissal (ARD) committees wrote Individualized Education Programs (IEPs) that placed them in Mr. Huerta's class. Both boys' IEPs require that they participate in all classroom activities for the time that they are in their inclusion classes, and that individual support be provided as necessary in order to assure them an appropriate education.

56.   What are the likely reasons that Dave and Norman rejected the motion?

(A)   They do not like Elena.

(B)   They do not want to have to do something that requires them to write and they probably don't know what a pen pal is.

(C)   They do not like the class.

(D)   They are prejudiced against people from South America.

57.   Since Dave and Norman both have disabilities and don't want to participate, what should Mr. Huerta do?

(A)   Exempt them from participating in the activity and have them spend pen pal time in the resource room.

(B)   Exempt them from participating in the activity but let them stay in the classroom with the rest of The Family during pen pal time.

(C)   Require them to participate, but encourage them and tell them just to do the best that they can.

(D)   Require them to participate, but provide them with individual assistance if needed.

After the vote, Mr. Huerta assumes leadership of the class. "We are going to be studying South America this semester," he says. "Would you like to go ahead and start our South America unit next week so that we can all learn more about South America before we write?" Mr. Huerta then tells each sib-group to discuss this idea and report back. All of the groups respond positively.

"Fine," he says. "Each sib-group will choose one country in South America. Your group will study your chosen country and become our resident experts on it. You may approach this in any way you like. For example, you may want to tell about folkways of the country. You may want to wear clothing or bring food from the country. Perhaps you'd like to make a papier-mache map of the country or show a short video about it. Or see if you can find a laser disk. There is no right or wrong way to do this. Each person in your group might do a different part, or you might choose to all work on each part together. Your group will then teach a lesson to the rest of the class about your country."

58. Why does Mr. Huerta choose to approach the unit in this way when he could present the material more quickly and complete the unit faster than the students can work in teams?

    (A) He employs a constructivist perspective of learning.

    (B) He knows that the children will enjoy the project more if they work in teams.

    (C) He is constrained by state curriculum, which mandates that students work in groups on social studies assignments.

    (D) He is required by the Individual Education Programs (IEPs) of Dave and Norman to organize his class into cooperative groups since this is the way in which Dave and Norman learn best.

59. What term best describes the type of cooperative grouping activity that Mr. Huerta is using for this unit?

    (A) STAD   (C) Jigsaw

    (B) TGT   (D) Group Investigation

On the first Wednesday of the South America unit, Mr. Huerta loads all the students into a school minivan and drives them to the local library. He asks Ms. Kelly, the librarian, to take eight of the students to the periodical section to teach them how to use the *Readers' Guide to Periodical Literature*. He takes the other eight students and teaches them how to find material in the library. Mr. Huerta and Ms. Kelly then exchange students.

60. Why does Mr. Huerta take the class to the local library?

    (A) He understands the relationship of the school to the larger community in general and to the library in particular. He wants to develop a mutually supportive relationship between his students and the community.

    (B) He cannot provide his students with the variety of materials that they need in order to complete their four units of study. Taking them to the library to secure resources is the only way he can provide his students with a sufficient variety of learning materials.

    (C) He wants to make use of the library in order to forge strong home-school relationships.

    (D) He appreciates student and family diversity and wants to promote it through the use of the local library.

61.   Why does Mr. Huerta ask Ms. Kelly to take half of the students while he takes the other half?

   (A)   He does not know how to use the periodical section of the library as well as the librarian does.

   (B)   He needs to keep closer track of his special needs students than he can do if he has all 16 children at once.

   (C)   He knows how to use a variety of resources and grouping to maximize student learning.

   (D)   He wants to promote outcome-oriented behavior in his students.

At the library, Mr. Huerta shows the students how to find books and non-print materials on their South American countries. He helps his students select 14 books, two laser videodisks, one software game that teaches basic Spanish, and the computer game "Where in the World is Carmen San Diego?" Ms. Kelly helps the students select 17 magazine articles about their South American countries. At the front desk, a bystander criticizes Mr. Huerta's decision to allow the students to check out non-print materials. "You know, young man, it's no wonder that youngsters these days can't read. They ought to be checking out books and magazine articles exclusively. Checking out computer games and videos doesn't teach children how to read. If we don't get back to the basics of reading and writing, we're going to become a third-world country. Teach the children how to read. They have enough time to play at home, when our tax dollars aren't paying for it."

62.   Which of the following statements are true?

   (A)   The bystander is right. Instructional time should be spent on printed material rather than on computer games and video material. Children spend many hours engaged in these activities on their own time. School time must be reserved for books and traditional printed matter.

   (B)   The bystander is wrong. It is important to use a variety of instructional materials to support student learning.

   (C)   The bystander is wrong about getting back to the basics because that approach never worked anyway.

   (D)   The bystander is right. Computers and laser disks are not important technologies for students to master.

On the morning after the library visit, Mr. Huerta asks his students if they would like to invite their family the day they give their presentations. The class discusses this idea at length. Although Marianne Griego is a developmentally advanced, mature child who comes from a supportive, well-educated family, she leads the resistance to inviting family members. Four other girls of varying degrees of maturity join Marianne's camp, but the majority votes to invite their family.

63.   Based on the information provided, what is the most likely reason that Marianne does not want to invite her parents?

    (A)   Marianne is embarrassed because her parents are more educated and dressed better than the parents of many of the other children.

    (B)   Marianne's parents want to move her to a private school. She is afraid that when they find that she is working in a group with students who are less able than her they will pull her out of public school.

    (C)   Marianne has moved into the developmental level in which she is beginning to separate from her family and emotionally move toward her peers. She feels embarrassed when her parents treat her like a child in front of her peers and teachers.

    (D)   Marianne has a crush on Mr. Huerta. She is afraid that her parents will tell him and thereby embarrass her in front of him and her friends.

64.   Why does Mr. Huerta suggest that the students invite their family to watch them present their projects?

    (A)   He wants to promote strong home-school relationships.

    (B)   He knows that the students will be nervous since this is their first class presentation. He wants to make them feel less anxious by having their family there.

    (C)   He understands the interrelationship between the school and the larger community. He wants to create strong school-community bonds.

    (D)   He knows that having their family present will provide a strong motivator for excellence on the part of his students.

On the day of the first class presentation, Mr. Huerta develops the following form to complete on each group:

Did a sib-group demonstrate –

1. Higher level thinking skills? How?
2. Ability to use technology? How?
3. Involvement of all sibs? How?
4. Use of in-school resources? Which?
5. Evidence of problem-solving skills? How?
6. Which of these should I target next time?

---

65. Mr. Huerta develops this form in order to conduct what type of assessment?

    (A) Informal assessment to assess and reform instruction

    (B) Informal assessment to understand individual learners

    (C) Formal assessment to monitor instructional effectiveness

    (D) Formal assessment to understand individual learners

Mr. Huerta asks the school counselor, the resource teacher, the principal and her staff, and Ms. Wilson and her music class to also attend his students' presentations. Unknown to his students, he gives each colleague a question to ask, and requests that each preface the question with a statement somewhat similar to the following: "I would like to know more about what you said regarding _____ in your presentation. This is a topic of interest to me and about which I would like to learn more."

66. What was Mr. Huerta's purpose in using his colleagues in this way?

    (A) He wants to use a variety of instructional strategies in order to help his students become self-directed problem solvers.

    (B) He wants to use the questions as a form of formal assessment.

(C)   He wants his colleagues to become reflective professionals who know how to promote their own intellectual growth.

(D)   He wants his students to see adults model the behavior of being lifelong learners.

The day following the last of the group presentations, Mr. Huerta gives direct instruction to the class in order to fill in any gaps which he thinks are important to the students' understanding of the unit on their South American countries. Then, on the following day, he allows the students to work in their cooperative groups on a review for a test to be given the next day. The test is an objective multiple-choice test covering all four countries. Here is the first page showing the first five of the 25 multiple-choice items on the test.

---

1. **Which country has Bogotá as its capital?**
    a. Colombia   b. Argentina   c. Chile
2. **Which country is most likely to directly affect the climate of the United States?**
    a. Brazil   b. Chile   c. Paraguay
3. **Where would the people be most likely to wear little clothing?**
    a. Southern Colombia   b. Central Chile   c. Southern Argentina
4. **Which country is the largest?**
    a. Colombia   b. Argentina   c. Brazil
5. **Which of these things most closely ties together Brazil and Argentina?**
    a. Religion   b. Language   c. Vegetation

---

67.   Based upon these sample questions, what type of knowledge does the multiple-choice section of the test assess?

(A)   Lower-level thinking only

(B)   Higher-level thinking only

(C)   Both higher- and lower-level thinking

(D)   Informational knowledge only

68.   Which one of the following best describes the purpose of this assessment?

(A)   A summative assessment of individual learners

(B)   A summative assessment of group performance

    (C)   A formative assessment to shape future instruction

    (D)   A formative assessment to understand individual learners

69.   For his next social studies unit, what factors should Mr. Huerta take into consideration in planning instruction for the entire group?

    (A)   State curriculum guidelines, results of the assessment conducted in sample tests, and his proposed learner outcomes

    (B)   State curriculum guidelines, results of the assessment conducted in sample tests, and the IEPs of his students with disabilities

    (C)   Results of the assessment conducted in sample tests and the IEPs of his students with disabilities only

    (D)   The IEPs of his students with disabilities only

Ms. James, a first-year teacher, teaches fourth-grade in a small east Texas town where she has a class of 23 ethnically mixed students. She conducts a daily fifteen-minute spelling lesson consisting of the teacher placing the words on the board, pronouncing them, and then defining each. The students are then given five minutes for "group practice." They read the words, spell the words, and practice repeating the meanings to each other. During the last part of the lesson, Ms. James calls on individual students to spell words from the previous lesson and gives them feedback on their performance. During one of these feedback sessions, Ms. James calls on Amy to define and spell the word "believe." After defining it correctly, Amy reverses the "i" and the "e" when she spells it. Ms. James says, "Amy, what's the matter? I'm surprised at you. This is such a basic word, and we've gone over it so many times."

70.   How should Ms. James have responded?

    (A)   She should be non-judgmental and say, "Amy, you spelled it, 'b-e-l-e-i-v-e' instead of 'b-e-l-i-e-v-e,'" writing the correct spelling on the board. "Remember, 'i' before 'e' except after 'c.'"

    (B)   She should have said, "Amy, you will have to study your spelling words during recess today."

    (C)   She should ask, "Amy, are you sure you can handle these types of words?"

    (D)   She should tell Amy to sit down and practice this type of word for the rest of the lesson.

Mr. Small is an experienced fourth-grade teacher in a large Texas urban school. This year, after doing some research, he decides to reduce the number of language arts quizzes and written exams he prepares for his students. Instead, he develops several performance tasks and projects to assess using rubrics he gives to the students at the beginning of each assignment.

71.   Mr. Small uses performance tasks for assessment because he knows

(A)   he causes too much work for his students by using too many quizzes and written tests.

(B)   performance tasks can be assessed authentically and provide evidence of enduring understanding of the targeted material.

(C)   he is working too hard by grading all the assignments himself.

(D)   performance tasks usually are scored holistically.

Tammy Grimes, a teacher in a large suburban elementary school in southeast Texas, enjoys her first year teaching 25 fourth-grade students in spite of the hard work and newness of the job. One day, Patty, one of Ms. Grimes' students, is acting strangely in class. She seems quieter than usual. Ms. Grimes asks her if she feels ill. Patty replies, "No, Miss Grimes." As Ms. Grimes gets closer to Patty, she notices several bruises on her arms and legs. She says, "Patty, how did you get these bruises on your arms and legs?" Patty responds, "I was out playing on Saturday, and I fell down."

72.   Ms. Grimes should

(A)   phone Patty's parents and ask them what happened to make sure they know about the bruises.

(B)   tell Patty to go and see the nurse as soon as class is over, so that the nurse can check her.

(C)   trust Patty and do nothing, so she will not lose confidence in her teacher.

(D)   personally report this to the school nurse as soon as possible.

Lacie Parks teaches fifth grade in a community of 100,000, which includes the residents of a military base. Whenever a new student enrolls in her class, Ms. Parks encourages the student's family to complete a paper, listing 1) places they have lived about which they would be willing to participate in helping their child to present a program to the class; and 2) other topics or hobbies about which they would be will-ing to present a program to the class. Then, when a new student arrives, Ms. Parks quickly makes a point to incorporate whatever topics this new student's family may present to the curriculum. When Renee Bonaly transfers into the class in January, her mother, Captain Bonaly, lists Turkey as a country in which the family has lived. She agrees to come February 10 and, along with her daughter, present a program on Turkey. "Be sure to talk about the Islamic religion," Ms. Parks tells Captain Bonaly. "And it would be wonderful if you could help Renee prepare a Turkish dish that the students could taste!"

73. What is likely to be the most important consequence of this activity for Renee?

    (A) Her mother will become more involved with the school.

    (B) She will learn more about Turkey.

    (C) She will appreciate the diversity of her classmates.

    (D) She will promote her own social and cognitive growth.

74. Why does Ms. Parks tell Captain Bonaly to make certain to include information about the Islamic religion?

    (A) She knows that a study of comparative religions is a requirement of the fifth-grade curriculum in Texas.

    (B) She wants her students to understand that not all peoples have the same religious beliefs.

    (C) She knows that students are highly motivated to learn about religions.

    (D) She uses good planning in order to create students who are self-directed learners.

On the following Tuesday, Summer Rawlings comes to see Ms. Parks before school. "Ms. Parks, I saw Renee at the skating rink over the weekend. She told me that her mom is going to come to school in a couple of weeks. She said her mom is going to tell us about the Islamic religion. Is that right?" Ms. Parks nods. "Yes, Summer. Isn't that exciting?" "I guess so," says Summer. "Ms. Parks, since Renee's mom is going to tell us about the Islamic religion, can my minister come and have a little prayer service with our class afterwards?"

75. How should Ms. Parks respond?

    (A) She should contact Captain Bonaly immediately. She should apologize for having offered the invitation to speak to the class and withdraw the invitation.

(B)   She should contact Captain Bonaly immediately. She should apologize for having asked Captain Bonaly to speak about the Islamic religion. She should ask Captain Bonaly to present the program about Turkey, but omit information related to the Islamic religion.

(C)   She should say that since Captain Bonaly is going to tell about the Islamic religion, it is only fair that Summer's minister should come to have the prayer service as long as it is a nondenominational service.

(D)   She should explain that while teaching about different religions is appropriate at school, having a minister come to conduct a prayer service is not allowed.

In Ms. Parks' science class, the students are studying sound. Ms. Parks is using level four interactive videodisk technology. Using computers, appropriate software, and the videodisk player, each cooperative group is to create a lesson on a particular facet of sound, such as volume or pitch. Each group will then teach a lesson to the rest of the class.

76.   What is the major benefit of having the students teach a lesson about sound to the rest of the class?

(A)   When students prepare a lesson to teach peers, students learn about learning theories and subsequently become better students.

(B)   When students prepare a lesson to teach peers, students learn to better appreciate the efforts of the classroom teacher.

(C)   When students prepare a lesson to teach to peers, students are highly motivated to learn the subject matter involved.

(D)   When students prepare a lesson to teach peers, students learn organizational skills that generalize to improve academic performance in other areas.

One advantage of using the interactive videodisk technology is that students have the opportunity to actually observe demonstrations of how such phenomenon as sound waves work.

77.   Teaching students by allowing them to see the natural phenomenon of sound waves taking place instead of merely offering complex theoretical descriptions of sound waves is most important for students at what stage of cognitive development?

(A)   Piaget's sensorimotor stage

(B)   Piaget's concrete operational stage

    (C)   Piaget's formal operational stage

    (D)   Piaget's interpersonal concordance stage

Following the successful completion of the sound unit, Ms. Parks wants to learn other ways to use the technology in her school to increase her students' learning and technological literacy.

78.   She can best do this by

    (A)   asking her mentor teacher to help her find out about technologies available in her district.

    (B)   enrolling in a computer-technology course at her local university or community college.

    (C)   reading the computer and technology books and periodicals available in her school library.

    (D)   asking the media center specialist to teach her how to use the available technologies.

As Ms. Parks and her fifth-grade students become more and more technologically literate through their science-technology classes, she asks her students how their class can use the technological skills that they have developed to help the school. Several of the students suggest that the class adopt a class of second-graders to introduce the use of interactive videodisk technology within the context of language literacy. The class enthusiastically votes to undertake this project.

79. What is the most likely outcome of the project?

    (A)   The students will gain an appreciation of their ability to communicate effectively with peers, younger students, and teachers.

    (B)   The students will develop a sense of responsibility toward their school community and a sense of the interrelatedness of the school community.

    (C)   The students will develop an appreciation for the potential of technology as a teaching tool.

    (D)   The students will make a personal commitment to learn more about technology and to increase their technological skill.

Ms. Parks is interested in teaching in an interdisciplinary way. For example, she wants her students to understand how science impacts the community in which they live. The state curriculum guide for her grade focuses on scientific methods, such as data collection, organization, and reporting. She wants her program to stress real-life examples of scientific methods used in local businesses. She decides to contact businesses in the community and arrange for field experiences for her students. First, she wants each business selected to have someone come and talk to her students about science's role in their field. Then she wants to spend several days helping the students do library and computer database research on the topics introduced by the speaker. Next, she wants to use the school science lab to practice using the data collection and other scientific procedures employed by the business. Finally, thus prepared, she wants to take her students to see science in action at the work site.

She lists the community businesses that she has selected on a sheet of butcher paper that she posts on a bulletin board.

Local Businesses That Use Science

Chemistry	Biology	Physics
Soda pop bottling factory	Hospital Medical Lab	Geotech Architecture, Inc.
ABC Concrete Contractors	Ms. Grant's truck farm	Marid's Auto Shop

---

80.   What is most likely to be a benefit of making community businesses a part of Ms. Parks's students' science program?

(A)   The community would become aware of the importance of their involvement in the education of the students.

(B)   The community would increase their understanding of the problems facing today's students.

(C)   The community would increase their understanding of the problems facing today's teachers.

(D)   The students would be more likely to stay in the community upon graduation rather than leave for more lucrative employment in metropolitan areas.

During the period of community-involvement field experiences, Ms. Parks continually directs her students' attention to the fact that science is a way of solving problems. Following the period of field experiences, Ms. Parks asks her students to identify a problem in their school and to devise a scientific way of studying and solving that problem. The students work in groups for two class periods and select the following problem for investigation: It is late spring, and the classroom gets so hot during the afternoon that the majority of the students are uncomfortable. Their research question becomes, "Why is it hotter in our classroom than in the music room, art room, or library? How can we make our classroom cooler?"

81. Of the following choices, what is the most important benefit of allowing the students to select their own problem to investigate, rather than having the teacher assign a problem?

    (A) Students become self-directed problem-solvers who can structure their own learning experiences.

    (B) The teacher can best assess each student's academic and affective needs in a naturalistic setting.

    (C) Students will have the opportunity to work with a wide variety of instructional materials.

    (D) Students will learn to appreciate opposing viewpoints.

82. Which of the following is the most important force at work when students are allowed to select their own problem for investigation?

    (A) Increased student motivation

    (B) Increased student diversity

    (C) Increased structure of student groups

    (D) Increased use of self-assessment

Mr. Simmons, an eighth-grade social studies teacher, teaches a diverse class of 28 students. He plans a history project for his students and their parents or caretakers to reinforce the class's study of America at the turn of the 20th century. Mr. Simmons' plan is to have history students give a "tea party," in which they dress-up in the clothes of the early 20th century and discuss the issues of the day. Students write elaborate invitations to send to their family. The family members sit at tables interspersed among the students' tables, so that they can follow closely what is taking place during the presentation. Each student takes the part of either a famous or a common person from that time period; for example, President McKinley, members of the president's cabinet, social activists, writers, and workers. The participants make presentations to the group and discuss issues in groups at their tables. The event is held in the school cafeteria, where tea, coffee, and cake are served.

During the tea, one of the parents comes up to Mr. Simmons and says, "Hi, Mr. Simmons. I'm Mrs. Johnson, James's mother. Are you modifying the tests for James, as was decided in his Admission, Review, and Dismissal Meeting?" Mr. Simmons replies, "Mrs. Johnson, I can't talk to you about that right now. When would be a good time tomorrow for me to call you to discuss James's IEP?"

83.   Mr. Simmons invites family members to the tea to

    (A)   involve them in their children's education.

    (B)   help the students feel more comfortable during their presentations.

    (C)   help them get to know each other.

    (D)   let them see what an effective teacher looks like.

84.   The most important reason Mr. Simmons declines to talk to Mrs. Johnson about her son's IEP is because

    (A)   discussing the plan would have distracted from the tea.

    (B)   it could violate rules of confidentiality.

    (C)   it might have made James nervous.

    (D)   he wanted to pay attention to what was going on at the tea.

Mr. Joseph is a fifth-grade math and science teacher working in a large suburban middle school. At the beginning of each of his classes, he stands outside of his classroom and greets his students as they walk into his classroom. Mr. Joseph notices students coming into his class who appear upset or angry and show signs of poor self-esteem. Sometimes he overhears his students arguing with other students before class. Often, these students seem to "shut down" during class and do not follow along with the work. He knows this is a problem, but he is not sure what he should do to solve it. He wants to keep these students from getting behind in their learning.

85.   To reduce this problem, Mr. Joseph should

    (A)   inform the school counselor of the problem and send each student with these symptoms to see the counselor as soon as class starts.

    (B)   call the parents of students who seem upset or angry and try to persuade them to fix the problem.

    (C)   send students with these kinds of problems out in the hall so they can get themselves together and learn.

    (D)   create an environment in his classroom where students feel safe and let them know he is aware of their problems and will do all he can to help them learn.

Ms. Wallace, a first-year, sixth-grade teacher in a central Texas town of 80,000 people, teaches a diverse class of 25 students, organized into cooperative groups. Each September, the principal has teacher-parent conferences scheduled for two days. Classes are ended early, and from noon until 3:30 p.m. teachers meet with the parents or caretakers of their students. Ms. Wallace looks forward to these conferences. She prepares by sending reminders home with the students and calls all of the families just prior to the day of the first conference.

86.   In order to further prepare for the conferences, Ms. Wallace could

   (A)   limit preparations and adjust to situations as they arise.

   (B)   arrange the environment to include comfortable seating, eliminate distractions, review each child's folder, gather examples of work, and be familiar with each student's work before the parent or caretaker arrives.

   (C)   prepare "packaged" answers for those parents/caretakers who will want to vent because their children are not doing well in her class.

   (D)   arrange for cookies and tea to be served during each conference and sit behind a desk to emphasize the fact that she is in charge.

87.   For the actual conference Ms. Wallace should

   (A)   welcome the parents or caretakers, establish rapport by listening to what they have to say, and begin and end on a positive note.

   (B)   tape the conference, in case there are any problems later.

   (C)   make sure the student attends the entire conference with his/her parents or caretakers.

   (D)   get straight to the point by telling the parent or caretaker all that is negative about the student so that they can take action to correct the situation.

Ms. Wallace has seven students identified as requiring special education services in her classroom. At the beginning of the year, she receives a packet containing instructions and IEPs for each student. She knows she has to do specific things with the IEPs. They have been sitting in the top drawer of her desk waiting for her action. She decides to go the principal, Ms. Summers, to learn more about these IEPs.

88. What kind of direction should Ms. Summers give Ms. Wallace about the IEPs?

   (A)   She has thirty days to implement the modifications in the IEPs.

(B)   IEPs are optional and can be used only if needed.

(C)   The IEPs must be kept in the classroom at all times.

(D)   IEPs are legal documents, and the modifications must be implemented immediately, or the school district is subject to lawsuit.

While in the meeting with Ms. Summers, Ms. Wallace asks her about what the IEPs should contain.

89.   Ms. Summers tells Ms. Wallace that an IEP contains

(A)   what the teacher should say to the parents or caretakers of a special education child and the amount of time a child will spend in the regular classroom.

(B)   information concerning the identified father of the child, specific child protective services information, and information about the child's level of academic performance.

(C)   information about the child's level of academic performance, his/her age, and the child's religious background.

(D)   information about the child's level of academic performance, the amount of time a child will spend in the regular classroom, and possible technology activities/accommodations for the child.

In an effort to get her students to recognize the roots of the American Revolution, Mrs. Johnson, a first-year teacher, plans a discovery lesson for her seventh-grade social studies class. After her students read an article concerning economic, social, and political conditions in the pre-Revolutionary War colonies, they are placed in groups and instructed to brainstorm possible causes of the war that followed. Mrs. Johnson notices that some group participants are socializing, but apparently are not on-task. She wants to re-direct the off-task behavior, but is unsure how to proceed.

90.   Mrs. Johnson should

(A)   pull all students not on-task aside and assign them extra homework.

(B)   intervene and provide all students not on-task extra help with the activity.

(C)   stop the activity and cover the assignment using another instructional method.

(D)   stop the activity and reform the groups.

ANSWER KEY

1.	(C)	24.	(A)	46.	(C)	68.	(A)
2.	(C)	25.	(B)	47.	(B)	69.	(A)
3.	(A)	26.	(A)	48.	(A)	70.	(A)
4.	(C)	27.	(C)	49.	(D)	71.	(B)
5.	(A)	28.	(D)	50.	(B)	72.	(D)
6.	(C)	29.	(B)	51.	(B)	73.	(A)
7.	(C)	30.	(B)	52.	(A)	74.	(B)
8.	(A)	31.	(D)	53.	(D)	75.	(D)
9.	(C)	32.	(C)	54.	(D)	76.	(C)
10.	(D)	33.	(C)	55.	(C)	77.	(B)
11.	(A)	34.	(C)	56.	(B)	78.	(D)
12.	(B)	35.	(B)	57.	(D)	79.	(B)
13.	(D)	36.	(C)	58.	(A)	80.	(A)
14.	(B)	37.	(B)	59.	(D)	81.	(A)
15.	(C)	38.	(A)	60.	(A)	82.	(A)
16.	(B)	39.	(C)	61.	(C)	83.	(A)
17.	(C)	40.	(B)	62.	(B)	84.	(B)
18.	(B)	41.	(D)	63.	(C)	85.	(D)
19.	(A)	42.	(A)	64.	(A)	86.	(B)
20.	(A)	43.	(C)	65.	(A)	87.	(A)
21.	(A)	44.	(B)	66.	(D)	88.	(D)
22.	(C)	45.	(A)	67.	(C)	89.	(D)
23.	(B)					90.	(B)

To determine in which domains your strengths and weaknesses lie, use the table on page 275.

DETAILED EXPLANATIONS OF ANSWERS

1.   (C)   The correct answer is (C). Teachers apply knowledge of appropriate ways (including electronic communication) to work and communicate effectively with families in various situations. When teachers have a good relationship with parents, students benefit. Initiating contact in a positive way creates a good first impression. (A) is incorrect because getting parents to like the teacher is not an end in itself. (B) is incorrect because it would be somewhat difficult to get a sense of what parents are like over the phone. (D) is incorrect because it is a negative action.
    Competency 011

2.   (C)   The correct answer is (C). Utilizing cooperative learning to teach an understanding of diversity is proven by research to be effective. Students placed in cooperative groups improve their social skills and increase their understanding of different and diverse groups of students. (A) is incorrect. Separating the students prevents them from opening lines of communication with each other, which could increase misunderstanding. (B) is incorrect because free time to socialize that is relatively unsupervised can increase the chance of conflict. (D) is incorrect. Research shows that lecturing on this topic is not as effective as working together in cooperative groups. Lecture does not give students the chance to interact.
    Competency 002

3.   (A)   The correct response is (A). Research demonstrates that creating a learner-friendly classroom is a useful tool to help reach all students in the classroom. This means designing instruction to fit the way students learn. (B) is incorrect because although direct instruction is a useful instructional tool, it is not effective for addressing the issue of diversity in the classroom. (C) is not correct because the response does not address the question. (D) is incorrect because "lecture" is a primary feature of direct instruction, which does not effectively address the diversity issue.
    Competency 002

4.   (C)   The correct response is (C). Performing tasks gives students the opportunity to do hands-on activities that allow them to work together. Placing students in cooperative groups encourages tolerance and understanding between students. (A) is incorrect. Traditional tests and quizzes do little to enable teachers to demonstrate the significance of student diversity for assessment. (B) is incorrect because while

spelling tests can help children to learn, they do not address diversity issues. (D) is incorrect because the answer does not address the question of diversity.

Competency 002

5.   **(A)**   The correct response is (A). At this grade level, awareness of job roles and developing good attitudes about work ethics related to all forms of employment are major goals of the curriculum. To help accomplish these goals, Ms. Felder's invitation to the parents of children in her class to visit and talk about their careers continues her effort to build a close working relationship with the parents. With three or four parents visiting on a given day, she will have the opportunity to talk with each and strengthen her own communication with each child's family. Even if a parent cannot participate in the project, Ms. Felder will have the opportunity to talk with the parent and perhaps encourage the parent to send some information about his or her career to the class. Certainly, some parents will be unable to leave work for the project, others may be apprehensive about talking to the students in the class. Having only a few parents a day will enable Ms. Felder to plan her lesson well so that she can focus upon the role each worker plays in benefiting the students in her class. (B) is incorrect because it focuses on an unimportant aspect of the career awareness unit. (C) is incorrect because it is not based upon the goals of career awareness at this stage of schooling. The teacher is not trying to get 11-year-olds to choose a career; she is just trying to make them aware of the career choices available to them. (D) is incorrect because it places an invalid inference on the parent's being able to speak to the class.

Competency 011

6.   **(C)**   The correct response is (C). Mrs. Kresmeier uses effective communication strategies to teach students and encourages them to interact for the same purposes. Mnemonic devices are apparently a new technique for most of the students; the teacher's own creative spelling clues are often new ones matching the age-level interests and patterns of humor enjoyed by her students. The most success is probably derived from her encouragement to examine the words to find a feature that can be turned into a mnemonic device. (A) is incorrect since there has been no attempt to rule out other techniques of learning to spell. (B) is incorrect because certainly other teachers have also impressed upon the students that spelling is important. The creative methodology is probably the major difference between Mrs. Kresmeier's method and those that students have encountered in the past. (D) is incorrect since no evidence exists to show that Mrs. Kresmeier is especially selective in choosing her spelling lessons.

Competency 007

7.   **(C)**   The correct response is (C). Formative assessment is continuous and intended to serve as a guide to future learning and instruction. Summative evaluation (A) and summative assessment (B) are both used to put a final critique or grade on an activity or assignment with no real link to the future. Peer assessment would require students to critique each other (D).

Competency 010

8.   **(A)**   The correct response is (A). Meeting one-to-one to discuss a student's strengths and weaknesses creates a feeling of trust and confidence between the students and the teacher. Grading papers solely on the content of a conference (B) is not an efficient means of grading. The student/teacher conference should not focus on only one part of the writing process, such as careful editing (C) or pre-writing (D).

Competency 007

9.   **(C)**   The correct response is (C). The role of the resource teacher is to provide individual instruction for students who qualify for services and, through collaborative consultation, work with the classroom teacher to adapt instruction to match student needs. A resource teacher should not be entirely responsible for teaching a learning-disabled student (A) and is also not responsible for tutoring outside of the scheduled class meetings (D). A learning-disabled student should not be totally excused from assignments (B).

Competency 012

10.   **(D)**   The correct answer is (D) because it demonstrates that the teacher understands the learning processes and factors that impact student learning. When earlier learning is repeated, neural pathways become more efficient through mylination, a process of adding a fatty coating to axons. (A) is incorrect because preventing boredom, although important, is not necessarily the result of rap or poetry. (B) is incorrect; although keeping students busy may be valuable for classroom management purposes, it is not directly related to the understanding of student learning processes. Having student presentations does not ensure student learning (C). The learning is dependent on the type of presentation.

Competency 004

11.   **(A)**   The correct answer is (A). This demonstrates the teacher's understanding of the learning process and factors that impact student learning. Singing a new song, visiting a new place, or solving a new problem can stimulate the brain and prime it for learning. There is no research that shows a fast-paced classroom stimulates learning, making (B) incorrect. Varying the daily routine by itself does not stimulate the brain (C). (D) is incorrect because managing students on a field trip is often more difficult than in the classroom.

Competency 004

12.   **(B)**   The correct answer is (B). Teachers need to use productivity tools to communicate information in various formats, including multimedia presentations. (A) is incorrect. Her mastery of the technique is important, but student learning is the most important objective. (C) is incorrect because even though it is an easy technique to master, student learning remains the most important objective in a classroom. (D) is not correct. It is a good idea to develop techniques and plans that can be utilized from year to year, but this is not the most important reason for incorporating PowerPoint in a class.

Competency 009

13. **(D)** The correct answer is (D). Teachers should teach, model, and monitor age-appropriate study skills (e.g., using graphic organizers). Research shows that notes or other information put in mind-mapping form is brain-compatible. (A) is incorrect. Although this may be true, it does not relate to learning processes or factors that impact students' learning. (B) is incorrect because the markers add color to the notes, which enhances learning. (C) is incorrect since Ms. Garcia can use direct instruction at any time. The key here is the mind-mapping exercise.
   Competency 004

14. **(B)** The correct answer is (B). Teachers need to plan instruction according to students' variety of approaches to learning. By varying her instructional methods to include auditory, visual, tactile, and kinesthetic approaches, Ms. Garcia attempts to give all students in her classroom a chance to learn. Just providing variety (A) does not reach all students. (C) is incorrect since the question is about the teacher's understanding of learning processes. (D) is incorrect. Hopefully, Ms. Garcia will not allow herself to become bored. The issue is planning effective and engaging instruction for the students.
   Competency 004

15. **(C)** The correct response is (C). A well-organized classroom with established behavior expectations reduces student stress. (A) is incorrect because inducing stress on the students will certainly be counter-productive. (B) is incorrect because stress from outside sources should be dealt with swiftly. (D) is incorrect because teachers must address the problems experienced by students to reduce stress.
   Competency 005

16. **(B)** The correct response is (B). The variance in fifth-graders' physical size and development has a direct influence on their interests and attitudes, including their willingness to work with others and a possible preference for working alone. Working in small groups enhances student achievement. It is a learned skill that must be practiced. (A) is incorrect because fifth-graders do have the physical and mental maturity to work in small groups. (C) is incorrect because not all fifth-grade students lack the ability for internal control. (D) is incorrect because although Mr. Dobson might need to be more specific in his directions to the students, this is not the main reason for the behavior.
   Competency 001

17. **(C)** The correct response is (C). Students who are naturally shy are usually more willing to participate in small groups rather than in discussions involving the entire class. (A) is incorrect because calling on each student once per day will not necessarily convince shy students to participate in class discussions even if participation grades are assigned. (B) is incorrect because even though students may become less shy as the year progresses, the teacher still has a responsibility to encourage students to participate. (D) is incorrect. Although speaking to each student individually

may help some students participate, it is likely that more students will participate if the procedure outlined in (C) is implemented.

Competency 005

18. **(B)** The correct response is (B). Students who are overly talkative are usually flattered to be asked to take a leadership role. Asking these students to take notes also assigns them a task that allows other students to voice their opinions uninterrupted. (A) is incorrect because calling on these students only once during the class period will most likely frustrate them and create problems. (C) is incorrect because placing overly talkative students in a group by themselves does not teach them to listen to other students' opinions. (D) is incorrect because although overly talkative students usually need attention, they must be helped to recognize that other students also have opinions, even though they may not be assertive in voicing them.

Competency 005

19. **(A)** The correct response is (A). Students who tutor peers or younger students develop their own proficiency as a result of assisting other students. (B) is incorrect because although some students may view teaching as a possible career, this is not the intended purpose of the tutoring. (C) is incorrect because helping first-graders learn addition and subtraction is the goal, not necessarily learning specific tutoring techniques. (D) is incorrect because becoming friends with younger children is not the main goal of the activity.

Competency 006

20. **(A)** The correct response is (A). Planning lessons that enable students to experience a high rate of success during independent practice is directly related to enhanced student achievement and heightened self-esteem. (B) is incorrect because although parents are often happy as a result of a student's academic success, this is the result of structuring lessons so that students will be successful. (C) is incorrect because although students are more likely to complete homework if they are successful during practice, this is only part of the correct answer. (D) is incorrect because students who are successful in independent practice may or may not ask more questions.

Competency 003

21. **(A)** The correct response is (A). It is a general rule that if student questions require lengthy responses then the initial explanation was probably faulty. (B) and (C) are incorrect because there is insufficient information to suggest that students were not paying attention, or that they have below-average listening skills. (D) is incorrect because a teacher should direct all explanations of new information to the level of the students. If students did have poor backgrounds in mathematics, the teacher should take that into account when explaining new information.

Competency 003

22. **(C)** The correct response is (C). This is an example of working with other teachers to plan instruction. (A) is incorrect because it is incomplete. This activity may complete the school year, but it is not necessarily an end-of-the-year project. (B) is incorrect because problem-solving and inquiry teaching are only small components of the activity. (D) is incorrect because asking students to research Galileo and asking the PTA for science equipment are not necessarily related.
   Competency 003

23. **(B)** The correct response is (B). Grouping patterns affect a student's perceptions of self-esteem and competence. Maintaining the same groups throughout the year encourages students in the average group to view themselves as average, students in the above average group to view themselves as above average, and students in the below average to view themselves as below average. (A) is incorrect because most students do not like unpredictable teacher behavior. (C) is incorrect because changes in the classroom often create an atmosphere of mistrust and uneasiness and do not cause students to be more alert. (D) is incorrect because the explanation is incomplete when compared to (B).
   Competency 005

24. **(A)** The correct response is (A). Visiting teachers in other schools will promote collaboration and cooperation. (B) is incorrect because there is no reason to believe that the principal is encouraging these teachers to apply for a job in the middle school. (C) is incorrect because although using computers in math classes may be a topic on which teachers choose to collaborate, (A) is the more complete answer. (D) is incorrect because the middle school math curriculum is not intended for use in the fifth grade.
   Competency 012

25. **(B)** The correct answer is (B). When correctly implementing "cooperative learning," the teacher establishes a classroom climate that promotes learning and emphasizes collaboration and supportive interactions. Research shows the power of cooperative learning. When appropriately practiced, everyone is equally involved. Students learn how to get along with one another and willingly work together. They learn social skills and demonstrate higher academic achievement. (A) is incorrect because this technique is research-based. (C) and (D) are incorrect because cooperative learning does not emphasize or promote competitiveness.
   Competency 005

26. **(A)** The correct response is (A). The teacher knows how to establish a classroom climate that fosters learning, respect for diversity, and awareness of how their actions effect others. Research indicates that cooperative learning improves ethnic relations. The groups that are formed are heterogeneous by ability, gender, and ethnic group. Students work with and get to know each other, thus breaking down ethnic barriers. (B) is incorrect. Punishment does not teach people to get along with one another. (C) is incorrect. Negative sanctions are not going to avoid ethnic

conflict. (D) is incorrect because assemblies and speakers can be food for thought, but are not the solution for preventing ethnic conflict. There is no research to show this has a positive effect.

Competency 005

27.   **(C)**   The correct answer is (C). Teachers schedule activities and manage time in ways that maximize student learning, including coordinating the performance of non-instructional duties (e.g., taking attendance) with instructional duties. Ms. Rodgers starts her class with the students working and takes attendance with little disruption and loss of time. (A) is not correct because preparing for daily activities during class time does not reflect effective use of time. (B) is incorrect because showing how much control of the class she has is not related to time management in the classroom. (D) is incorrect because it is not related to maximizing students' learning.

Competency 006

28.   **(D)**   The correct answer is (D). The teacher understands strategies for creating an organized and productive learning environment. There are excellent technological tools available that enable teachers to keep up with grades. This can reduce grading errors and save time, and the appearance is professional. There is no need for Mr. Brand to impress anyone (A). (B) is incorrect because although others might be impressed, it is not a valid reason. (C) states another wrong reason for putting grades on computer.

Competency 006

29.   **(B)**   The correct answer is (B). When teachers provide an enriched environment in their classroom, they understand learning processes and factors that impact student learning, such as activities that include problem-solving, critical thinking, relevant projects, and complex activities. (A) is incorrect because adequate instruction is a basic element of all classrooms, and thus not an indicator of an enriched classroom. (C) is incorrect because a classroom can be full of posters and pictures and not contain an enriched environment, if problem-solving, critical thinking, relevant projects, and complex activities are not provided. (D) is incorrect because hugging each child daily does not contribute to an enriched classroom.

Competency 004

30.   **(B)**   The correct answer is (B). Teachers need to apply procedures for organizing and managing groups to ensure that students work together cooperatively Cooperative activities need to be timed and monitored in order to be successful. When students form special groups, they need close facilitation. (A) is incorrect because students can be off-task for short periods of time in this form of instruction for socialization purposes. (C) is incorrect since gifted and talented students may or may not take on leadership roles in the groups. It is just as feasible for students with special abilities to be the leaders in many cases. (D) is also incorrect. The teacher

should not plan for a "dog and pony show," but should always plan and implement good, research-based instructional strategies instead.

Competency 006

31.   **(D)**   The correct response is (D) because careful planning includes checking on the availability of resources and materials. (A) is incorrect because Mrs. Doe's reflective thinking is merely a component of communication and may not have contributed to student involvement. (B) is incorrect because personal acquaintances with Native Americans might have helped shape the student's attitude toward that ethnic group but may not have contributed to their involvement in the study. (C) is not correct because students do not have natural abilities to perform research but, instead, must be motivated through careful teacher planning to perform such tasks and must be exposed to the availability of resources and materials relevant to the topics to be studied.

Competency 003

32.   **(C)**   The correct response is (C). Multiple strategies are planned for the motivation of the students, but a result of the strategies is that the unit is integrated into other subjects through library assignments, reading, writing, music, and dance. Using multiple techniques in the classroom motivates each student to participate in a meaningful way; it is only when all students participate that the entire group will be motivated. The attitudes and beliefs developed in the project may become the foundation upon which the students will build their philosophy of American history. (A) is not correct because developing a foundation for teaching American history is not even a long-range goal. (B) and (D) are incorrect because those statements are egocentric to the teacher and have nothing to do with learner-centered instruction.

Competency 008

33.   **(C)**   The correct response is (C). Working collaboratively with other teachers is the avenue through which the talents of the students are identified. (A) is incorrect because it is a false statement since no risks were taken. (B) is incorrect. The board's approval is not required. (D) is not correct because written parental/caretaker permission is not needed for these activities.

Competency 003

34.   **(C)**   The correct response is (C). The external factors of the field trip can create a positive motivation and will allow the students to make the connection between their existing skills and the new skills they are just learning. (A) is not correct since no mention is made of community involvement in the field trip. (B) is not correct because the statement is not relevant. (D) is incorrect because the students do not take responsibility for their own learning. They are given instructions concerning what they are to do before they leave for the field trip.

Competency 001

35. **(B)** The correct response is (B). By allowing the students a choice of field trips, respect is shown to the students. Each student chooses to visit the area to which he/she can relate, helping him/her to better understand the society in which he/she lives. It is but one of an array of strategies used throughout the unit. Fostering learning as a purposeful pursuit is the result of respecting differences and understanding the society in which we live. (A) is not correct because, while the students are to decide where they wish to go, this is not a part of the instructional objective. (C) is incorrect since the decision allowed through this strategy does not limit the view of learning as a purposeful pursuit. (D) is inaccurate because direct instructional strategies are not utilized here.

   Competency 002

36. **(C)** The correct answer is (C). The teacher understands strategies for managing student behavior. Students are much more likely to follow rules and procedures if they help develop them. (A) is incorrect because the teacher wants the students to be a part of the rule-making process. (B) is incorrect since parents will still be notified for repeated violation of rules. (D) is incorrect. There are many other ways to earn the students' respect. This is a classroom management issue.

   Competency 006

37. **(B)** The correct answer is (B). "Think-pair-share" is a cooperative learning structure that increases student participation. It is also a way to slow down the pace of the lesson and extend student thinking. The "buzz groups" strategy is another effective means of increasing student participation. Singling out individual students during class could be embarrassing, making (A) incorrect. (C) is not correct since external rewards might encourage the already active responders to respond more frequently. (D) is not correct because effective strategies can be employed to improve the situation.

   Competency 007

38. **(A)** The correct answer is (A). When giving directions, teachers should always give one direction at a time and wait until each step is completed before moving on to the next direction. (B) is incorrect; this is time that could be used better. Giving effective oral directions will solve the problem. (C) is incorrect because directions need to be given one at a time. External rewards (D) are not going to solve the problem; giving one direction at a time will.

   Competency 007

39. **(C)** The correct answer is (C). Students must make several mental adjustments before responding immediately to the direct-teach method of instruction. They have been listening, processing the information, and making their own mental connections to the material. When the ten-minute direct-teach is over the teacher might ask, "What thoughts or ideas do you have about the lecture? What comments would you like to make?" Next, the teacher could say, "Thank you, now turn to one or two people near you and briefly discuss this issue." After allowing the students to

debate briefly the teacher would say, "Please thank your partners and turn towards me. What comments or questions do you have?" This entire process should take about ninety seconds and gives students a chance to verbally prepare their thoughts in a safe way, before beginning the discussion. (A) is incorrect because generally, these kinds of questions do not give students time to process the information needed to reply and may cause them to freeze up. (B) is incorrect since this kind of challenge is not a motivator. Students do not need this kind of questioning at any stage of development, making (D) incorrect.
> *Competency 008*

40.   **(B)**   The correct answer is (B). Teachers need to know how to give effective directions. The teacher should have said, "Raise your hand if you have been to Promontory Point, Utah." This change in the phrasing of the question eliminates guessing what the teacher wants. Everyone is clear as to what is expected. The other question forces the students to guess at what response the teacher wants, reducing the students' willingness to respond. (A) is incorrect since the question is not straightforward. Students do not know how to respond to the question. (C) is incorrect because this kind of question only causes confusion. (D) is also incorrect. It does focus on the topic, but the issue here is the type of question being asked.
> *Competency 007*

41.   **(D)**   The correct answer is (D). Lessons based on the use of computers and the World Wide Web are most effective in settings in which students are working on small-group projects. Ms. Randal has an ideal situation in her classroom to facilitate these activities. All of them are interactive and allow students to construct their own knowledge. (A) is incorrect; there is much more Ms. Randal can do with the computers and the students in her classroom. There is no set time that students should be on the computer each day (B). Access to controversial information (C) can be controlled; students should be allowed access to the World Wide Web.
> *Competency 009*

42.   **(A)**   The correct answer is (A). No software can legally be copied without obtaining a license. There are high fines, and this behavior sets a bad example for the students. Schools are not exempt from copyright laws (B). (C) is simply not true and thus incorrect. Most software can be copied (D).
> *Competency 009*

43.   **(C)**   The correct response is (C). The teacher is allowed to seek opportunities to grow professionally by using different sources of support and guidance to enhance his/her own professional skills. The ability to reflect and self-evaluate (A) is implied within the correct response (C). (B) is not true. The issue is not assessing the learners (D), but cooperative reflection and self-evaluation.
> *Competency 012*

44.   **(B)**   The correct response is (B). The teacher is familiar with the various

expectations, laws, and guidelines relevant to education. (A) is a subjective statement and not the issue. The statement made by the teacher is that he knows of the expectations of the state for his class each year. (C) is also a subjective statement and is not germane to the question. (D) may or may not be a true statement. It is not relevant to the question.

Competency 013

45.   **(A)**   The correct response is (A). The teacher is to constantly monitor and adjust strategies in response to learner feedback. (B) is an untrue statement. A teacher does not design instruction for different situations, but monitors and adjusts instruction as situations change. (C) is a true statement; a teacher should be able to recognize factors that promote or diminish motivation. This skill comes from monitoring and adjusting instructional strategies. (D) is also true. The teacher becomes aware of external or internal factors through monitoring and adjusting instructional strategies. However, answers (C) and (D) are both included in response (A), making it the more complete and correct answer.

Competency 008

46.   **(C)**   The correct response is (C). The teacher recognizes signs of stress in students (e.g., a drop in grades) and knows how to respond appropriately to help the student. The teacher understands that factors outside the classroom may influence students' perceptions of their own self-worth and potential. (A) is a generic statement and cannot be proven to be right or wrong. Although (B) is true and individualizing may have occurred, the demonstration by Mrs. Sivart shows that modifying the text and tests is necessary. (D) is true, but diversity in the classroom does not cause the text to be written three years above grade level. The statement is not germane to the question.

Competency 005

47.   **(B)**   The correct answer is (B). Cooperative learning and computer workstations allow students to work together. Teachers should know how to use technology in problem-solving and decision-making situations. (A) is incorrect because Mr. Harris is using the computers properly. (C) is incorrect because Mr. Harris is providing the software free of charge. He can still use the school software for other activities. (D) is incorrect because the goal should not be to use this activity to reduce boredom.

Competency 009

48.   **(A)**   The correct answer is (A). The teacher incorporates the effective use of technology to plan, organize, deliver, and evaluate instruction for all students. All of these software packages are available for teachers to use. (B) and (D) are incorrect because these types of software are designed for student use and will not add to the effective time management of the teacher in organizing her class. (C) is incorrect because there is no software that will compose original essays.

Competency 009

49.   **(D)**   The correct answer is (D). Teachers create assessments that are in line with the instructional goals and objectives. The student presentations of essays and posters are authentic assessments. They are the application of a skill within a real-life situation. A portfolio assessment (A) evaluates samples of students' work over time. (B) is wrong because it supports the idea that the total essay written by a student is more than the sum of its parts. (C) is incorrect because a performance assessment has students demonstrate their abilities to perform tasks in a testing situation.
   Competency 010

50.   **(B)**   The correct response is (B). By allowing Elena and the class to feel that the pen pal activity that they initiate results in the class's study of South America, the students will feel ownership of the activity and will therefore be more highly motivated to learn the material. There is no research that suggests that surprise provides strong motivation for students (A). It is unlikely that the class would become so excited about the South American unit that their attention to the current unit of study would suffer (C). In addition, Mr. Huerta plans to allow the class to vote on the pen pal project the next day, and this information would probably be more stimulating to the students than thinking about a social studies unit. If Mr. Huerta feared that the students would be sidetracked by the pen pal information, he would have likely asked Elena to wait until the current unit was completed to ask them to vote on it. While teaching students to self-assess is important, self-assessment is not germane to the question of why Mr. Huerta did not tell Elena about the South American unit (D).
   Competency 008

51.   **(B)**   The correct response is (B). Mr. Huerta's response calls for Elena to self-assess, which in turn promotes active inquiry. This is not a poor strategy. By encouraging her to think about her idea and subsequently suggesting that she take the idea to the group meeting, Mr. Huerta is reinforcing her for bringing the idea to him (A). While asking Elena what she thinks about her idea may help Mr. Huerta assess her cognitive development in a small way, the important factor involved is in teaching her to evaluate her own thinking (C). Assessing the outside influences that affect a child's learning is not relevant to this question (D).
   Competency 007

52.   **(A)**   The correct response is (A). Gagne's concept of scaffolding subsumes choices (B) and (C). By scaffolding her, Mr. Huerta helps Elena to consider all of the alternatives available to her and to make her own decision about the project (B and C). Therefore, (A) is the preferred answer. While pleasant interaction with an adult is considered to be reinforcing to a child, Mr. Huerta's purpose in asking Elena what she should do first would not have been to reinforce her by prolonging a pleasant interaction, but to scaffold her as she plans a course of action (D).
   Competency 008

53.   **(D)**   The correct response is (D). Telling a student that she has expressed a good idea reinforces the idea, which is positively evaluated. The expression of ap-

proval will reinforce the antecedent to the comment. In this case, the antecedent is Elena's suggestion to ask the class to vote on the pen pal idea. Therefore, this is the behavior that is reinforced. While such reinforcement enhances student self-esteem, it is only a by-product of the reinforcement and not the purpose of it in this scenario (A). While the conversational transaction is coming to an end, Mr. Huerta's purpose in saying "Good idea" is not to signal the end of the transaction, but rather to reinforce a behavior (B). Although Elena does self-evaluate in this transaction, this is not the behavior reinforced, since it is not the antecedent to the reinforcing remark (C).

Competency 007

54. **(D)** The correct response is (D). Eating together is an important way of developing social bonds. By eating with his colleagues, Mr. Huerta is promoting collegiality, which in turn creates a positive school culture. It is true that first-year teachers are at increased risk of illness; however, there are a variety of ways of maintaining good nutrition that do not include eating in the cafeteria with one's colleagues (A). Nothing in the scenario suggests that Mr. Huerta is trying to encourage students to eat in the cafeteria (B). The scenario explains that Mr. Huerta is not interested in music; therefore, he would not have eaten lunch in the cafeteria in order to learn about the elements of Latin music (C).

Competency 012

55. **(C)** The correct response is (C). Students who share the African-American or the Hispanic culture tend to be social learners. The family metaphor is a culturally appropriate structure for teaching these learners. Nothing in the scenario suggests that Mr. Huerta does not have a family of his own. If this was the case, it would be irresponsible to organize his classroom for the express purpose of meeting his own emotional needs (A). Although organizing the classroom by the family metaphor is the most culturally appropriate structure for teaching social students, it is not necessarily the best organizational framework to cover the most material in the least amount of time (B). While it is important for students to bring their own experiences into the classroom, it is crucial that the teacher's expectations for learning and for classroom behavior are explicitly outlined; (D) is incorrect.

Competency 002

56. **(B)** The correct response is (B). Students who were previously enrolled in a special class for the majority of the day are likely to want to avoid activities that require them to engage in activities perceived to be difficult, such as writing. In addition, it is unlikely that Dave and Norman know what a pen pal is. Many teachers assume that special students have knowledge of common words that they in fact do not understand. There is no reason to assume that Dave and Norman dislike either Elena or the class in general or are prejudiced against persons from South America (A, C, and D).

Competency 001

57. **(D)** The correct response is (D). Dave and Norman have IEPs that require that they participate in all classroom activities and that individual assistance be provided as necessary. It is required that Mr. Huerta complies with the boys' IEPs. The IEPs do not state that the boys may be exempted from activities in which they do not want to participate (A and B). In addition, sending them to the resource room when the IEP states that they should be in the regular classroom is segregation on the basis of their disabilities (A). While they are to engage in the activity, the IEPs also require that Dave and Norman be given whatever individual support is needed in order to assure that they receive an appropriate education. It is not enough to tell them to do the best that they can and then not provide individual support (D).
> *Competency 013*

58. **(A)** The correct response is (A). The teacher knows that people construct their own knowledge and, therefore, Mr. Huerta employs a constructivist perspective of learning. Having the children develop their own units to teach to the class employs such a perspective. While children typically do enjoy work more when they work in teams, their enjoyment would not be Mr. Huerta's primary motivator for using this particular instructional approach. Their enjoyment should be a result of good instructional strategy, rather than a reason for employing a particular instructional strategy (B). The state curriculum guide does not mandate instructional strategies (C). The IEPs of special students are not mandates governing the organization of mainstream classrooms. The needs of the special students are to be met within the framework of the mainstream classroom (D).
> *Competency 004*

59. **(D)** The correct response is (D). Mr. Huerta's unit of study employs the cooperative learning activity Group Investigation, because each group of students works on one project in any way in which they choose. STAD, or Student Teams Achievement Division (A), does not describe this activity; STAD places heterogeneously grouped students in teams in which they study material together. Each member then competes for her/his team against members of other teams who resemble her/him in ability. TGT, or Teams Games Tournaments (B), describes a cooperative group activity in which groups compete with other groups on mastery of the same material. In Mr. Huerta's activity, teams become resident experts on their country and are not competing with other groups. Jigsaw (C) is an organizational arrangement in which students are arranged in cooperative groups, and then each person in the group is assigned to become an expert on one facet of a unit of study. This person meets with students from other groups who are to become experts on the same facet. Once these students have mastered the material, they report back to the group. The facets of study then fit together like a jigsaw puzzle.
> *Competency 008*

60. **(A)** The correct response is (A). Students should view their school as an integral part of their community, rather than as an isolated entity unto itself. As such, students should view the entire community as both a source of knowledge and

a source of problems to investigate and solve. By taking his students to the library, Mr. Huerta is affirming the relationship between the community and the school in general, and the library and the school in particular. He could have gone to the library himself and borrowed the necessary resources if the school was unable to supply sufficient resources; this would have been faster and less complicated than taking the entire class, so (B) is not a good answer. Taking the students to the library is not likely to forge strong home-school relationships except for the child whose parent is the librarian (C). Using the library does not promote student and family diversity (D).

Competency 012

61.   **(C)**   The correct response is (C). The librarian is a human resource for helping Mr. Huerta's students learn. As a graduate of a teacher education program, Mr. Huerta should know how to use the periodical section of the library (A). While Mr. Huerta needs to keep track of his special students, his primary reason for asking the librarian to help half of the students would be to maximize the learning of all students by using her as a learning resource, rather than to more closely supervise two students (B). While using the librarian as a resource may well promote the children in learning to problem-solve, Mr. Huerta's immediate concern would be in using her as a resource for student learning (D).

Competency 009

62.   **(B)**   The correct response is (B). The bystander is wrong. By using a variety of instructional materials, Mr. Huerta offers students with diverse learning styles and interests more opportunities to learn content matter than by using only one type of instructional material. In addition, students must master new technologies in order to be prepared for adult living, and such technologies are best mastered within the context of academic subjects. While books and traditional printed matter are important learning resources, technologies and appropriate software are also important learning resources that a good teacher will not overlook. (A) is incorrect. New teachers may find that some members of the community will fail to appreciate the role that new technologies play in classroom instruction. Technology and traditional printed matter can be equally important to the learning process. (C) is not correct since the "basic" approach may have worked nicely in a former time even though there are better approaches today. (D) is incorrect because computers and laser disks are important technologies for students to master.

Competency 009

63.   **(C)**   The correct response is (C). As students developmentally enter the adolescent years, they begin to separate from family and move toward peers. Even students who are close to their family suddenly find themselves embarrassed to be seen with them, because they want to be seen by their peers as an adult, rather than a child. Students whose parents or caretakers are less educated and less well-dressed than the family of their peers would be far more likely to be embarrassed to have their family members come to school than a student whose family members, com-

pared to others, are better educated and better dressed (A). Nothing in the scenario suggests that Marianne's parents want to move her to a private school, and nothing suggests that her parents object to her working in a group with children who are less able than she (B). While students frequently have crushes on teachers, nothing in this scenario suggests that this issue is true (D).

    Competency 001

64. **(A)** The correct response is (A). Asking family members to come to school for positive reasons does curry strong home-school relationships. Many parents or caretakers are asked to come to school only when problems arise; this weakens the home-school relationship. Parents need to see the school showcasing their children and valuing their strengths. Having a family member present at a classroom presentation is more likely to increase a student's anxiety rather than to allay it (B). While improving home-school bonds also improves school-community bonds, school-community bonds are secondary to the home-school bonds in this scenario (C). While having their parents or caretakers present should be a strong motivator for students to do good work, it could also increase pressure and stress on the students (D).

    Competency 011

65. **(A)** The correct response is (A). The assessment is informal since it is not standardized and normed. It is designed to shape instruction since Mr. Huerta's last question specifically asks how future instruction should be shaped. The performance of individual learners is not addressed. Only the performance of the group as a whole is assessed (B and D). Formal assessments must be standardized and normed (C and D).

    Competency 010

66. **(D)** The correct response is (D). By seeing adults model the behavior of being active inquirers, the students will learn to value lifelong learning. Having adults ask students questions at their presentation does not facilitate the students in becoming self-directed problem-solvers (A). The questions do not constitute formal assessment of the student's learning outcomes for this project (B). Mr. Huerta is not helping his colleagues to become reflective professionals by having them ask his students questions (C).

    Competency 006

67. **(C)** The correct response is (C). The test assesses both lower- and higher-level thinking. Item 5 requires analytical thinking, a higher-level thinking skill. Items 1 and 4 assess factual knowledge, the lowest level of thinking, and 2 and 3 assess comprehension, also a lower-level thinking skill. Therefore, Mr. Huerta's test assesses both higher- and lower-level thinking skills.

    Competency 010

68. **(A)** The correct response is (A). Summative assessments occur after learning has taken place. Summative assessments are employed to measure the end result

of instruction. They are typically used to grade students. This assessment is taking place after the South American unit of study has been completed. The students will be given grades based upon this assessment. Therefore, it is a summative assessment. The students take the test individually. Therefore, this is a summative assessment of individual learners. Since the group does not complete the assessment, it is not a group assessment (B). In contrast to summative assessments, formative assessments take place during the teaching/learning process while skills are being formed. Formative assessments, such as the one that Mr. Huerta conducted during the group presentations, are designed to help a teacher monitor the teaching process and make changes. Since Mr. Huerta will continue to work on the complex skills assessed in the group presentation, he uses a formative assessment. However, since the class has completed the informational unit on South America, this individual test is a summative assessment of the content matter (C and D).

Competency 010

69. **(A)** The correct response is (A). Mr. Huerta must consider state curriculum guidelines and proposed learner outcomes in developing his next unit of study. He should also take into consideration the findings from the assessment of his previous unit of study. He does not have to take into consideration the IEPs of Dave and Norman in developing his next unit of study (B, C, and D).

Competency 003

70. **(A)** The correct answer is (A). The teacher provides students with high-quality feedback. Feedback should be nonjudgmental; teachers should focus on the errors and how to correct them without any negative comments. (B), (C), and (D) are punitive in nature and unfairly single out Amy for ridicule and embarrassment. Teachers should emphasize effort or lack of it, not lack of ability.

Competency 010

71. **(B)** The correct answer is (B). Teachers demonstrate knowledge of the characteristics, uses, advantages, and limitations of various assessment methods and strategies. When teachers assess performance tasks, they are better able to gage student understanding. (A), (C), and (D) are incorrect. (A) and (C) bear little relationship to seeking useful assessments. (D) is only partially correct since holistic grading is best for scoring essay questions or other types of writing rather than performance tasks.

Competency 010

72. **(D)** The correct answer is (D). The teacher knows the legal requirements related to child abuse for educators. Texas teachers are required to report possible cases of child abuse immediately. Failure to do so can result in criminal charges being filed against the teacher and could lead to further harm to the student. Phoning Patty's parents (A) would probably not determine what happened to the child and could place her in further jeopardy. (B) is incorrect because trusting Patty in this matter is a big mistake. If Patty does not go to the nurse, Ms. Grimes may be subject

to criminal charges. (C) is incorrect. Doing nothing is the worst thing Ms. Grimes can do. She might become subject to criminal charges, and Patty could receive more injuries.

   Competency 013

73.   (A)   The correct response is (A). When Captain Bonaly becomes involved in her child's schooling, Renee derives important benefits. Communication between home and school is enhanced; Renee will have increased pride in her academic achievements. Her self-esteem will grow. Captain Bonaly will have increased interest in Renee's school activities. Although Renee will probably learn more about Turkey, this limited benefit pales in comparison to the benefit of having her mother become involved with her school (B). Although Renee has lived in Turkey, it is more likely that the activity will help her learn to better appreciate the diversity of the Turkish people than to appreciate her own diversity (C). Completing the project will promote Renee's growth, but this benefit is secondary to the benefit of having her mother become involved in her new school (D).

   Competency 011

74.   (B)   The correct response is (B). Fifth-graders are beginning to move from concrete thinking to abstract thinking. Learning that not all peoples have the same religious beliefs is an important diversity notion for new abstract thinkers to understand. A study of comparative religions is not a curricular requirement for Texas fifth-graders (A). While some students may be highly motivated to learn about religions, this interest is not necessarily widespread (C). Using good planning to create self-directed learners is not a reason to ask Captain Bonaly to be sure to tell students about the Islamic religion (D).

   Competency 002

75.   (D)   The correct response is (D). Having Summer's minister come conduct a prayer service is a violation of the separation of church and state (C). In contrast, teaching about different religions does not violate the separation of church and state. Ms. Parks should explain the difference in the two activities to Summer. There is no reason to withdraw the invitation to Captain Bonaly to come speak to the class (A), nor is there a reason to ask Captain Bonaly to omit information about the Islamic religion (B).

   Competency 013

76.   (C)   The correct response is (C). Teaching others requires active learning and promotes greater understanding of material. Although students may teach a unit to their peers, it is highly unlikely that the students will learn about learning theories in the process (A). Although learning to appreciate their teacher's efforts (B) might be a pleasant benefit of teaching a lesson to the class, it is not a major benefit of the activity. Students should learn organizational skills when they prepare a lesson for the class; however, the extent to which this learning would generalize to improve academic performance in other areas (D) is questionable.

   Competency 008

77. **(B)** The correct response is (B). Children operating at the concrete operational stage greatly benefit from direct observation. Infants operate at the sensorimotor stage; observing a demonstration of how sound waves work would be of no use to infants (A). While students operating at the formal operational level would greatly benefit from direct observation of sound waves in addition to complex theoretical descriptions, the direct observation is absolutely essential to the understanding of the concrete thinker (C). There is no Piagetial interpersonal concordance stage. Interpersonal concordance is a stage of moral development described by Lawrence Kohlberg.

Competency 001

78. **(D)** The correct response is (D). The media specialist would be Ms. Park's best resource for learning about the technologies available in her school. The mentor teacher may not know the capabilities of available technologies; in addition, teaching new teachers how to use school technologies is the responsibility of the media specialist, not mentor teachers (A). While Ms. Parks would benefit from enrolling in a computer-technology course at her local university or community college, the courses would not necessarily teach her how to use the technologies available in her school (B). Reading computer and technology books and periodicals available in her school library (C) would also not necessarily teach her how to use her school's available technologies.

Competency 012

79. **(B)** The correct response is (B). By taking responsibility for teaching younger students, Ms. Park's students will develop a sense of responsibility for their school community. While they may communicate effectively with other members of the school community in the course of this project, it is unlikely that the students will learn to appreciate their communication skill (A). The students may develop an appreciation of the potential of technology as a teaching tool, but this outcome is less likely than their development of a sense of responsibility toward their school community (C). Although a few students may make a personal commitment to developing technological skills as a result of teaching younger peers, making a personal commitment as a result of this activity is a morally advanced action that few fifth-graders would be capable of making (D).

Competency 006

80. **(A)** The correct response is (A). By participating in the students' education, the community members will learn that their involvement in the students' education is important. The businesses' involvement is unlikely to help the community to better understand the problems of students (B). Although the community may come to understand something about discipline problems facing teachers as they interact with Ms. Park's students, this is not the most likely benefit of their involvement (C). Having the businesses involved in the students' education in fifth grade is unlikely to persuade them seven years later to remain in the community in lieu of seeking lucrative employment somewhere else (D).

Competency 012

81. **(A)** The correct response is (A). When students are allowed to select their own problems for study, they become self-directed problem-solvers. As such, they have the opportunity to structure their own learning experiences. Assessing students' needs in a naturalistic setting is highly time-consuming and not an important benefit of having students select their own problem to investigate (B). There may or may not be a wide variety of instructional materials available to the students as they engage in studying the temperature problem (C); this is not likely to be a major benefit. Learning to appreciate opposing viewpoints is a competency that would be better addressed in social studies and language arts rather than in an activity that deals with a natural empirical science (D).
Competency 003

82. **(A)** The correct response is (A). People are more highly motivated to solve problems that they choose, rather than problems that are chosen for them. Choosing a problem for investigation does not increase student diversity (B). Problem selection has nothing to do with the structure of student groups (C). Although students may engage in more self-assessment, this is not the most important force at work (D).
Competency 005

83. **(A)** The correct answer is (A). Teachers engage parents, guardians, and other legal caregivers in various aspects of educational life. An event such as the tea is a good way to get family members involved in their children's education. (B) is incorrect because the presence of children's parents does not necessarily make the children more comfortable. This is especially true of eighth-graders. (C) is incorrect. This is about the relationship between home and school, not about the families getting to know each other. (D) is incorrect because having family members come to class for this reason would be self-serving.
Competency 011

84. **(B)** The correct answer is (B). All information regarding special education students is confidential. By discussing James' IEP in public where anyone else might overhear what is being said, Mr. Simmons could be violating rules of confidentiality. Although (A) might be true, the confidentiality issue is of greater importance. This discussion probably would have made James nervous (C), however, the issue here is confidentiality. (D) is incorrect because teachers in this position are always going to be approached by parents. To ignore them for selfish reasons is not advisable.
Competency 013

85. **(D)** The correct response is (D). During late childhood and early adolescence, students often exhibit problems with self-image, physical appearance, eating disorders, feelings of rebelliousness, and other similar problems. Teachers of these students should be aware of these developmental problems and do all they can to minimize them in their classrooms. Providing a safe learning environment and letting students know that the teacher is aware of these issues will assist in keeping

these students on-task. (A) is incorrect. Many students at this age exhibit these kinds of problems. The counselors do not have time to address all of them, and this reaction would cause a major disruption in the learning process. (B) is incorrect. Although parents can sometimes help, this solution should be used only for the most severe cases. (C) is incorrect because calling students' attention to these kinds of problems in this way often only makes the problems worse by isolating and ostracizing individuals.

Competency 001

86. **(B)** The correct response is (B). Teachers conduct effective conferences with parents, guardians, and other legal caregivers. Parents should feel comfortable with their surroundings at a parent-teacher conference. Any advanced planning the teacher can do will relieve some of the stress associated with parent-teacher conferences. By having examples of students' work, teachers can knowledgeably discuss each student. (A) is incorrect; there is very little that teachers should allow to just happen. (C) is incorrect. Teachers should plan for situations whenever possible and not limit preparations to "packaged" answers. However, teachers should point out positive behaviors observed in their students and encourage the parents/caretakers to take an active, positive role in the children's education. (D) is not correct because in a conference, teachers should make sure that both parties are on the same plane to avoid power implications. This is accomplished by sitting side by side.

Competency 011

87. **(A)** The correct answer is (A). Teachers conduct effective conferences with legal caregivers. Ms. Wallace needs to welcome parents and caretakers to her conferences and make them feel comfortable. It is important to listen carefully to what the parents or caretakers say and to end the conference on a positive level. (B) is incorrect. Taping is going make it difficult to establish a good rapport. A tape recorder often makes people uncomfortable. (C) is incorrect. Generally, parent-teacher conferences should allow time for confidential discussion between the teacher and parent. The student may attend the conference a portion of the time. (D) is incorrect because a positive rapport cannot be established by emphasizing the negative. Parents/caretakers will naturally take a defensive posture if the conference has a negative tone.

Competency 011

88. **(D)** The correct answer is (D). The teacher must know the legal and ethical requirements for educators (e.g., those related to special education). Ms. Wallace has made a critical error in not implementing the IEPs immediately. She and the school district can be sued for not implementing special education modifications determined in an ARD meeting. (A) is incorrect because there is no grace period for the implementation of the modifications in IEPs. IEPs are not optional (B). IEPs are confidential (C) and should be kept in a safe place, where other students or anyone else cannot see them.

Competency 013

89.   **(D)**   The correct answer is (D). Teachers know the legal requirements for educators related to special education. IEPs must contain information about the child's current level of academic performance and the amount of time that a child will spend in the regular classroom. An IEP must have an evaluation plan and may include technology modifications such as allowing the student the use of computer software in the classroom for designated activities. (A) is incorrect. The IEP does not contain verbiage to be used in discussions between the teacher and parent. (B) is incorrect because some family information may be protected by court order or by FERPA (Federal Education Right to Privacy Act), and specific CPS investigative information is protected information. (C) is not correct because religion has little or no impact on the special education concerns of a child, except in some health cases; i.e., some religious orders refuse the use of blood transfusions. The religious beliefs of a child and his/her family may be kept confidential.

   Competency 013

90.   **(B)**   The correct response is (B). Students in the seventh grade are character-ized by a wide variety of developmental differences. The discovery assignment's level of difficulty could explain some students not remaining on-task. Once the students who do not understand the discovery method are given extra help, they should suc-ceed. (A) is incorrect. Assigning extra homework would be punitive because students not on-task could be developmentally behind. (C) is incorrect. There is no reason to change the method of instruction because some students are off-task. (D) is incor-rect. Forming new groups would not alter the fact that some students are having difficulties because of developmental differences.

   Competency 001

Practice Test 2: PPR 4–8
Answers, Sorted by Competency

Question	Domain	Compe-tency	Answer	Did You Answer Correctly?	Question	Domain	Compe-tency	Answer	Did You Answer Correctly?
16	I	1	B		40	III	7	B	
34	I	1	C		51	III	7	B	
56	I	1	B		53	III	7	D	
63	I	1	C		32	III	8	C	
77	I	1	B		39	III	8	D	
85	I	1	D		45	III	8	A	
90	I	1	B		50	III	8	B	
2	I	2	C		52	III	8	A	
3	I	2	A		59	III	8	D	
4	I	2	C		76	III	8	C	
35	I	2	B		12	III	9	B	
55	I	2	C		41	III	9	D	
74	I	2	B		42	III	9	A	
20	I	3	A		47	III	9	B	
21	I	3	A		48	III	9	A	
22	I	3	C		61	III	9	C	
31	I	3	D		62	III	9	B	
33	I	3	C		7	III	10	C	
69	I	3	A		49	III	10	D	
81	I	3	A		65	III	10	A	
10	I	4	D		67	III	10	C	
11	I	4	A		68	III	10	C	
13	I	4	D		70	III	10	A	
14	I	4	B		71	III	10	B	
29	I	4	B		1	III	11	C	
58	I	4	A		5	III	11	A	
15	II	5	C		64	III	11	A	
17	II	5	C		73	III	11	A	
18	II	5	B		83	III	11	A	
23	II	5	B		86	III	11	B	
25	II	5	B		87	III	11	A	
26	II	5	A		9	IV	12	C	
46	II	5	C		24	IV	12	A	
82	II	5	A		43	IV	12	C	
19	II	6	A		54	IV	12	D	
27	II	6	C		60	IV	12	A	
28	II	6	D		78	IV	12	D	
30	II	6	B		80	IV	12	A	
36	II	6	C		44	IV	13	B	
66	II	6	D		57	IV	13	D	
79	II	6	B		72	IV	13	D	
6	III	7	C		75	IV	13	D	
8	III	7	A		84	IV	13	B	
37	III	7	B		88	IV	13	D	
38	III	7	A		89	IV	13	D	

TExES

Texas Examinations of Educator Standards

Practice Test 3: PPR 8–12

This test is also on CD-ROM in our special interactive TExES TEST*ware*®. It is highly recommended that you first take this exam on computer. You will then have the additional study features and benefits of enforced timed conditions, individual diagnostic analysis, and instant scoring. See page 3 for guidance on how to get the most out of our TExES book and software.

PRACTICE TEST 3:
TExES PPR 8–12
(Answer sheets begin on page 392.)

TIME: 5 hours
90 questions

> **DIRECTIONS:** Read each stimulus carefully, and answer the questions that follow. Mark your responses on the answer sheet provided.

Ms. Brooks is a secondary special education teacher and reading specialist. Her teaching assignment requires her to provide for the special needs of students who have difficulty reading. At the beginning of the semester, she has her students read together in class. Initially, she reads a paragraph and then asks the students to find answers to the following questions: "Who/What... is the paragraph about?," "What . . . does the paragraph say about the person, event, or action?," "When... did it take place?," "Where... did it occur?," "Why... did it happen?," and "How . . . did it happen?" For several weeks, she leads the class through this protocol. After weeks of practice, students are expected to follow this protocol on their own.

1. Ms. Brooks is attempting to teach her students

    (A) an elaboration strategy to help them monitor their reading comprehension.

    (B) about the importance of topic sentences in paragraphs.

    (C) about the importance of topic sentences and supporting details in paragraphs.

    (D) important decoding skills.

Ms. Brooks wants her students to feel better about themselves and to develop positive attitudes about reading.

2. Therefore, when she gives them a reading assignment she

    (A) sends them to the library and allows each student to select whatever he or she would like to read.

(B)   tends to guide students in their selection of reading materials, pointing out all books on topics about which they have expressed an interest.

(C)   ensures that students read only worthwhile material, such as literary classics.

(D)   makes certain that students do not select books that are written at too high a level, which could result in reading frustration.

Ms. Brooks spends much of her instructional time teaching her students different reading strategies and giving them opportunities to practice these strategies in class.

3.   By teaching her students reading strategies they can use on their own, she is

(A)   creating a quiet classroom environment conducive to the learning of all students.

(B)   able to spend more class time grading students' work.

(C)   stressing to her students the importance of reading as a social activity.

(D)   promoting students' sense of responsibility for their own learning and equipping them to become independent readers.

Ms. Brooks determines that she will base her students' grades on their performance on homework, daily work in class, and informally-constructed (teacher-made) tests. However, the deciding factor as to whether or not students have made sufficient progress to exit her special reading class will be the students' performance on standardized reading tests.

4.   This decision is based on the proposition that

(A)   standardized tests are easier to grade than informally-constructed tests.

(B)   standardized tests are more subjective than informally-constructed tests.

(C)   statistical procedures used in the construction of standardized tests result in greater test validity and reliability as measures of overall reading achievement.

(D)   standardized tests are more economical in terms of both time and money.

◆◆◆◆◆◆◆◆

Mrs. Smith teaches ninth-grade English. Her class is made up of a very diverse group of students, including an almost even distribution of male and female students from various ethnic backgrounds. The students also vary widely in socioeconomic status. When teaching her class, Mrs. Smith uses instructional methods that include note-taking, graphics, hands-on activities, and listening exercises.

5.   By using this variety of activities, Mrs. Smith is demonstrating her awareness that

   (A)   students who have similar learning styles work well together.

   (B)   students represent a wide range of learning styles, including auditory, visual, and tactile.

   (C)   she should speak slowly and clearly as she delivers her lectures.

   (D)   she should seek to learn the most common learning style among her students and deliver her instruction according to the needs of that style.

Mrs. Smith notices that one of her students is unusually quiet and reserved, and her schoolwork has become of lower quality than usual. Mrs. Smith also notices that the student has a number of bruises on her arms and legs. Upon talking to the student, Mrs. Smith learns that the student has recently had several heated arguments with her mother. She also knows from previous parent conferences that the student's mother has an explosive temper and uses threatening language as a disciplinary tactic. Based on this evidence, Mrs. Smith suspects that the student is being abused.

6.   The one thing Mrs. Smith must do is

   (A)   call Child Protective Services to report suspected child abuse.

   (B)   call the child's mother and ask if there is a problem with the student.

   (C)   tell the principal that the child might be abused and thus at risk of failing.

   (D)   ask the child to elaborate about what problems she is having at home.

Mrs. Chavez notices that a few of the students in her class have exchanged heated words as class begins. She also notices during class that the interactions among these students appear strained.

7.   Her best response to these behaviors is to

   (A)   address the issue in front of the entire class, so that all students may hear.

   (B)   ignore the comments completely.

(C)   put the students in groups so that they must learn to work together.

(D)   communicate clear guidelines for behavior in class.

Mr. Clayton has arranged the desks in his high school speech classroom into small clusters of four desks, each facing one another so that students can work in cooperative groups. He has a podium at the front of the room for students to use as they deliver their speeches. He also has a resource wall in the classroom, including computer stations and a large collection of magazines and books that students use to find resources to prepare their speeches.

8.   This classroom arrangement demonstrates Mr. Clayton's awareness of effectively using

(A)   the strengths of individual students.

(B)   the state's curricular guidelines.

(C)   the physical space of the classroom.

(D)   his academic freedom as an educator.

Mrs. Roberts has her students work in cooperative learning groups on a regular basis. When doing so, she walks around the room to check and make sure all group members are on-task and participating in the assignment. In addition, all group members have to keep a log of how everyone participated in the project. All members of the group receive the same grade for the project.

9.   Another technique for effectively managing group activities would be to

(A)   develop task-appropriate activities for group work.

(B)   ensure that students choose their own groups.

(C)   require groups to meet outside of class.

(D)   assign groups so that they are as homogeneous as possible.

Mr. Williams wants to ensure that his first-period English I students learn the correct meanings for the vocabulary words he assigns them each week. These words accompany the required readings he assigns to students; understanding the meanings of all the words is essential for quality reading comprehension. In fact, Mr. Williams feels so strongly about the vocabulary words that he wants students to have class time each week to look up definitions and practice using the new words in a sentence. However, each week he gets so busy with the other activities planned for class that sometimes the students don't have time to look up their vocabulary words in class.

10. The best way for Mr. Williams to alleviate this problem is to

   (A) set a routine in which students use 15 minutes on the same day each week to study vocabulary words.

   (B) rely on the reading assignment to develop students' understanding of the vocabulary words.

   (C) give the students a list of the definitions for all vocabulary words.

   (D) assign one student each week to be responsible for looking up the words for that week.

Mr. Reams's science class of ninth-graders range in abilities from gifted (Joe and Sue) to low-average (Hank). The previous day has been recognized as Earth Day, focusing the students' attention upon the environment. Mr. Reams wants to extend this subject to portray the significant difference one small group can make toward a cleaner environment. The class reviews Earth Day and the need for its existence. Mr. Reams follows by asking: "What are some of the pollution problems present in our own school?" Class responses include a tobacco-polluted environment, the use of non-biodegradable Styrofoam containers, and the lack of recyclable aluminum soft-drink cans. Mr. Reams forms small, heterogeneous groups. Each is charged with determining which offenses can be changed, how they can be changed, the resources needed for the change, and the benefits that can be derived from the change.

While monitoring the groups as they brainstorm, Mr. Reams observes that both Hank and Joe are actively involved in making suggestions, while another group member takes notes. Mr. Reams pauses with each group, listening, reiterating, and encouraging students.

11. Which of the following learning environmental factors is Mr. Reams using for this phase of his class?

   (A) Small groups are unstructured; therefore, he is without a role.

   (B) By making use of small groups, he has assured the students of success in the classroom.

   (C) He is modeling effective communication strategies of reflective listening, simplifying, and restating.

   (D) He has made the instruction relevant to the students' own needs.

12. When Mr. Reams divides the class into small, heterogeneous groups, he is attempting to

(A)   select appropriate materials and resources for particular situations and purposes.

(B)   use observation as an informal assessment.

(C)   use an array of instructional strategies to actively engage students in learning.

(D)   prevent any social/emotional atmosphere from developing in the classroom.

Ideas generated in small groups are written on the chalkboard. Each entry is discussed according to the four criteria given by Mr. Reams. It is concluded that a smoke-free environment requires the legislation of a group with more power than the ninth-grade class. The use of non-biodegradable Styrofoam containers requires research as to why the school chose to use such containers. Research is also required to answer why there has been no aluminum can recycling effort by the school.

Three days later, the class presents their research in class. The school's choice to use non-biodegradable containers was based on economics. Non-biodegradable containers are less expensive and it is felt that most of them will be placed in the trash and hauled to the landfill and, thus, pose no problem. Therefore, the school will continue its present policy. Research also reveals that the school has no recycling program because there has been no interest by the students, faculty, or staff for such a program. Hank volunteers to question the soft-drink man and make a line-graph showing the number of cans delivered weekly to the school. Sue volunteers to contact the Ace Manufacturing Company and prepare a speech to give to the class to explain how the cans are collected and recycled. Other students agree to interview other students, the principal, custodians, and cafeteria workers and write reports summarizing the interviews.

13.   As the students conduct the research and begin the interview process, Mr. Reams feels he has successfully

(A)   developed an interdisciplinary activity for the class.

(B)   designed the instruction taking into account the learners' backgrounds and abilities.

(C)   almost achieved his goals for the class.

(D)   helped the students understand the role of technology as a learning tool.

One week later, the students report that collection of the cans will be accomplished by placing receptacles purchased by the administration in strategic places. The custodians will deliver weekly the cans for recycling, and the school will receive $.023 per pound for them.

14. Mr. Reams is congratulated by the principal for having

    (A) presented a new and unique problem to the students.

    (B) made the instruction relevant to the students' own needs.

    (C) helped the students feel that they are responsible members of a smoothly functioning community.

    (D) used an on-going assessment as an instructional tool.

The class begins to discuss ways that the recycling money could be used. It is concluded that the class will purchase trees to be planted on campus. Mr. Reams asks if the class has considered how to care for the trees. No one has thought of the care that must follow the planting. Hank says that his father is a gardener and knows all about trees. Sue asks if Hank's father could speak to the class about tree care. As the trees are being planted on Arbor Day, Mr. Reams has asked several parents and community members to be present to encourage the class in its endeavor.

15. Mr. Reams has

    (A) gotten the students to work with members of the community.

    (B) conferenced with parents to explain what the students have yet to do.

    (C) taken advantage of community strengths and resources to foster student growth.

    (D) used a variety of strategies to achieve his goal of trees being planted on campus.

Mrs. Webb has a number of students in her tenth-grade history class who are also enrolled in English as a Second Language (ESL) classes. As she analyzes student assignments, she realizes that the lowest scores in the class on any given assignment are consistently found among these students.

16. Mrs. Webb's best reaction to this discovery would be to

    (A) ensure that assignments reflect students' academic abilities and not their limited English proficiency.

    (B) provide assignments to the ESL students that are easier than the assignments given to other students.

    (C) have another student translate everything she says into Spanish.

    (D) refer these students to special education so that they can receive additional help.

Mr. Moore wants his ninth-grade students to configure chemical equations for a number of particular substances on the computer. The equations require that students enter several elements and conduct mathematical computations on them to derive the results.

17.   For this particular assignment, the most appropriate type of software to use would be

  (A)   simulations.

  (B)   word processing.

  (C)   spreadsheets.

  (D)   graphics.

Mr. Moore requires his students to complete an additional project that involves noting the changes in chemical substances over time. Students must develop charts that graphically display the changes. They must also write a two-page report explaining the changes. The assignment is to be completed out of class, and Mr. Moore recommends to all students that they complete their project with the use of a computer.

18.   When making this type of assignment, Mr. Moore should

  (A)   make sure that all students have a computer available to complete their project.

  (B)   allow some students to borrow the school's computer over the weekend so they can finish their project.

  (C)   offer extra points for projects that are completed with the use of a computer.

  (D)   eliminate using computer-assisted assignments since not all students have a computer at home.

Mr. Moore wants his students to learn to acquire information through the use of technology. He demonstrates how to use several chemistry-specific software programs, and he helps students use Web sites with strong scientific information, such as those developed by Encyclopedia Britannica, Scientific American, and the American Medical Association.

19.   Before having students search on their own for Web-based resources, Mr. Moore should also

    (A)   warn students not to use major search engines since they produce too many results for students to choose from.

    (B)   advise students that not all Internet sources are accurate and that they should use discretion in using these sites as resources.

    (C)   require students to obtain parental permission for accessing the Internet.

    (D)   have students practice looking for information on the Internet by looking for the answers to specific questions.

Mr. Moore explains that students are to develop a multimedia presentation to explain a given topic. He develops a grading rubric for the project and goes over the rubric with students when making the assignment. The rubric explains that 70% of the student's grade will be based on the accuracy of the information, its clarity, and its comprehensiveness. The remaining 30% of the grade will be based on the student's actual presentation skills using the multi-media tools, including the presentation design, use of graphics, and other non-content based features.

20.   Mr. Moore develops this rubric and explains it to students in order to

    (A)   encourage students to make their presentations as interactive as possible.

    (B)   clarify any questions students have about their topics for the project.

    (C)   minimize the amount of grading he will have to do.

    (D)   ensure that students focus on the content of their presentation.

The social studies department of an inner city high school wants to change to a more relevant curriculum. The department wants to have units on economics throughout the world instead of only regions of the U.S. Mrs. Dunn is asked to submit a proposal for the new curriculum, related activities, sequencing, themes, and materials. In consultation with the other teachers in the department, a needs assessment of the students is planned.

21.   The group feels that the needs assessment will

    (A)   help students make a connection between their current skills and those that will be new to them.

    (B)   reveal community problems that may affect the students' lives and their performance in school.

(C) foster a view of learning as a purposeful pursuit, promoting a sense of responsibility for one's own learning.

(D) engage students in learning activities and help them to develop the motivation to achieve.

A second needs assessment, which focuses on the students' environment, is prepared. When this assessment is evaluated, it reveals an ethnically diverse community. Student interests and parental expectations vary, different language backgrounds exist, student exceptionalities are common, and academic motivation is low. The question confronting the teachers is how to bridge the gap from where the students are to where they should be.

22. The available choices are

(A) change the textbooks only.

(B) relate the lessons to the students' personal interests.

(C) create a positive environment to minimize the effects of the negative external factors.

(D) help students to learn and to monitor their own performance.

It is decided that students will be administered an interest inventory at the beginning of the semester. The questions will range from "Are you currently working?" "What is your salary?" to "What salary do you want to earn in ten years?" "What skills will you need for earning that salary?" and "How are salaries determined?"

23. The results of the interest inventory will allow Mrs. Dunn to

(A) nurture the students' academic growth through developmentally appropriate instruction.

(B) plan instruction that will enhance their self-esteem.

(C) invite community professionals to speak to the class.

(D) plan instruction that will lead students to ask questions and pursue problems that are meaningful to them.

An activity is planned to follow the interest inventory. Mrs. Dunn contacts various members of the business community. Each agrees to send a representative to the class to discuss those jobs that require the minimally skilled, those that require the semi-skilled, and those requiring the highly skilled. A question-and-answer period would be the format.

24. The above planning reveals that Mrs. Dunn is aware of

(A) problems facing the students and how these problems may affect their learning.

(B) the multiplicity of roles that teachers may be called upon to assume.

(C) being a member of a learning community, knowing how to work effectively with members of the community to solve problems and accomplish educational goals.

(D) the need to establish a relationship of trust with the parents/guardians from diverse backgrounds to develop effective parent-teacher partnerships that foster students' learning.

It is determined that at the end of the question-and-answer period, the students will have an awareness of the correlation between their skills, or lack of skills, and their salaries. A parental guardian support group will be established to enhance the students' motivation to master new skills. Strategies for use at home and in the classroom will be developed.

25. Mrs. Dunn feels that with the aid of family members

(A) she can promote her own professional growth as she works cooperatively with professionals to create a school culture that enhances learning and results in positive change.

(B) she will meet the expectations associated with teaching.

(C) she will foster strong home relationships that support student achievement of desired outcomes.

(D) she will exhibit her understanding of the principles of conducting parent-teacher conferences and working cooperatively with families.

Ms. Spencer teaches ninth-grade chemistry. Before her students begin an experiment, she usually asks them to write down a brief explanation of the experiment's objective. Students also have to explain how the procedures will help accomplish the objective.

26. Which of the following is the greatest benefit of Ms. Spencer's teaching strategy?

(A) It ensures that most of the experiments will yield the desired outcome.

(B) It enables students to work more quickly so that Ms. Spencer can go home earlier.

(C)   It helps students to develop a conceptual framework for the work they are about to do.

(D)   It makes sure that all students start the experiment with an equal chance of success.

Mr. Brown feels very uncomfortable when he has to make decisions about the assessment of students. He has had some difficulty with various types of assessment. He decides it is time to talk to Mr. Croft, the principal.

27.   Which of the following would be the most effective way for Mr. Brown to document his teaching in an authentic setting and to be aware of students' efforts, progress, and achievements in one or more areas?

(A)   Standardized tests   (C)   Observation

(B)   Teacher-made tests   (D)   Portfolio

28.   A common way to assess student learning of specific objectives and specific content is through the use of

(A)   self- and peer-evaluations.   (C)   teacher-made tests.

(B)   portfolios.   (D)   observations.

29.   What type of assessment is rated against the performance of other students and are reported in terms of percentiles, stanines, and scaled scores?

(A)   Portfolios   (C)   Observations

(B)   Teacher-made tests   (D)   Standardized tests

30.   When students are asked to use their knowledge and understanding of specific evaluation criteria, they are using what type of assessment?

(A)   Portfolio   (C)   Self- and peer assessment

(B)   Teacher-made test   (D)   Observation

◆◆◆◆◆◆◆◆

Mr. Jones is asked to improve the remedial reading curriculum for ninth-grade students. He finds that students are continually tested and evaluated on reading, the current objectives are unclear, and the teaching materials are inappropriate. Following a lengthy observation of his colleague Mrs. Ratu's teaching strategies, Mr. Jones concludes that she is teaching basic reading skills in the same manner as lower elementary teachers. Mrs. Ratu uses a controlled vocabulary and simple sentences as teaching materials. The students are being taught to rely heavily upon pictures and illustrations for the story. Most of the material is fictional in genre. Rote is Mrs. Ratu's preference for learning.

31. Mrs. Ratu's method of teaching remedial reading focuses upon

    (A) the level at which the students should learn basic reading skills.

    (B) sound instructional design and evaluation.

    (C) her lack of understanding of the learners in her class.

    (D) her desire to make remedial reading easy for the students.

Mr. Jones analyzes the test results and finds that many of the students in Mrs. Ratu's class have average scores in the areas of art, math, and music. He concludes that, with the exception of reading, most are average-ability students and will be successful when their remediation is complete. Mr. Jones makes several decisions: (1) the students will be evaluated annually with an achievement test; (2) reading materials of interest to teenagers will be substituted for elementary materials; (3) each student will be encouraged to read about the subject of his or her choice; (4) roundtable discussions will be developed for each "favorite subject."

32. Having reviewed the students' scores in other classes, Mr. Jones can justify his decisions with all of the following reasons *except*

    (A) development in one area can foster development in another area.

    (B) using a variety of techniques helps develop intrinsic and extrinsic motivation.

    (C) allowing students to have choices in their learning will create camaraderie.

    (D) roundtable discussions will increase student interactions and help develop oral language skills.

An interest inventory is conducted with the students to identify subjects of interest. New materials are ordered. While students are waiting for the new materials, they are instructed to bring to class materials that deal with the subject of their choice. If there is a deficiency of materials in the home, the student is to go to the library for magazine articles to bring to class. After some debate the students decide that the first roundtable discussion should be about gun control, an issue about which many students have very strong feelings. Ray is the first student to speak. "Guns have always been a right in this country. Now people are trying to take them away, just when people need them more than ever to protect themselves." Stan supports Ray's opinion but for different reasons. He adds, "Yeah, every year around this time my father and I take a hunting trip. If we weren't allowed to have guns, we couldn't go." At this point, Tracy enters the discussion. "It's not hunting guns they want to ban, it's machine guns. Nobody needs a machine gun to go hunting." When Tracy is finished speaking, Brian raises his hand. When he is given permission to speak, he states: "But if you take away those guns, then the only people who would have them would be the gangs and the drug dealers." "And the government," Tracy adds. As the discussion draws to a close, Mr. Jones asks students to continue reading about this subject.

33. The roundtable discussion, as described, demonstrates that

(A) diversity of opinion does not always mean disruption of meaningful classroom activity.

(B) students are easily aroused by emotional issues, diminishing their concentration and learning.

(C) students recognize factors having a negative impact on motivation.

(D) students can respect differences of opinion and establish a learning community.

34. When Mr. Jones institutes the roundtable discussion, he is using a process that will

(A) ensure his control over the discussion.

(B) serve as one form of assessment.

(C) design outcome-oriented learning experiences that foster understanding.

(D) structure the learning environment to maintain a lifelong pursuit of learning.

35. As the facilitator of the roundtable discussion, Mr. Jones is able to

(A) manage the classroom environment as he chooses.

(B) model effective communication strategies, thereby leading the learners into active inquiry.

(C) determine the socioeconomic level of the home.

(D) monitor student input on the subject and assess student learning.

Ms. Johnson is a junior high school teacher who has chosen human diversity as the topic for a lesson unit. She has decided to approach the topic, initially, by asking students to engage in introspective activities. On the day she introduces the topic to the class, she asks her students to make a list of the things they like about themselves. Then, she asks them to write two paragraphs in class, describing their personal strengths in terms of (A) their classroom behavior, and (B) their behavior (or relationships) with others outside class.

36. By asking her students to make a list of the things they like about themselves, Ms. Johnson is

    (A)   giving the class an easy assignment—something that everyone can do.

    (B)   making sure that everyone writes something.

    (C)   stimulating students' thinking and providing the class with a pre-writing activity to help students identify ideas to include in their paragraphs.

    (D)   specifically teaching the students the importance of outlining.

37. By asking her students to think about their own characteristics, Ms. Johnson is promoting her students' cognitive development by helping them to

    (A)   activate prior knowledge as a basis for understanding new concepts.

    (B)   demonstrate their ability to write personal narratives.

    (C)   practice their grammar and sentence structure.

    (D)   develop positive self-esteem by identifying their assets and skills.

38. In asking her students to think about their behavior both in class and outside class, Ms. Johnson is acknowledging that her students

    (A)   are entitled to their own opinions.

    (B)   are affected by multiple factors, some that she can control and others she cannot.

    (C)   are sure to have some strengths they can write about.

    (D)   possess analytic skills to compare and contrast their skills to those of others.

39. When Ms. Johnson asks the students to write about their behavior in class and their behavior (or relationships) outside class, she is taking into consideration a pervasive aspect of human development theory by

    (A)   stressing that, according to Piaget, some students are concrete thinkers in adolescence.

    (B)   noting that, according to Piaget, most adolescents are thinking at the stage of formal operations.

    (C)   observing that students' cognitive functioning is a product of both their innate intellectual characteristics and their environment.

    (D)   pinpointing that adolescent students tend to be socially unaware and cognitively insensitive to the thoughts of others.

40.   The pedagogical rationale for Ms. Johnson's assignments, which require students to write about themselves, is to

    (A)   fulfill her responsibilities as an English teacher.

    (B)   prepare her class to create autobiographies.

    (C)   utilize a Language-Experience-Approach (LEA) for instruction.

    (D)   prepare her class to read biographies about great Americans from diverse cultural backgrounds.

Ms. Johnson collects the students' papers at the end of class.

41.   As she reads the papers, she decides that the best way to give her students meaningful feedback is to

    (A)   not mark errors on the paper so as not to discourage or inhibit their creativity.

    (B)   make at least one positive comment about each paragraph.

    (C)   begin with one or two positive comments about the paper and then suggest how students could improve their writing.

    (D)   give everyone a high grade on the paper for participating in the assignment.

The next lesson in Ms. Johnson's unit on diversity is a library project. In order to determine what kind of project students will undertake, Ms. Johnson leads the class through a brainstorming activity, allowing the students to generate a list of possible topics for the library project.

42.   The choice of brainstorming is to

    (A)   determine the students' interests.

    (B)   give everyone a chance to participate in class.

(C)   demonstrate an approach for solving problems creatively.

(D)   avoid giving everyone in class the same assignment as it might not appeal to every student and might result in some students cheating.

Students decide that they would like to read about an American they admire. Asking the members of the class to work together in pairs, Ms. Johnson requests that the students select and find a magazine article about the person they have chosen. Ms. Johnson decides that the approach that will allow students to be most productive is to pair students with compatible learning preferences and learner characteristics.

43.   In choosing this approach, Ms. Johnson

(A)   avoids having students simply pick someone they like to be their partner.

(B)   takes advantage of the information she has about students' individual learning styles so as to maximize student learning effectiveness and efficiency.

(C)   avoids randomly assigning students to pairs.

(D)   risks having incompatible students working together in pairs.

Before the class goes to the library, Ms. Johnson asks the students to predict how they will find the information they need for the assignment.

44. The instructional purpose for this is to

(A)   engage the students in hypothetical thinking and inductive reasoning.

(B)   save time so that the students will be able to go straight to work once they get to the library.

(C)   help her students acquire good self-management skills.

(D)   assist the librarian by covering important information in class.

Ms. Woods has two years of teaching experience at a large urban high school. This is her first year teaching ninth-grade English at a small, suburban, ethnically mixed high school. She wants to take advantage of the week of faculty meetings before school opens to become better acquainted with the school grounds, faculty, curriculum, and available materials.

45.   How could she best utilize her time?

(A)   Tour the school, noting the teacher's room, materials room, and other important rooms.

(B)   Talk to the principal about what is expected of her.

(C)   Talk with a willing teacher, who has spent several years at the school, about community characteristics and available materials as they apply to the curriculum, and then investigate other resources.

(D)   Obtain a copy of the curriculum to take to the materials room where she can determine what materials are available for classroom use.

Ms. Woods is reviewing her class lists and curriculum guide wondering what to plan for the first day of school.

46.   Taking into account her goal of establishing a risk-free environment that promotes active student learning, Ms. Woods would most likely

(A)   present the class with a yearlong outline of the novels they will be reading and when they will be reading them.

(B)   have the class fill out a questionnaire to ascertain what types of literature they like best.

(C)   have each student introduce him- or herself to the class and suggest a favorite book.

(D)   give pairs of students an interview to conduct with one another, asking about their favorite books and their favorite English class activities.

Three months have passed, and Ms. Woods is preparing to submit grades and conference request forms. Although students have done well in reading, grades in writing are low. Ms. Woods has come to the conclusion that her students are having trouble assessing their own writing strengths and weaknesses.

47.   Which of the following would *not* be an appropriate way of monitoring and improving the students' writing?

(A)   Have students identify, with the help of the teacher, one area of writing in which they feel they need improvement, then focus on this area until their goal has been reached and a new area has been identified.

(B)   Keep all draft and final copies in a portfolio from which the student will pick a piece to discuss with the teacher at a teacher-student conference.

(C)   Read a quality composition written by a class member once a week.

    (D)   Have students submit daily an original work on the topic of their choice that will be graded.

It is time for parent-teacher conferences. Ms. Woods has prepared a discussion checklist so that she is certain to cover all essential topics during the conference.

48.   Which of the following will she need to remember?

    (A)   First address the problems, then address the positive aspects with whatever time is remaining.

    (B)   Begin with a positive note about the student, then ease into concerns about the negative aspects.

    (C)   Present as many technical facts as possible, so that the parents sense an air of confidence and experience in her ability as a teacher.

    (D)   Present the solutions that she, the teacher, feels are most advantageous and continue to support this issue until the parents have agreed to the recommendations.

Ms. Woods attends a seminar on improving the classroom environment. She is looking for more interaction and participation in her classroom. The seminar suggests changing one thing at a time to see what works best.

49.   Which of the following would make the fastest change in class participation?

    (A)   Assigning seats row by row, alternating boys and girls.

    (B)   Having the industrial arts teacher build new bookshelves for the classroom.

    (C)   Presenting a new policy where each person must bring one debatable question to class each day.

    (D)   Arrange the desks into a circle so everyone can see one another.

The seminar stresses a multicultural classroom. Every student should be recognized as having important values and ideas.

50.   What can Ms. Woods include in her syllabus that would both fit her curriculum and celebrate the cultural diversity in her classroom?

    (A)   She can have students choose to read an author from their cultural background or a different one that interests them. Then she can have each student present an informal oral report on the cultural aspects found in the book.

(B)   Each month she can introduce a new author, focusing on non-American authors.

(C)   The students can find their ancestral country on the classroom map during a discussion of a book in which a character takes a journey to this country.

(D)   A day will be declared "Cultural Diversity Day," and the teacher will display novels by authors of varied ethnic backgrounds.

Ms. Woods uses a seminar suggestion, cooperative grouping, to complete a class project.

51.   This project allows students to engage in all of the following activities *except*

(A)   demonstrate leadership ability.

(B)   organize and distribute appropriate work for all members of the group.

(C)   self-evaluate the role each has played in the learning activity.

(D)   work together with students of like abilities.

The cooperative learning exercise is based on an historical novel of the group's choice. They will need to present information to the class about the history that took place in the time around the setting of the novel. Ms. Woods has asked a social studies teacher to demonstrate how the students can prepare a timeline of historical facts simply by reading a novel. In addition, the librarian speaks to the class about the many uses the library serves while students are working on a project such as this.

52.   What was Ms. Woods' instructional objective for organizing these speakers?

(A)   To give herself a free period to prepare other lessons

(B)   To acquaint the students with other faculty members whom they may not have met

(C)   To minimize the amount of time students have to spend on preparing their projects

(D)   To acquaint the students with material at their disposal and how they can access it

Ms. Woods notices the same problem continually surfacing among students working in groups.

53.   Ms. Woods would best handle this situation by

(A)   listening to students as they describe the problem and ways to solve it while she organizes the discussion.

(B)   speaking to the group leaders and telling them to overlook the problem and then continue the activity.

(C)   letting the groups work out the problem at their own pace and in their own way.

(D)   stopping the group work, stating that it is not working out as planned, and that the class is not finishing the project.

In her English class, Mrs. Lorenzo includes literature from authors such as Harriet Beecher Stowe, Toni Morrison, Rudolfo Anaya, Richard Wright, and Zora Neale Hurston.

54.   Her main purpose for including this variety of authors is to ensure that students read texts that

(A)   demonstrate diverse cultures represented in literature.

(B)   exhibit both high and low levels of writing skill.

(C)   reflect current events and political opinion.

(D)   identify well-known literary characters.

Miss Taylor is a first-year American history teacher. Her first assignment for students requires that they write a 10-page research paper about a historical figure of their choice. When announcing the assignment, Miss Taylor explains how students can make the project fun and exciting by learning new information about how the historical figure they choose has had a lasting impact on America. She also gives students specific criteria for writing their papers, reminding students that their papers should have no grammatical or technical errors. Lastly, Miss Taylor asks students to come to her with any questions or concerns they have as they engage in their research and writing for this project.

55.   Based on her behavior, Miss Taylor believes that when making assignments, teachers should

(A)   require students to conduct research and write papers.

(B)   reflect high expectations and enthusiasm for student learning.

(C)   ensure that students work independently.

(D)   engage in activities that the teacher enjoys.

As students turn in their essays, Miss Taylor notices that although most of the student papers are ten pages, some are typed in a large font and thus actually contain much less content than she expected. Other papers include a number of pictures and diagrams, which she did not expect students to include. A few students did not include any resources or references with their paper, although Miss Taylor wanted the papers to be research-based.

56. From this experience Miss Taylor knows that with future assignments she must

 (A) articulate detailed, clear directions for student work.

 (B) be more flexible with her expectations.

 (C) provide a sample product for students to use as a model.

 (D) allow no room for student originality in important work.

The research papers Miss Taylor assigns have to be typed, with double spacing and one inch margins. Italics, underlining, and other formatting techniques are required as necessary. Students also have to make a brief presentation of their research to the class using PowerPoint.

57. By making this requirement, Miss Taylor is demonstrating her ability to

 (A) stir students' interests in history.

 (B) require students to learn new computer techniques.

 (C) increase the amount of research conducted by students.

 (D) integrate technology into her course assignments.

Mrs. Fisher notices that one of her female ninth-grade students, Lisa, always asks to go to the restroom during class, which is immediately following lunch. Lisa typically makes good grades, and she is active in extra-curricular activities. Mrs. Fisher also notices that Lisa has been more conscious of her weight lately, making comments like "if I weren't so fat" and "if I were skinny." Mrs. Fisher suspects that Lisa has an eating disorder and is going to the restroom in order to purge.

58. Based on this suspicion, Mrs. Fisher should

 (A) share her concerns with the school counselor.

 (B) send another student to check on Lisa the next time she is in the restroom.

(C)   call Lisa's parents to express her concerns.

(D)   confront Lisa with her suspicions in order to find out the truth.

Mr. Shahid wants his students to understand how water is formed from the two elements of hydrogen and oxygen. He uses a manipulative of two blue balls labeled hydrogen and one white ball labeled oxygen. The balls are connected with wooden rods. Mr. Shahid briefly uses this manipulative, but then continues his explanation with an in-depth description of how water is formed and the theoretical underpinnings for this scientific discovery.

59.   In order for students to understand this lesson, they must be at Piaget's _____ stage of development.

(A)   concrete operational

(B)   formal operational

(C)   preoperational

(D)   sensorimotor

Mrs. Stretcher is disappointed with her class because they all performed poorly on a test she recently gave them. They had reviewed for the test in great detail, but it is clear to Mrs. Stretcher that the students simply did not study or prepare for the exam. She angrily places samples of student responses on the overhead projector and critiques them. She also calls out the grade each student made to demonstrate how poorly the class performed.

60.   The main problem with such a strategy is that it is

(A)   embarrassing for students because they should have earned better grades.

(B)   illegal to use student work samples without permission.

(C)   inappropriate to be upset by students' choice not to study.

(D)   unethical because it violates student confidentiality of grades.

Mrs. Goodbody has just averaged her students' grades for the midpoint of the grading period. She has five students who are failing and three whose current average is within five points of failing. There are three weeks remaining in the grading period. Mrs. Goodbody would like to schedule a conference with the parents of all the students who are failing, as well as those students who are within five points of failing.

61. Her reason for wanting to visit with parents of students whose averages are passing is to

    (A) use proactive methods to keep parents informed about their child's potential for failure.

    (B) protect her from parent complaints for students who might fail that grading period.

    (C) require that the parent check the student's homework each night.

    (D) improve her rating on the parent communication portion of the Professional Development and Appraisal System (PDAS) evaluation.

In addition to conferencing with parents of students who are failing or near failing, Mrs. Goodbody also makes a quick phone call to the parents of students who are doing well in her class. She leaves a brief message with these parents stating how well their child is doing and how much she appreciates the child's hard work.

62. The main benefit of this type of parent contact is that it

    (A) helps Mrs. Goodbody learn the names of all her students' parents.

    (B) allows Mrs. Goodbody to communicate positive feedback with parents.

    (C) requires parents to be involved with their child's teacher.

    (D) decreases the number of discipline problems in Mrs. Goodbody's class.

Mrs. Goodbody assigns her students a family research project. They are required to interview the oldest family member they know, and they must complete a detailed family tree. Students are asked to look for interesting family stories, whether these stories be happy, sad, or funny. Students will ultimately write their own autobiography to accompany this project.

63. The purpose of this type of assignment is to

    (A) help the teacher understand her students' background.

    (B) engage families in student learning.

    (C) develop a class cultural awareness project.

    (D) increase students' abilities to conduct interviews.

Marcela Dominguez is an eighth-grade mathematics teacher. She plans a unit of geometry incorporating an upcoming school event, "Literature Across the Curriculum." The administration is encouraging the entire school to focus on the importance of reading in all academic fields. Ms. Dominguez has read an excerpt from an article in a recent architecture magazine at the beginning of class everyday this week.

64. What was her main rationale for doing this?

(A) She finds the article to be personally interesting.

(B) By modeling fluent reading skills to the class, she helps build students' reading skills.

(C) It demonstrates how skills learned in mathematics can be applied to real-life situations.

(D) It will serve to motivate students to become architects.

Ms. Fields, a computer teacher, is passing by Ms. Dominguez's classroom while she is teaching her lesson. Later that day, Ms. Fields asks Ms. Dominguez if she would like to teach her class a lesson using the computers in the lab. Ms. Domiguez politely responds that she thinks she will pass on the offer.

65. Which best evaluates Ms. Dominguez's response?

(A) It was correct because classes should always be taught in the same environment since retention occurs best when in a familiar setting.

(B) It was correct because using the room once would provide little knowledge to the students and important instructional time would be lost.

(C) It was incorrect because by utilizing the computers Ms. Dominguez's lesson planning would be eased since one lesson would not have to be planned.

(D) It was incorrect because Ms. Fields can serve as an excellent resource since computer programs can be conducive to understanding and retention of mathematical concepts.

Ms. Dominguez has just returned an exam. One student, Shane, received a failing grade and a note to be signed by his parents. He is afraid of the repercussions he might receive from his father who expects perfection. Shane is not a straight A student, but usually earns B's.

66. What should Ms. Dominguez do about this situation?

(A) Exempt him from having to return a signed exam, assuming that he is certain to improve in the future.

(B) Call his parents personally.

(C)   Write a note explaining the failing grade, but detail as many of the student's positive qualities as are applicable, as well as the confidence the teacher has in the student's future success in the class.

(D)   Counsel Shane on how to better cope with a demanding household.

While on after-school hall duty, Ms. Dominguez notices a boy showing another student a shiny object. On further inspection, she notices that it is a hunting knife.

67.   The best plan of action would be for her to

(A)   tell the boys that they must get on the bus immediately or leave school grounds, ignoring the knife.

(B)   take the knife from the boy and escort him to the principal's office.

(C)   take the knife from the boy with the stipulation that his parents must contact her if he wants it back.

(D)   lecture the boy on the dangers of bringing a knife of any sort to school and warn him not to bring it again on penalty of losing the knife permanently.

One of Ms. Dominguez's students has been repeatedly playing practical jokes during class. She has arranged for a parent-teacher conference.

68.   During the conference, Ms. Dominguez should

(A)   ask the parents to meet with the principal.

(B)   express concern for the class and the student's learning.

(C)   convey to the parents that the student is disruptive and disrespectful.

(D)   set up a discipline plan for the home and school to which the parents must agree before they leave.

Ms. Eagleton is a first-year history teacher in a high school. Her first-period class has 30 students, all of whom are in tenth or eleventh grade. She is preparing a unit on immigration to the United States. Ms. Eagleton plans to include cooperative learning activities that incorporate group goals and require individual accountability.

69. Which of the following results would *not* be expected?

(A)   An increase in competition for grades

(B)   An increase in students' self-esteem

(C)   An increase in the amount of time students spend on academic tasks

(D)   An increase in positive attitudes toward other class members

Soon after beginning the cooperative learning activity, Ms. Eagleton receives a call from a parent who is concerned that the students will not be prepared for the college entrance exams, which must be taken individually.

70.   Which of the following would be the best response for Ms. Eagleton to this concern?

(A)   Explain that students can take a review course for the college entrance exams during their junior year.

(B)   Explain that colleges are more concerned about high school grades than college entrance exam scores.

(C)   Explain that each student is individually responsible for the course content even though the students work cooperatively to learn the information in order to develop skills needed for the exam.

(D)   Explain that learning U.S. history and taking college entrance exams are two very different tasks.

Ms. Eagleton has noticed that during class discussions, many students answer her questions with one or two words or a short phrase. She makes certain that she provides enough time for students to consider the question and prepare an answer before calling on a student to respond.

71.   Which of the following reasons is probably the cause of the students' short answers?

(A)   The students are too intimidated to provide lengthy answers.

(B)   The questions usually require factual recall.

(C)   The students are uncertain about the answer, so they keep their comments short.

(D)   The questions are probably too difficult for these students.

Ms. Eagleton can reserve the use of the computer lab during the first period. As the students complete their research about immigration, she has assigned a 500-word essay, in which they are required to summarize their findings. Ms. Eagleton has asked the students to prepare a handwritten rough draft and make the final copy using the computer. She has encouraged students to make as many changes on their own rough copies as necessary.

72.   Which of the following terms best describes this activity?

   (A)   Revising and editing

   (B)   Peer group work

   (C)   Process-writing

   (D)   Cooperative learning

The students in Ms. Eagleton's first-period class have become interested in the local election for mayor. Both mayoral candidates have proposed a curfew of 10:00 p.m. for Sunday through Thursday and 1:00 a.m. on Friday and Saturday for anyone under the age of 18. The students complain to Ms. Eagleton for several days. She decides to have the students write individual letters expressing their point of view to the mayoral candidates.

73.   What would most likely be the effect of this activity?

   (A)   Promoting a sense of civic responsibility

   (B)   Causing individual students to analyze the pros and cons of the curfew

   (C)   Encouraging student to plan a sidewalk protest of the curfew

   (D)   Causing parents to express concern over a youngster's involvement in politics

Mr. Johnson, a tenth-grade history teacher, decides to include more group work in his class assignments. He assigns students to work in small groups of four on their World War II project. Groups have to research a topic, write a paper, and make a presentation to the class of what they have learned. The presentation must include the use of technology, a handout for all students, and techniques for involving the class in discussion. The groups must also document every member's participation in all parts of the project, and each group will receive a single grade.

74.   Mr. Johnson is using this assignment as a tool to

   (A)   encourage cooperative learning techniques among students so that they know how to work responsibly with peers.

   (B)   help control disciplinary problems with certain students so that students can focus on learning.

   (C)   reduce the amount of individual work that will need to be graded so that he has more time to give constructive feedback.

   (D)   teach students the role of particular heroes in the world wars so that they can learn about these individuals.

Mr. Davis has just completed his first year of teaching. He takes time one afternoon to examine the lesson plans he created for each week of this first year. He carefully analyzes what he did each week and how his style of teaching might have changed. For each major lesson, he reevaluates what was good about the lesson and what he could have done to make the lesson better. He also writes notes about certain experiences that he feels are particularly positive or negative. Overall, he thinks that during this year he has made a few mistakes but has also learned a great deal. He feels that he has improved in his abilities to integrate technology into the curriculum and to deliver effective instruction. Two areas he still wants to improve in are classroom management and innovative evaluation techniques.

75. By engaging in the activity described above, Mr. Davis demonstrates how important it is for teachers to

   (A)   revise all lesson plans each year.

   (B)   engage in self-reflection for personal and professional growth.

   (C)   integrate technology into the curriculum.

   (D)   seek out staff development opportunities.

The school district offers a number of professional development workshops for teachers each year.

76. Based on Mr. Davis's analysis of his first year, he should attend the workshop being offered on

   (A)   encouraging student use of Internet resources.

   (B)   using holistic scoring methods for student products.

   (C)   developing new teaching techniques.

   (D)   recognizing cultural differences in students.

Ms. Scott's senior English class begins each instructional period with five minutes of journal-writing. As students enter the classroom each day, they know to pick up their journal from the fourth-period box on the far wall. A new prompt is written for them on the chalkboard so that when the bell rings they are to immediately begin responding to the prompt.

77. The purpose of this technique is to allow Ms. Scott to

   (A)   finish last-minute preparations for class.

   (B)   have the first few minutes of class to take roll.

(C)   use available class time to maximize learning.

(D)   check her lesson plans for the day's lesson.

Ms. Malony's eighth-grade English class is organized so that students have many grades. The class is exceptionally large, so these two factors together result in a great deal of grading that must be done by Ms. Malony. In order to help with this grading, she has the students check one another's daily work. After having students trade papers, she calls out the correct answers and has students mark each answer correct or incorrect. She then has students pass the papers to her so she can verify and record the grades.

78.   The best way for Ms. Malony to use this method of grading would be to

   (A)   use the practice for major tests only since those are the assignments that should be graded most efficiently.

   (B)   use the practice for all grades since that will give her more time to prepare future lessons rather than spending all her time grading.

   (C)   use the practice only for daily grades that make up a small portion of the students' final grades.

   (D)   use the practice for assignments that are true/false or multiple choice only.

Spring Creek High School requires that all teachers use an electronic gradebook to maintain their class records. Mr. Hernandez doesn't like to use gradebook software, so he keeps all of his grades in a paper gradebook until the final week of the grading period. At the end of the grading period, Mr. Hernandez finds himself rushed to enter all of his grades in the electronic gradebook at the last minute.

79.   The best way to solve this problem is to

   (A)   have one of his most dependable students enter the grades for him.

   (B)   enter all of the grades and then keep up with grade entry on a more regular basis.

   (C)   enter only the major test grades since they are weighted the heaviest.

   (D)   estimate all the grades so that they can be entered more quickly.

Ms. Fuentes asks her English students to write an essay in class in response to a story they have just read and discussed. Students are required to reply to the following prompt: "Analyze the conflict between the two main characters in this story. Develop a solution for this problem, and rewrite the end of the story to reflect your solution."

80. This type of assignment is designed to

    (A)   have students use higher-order thinking skills.

    (B)   ensure that students can recognize the conflict of a story.

    (C)   check for reading comprehension.

    (D)   engage students in creative writing techniques.

Ms. Allen is a first-year English teacher. She is teaching two sections of ninth-grade English and three sections of tenth-grade English. She has implemented a process writing model of instruction. Her students have just completed their first essay of the year. As she is reading the students' papers, she realizes that one ninth-grade student and one tenth-grade student have turned in exactly the same essay.

81. What should she do first?

    (A)   Report the students to the principal

    (B)   Call their parents

    (C)   Talk with each student individually

    (D)   Assign an "F" to each paper

Later, both students admit to Ms. Allen that they wrote the paper together.

82. Which of the following would most likely be the best response for Ms. Allen?

    (A)   Assign both students seven days detention and schedule a conference with their parents

    (B)   Require each student to write an essay on why cheating is negative

    (C)   Require each student to write another paper, but assign each student a zero

    (D)   Require each student to write another paper, but assess a penalty consistent with school policy to each student

Ms. Allen and Mr. Ramirez, a history teacher, plan to teach an integrated unit on the American Revolution. All of Ms. Allen's second-period class is with Mr. Ramirez for sixth period world history. They plan to coordinate their lessons so that the topics the students study in world history are the topics that the students read and write about in English.

83. What will be the most likely consequence of the integrated unit?

    (A)   The students will be totally confused and frustrated by so much emphasis on the same topics.

(B)   The students will remember more about this topic for a longer period of time.

(C)   The students will believe that they are doing one assignment for two teachers.

(D)   Ms. Allen and Mr. Ramirez will appear to be over-teaching the topic because they are both discussing the same topics although they teach in different subject areas.

Mr. Stephens, a science teacher, has the students in Ms. Allen's second-period class during first-period physical science. He tells Ms. Allen and Mr. Ramirez that he would like to collaborate with them by integrating some science topics into their unit on the American Revolution.

84.   This will most likely

(A)   frustrate Ms. Allen and Mr. Ramirez because they will now have to discuss science.

(B)   cause the students to develop a broader view of the Revolutionary time period.

(C)   irritate the school librarian who must put all the books related to the revolution on reserve.

(D)   cause the students to do English homework in science class and science homework in history class.

Mrs. Kopak notices that the boys in her class always seem to call out the answers to the questions. Although girls make up almost half the class, they rarely seem to answer questions introduced in class discussion.

85.   To help remedy this situation, Mrs. Kopak should

(A)   modify her class discussion questions so that they are not as difficult for girls to answer.

(B)   ask the boys to stop responding to discussion questions in class, so that the girls have a chance to respond.

(C)   have students write down their responses, taking up the written responses to check for accuracy.

(D)   call on students for responses in class, making sure she calls on girls as often as boys.

After reviewing his lesson plans for the school year, Mr. Bradshaw ultimately determines that he needs to completely revamp the content he teaches in his class. While he feels he is using sound instructional strategies, he worries that he was not able to teach students all of the major concepts that he should have. Some important concepts had to be omitted due to lack of time, and he would like to ensure that this problem does not happen again.

86. The most important step Mr. Bradshaw should take in beginning this process is to

   (A) ask the principal for permission to begin changing his lessons.

   (B) survey the students to determine what they think should be taught.

   (C) consult the TEKS to ensure that he is including the appropriate content areas.

   (D) model his lessons after another teacher who has a great deal of experience.

An assignment for Mr. Reyes' ninth-grade science class requires students to develop a collection of insects. The assignment calls for students to collect 30 types of insects and turn in their collection neatly stored and labeled. As students turn in their assignments for evaluation, Mr. Reyes notices that although all the collections appear to be neatly stored and labeled, some students have placed their collections in wooden cases with professionally printed labels, while other students have pinned their insects to cardboard and taped handwritten labels to them.

87. From his observations Mr. Reyes can likely infer that

   (A) some students put forth more effort than others with the project.

   (B) his students come from varying socioeconomic backgrounds.

   (C) insect collections are not an effective assignment to use with students.

   (D) he should include a grade for how nicely the collection is presented.

Mr. Reyes is careful as he evaluates the insect collections to use a rubric he created for this project. The rubric contains each assigned point value for the specific criteria of the assignment. He gave students a copy of the rubric at the project's outset, along with a detailed description of procedures for properly completing the project; these procedures included the TEKS related to the project, the purpose of the project, and the criteria for evaluation.

88. By developing and using this rubric, Mr. Reyes is making sure that he

    (A) avoids questions later about his grading procedures.

    (B) helps reduce his grading load as students turn in their projects.

    (C) awards only a set number of As and a set number of Fs.

    (D) aligns his grading standards with goals and objectives.

Mr. Fisher's science class has four students who are receiving special education services. The school counselor provides Mr. Fisher with a copy of modification sheets that specify academic and social modifications for each student in order for that student to experience success in the science classroom.

89. Mr. Fisher's best approach to meeting these students' needs is to

    (A) make modifications only when the students' performance falls below a passing grade.

    (B) make modifications with all assignments and document the students' performance.

    (C) make modifications based on the difficulty of the content being covered.

    (D) make modifications that the parents specifically request.

Mrs. Torres is a proctor for the exit-level Texas Academic Knowledge and Skills (TAKS) test. One student asks Mrs. Torres to help her understand the meaning of a particular question. The student does not ask for the answer of the question, but simply for clarification of what the question means. Mrs. Torres knows that the student's eligibility for graduation depends on the results of this test, as does the school's accountability rating.

90. The appropriate response for Mrs. Torres is to

    (A) help the student understand the meaning of the question.

    (B) offer help with choosing the correct response since the question is confusing.

    (C) clarify the meaning of the question for all students in the room.

    (D) neither clarify the meaning of the question nor offer help with the answer.

ANSWER KEY

1.	(A)	24.	(C)	46.	(D)	68.	(B)
2.	(B)	25.	(C)	47.	(D)	69.	(A)
3.	(D)	26.	(C)	48.	(B)	70.	(C)
4.	(C)	27.	(D)	49.	(D)	71.	(B)
5.	(B)	28.	(C)	50.	(A)	72.	(C)
6.	(A)	29.	(D)	51.	(D)	73.	(A)
7.	(D)	30.	(C)	52.	(D)	74.	(A)
8.	(C)	31.	(C)	53.	(A)	75.	(B)
9.	(A)	32.	(C)	54.	(A)	76.	(B)
10.	(A)	33.	(A)	55.	(B)	77.	(C)
11.	(C)	34.	(C)	56.	(A)	78.	(C)
12.	(C)	35.	(B)	57.	(D)	79.	(B)
13.	(A)	36.	(C)	58.	(A)	80.	(A)
14.	(C)	37.	(A)	59.	(B)	81.	(C)
15.	(C)	38.	(B)	60.	(D)	82.	(D)
16.	(A)	39.	(C)	61.	(A)	83.	(B)
17.	(C)	40.	(C)	62.	(B)	84.	(B)
18.	(A)	41.	(C)	63.	(B)	85.	(D)
19.	(B)	42.	(C)	64.	(C)	86.	(C)
20.	(D)	43.	(B)	65.	(D)	87.	(B)
21.	(A)	44.	(A)	66.	(C)	88.	(D)
22.	(C)	45.	(C)	67.	(B)	89.	(B)
23.	(D)					90.	(D)

To determine in which domains your strengths and weaknesses lie, use the table on page 334.

TExES PPR 8–12

DETAILED EXPLANATIONS OF ANSWERS

1.   **(A)**   The correct response is (A). Ms. Brooks has attempted to increase students' metacognitive awareness and fluency by directly teaching them an elaboration strategy to aid and monitor their reading comprehension. This is a holistic approach to teaching reading versus a specific skill or component approach as referred to in (B), (C), and (D).
   Competency 004

2.   **(B)**   The correct response is (B). As a reading specialist, Ms. Brooks understands the important role that motivation plays in reading comprehension. Students are more likely to both read and understand things that they enjoy and are interested in—not necessarily literary classics (C). Readability studies reveal that students can comprehend material written at very high levels when they are interested in the material (D). The teacher certainly has a responsibility to guide students' choices and not to simply send them to the library (A).
   Competency 008

3.   **(D)**   The correct response is (D). When students are taught effective strategies to use as tools, they can become independent learners. A quiet classroom (A) is not conducive to the learning of all students; research on learning styles indicates that only some students prefer a quiet surrounding when reading or studying. Ms. Brooks must be actively involved in each class, monitoring students' performance, so she does not have any extra time for paperwork in class (B). Although reading can be a social activity, the most important reading done by students (in and out of school) is accomplished as a solitary activity (C).
   Competency 008

4.   **(C)**   The correct response is (C). Statistical procedures used to standardize tests usually result in high validity and reliability; reading tests in particular are usually good measures of overall reading achievement as compared to the more specific and narrow purview of most informally-constructed tests. Standardized tests are not always easier to grade (A), nor are they more subjective (B), nor are they usually more economical (D) than informally-constructed tests.
   Competency 010

5. **(B)** The correct response is (B). Instructional activities for all major topics should include things that address as many varied learning styles as possible. Graphics and note-taking may help visual learners, hands-on activities help tactile learners, and listening exercises help auditory learners. Grouping students with similar learning styles together (A) does not address all students' needs, nor does using the most common learning style for all instruction (D). Speaking slowly and clearly (C) has nothing to do with using strategies that address a variety of student needs.
   Competency 007

6. **(A)** The correct response is (A). All educational professionals, including teachers, are obligated by Texas law to notify Child Protective Services of suspected child abuse. Calling the student's mother about the abuse (B) could have negative repercussions for the student. Telling the principal about the situation (C) might be a good thing to do, but it is secondary to the state law mandating a report to CPS. Asking the child about problems at home (D) is a job for the school counselor more so than the classroom teacher.
   Competency 013

7. **(D)** The correct response is (D). To maintain order and avoid student disruptions in class, the teacher must establish, communicate, and enforce clear behavior expectations to students. (A) might embarrass students, which could have negative repercussions, and it involves correcting the students who have done nothing wrong. (B) does nothing to resolve the problem, rather, there is the possibility that the situation escalates. (C) could also cause the problem to escalate. Only (D) addresses the inappropriate student behaviors in an effective manner.
   Competency 005

8. **(C)** The correct response is (C). Mr. Clayton has arranged his room in order to best serve the needs of his students, thus effectively utilizing the physical classroom space available to him. Nothing in the prompt indicates his use of student strengths (A) or the TEKS, the state curriculum guidelines (B). Use of his academic freedom as a teacher (D) would be better demonstrated by instructional decisions rather than room arrangement; the description given in the prompt clearly demonstrates his use of physical space rather than academic freedom.
   Competency 005

9. **(A)** The correct response is (A). Not all tasks are effective for group work. The teacher should be sure to assign a task in which working cooperatively with a group is the most effective technique for completing it. Allowing students to choose their own groups (B) is probably not an effective technique, as students normally choose to work with their friends and may wind up socializing rather than learning. This could also leave some students without a group. Requiring groups to meet outside of class (C) is not necessary as an effective management tool. Homogeneous groups (D) might be occasionally appropriate, but normally heterogeneity is a better guideline for developing student-cooperative groups.
   Competency 006

10.   (A)   The correct response is (A). Routines and procedures are a key component of an organized and productive environment. If Mr. Williams values the importance of the weekly vocabulary words, then he should make those words part of a regular class routine. For example, he could devote the last 15 minutes of class every Friday to vocabulary words. If the teacher does not value the vocabulary words enough to set aside regular class time for them, then students will fail to recognize the importance of these words as well. Relying on the reading to define the words (B) is ineffective, since the prompt states that the vocabulary words are prerequisite to understanding the reading. Simply giving the students the words and definitions (C) is less effective than having students look up the definitions on their own. Having one student look up all the words each week (D) and share the information with the class is also less effective for all students.
     Competency 006

11.   (C)   The correct response is (C). Mr. Reams is modeling effective communication techniques. (A) is incorrect because the teacher's role changes from structured to unstructured situations, but it is never minimized. (B) is false because no teaching strategy can assure success. (D) is incorrect because at this point, students are not aware of environmental needs. They are still in the brainstorming section of the instruction.
     Competency 007

12.   (C)   The correct response is (C). The instructor is attempting to vary his instructional strategies to keep students involved. (A) is incorrect because no selection of materials and resources has occurred at this point. Small, heterogeneous ability groupings allow for input from all students. (B) is wrong because in a brainstorming situation, assessment is not used and creativity is encouraged. (D) stifles, rather than encourages, the positive social and emotional climate in the classroom that the instructor wishes to create at all times.
     Competency 008

13.   (A)   The correct response is (A). Mr. Reams has developed a successful interdisciplinary activity for his class. (B) is incorrect because Mr. Reams may not be familiar with each learner's individual background and abilities regarding recycling and pollution. (C) is incorrect because he would not yet know the outcome of his efforts. (D) is incorrect because technology as a learning tool has not been introduced at this point.
     Competency 008

14.   (C)   The correct response is (C). The instructor has made the students feel as though they are members of a smoothly functioning community. (A) is a false statement. Environmental pollution is not a new or unique problem. (B) expresses only part of the complete and correct answer. (D) is incorrect because there has been no assessment thus far.
     Competency 006

15.   **(C)**   The correct response is (C). The instructor has taken advantage of community strengths to foster student growth. (A) is incorrect because the teacher is a role model and has worked cooperatively with the community himself. (B) is incorrect because parent-teacher conferences are not necessary for the successful completion of this activity. (D) is incorrect because achieving teacher-determined personal goals indicates student manipulation rather than student problem-solving.
  Competency 012

16.   **(A)**   The correct response is (A). The teacher will have to modify her class to accommodate the needs of all learners, including those who have limited English proficiency. Modifications for these students should include making sure that assignments reflect the students' academic abilities to the greatest extent possible. It does not mean that students should receive easier assignments (B). Translating information for students in ESL classes (C) might be necessary on occasion, but as a general rule this is an ineffective technique; (C) also incorrectly assumes that all ESL students speak Spanish. Students in ESL classes are not eligible for special education services (D) simply because they have trouble with English. To assume that students with limited English proficiency also have learning disabilities is an inappropriate teacher behavior.
  Competency 002

17.   **(C)**   The correct response is (C). Teachers should be able to advise students on the appropriate use of technology. Because this assignment involves rows of numbers and mathematical computations, using a spreadsheet would be the most effective type of program for students to use. Simulations (A), word processing (B), and graphics (D) would be appropriate tools for other types of assignments, but not for this one.
  Competency 009

18.   **(A)**   The correct response is (A). A major consideration in the use of technology among students is that of equity. All students must have access to the technology being required. While integrating the technology into his chemistry assignments is a good idea, Mr. Moore must be sure that all students have appropriate access to the technology required to complete such a project. (B) would be quite problematic and likely against school policy. (C) is not a good choice, since offering bonus points on the basis of using a computer does not address the equity issue around which this problem centers. Eliminating the use of technology (D) is not an appropriate choice since it does not fulfill the TEKS requiring integrated use of technology.
  Competency 009

19.   **(B)**   The correct answer is (B). Mr. Moore should warn students that while the Internet is an excellent source of quick information, it is not governed by tight standards that ensure all the information it offers is accurate. Offering an example of incorrect information found on the Internet might also be helpful. (A) is not a good option because major search engines would actually be an excellent way for

a student to begin his/her search. (C) should be unnecessary because parents have already given consent through the district's acceptable use policy. (D) is of little help for this assignment; Mr. Moore wants students to learn to explore the Internet, so having them look for specific answers offers little or no benefit that the assignment itself would not equally cover.

Competency 009

20. **(D)**   The correct response is (D). Explaining the rubric for grading standards on this project will help students understand the relative importance of the project's content as opposed to design. Sometimes, students become so engrossed in the types of technology they can use for technology-enhanced projects that they forget to focus on the project's content. By using the rubric to explain the grading criteria on the project, Mr. Moore hopes to avoid this problem with his students. Encouraging students to make the project as interactive as possible (A) only increases the chance that they will focus too much on design instead of content. The rubric is designed as a clarification tool (B) but not necessarily for clarifying questions about topics. Also, rubrics do help with grading (C) but they do not minimize the amount of grading, nor is grading the purpose for introducing the rubric to students at this point.

Competency 009

21. **(A)**   The correct response is (A). A needs assessment will help students make the connection between their current skills and those that will be new to them. (B) is wrong because a needs assessment focuses on the skills a student currently possesses. (C) is incorrect because the needs assessment is designed to determine what is required to be taught and included in the curriculum. (D) is a false statement. A needs assessment is not designed to motivate students.

Competency 004

22. **(C)**   The correct response is (C). A positive environment must be created to minimize the effects of negative external factors. (A) is inappropriate because changing the textbooks but allowing the environment to remain the same only results in maintaining the status quo. (B) is incorrect because relating the students' personal interest to the new material is only a part of creating a positive environment. (D) is wrong because again it is only a small part of maximizing the effects of a positive learning environment.

Competency 005

23. **(D)**   The correct response is (D). The instructor should plan instruction that will lead students to ask questions and pursue problems that are meaningful to them. (A) is part of (D). Meaningful instruction will nurture student growth and the instruction will be developmentally appropriate. (B) is incorrect because it is incomplete. The type of instruction indicated in (D) would enhance students' self-esteem. (C) is incorrect because meaningful instruction may or may not include an invitation to community professionals to speak in class.

Competency 002

24. **(C)** The correct answer is (C). The instructor knows how to work effectively with all members of the community to solve problems and accomplish educational goals. (A) is encompassed in (C). Working with community leaders, identifying community problems and, if possible, solving those problems with the students will motivate students and affect their learning. A teacher's role does change from situation to situation (B), but in this question, it is not the most important point and therefore not the best answer. (D) is incorrect because before any community change can occur, there must be a bond of trust between the parent and the teacher.
    Competency 012

25. **(C)** The correct response is (C). The teacher would be fostering strong home relationships that support student achievement of desired outcomes. (A) is the result of (C); as the teacher interacts with professionals in the community, her own professional growth will be promoted. (B) is also the result of (C); all teachers are expected to interact with the community and work to develop strong home relationships that will support student achievement of desired outcomes. (D) is incomplete since strong home relationships are developed through the principles of conferences, trust, and cooperation.
    Competency 011

26. **(C)** The correct response is (C). Writing down the objectives and procedures of an experiment helps students develop a conceptual framework for the work they are about to do. By assigning this work, Ms. Spencer actively engages all of her students in the learning process. This strategy does not ensure that all experiments yield the desired outcome (A). Ms. Spencer should make sure that every student has enough time to finish the experiment; looking out for her own advantage should not be her objective (B). Though this strategy might help students better understand what they are supposed to do and be successful, this is not the most important reason for this teaching strategy (D).
    Competency 008

27. **(D)** The correct response is (D). This question relates to enabling teachers to document their teaching and to be aware of students' efforts, progress, and achievements. A portfolio is a purposeful collection of work that exhibits efforts, progress, and achievement of students and enables teachers to document teaching in an authentic setting. Standardized tests are commercially developed and are used for specific events; (A) is incorrect. A teacher-made test is used to evaluate specific objectives of the course; (B) is not the best choice. Observation is used to explain what students do in classrooms and to indicate some of their capabilities; therefore, (C) is not correct.
    Competency 010

28. **(C)** The correct response is (C). This question relates to evaluating specific objectives and content. Teacher-made tests are designed to evaluate the specific objectives and specific content of a course. (A) is incorrect because self- and peer-

evaluation utilizes a student's knowledge according to evaluation criteria that are understood by the student. A portfolio is a purposeful collection of work that exhibits effort, progress, and achievement of students and enables teachers to document teaching in an authentic setting; thus, (B) is incorrect. Observation is used to explain what students do in classrooms and to indicate some of their capabilities; (D) is not correct for this situation.

Competency 010

29.   (D)   The correct response is (D). This question refers to student performance in terms of percentiles, stanines, and scaled scores. Standardized tests rate student performance against the performance of other students and report the scores in terms of percentile, stanines, and scaled scores. A portfolio is a collection of student effort, progress, and achievement; thus, (A) is incorrect. Teacher-made tests evaluate specific objectives and content; therefore, (B) is incorrect. Students' capabilities and what they do in classrooms are evaluated through observation, making (C) incorrect.

Competency 010

30.   (C)   The correct response is (C). This question relates to a form of assessment that utilizes students' knowledge and understanding of specific criteria. Self- and peer-assessment requires that the student be aware of and understand the evaluation criteria. A collection of work that exhibits students' success and enables teachers to document teaching is a portfolio; thus, (A) is incorrect. A teacher-made test evaluates specific objectives and content; therefore, (B) is not correct. Observation is used to indicate capabilities and actions of students; so, (D) is not correct.

Competency 010

31.   (C)   The correct response is (C). Mrs. Ratu's lack of competency is exhibited through her lack of understanding her students. The effect of Mrs. Ratu's minimal competency results in her teaching on the elementary level (A). If Mrs. Ratu understood the learners, she would have recognized her lack of competency in both teaching and evaluating of the students. Mrs. Ratu's desire to make remedial reading easy for the students by teaching them on a lower elementary level (D) again exhibits lack of competency.

Competency 001

32.   (C)   The correct answer is (C). Camaraderie cannot be fostered by choice alone. However, roundtable discussions will increase student interaction and help each student develop oral language skills (D). A variety of techniques can promote student motivation (B) and the finding that students have average scores in many areas emphasizes the importance of development in one area transferring to another (A).

Competency 008

33.   **(A)**   The correct answer is (A). Students are aroused by emotional issues, but as described, this roundtable discussion does not distract them from reading and learning (B). The example does not describe a negative impact on motivation (C), nor does it provide enough proof of a learning community being established (D).
    Competency 002

34.   **(C)**   The correct response is (C). Mr. Jones has planned the discussion as an outcome-oriented learning experience. In the discussions, Mr. Jones is the facilitator and should not control the discussion (A). The activity does not function as an assessment tool (B), since Mr. Jones has already made the decision to evaluate the students yearly by an achievement test. Maintaining a lifelong pursuit of learning is the ultimate goal for all education; however, the immediate and more pressing goal is to improve the reading skills of the concerned students (D).
    Competency 003·

35.   **(B)**   The correct response is (B). As a facilitator, Mr. Jones listens and monitors the discussion. His duty as facilitator is to model effective communication strategies, to monitor the students' input, and to encourage all students to participate. Mr. Jones will be able to manage the classroom environment (A), but that is a part of shaping the learners through effective communication strategies. The amount of information each student has collected can be indicative of the homes' socioeconomic level (C), but this statement is not an absolute. The student could have forgotten to look for material at home. Mr. Jones is able to monitor student input, but the roundtable discussion should not be used as an assessment tool (D).
    Competency 007

36.   **(C)**   The correct response is (C). A pre-writing activity stimulates students' thinking and helps them with the writing process. (A) and (B) are too general and superficial. (D) refers specifically to outlining, something not mentioned in the context of the problem set.
    Competency 004

37.   **(A)**   The correct response is (A). Introspective activities help students to connect new information to previously learned information, an important cognitive process. (B) refers to personal narrative, whereas the writing assignment is a personal description. (C) is inappropriate at this point in the learning process. (D) is an effective goal for instruction, but the question specifically asks about cognitive development.
    Competency 004

38.   **(B)**   The correct response is (B). Students are affected by multiple factors, including environmental factors both inside and outside class. (A), (C), and (D) are too general and broad. (A) is a broad generalization that has no direct application to Ms. Johnson's request that students think about their own behavior inside and outside class. (C) is superficial and assumes that students can easily identify their

own strengths when research shows that students (and adults) often have difficulty identifying their specific strengths and assets. (D) is incorrect because of the same rationale.
> *Competency 004*

39. **(C)** The correct response is (C). One of the central tenets of human development is the constant interaction and precarious balance of nurture and nature. (A) and (B) specifically refer to Piaget's theory of cognitive development, a particular subset of human development theories. (D) is a false statement; theories of human development support the notion that adolescence is a time of increased social cognition and the awareness of the thoughts of others. (Hence, the adolescent phenomena of "personal fable" and "imaginary audience" as identified by Elkind.)
> *Competency 001*

40. **(C)** The correct response is (C). The Language-Experience-Approach (LEA) is a proven pedagogy for increasing students' reading and writing proficiency and their overall language competency. It requires that students write about what they know. (A), (B), and (D) are irrelevant. (A) superficially addresses that Ms. Johnson is an English teacher; (B) refers to autobiographies, something that is not mentioned in the preceding information, and (D) foreshadows a library project that has not yet been introduced into the context of these questions.
> *Competency 005*

41. **(C)** The correct response is (C). A basic principle in providing students with appropriate feedback is to first note the students' strengths (or positive aspects of the students' work and/or performance) and then point out specific ways they can improve their work and/or performance. Therefore, the best approach for a teacher to take when providing students with feedback on written work is to first note the good things about a student's writing and then suggest ways to improve. (A) and (B) are in essence the same; both choices indicate that only students' strengths would be acknowledged, omitting the important aspect of addressing ways students can improve. Neither action would enhance students' cognitive skills or their metacognitive skills (or self-awareness). (D) is unacceptable because it denigrates the teacher's responsibility to evaluate students' performance on the basis of individual merit against the standards established by particular disciplines.
> *Competency 004*

42. **(C)** The correct response is (C). Although brainstorming activities benefit learning by determining students' interests (A) and giving everyone a chance to participate (B), these aspects are merely benefits, not the real purpose of the activity. (D) is incorrect because it is irrelevant to the situation described; brainstorming, as an activity, has no direct relationship to honesty or cheating.
> *Competency 004*

43.   **(B)**   The correct response is (B). Although (A), (C), and (D) are possible choices, the best answer to the question is (B). (A), (C), and (D) basically restate the same idea: the teacher forms the groups instead of the students. This is specified in the context of the question. The only option that gives a rationale for the teacher choosing her action is (B).
      Competency 002

44.   **(A)**   The correct response is (A). Only (A) recognizes the cognitive principle underlying the teacher's assignment. (B) and (D) are essentially the same; although the assignment may result in these time-saving features, they are not the instructional principle guiding the teacher's practice. (C) is irrelevant; asking students to hypothesize is not directly related to inculcating self-management skills in learners.
      Competency 001

45.   **(C)**   The correct answer is (C). The most efficient way to gain information about a new setting is to speak with someone who is familiar with the circumstances. Orienting oneself with the physical layout (A) is helpful, but cannot tell the teacher about the student population or materials. Although communication with the principal (B) is always a good idea, the principal usually will have little time to have an in-depth discussion and will not be able to tell specifically what materials are available. Eventually, Ms. Woods will need to match curriculum guidelines to the material available (D), but sitting in the materials room will not introduce her to staff and student characteristics.
      Competency 012

46.   **(D)**   The correct response is (D). By having students interact with each other on the first day, the nervousness is broken, and Ms. Woods will have quality student profiles to use when preparing suitable lessons. Handing out an outline (A), which will probably change greatly by year's end, does nothing to introduce the students to each other or the teacher to the class. A questionnaire of favorite literature (B) will help the teacher prepare topics around student interests, but the individual questionnaire does nothing to involve students in familiarizing themselves with one another. Individually introducing oneself by name and his/her favorite book (C) puts the students on the spot, which may make a new high school student nervous. In addition, one book will not help the teacher develop a good student profile.
      Competency 005

47.   **(D)**   The correct response is (D). Forcing a student to write every night, particularly for a grade, will do little to create quality work. The students have set goals toward which they will work bit by bit until they reach them (A). The teacher and student have an opportunity to discuss good and bad points of the student's writing in a non-threatening atmosphere (B). It is always helpful to have a model of good writing (C), and by choosing students' papers, self-esteem is enhanced.
      Competency 010

48.   **(B)**   The correct response is (B). Parent-teacher communication should always begin and end on a positive note, so as not to offend parents and turn them off to future suggestions. Never leave problems for the end (A), because parents may be put on the offensive if they sense a negative attitude from the teacher. Parents do not want to feel as if they are being put down, which will often occur if the teacher uses too much technical jargon (C). Teachers must gain the parent's cooperation (D), so that both parent and teacher feel comfortable with the plan of improvement at home and at school.
   Competency 011

49.   **(D)**   The correct response is (D). The classroom arrangement can control how the students respond in class. Students tend to respond more openly if they are communicating face to face with each other, which makes a circle the optimal desk arrangement. Putting students in rows by sex (A) does little to stimulate discussion. The physical aesthetics of the classroom are important (B), but nice-looking bookcases will not encourage participation. A new topic each day may spur limited conversation at the time, but does little to encourage continual class participation.
   Competency 006

50.   **(A)**   The correct response is (A). Many authors include cultural aspects in their books. By reading an author from an appealing culture, a student not only learns about the character, but also the character's culture. By presenting their findings to the class, classmates are exposed to this information as well. Exposure to new authors is important, but highlighting a new author once a month (B) is not enough exposure to be significant. Although knowing geographical locations of countries is important (C), cultural diversity encompasses much more. Mere exposure to varied authors is necessary, but multicultural awareness is meant to be integrated into the entire curriculum, rather than relegated to one day (D).
   Competency 002

51.   **(D)**   The correct response is (D). Cooperative grouping should give the students a chance to display leadership abilities (A), to organize and distribute materials so that all members play a vital part in the final product (B), and to evaluate for themselves how the group functioned and whether or not it did the best job it could (C). However, the teacher should have a way to group the students so that they are balanced for optimal learning by everyone; groups should allow students with different strengths and weaknesses and of different ability levels to work together (D).
   Competency 008

52.   **(D)**   The correct response is (D). The social studies teacher demonstrates how material from curriculums can be synthesized and how students can use prior knowledge and non-novel resources to aid them in their project. Students new to a school need to know how to gain access to information, which is best done with the help of the librarian. Ms. Woods has used her faculty resources to enhance her

teaching and build a good working environment among faculty members. Although Ms. Woods will not be teaching class at the time, it is not necessarily free time, and this is not her main objective (A). The students will become more familiar with other faculty members (B), but they will gain more than just this. If the students listen carefully, they will learn time-cutting information and gathering techniques (C), but the discussion will not serve as a way to get out of doing work.

Competency 012

53. **(A)** The correct response is (A). Ms. Woods will best serve as a facilitator in this situation. She knows how to let students solve the problem by discussing options while she guides and directs the students. She does this without overtly telling them how to solve the problem. By overlooking the problem (B), the teacher is setting an example that says that working problems out is not necessary. By not presenting a model to follow (C), the teacher may be letting the group flounder and waste precious time, even though they may solve the problem in the end. An activity should never be stopped with the explanation that it is not working (D).

Competency 007

54. **(A)** The correct response is (A). The authors mentioned in the prompt represent a variety of ethnic backgrounds, which is important exposure for students; traditional literature might not include these types of authors. (B) and (D) are not true statements and, therefore, cannot be correct. (C) could be a benefit of the selection, but not the teacher's main purpose in her selection.

Competency 002

55. **(B)** The correct response is (B). Miss Taylor's emphasis on how the assignment can be fun, but also top quality, demonstrates her high expectations and enthusiasm for student learning. A single assignment is not an indicator that Miss Taylor thinks all assignments should be research papers (A), nor does it indicate that she feels all assignments should require independent work (C). Choosing only assignments that the teacher enjoys (D) neglects the most important component of developing student assignments, which is the impact on student learning.

Competency 005

56. **(A)** The correct response is (A). The more detailed and clearer the directions for an assignment, the less chance of erroneous student interpretation of what should be included. Being flexible with expectations (B), particularly with major assignments, can result in student work that is below minimum standards or below what students are capable of doing. Providing a sample or model for student work (C) can be a good secondary tool for student assignments, but it is not an acceptable substitute for clear directions or instructions. Allowing no room for student originality (D) is also not a good choice, for even with clear instructions and expectations there is room for originality.

Competency 007

57. **(D)** The correct response is (D). The TEKS requires the integration of technology into a variety of settings, and Miss Taylor's requirement that students use specific format guidelines in their typing and development of a PowerPoint presentation are both methods for integrating technology into her course. The formatting requirements have little to do with students' interest in history (A), nor do they have a bearing on the amount of research students will conduct for this assignment (C). Most students will be fairly proficient at basic formatting requirements already, so it is not likely that the assignment will teach students new computer techniques (B).

Competency 009

58. **(A)** The correct response is (A). Mrs. Fisher's best option is to express her concerns and the reasons for these concerns with the school counselor, who is trained to help in matters of student concern such as this. Involving another student (B) is a poor choice in this instance: it places a large emotional burden on the second student. In addition, it makes the teacher's concern public rather than keeping it confidential among school officials. As (C) suggests, Lisa's parents do need to be notified soon. However, this call should be made by the counselor because he or she is a professional trained to deal with these types of concerns. Confronting Lisa directly (D) could cause her to be defensive about her actions and, if there is indeed an eating disorder, could cause her to hide her symptoms to avoid further detection.

Competency 013

59. **(B)** The correct response is (B). Students at the formal operational stage can understand complex theoretical descriptions with little or no direct observation. Students at the concrete observational stage (A) must have direct observation to reach understanding and have trouble with complex theoretical descriptions. The sensorimotor stage (D) applies to infants, and the preoperational stage (C) applies to children ages two to seven.

Competency 001

60. **(D)** The correct response is (D). Teachers have an ethical, sometimes legal, obligation to keep student grades confidential. This is particularly true with major grades that impact a student's course grade. The teacher's action probably does embarrass some students (A), but their embarrassment is less important than the breach of confidentiality. Using student work samples (B) is not illegal within the scope of the classroom, and it is certainly all right for a teacher to be upset when students do not perform at their level of ability (C). However, in this case, the teacher must find another means of responding to this frustration.

Competency 013

61. **(A)** The correct response is (A). Teachers should always respond as proactively as possible. Students who are within five points of a failing average at the grading period's midpoint have a strong potential for failing that grading period. The teacher is wise to inform parents of this possibility, along with an explanation

of why the student's grades are so low and what the teacher recommends be done about it (tutorials, completion of homework, etc.). This approach might help ward off parental complaints from those students who fail (B), but ultimately student success should be the reason for contacting parents rather than limiting the number of complaints. The same logic applies to (D), meaning that effective communication might help with the teacher's evaluation, but this should not be the impetus for contacting parents. Requiring parents to check their child's homework each night (C) is unrealistic for some parents, because of possible time and knowledge restraints.

    Competency 011

62. **(B)** The correct response is (B). It is recommended that teachers communicate regularly with parents, although this often means that teachers communicate only with the parents of students who are performing poorly in class. Positive communication is equally important, however, and it sends a strong sentiment to parents. Making these positive phone calls is unlikely to help Mrs. Goodbody remember her parents' names (A), nor does it mean that the parents will be more or less involved (C). Contacting parents with positive feedback also does not decrease the chance for discipline problems with students (D), although it does make a positive impression upon parents about how much the teacher cares about her students.

    Competency 011

63. **(B)** The correct response is (B). Increasing family involvement in student learning can be a key component of student success. This type of assignment is completely structured to involve family members to the maximum extent possible in each student's learning. The project will likely help the teacher understand her students' backgrounds (A), but this is clearly not the main purpose of the assignment. A class cultural awareness project (C) could be a culminating product for the assignments, but again it is not a good purpose. Students' ability to conduct interviews (D) is simply a part of the project but offers no insight as to the purpose of such a project.

    Competency 011

64. **(C)** The correct response is (C). Mathematical knowledge is used in numerous areas in the professional fields. By reading about a field that involves a math background, the teacher is fulfilling the request of the principal. Of course, reading a personally interesting article (A) and modeling fluent reading (B) are important, but they are not the main reasons behind reading the article. The article may spark an interest in architecture (D), but this will be a secondary reward.

    Competency 008

65. **(D)** The correct response is (D). For a computer teacher, hardware and software can serve as an excellent resource, even if it is utilized only occasionally. Although test-taking is usually more beneficial in a familiar place, classes do not always have to be in the same place (A) and minimal exposure (B) to new technology

is still beneficial. A lesson utilizing computers requires planning and would not be a free period for the teacher (C).
  Competency 012

66. **(C)** The correct response is (C). A teacher needs to know the best type of tone to take when conversing with parents. Knowing how parents feel about education and the fears the child has about failure, the teacher should do his or her best to show the student in a favorable light. Letting the student off the hook (A) would not solve the problem. In this case, calling the parents personally with news of a failing grade (B) would do more harm than good. Except in unusual circumstances, it is not the teacher's place to counsel a student on a family problem (D). The teacher can lend an ear, give support when it comes to raising self-esteem in the classroom, or suggest a talk with the school counselor.
  Competency 005

67. **(B)** The correct response is (B). It is against school policy to bring any sort of weapons to school. The only choice teachers have if they want to follow school rules is to turn the knife and the student over to the principal. Ignoring the incident (A), taking the weapon away but not reporting it (C), and letting the weapon remain in the boy's possession (D) would be a violation of school policy.
  Competency 013

68. **(B)** The correct response is (B). When discussing a behavior problem with parents, a teacher should always have documentation of the incidents so that the problem is presented in a fair and accurate manner. The best way to keep parents on the teacher's side is to convey concern (B) rather than aggravation (C). A teacher should work with parents' suggestions and not try to dictate how parents raise their children at home (D). It is inappropriate for the teacher to refer parents to the principal (A) without first trying to solve the problem.
  Competency 011

69. **(A)** The correct response is (A). Increased competition for student grades is not expected as a result of cooperative learning. Increased student self-esteem (B), increased time spent on academic tasks (C), and increased positive attitudes toward other students (D) are all expected results of properly-structured cooperative learning activities.
  Competency 006

70. **(C)** The correct response is (C). When cooperative learning activities are correctly implemented, individual students are responsible for content, even though the information was learned in a cooperative manner. (A) is incorrect because whether or not students can take a review course for the college entrance exam is irrelevant. (B) is incorrect because individual colleges have different admissions standards. Some colleges emphasize grades; some emphasize entrance exams. (D) is incorrect because it avoids the issue and does not respond to the parent's concern.
  Competency 011

71. **(B)** The correct response is (B). Questions that demand recall of factual information can be answered in one or two words or in a short phrase. If lengthy answers are desired, then the question format must change. There is no information to indicate that students are intimidated, therefore (A) is incorrect. Uncertainty about answers usually causes students to provide long, rambling responses, so (C) is incorrect. (D) is incorrect because the students are providing answers so it does not seem reasonable that the questions are too difficult.
    Competency 007

72. **(C)** The correct response is (C). The writing process is the term used for the steps described in preparing a written paper. The steps in the writing process include: prewriting, drafting, revising, editing, and writing the final copy, or publishing. (A) is incorrect because writing and editing are only parts of the writing process. The situation described does not include peer group work, so (B) is incorrect. This is not a description of cooperative learning, so (D) is also incorrect.
    Competency 009

73. **(A)** The correct response is (A). A sense of civic responsibility is promoted by a classroom discussion of civic events like, for example, local elections. (B) is incorrect because the situation described indicates that students have already determined their reasons for opposing the curfew. There is no reason to believe that students will stage a sidewalk protest as a result of the classroom activity, so (C) is incorrect. (D) is incorrect because the writing of letters, which is the response the teacher suggests, should cause no concern from parents.
    Competency 012

74. **(A)** The correct response is (A). Students must learn to work cooperatively and responsibly with one another in group assignments. Using cooperative learning projects will not necessarily reduce disciplinary problems, as mentioned in (B). The number of projects to be graded (C) should not be a determining factor in developing student assignments. The prompt does not specify that students must choose an individual for their project (D) nor does it mention that the topics chosen must involve war heroes (D).
    Competency 003

75. **(B)** The correct response is (B). Mr. Davis reflects on his first year and determines his strengths and weaknesses, as well as areas in which he has improved and areas in which he still needs further improvement. Engaging in such practices is critical for personal and professional growth. Revising lesson plans each year (A) is good practice, as are integrating technology into the curriculum (C) and seeking out staff development opportunities (D). However, there is little or no evidence of the importance of these practices based on the description of Mr. Davis's activity in the prompt.
    Competency 012

76. **(B)** The correct response is (B). One of the areas Mr. Davis recognizes as needing personal improvement is evaluation techniques; using holistic scoring methods directly impacts that deficiency area. Both (A) and (C) address areas in which Mr. Davis feels he is improving, so it would be less productive for him to attend these sessions at this time. Training in how to recognize cultural differences in students (D) is not mentioned in the prompt and therefore there is no basis for choosing this option.
    Competency 012

77. **(C)** The correct response is (C). The purpose of having students in a routine to begin journal-writing—or any other assignment—upon entering class is to have them focused and working as soon as possible. Thus, (C) is the correct response, because the purpose of this task is to use all available class time to maximize student learning. Although the five minutes in which students are working without direction might very well allow Ms. Scott to finish class preparations (A), take roll (B), or check her lesson plans (D), the actual purpose of such an activity is effective management and use of instructional time.
    Competency 006

78. **(C)** The correct response is (C). The Supreme Court has ruled that having students grade one another's work does not violate FERPA (Federal Education Rights and Privacy Act). However, the case did emphasize that the assignments being graded were a fairly small portion of the students' final grade, and thus not necessarily indicative of students' overall or final grade. Using the practice for all assignments (B) or major tests (A) would be unwise because these would be much more indicative of students' final grade and would thus be more likely seen as a violation of their guaranteed confidentiality rights. Although (D) is correct in its assumption that true/false and multiple choice tests are the most conducive to student-based grading because they leave so little room for error, it does not indicate whether these items might occur on daily work, minor quizzes, major examinations, or other types of assignments. Thus, (D) is too broad to be the correct response.
    Competency 013

79. **(B)** The correct response is (B). The only legal and ethical response to this problem is for Mr. Hernandez to enter all of the grades for this grading period. He should then receive more training on the gradebook program if necessary and develop a system for keeping up with grade entry on a regular basis, for example every Monday or Friday during his conference period. Allowing a student to have access to other students' grades (A) is a violation of FERPA (Federal Education Rights and Privacy Act). To select only the major test grades (C) is unfair to students and a violation of any grading policy including daily grades, one component that is explained at the beginning of the grading policy. Estimating grades (D) is also an unethical practice that unfairly inflates or lowers the grades that students have earned.
    Competency 013

80.   **(A)**   The correct response is (A). Analyzing and synthesizing information are the two highest levels on Bloom's taxonomy, and students should be able to use these levels in a writing assignment. Recognizing the conflict of a story (B) and checking for comprehension (C) are much lower-level skills that this particular prompt does not address. Although the assignment might involve some degree of creative writing (D), the purpose of the assignment is to engage students in the higher levels of thinking as they develop their new ending for the story.
   Competency 007

81.   **(C)**   The correct response is (C). If two students turn in the same essay for credit, the first thing the teacher should do is talk individually with each student. The teacher's next action should depend on what was learned from speaking with the students involved. (A) is incorrect because at this point it is unclear what the students have done and reporting their behavior would be premature. (B) is incorrect because until the teacher has spoken to each student individually there is not enough information to determine whether or not the parents should be notified. (D) is incorrect because assigning an "F" to the paper without first discussing the situation with the students would be unfair and would only serve to anger the students. Only after learning the reasons for the students' behavior should the teacher determine whether both students deserve a failing grade or not.
   Competency 013

82.   **(D)**   The correct response is (D). If both students admit that they wrote the paper together, the best response would be for the teacher to ask each student to write another paper and assess a penalty. The teacher has to make sure that this penalty is consistent with school policy. (A) is incorrect because even though the punishment may be appropriate, the issue of the duplicate paper for one assignment has not been resolved. (B) is incorrect because this is a mindless punishment and serves a very limited purpose. (C) is incorrect because there is no incentive to prepare another paper if the student knows in advance that he/she will receive a zero.
   Competency 005

83.   **(B)**   The correct response is (B). Teaching integrated lessons causes students to remember information for a longer period of time and in greater detail. (A) is incorrect because integrated lessons do not cause students to become frustrated or confused. Instead, integrated lessons have the opposite effect. (C) is incorrect because while lessons will be related, the classes will require individual assignments. (D) is incorrect because teachers who prepare integrated lessons must be very knowledgeable about the subject for which they are responsible.
   Competency 003

84.   **(B)**   The correct response is (B). Integrating another content area into the students' study of the American Revolution will develop a broader view of that period in history. (A) is incorrect because although the teachers are integrating their

lessons, they are each responsible for their own subject area. (C) is incorrect because librarians are usually pleased when books are used by teachers and students. (D) is incorrect because teaching integrated units does not mean that students will be doing homework for one subject during another's class period.

Competency 003

85. **(D)** The correct response is (D). It is Mrs. Kopak's responsibility to ensure that all students have the opportunity to respond in class. (A) is incorrect because it implies that the problem is a difference in intelligence or ability between girls and boys, which is an inaccurate assumption. (B) is not correct because it penalizes the boys for participating in class, which is a counterproductive reaction to the problem. (C) might be effective part of the time, but open class discussion is important for students to process and engage in effective learning; to do away with all discussion and student responses would greatly limit the effectiveness of the class.

Competency 002

86. **(C)** The correct response is (C). All curriculum decisions should be made based upon the required content outlined in the Texas Essential Knowledge and Skills (TEKS). There are required skills and objectives that have to be taught, so Mr. Bradshaw's first step must be to ensure that the changes he makes include all of these requirements. Mr. Bradshaw does not need the permission of the principal to make minor modifications in what or how he teaches (C); furthermore, he needs to know what types of changes he plans to make and how those changes will fit the TEKS before mentioning anything to the principal. Surveying the students (B) will not ensure that he meets state requirements for what content should be taught. Observing effective teachers (D) is a good practice, but it is not the most effective first step for Mr. Bradshaw's needs at this time. Observation would be a more helpful tool for problems with instructional techniques, rather than helping with the inclusion of required content.

Competency 003

87. **(B)** The correct response is (B). If all students turn in collections that are "neatly stored and labeled," as the assignment requires, then the difference in the quality of storage products and labels is most likely a sign of the students' financial and economic means. To assume that nicer storage cases are an indicator of effort (A) is faulty reasoning. Differences in presentations do not indicate that the assignment is ineffective (C). (D) does not take into consideration a student's socioeconomic status, which plays a large part in each student's ability to afford expensive wood cases; to tie the presentation to a grade based on anything other than neatness, correctness, and completeness would be unjustified.

Competency 001

88. **(D)** The correct response is (D). All evaluation criteria should be aligned with goals and objectives for both the course as well as the particular assignment. Using a rubric should help avoid questions over grading assignments (A) and should help Mr. Reyes as he grades the assignments (B), but aligning grading criteria to goals and objectives is a much more important reason to use a rubric than either of these choices. Awarding a predetermined number of high or low scores is a completely ineffective choice for student evaluation (D).

    Competency 010

89. **(B)** The correct response is (B). Modification sheets provided by the students' Admission, Review, and Dismissal (ARD) committee are mandatory. Teachers should also keep documentation of how the modifications are being implemented and how the students are performing with the modifications. To modify only when students are failing (A) is not meeting the students' needs; the modifications are designed to ensure that students are successful based on their abilities, not to remediate them after failure. Modifications should not be based solely on the difficulty of the content (C), nor should they be made solely at a parent's request (D). To be in compliance with special education law, modifications should be made exactly as specified by the ARD committee.

    Competency 013

90. **(D)** The correct response is (D). State guidelines are very specific as to what types of information the proctors for the TAKS can give. The proctor cannot offer help with understanding the question (A and C), nor with choosing the correct response (B). The only correct option is (D).

    Competency 013

Practice Test 3: PPR 8–12

Answers, Sorted by Competency

Question	Domain	Competency	Answer	Did You Answer Correctly?
31	I	1	C	
39	I	1	C	
44	I	1	A	
59	I	1	B	
87	I	1	B	
16	I	2	A	
23	I	2	D	
33	I	2	A	
43	I	2	B	
50	I	2	A	
54	I	2	A	
85	I	2	D	
34	I	3	C	
74	I	3	A	
83	I	3	B	
84	I	3	B	
86	I	3	C	
1	I	4	A	
21	I	4	A	
36	I	4	C	
37	I	4	A	
38	I	4	B	
41	I	4	C	
42	I	4	C	
7	II	5	D	
8	II	5	C	
22	II	5	C	
40	II	5	C	
46	II	5	D	
55	II	5	B	
66	II	5	C	
82	II	5	D	
9	II	6	A	
10	II	6	A	
14	II	6	C	
49	II	6	D	
69	II	6	A	
77	II	6	C	
5	III	7	B	
11	III	7	C	
35	III	7	B	
53	III	7	A	
56	III	7	A	
71	III	7	B	
80	III	7	A	

Question	Domain	Competency	Answer	Did You Answer Correctly?
2	III	8	B	
3	III	8	D	
12	III	8	C	
13	III	8	A	
26	III	8	C	
32	III	8	C	
51	III	8	D	
64	III	8	C	
17	III	9	C	
18	III	9	A	
19	III	9	B	
20	III	9	D	
57	III	9	D	
72	III	9	C	
4	III	10	C	
27	III	10	D	
28	III	10	C	
29	III	10	D	
30	III	10	C	
47	III	10	D	
88	III	10	D	
25	III	11	C	
48	III	11	B	
61	III	11	A	
62	III	11	B	
63	III	11	B	
68	III	11	B	
70	III	11	C	
15	IV	12	C	
24	IV	12	C	
45	IV	12	C	
52	IV	12	D	
65	IV	12	D	
73	IV	12	A	
75	IV	12	B	
76	IV	12	B	
6	IV	13	A	
58	IV	13	A	
60	IV	13	D	
67	IV	13	B	
78	IV	13	C	
79	IV	13	B	
81	IV	13	C	
89	IV	13	B	
90	IV	13	D	

TExES

Texas Examinations of Educator Standards

Practice Test 4: PPR EC–12

This test is also on CD-ROM in our special interactive TExES TEST*ware*®. It is highly recommended that you first take this exam on computer. You will then have the additional study features and benefits of enforced timed conditions, individual diagnostic analysis, and instant scoring. See page 3 for guidance on how to get the most out of our TExES book and software.

PRACTICE TEST 4:
TExES PPR EC–12
(Answer sheets begin on page 392.)

TIME: 5 hours
   90 questions

> **DIRECTIONS:** Read each stimulus carefully, and answer the questions that follow. Mark your responses on the answer sheet provided.

Mr. Drake is a first-grade teacher who is using the whole language approach when teaching about animals.

1.   Before reading a story to the students, Mr. Drake tells the students their purpose for reading the story and what they are expected to learn. What is his reason for doing this?

   (A)   The students should know why the instructor chose the story over any other.

   (B)   It is important for teachers to share personal ideas with their students in order to foster an environment of confidence and understanding.

   (C)   Mr. Drake wants to verify that all students are on-task before he begins the story.

   (D)   Mr. Drake is modeling a pre-reading skill in order to teach it to the young readers.

Mr. Drake's class has an extensive discussion on the needs of house pets. In response to a student who says that her family abandoned their cat in a field because it ate too much, Mr. Drake asks: "What is one way to save pets that are no longer wanted?"

2.   This exercise involves what level of questioning?

   (A)   Evaluation

   (B)   Analysis

    (C)   Comprehension

    (D)   Synthesis

Mr. Drake has students who read at different levels. He has the students in groups of two—one skilled reader and one remedial reader—reading selected stories to one another. The students read the story and question each other until they feel that they both understand the story.

3.   By planning the lesson this way, Mr. Drake has

    (A)   set a goal for his students.

    (B)   condensed the number of observations necessary, thereby creating more time for class instruction.

    (C)   made it possible for another teacher to utilize the limited materials.

    (D)   utilized the students' strengths and weaknesses to maximize time, materials, and the overall quality of the learning environment.

Mr. Drake is continuing his lesson on the animal kingdom. He wants to ensure that the students learn as much as they can about animals, so he incorporates information they are familiar with into the new information.

4.   Knowing that these are first-grade learners, what should Mr. Drake consider when planning their learning experience?

    (A)   Students will know how much information they can retrieve from memory experiences.

    (B)   Students will overestimate how much information they can retrieve from memory.

    (C)   Students will be able to pick out the information they need to study and the information that they do not need to study as a result of prior mastery.

    (D)   Students will estimate how much they can learn in one time period.

Before reading a story about a veterinary hospital, Mr. Drake constructs a semantic map of related words and terms using the students' input.

5.   What is his main intention for doing this?

    (A)   To demonstrate a meaningful relationship between the concepts of the story and the prior knowledge of the students

(B)   To serve as a visual means of learning

(C)   To determine the level of understanding the students will have at the conclusion of the topic being covered

(D)   To model proper writing using whole words

Vocabulary development is a key predictor of success in reading.

6.   Identify strategies that parents can use to promote vocabulary development in a fun and relaxed environment.

(A)   Use flash cards, pictures, and concrete objects to introduce vocabulary words.

(B)   Play hide-and-seek and watch television with the child.

(C)   Ask the child to write a summary of the events of the day in school and provide corrective feedback emphasizing appropriate grammar and vocabulary.

(D)   Ask the child to memorize a list of vocabulary words with their definitions.

7.   The *least effective* technique to promote literacy at home is to

(A)   read aloud to the child.

(B)   ask the child to read to you.

(C)   ask the child to invite friends home and encourage them to read together.

(D)   create a "quiet reading time" for the whole family.

Miss Sharp's fourth-grade class is studying a unit entitled "Discoveries" in social studies and science. Miss Sharp has prepared four learning centers for the class. In Learning Center #1, students use information from their science and social studies textbooks to prepare a time line of discoveries that occurred between 1800 and 1990. In Learning Center #2, students use a variety of resource materials to research one particular discovery or discoverer they have selected from a prepared list. Each student then records what they learned about this discovery or discoverer on an individual chart that will later be shared with the whole class. In Learning Center #3, students add small amounts of five different substances to jars of water and record the results over a period of five minutes. In Learning Center #4, students write a description of the need for a new discovery to solve a problem or answer a question. Then students suggest several possible areas of research that may contribute to this new discovery.

Miss Sharp introduces the learning centers by explaining the purpose of each center and giving directions for each activity. Next, she divides the class of 22 into four groups and assigns each group to a different center. After 20 minutes, some students are completely finished with one center and want to move on, but other students have only just begun working.

8.   What would be the best solution to this situation?

   (A)   Every five minutes students will rotate to work on a new activity.

   (B)   Students who finish one center early should be given additional work to complete before moving to the next center.

   (C)   Students should be permitted to move from center to center as they complete each activity so long as no more than six students are working at each center.

   (D)   Students should be permitted to work through the activities in each center as quickly as possible so that the class can move on to the next unit.

As the students work in the learning centers, Miss Sharp moves from group to group asking questions and commenting on each student's progress.

9.   This procedure indicates that Miss Sharp most likely views her role as a/an

   (A)   facilitator.

   (B)   supervisor.

   (C)   disciplinarian.

   (D)   evaluator.

10.   Which of the following would be the most appropriate concluding activity for the "Discoveries" unit?

   (A)   Students should have a class party celebrating the birthday of Marie Curie, Jonas Salk, and Thomas Edison.

   (B)   Each student should be required to prepare a verbal report detailing what they learned about an important medical discovery.

   (C)   Each student should take a multiple-choice test containing questions related to each learning center.

   (D)   Each student should design a concluding activity, or select one from a prepared list, that reflects what he or she learned about one discovery from those studied.

In selecting resource materials for Learning Center #2, Miss Sharp carefully chooses materials that present information about a variety of discoveries made by both men and women from several different countries.

11.	Her purpose in making these selections is most probably to ensure that materials

(A)	are challenging but written at the appropriate reading level.

(B)	demonstrate the diversity of individuals who have made discoveries.

(C)	contain information about discoveries included in the textbook.

(D)	will be of interest to the majority of the students.

12.	What is the main advantage of using hands-on activities to teach content areas in elementary schools?

(A)	Hands-on activities can promote higher-order thinking and increase intelligence among children from all linguistic groups.

(B)	Hands-on activities can lead to active learning and collegiality among children.

(C)	Hands-on activities can promote higher-order thinking skills and can guide students to construct their own knowledge.

(D)	Hands-on activities can promote equity and freedom among the diverse ethnic groups in the nation.

Mr. López is a fourth-grade teacher at Gaza Elementary. He presents a social studies lesson comparing the Apache and the Pueblo nations. Mr. López brings examples of the construction materials used in each type of housing and demonstrates the process used to build them. He also discusses the rationale for the use of temporary (Teepee) versus more permanent (Adobe) construction. After presenting the information and checking for comprehension, he asks students to think about the most important information learned about the two groups. He allows two minutes to think about it. Later, he asks them to share that information with a student sitting next to them. Following this activity, Mr. López uses a table on the blackboard to gather the information provided by the students. Partial results of the table are presented below.

> # What did we learn about the Pueblos and the Apaches?
>
> ## The Pueblos
>
> They built adobe houses
> They lived in New Mexico
>
> ## The Apaches
>
> They built teepees
> They lived in Texas

13. What is/are the instructional benefit(s) of allowing students to think about the answer for a few minutes and share the information with a peer before answering the question?

   (A) Students have sufficient time to think about the question, share information, and produce a better-prepared answer.

   (B) Students have opportunities to socialize with peers in a controlled and secured learning environment.

   (C) Students are allowed to interact with each other and learn to work in groups.

   (D) Students have more time to communicate and share cultural information in an open and relaxed instructional setting.

14. What part of the teaching cycle is Mr. López delivering when he presents examples of the construction materials used and demonstrates how to build each type of housing?

   (A) Motivation/focus   (C) Enrichment

   (B) Evaluation   (D) Closing

15. What part of the teaching cycle is Mr. López addressing through the information gathered in the table above?

   (A) Motivation/focus   (C) Enrichment

   (B) Reteaching   (D) Closing

Mr. López announces that the next day they are going to build a village. He organizes the class in groups of five students and instructs students to think about the location of their village and the type of structure they want to build. He asks them to use the information on the handout shown below as a foundation to make the decision. He also mentions that they need to provide a rationale for their decision.

Data about the Possible Sites

	Site A	Site B
Average temperature	70-101	30-101
Hunting Possibilities	Small animals – year-round	Large animals – June-Nov.
Type of Soil	Dry and fertile	Mixed fertile soil and rocky
Climate	Dry most of the time	Humid most of the time
Fresh Water	Available all year-round	Available all year-round
Terrain	Mountain and hills	Hills and flat land

16. What is the most important skill being addressed through the activity for the next day?

    (A) Problem-solving

    (B) Working in groups

    (C) Knowledge sharing

    (D) Study skills

◆◆◆◆◆◆◆◆

17. Identify the statement that best describes the Interactive/Experiential (Constructivism) model of teaching.

    (A) This model attempts to empower students from all cultural and linguistic groups by organizing classroom activities that value and accept the contributions of all children.

    (B) This model attempts to build students' experiences by involving them in activities designed to strengthen their background and guide them to assume greater control of their own learning.

    (C) This model attempts to promote the ability to communicate effectively in English and a second language with students from different ethnic backgrounds.

    (D) This model attempts to develop the cognitive academic language needed to succeed in school.

18. Identify one key consideration teachers must follow when implementing a classroom management program for kindergarten to second-grade students.

   (A) Guide children to share responsibilities with adults

   (B) Teach rules and procedures explicitly and practice them until students master them

   (C) Allow children opportunities to receive positive and productive feedback

   (D) Build students' self-image before implementing the program

The first step in organizing an effective classroom management is to understand students and their characteristics.

19. Identify the group of children described in the following statements:
   • Are compliant, eager to please teachers
   • Have short attention span, tire easily
   • Are restless and like to wander around the classroom
   • Might break rules because they forget about them

   (A) Kindergarten to sixth-grade students

   (B) Fifth-graders

   (C) Sixth- to ninth-graders

   (D) Kindergarten to second-grade students

20. Identify the statement that best describes the implementation of the Assertive Discipline management program.

   (A) It introduces an extensive set of rules that students recite until they are internalized.

   (B) Teachers employ coercion and physical contact to restrain and control children.

   (C) It begins with a clearly specified set of rules and is followed by specific behaviors that each child must exhibit daily.

   (D) Rules are linked to positive and negative consequences; negative consequences are linked to the action, not the child.

21. The key instructional benefit of using games such as the "Oregon Trails" and "Where in the World is Carmen San Diego?" is to

(A)   guide students to use the computer in a low-pressure environment.

(B)   promote the teaching of listening, speaking, reading, and writing in a relaxed environment.

(C)   teach maps skills and problem-solving skills in an enjoyable and sub-conscious manner.

(D)   force students to use technology.

22. A potential drawback of using presentation tools with multiple colors and animation is that

(A)   children might not be interested in this kind of approach.

(B)   children might be intimidated by the display of colors and animation.

(C)   children might pay more attention to the delivery system than to the content presented.

(D)   children might prefer more traditional forms of teaching that emphasize personal contacts with teachers and students.

23. Identify the productivity tools used to enhance instruction and facilitate ad-ministrative duties of classroom teachers.

(A)   Word processing, electronic grade book, and databases

(B)   Electronic encyclopedia, presentation tools, and instructional games

(C)   Simulations, instructional games, and drill-and-practice programs

(D)   Instructional videos, television, and CD players

Ms. Treen is a kindergarten teacher at Green Valley Elementary. Her students are primarily Hispanic. English is a second language for about one-third of the class. Ms. Treen wants to encourage her students to view themselves as successful readers and writers.

24. Which of the following instructional strategies would be *least effective* in ac-complishing this goal?

(A)   Providing a reading area in the classroom where students can select books to read in a relaxed and comfortable atmosphere

(B)   Reading at least two books aloud each day and discussing the story with the students

(C) Accepting invented spellings as the students write letters, grocery lists, telephone messages, and describe classroom events

(D) Requiring students to copy the alphabet using upper and lowercase letters at least once each day

25. During the first parent-teacher conference of the year, Ms. Treen should

(A) keep the conversation light and unemotional, saving any negative comments for the next conference.

(B) include positive comments about each child and make suggestions for how families can help the child at home.

(C) discuss the importance of speaking only English at home at all times and insisting that the child communicate with all family members in English.

(D) discuss the results of diagnostic testing using technical terms so that parents will understand her desire to help the children.

Ms. Treen has just finished teaching a unit on community helpers. She is disappointed because the children did not seem interested in the topic and did not want to discuss the community helpers she had listed on the bulletin board.

26. The best course of action for Ms. Treen would be to

(A) borrow another kindergarten teacher's unit on community helpers for use next year.

(B) evaluate each lesson in the unit and revise the lessons to make them more meaningful to the students.

(C) save discussions of community helpers for older children because the topic is too difficult for kindergarten students.

(D) show a filmstrip about community helpers and invite a policeman to visit the class.

Ms. Rivera uses colored blocks with kindergarten students to teach colors and counting from 1 to 20.

27. What is the educational principle implemented through this activity?

(A) Blocks are ideal for kindergarten students because they are inexpensive and easy to handle.

(B)   Children enjoy working with colorful and concrete objects.

(C)   Children at this stage are concrete learners and learn best with objects they can see and handle.

(D)   Children at this stage might not have the muscular coordination to handle objects with different shapes and colors.

In Ms. Adam's class, students are asked to interview family members to identify strategies they will use to solve a given mathematical problem.

28.   What might be the benefit of this strategy?

(A)   It will provide a multicultural view for problem-solving and will validate the students' native culture.

(B)   The teacher is acknowledging families, and their contributions will enhance the education of the students.

(C)   It will expose teachers to the culture of the students and will free them to address administrative duties.

(D)   It will involve the community in the learning process and will provide a medium to teach family members how things are done in the United States.

Ms. Hayek, a seventh-grade teacher, is having difficulties with Sheba, an Indian-American student. Sheba is extremely shy and refuses to turn in assignments and comply with simple classroom instructions. After exhausting all avenues to correct the problem, Ms. Hayek calls a conference with Sheba's parents. Ms. Hayek is very nervous about the conference and tries to prepare for it.

29.   Identify the strategy that is *least likely* to help Ms. Hayek to be successful in the conference.

(A)   Developing anecdotal records of the child's behavior and the intervention strategies used to address the situation

(B)   Bringing the district's bilingual translator to the conference and ask Sheba's parents to use this service to avoid communication problems during the conference

(C)   Gathering information about the parents' cultural background

(D)   Reviewing the student's permanent folder to have a better view of the student's performance and behavior in previous years

30. The Texas State Bilingual Education law allows for the use of two languages for instruction in

   (A) pre-K, middle school, and high school.

   (B) pre-K through upper elementary and middle school.

   (C) middle school through high school.

   (D) kindergarten through sixth grade.

Mr. Treskoski is a first-year teacher who has recently moved from another state to Las Palomas, a small town in rural west Texas. In his sixth-grade social studies class, Mr. Treskoski has his students read the local newspaper each Monday in order to increase their understanding of and involvement in civic issues at the local and national levels. In addition, the students are assigned to watch the local and national news at home on either Tuesday nights or Wednesday mornings, in order to use this information to supplement their understanding of the issues. For several weeks, the class has been following the upcoming mayoral election. The incumbent mayor, The Honorable Lucinda Griego, is running for re-election against a political newcomer, Tambra Crumpler. While Mayor Griego has a strong record of advocating for better living conditions for all the citizens of the town, Candidate Crumpler is an attorney whose platform is based upon taking a strong stand in combating the illicit gangs, which she says are creeping into the community. When the class is discussing the candidates' platforms, Molly Winters says, "My dad says that there isn't a gang problem here. He told me that it's just news media hype to sell papers and to get Ms. Crumpler elected. What do you think, Mr. T?" As one, the students turn their eyes to Mr. Treskoski. "That's an interesting thought," says Mr. Treskoski. "Let me think about that and get back to you tomorrow. I'll need to do some research before I decide what I think. But right now, let's talk about what you think."

31. Mr. Treskoski's statement about doing research before making a decision reflects

   (A) using planning processes to design outcome-oriented learning.

   (B) being a reflective practitioner who knows how to promote his own growth.

   (C) promoting diversity by allowing the students to express their opinions rather than expressing his own.

   (D) maximizing the amount of time that students spend on their own group discussions.

During his planning time, Mr. Treskoski goes to Mr. Hinojosa, the school librarian, and asks him to recommend sources for learning about gangs. He inquires whether the district has the technological capabilities to link with the nearest university in order to conduct a computer search for information related to gangs.

32.   What is the key advantage to Mr. Treskoski's asking Mr. Hinojosa for help, rather than seeking out the answers to these questions himself?

(A)   Mr. Treskoski can save a great deal of valuable planning time by having Mr. Hinojosa help him as opposed to finding the material himself, thus making better use of his limited time resource.

(B)   Mr. Treskoski can begin to develop a collegial relationship with Mr. Hinojosa in which each will view the other as a member of a mutually supportive learning community.

(C)   Mr. Treskoski can better understand factors outside the classroom that contribute to his students' growth.

(D)   Mr. Treskoski can make certain that his actions are in compliance with the school library regulations.

After Mr. Hinojosa helps Mr. Treskoski select a variety of materials on gangs from the school library, he explains to Mr. Treskoski that the Las Palomas schools do not have the technological capability to link with a university for a computer search. He suggests that instead Mr. Treskoski conduct a computer search of Infotrak at the local community college. Mr. Hinojosa calls Dr. Harvill, the librarian at the community college, and she gives Mr. Treskoski a set of instructions for selecting terms and setting limitations for an Infotrak search. The next day, Mr. Treskoski explains to his class about the computer search and asks the students to keep the computer search in mind as they examine the school's library materials on gangs. On Friday, after all students are thoroughly acquainted with the library materials, Mr. Treskoski has a "Town Meeting" of the class in order to decide how to structure the computer search. The class selects three terms for which to search, and limits the search to the most current 30 magazine and newspaper articles which contain a combination of these terms. After school, Mr. Treskoski meets with Dr. Harvill at the college to conduct the search.

33.   Mr. Treskoski's activities demonstrate

(A)   selecting appropriate materials to address individual students' needs.

(B)   knowing how to foster growth in each domain.

(C)   taking advantage of community resources to foster student growth.

(D)   understanding the relationship between planning and student growth.

During the following week, the students eagerly wait for all the articles to arrive through Interlibrary Loan at the community college. During this time, Mr. Treskoski's class begins to explore the idea of sensationalistic journalism. Casey Bradford raises her hand and says, "My aunt Tommie works for the paper as editorial director." Mr. Treskoski asks Casey whether she thinks Ms. Bradford would like to come and talk to the class. Casey suggests that she go to the office and call her aunt. She returns to the classroom with an affirmative answer and tells Mr. Treskoski that he is to call her aunt with a proposed date and time.

34. Mr. Treskoski's behavior demonstrates

    (A) using a variety of instructional strategies.

    (B) developing strong community/family/teacher partnerships.

    (C) an understanding of individual talents and abilities.

    (D) employing the use of preferred modalities in student instruction.

Molly Winters says that since her dad was the one who originally said that the notion of gangs in the town was hype put forth by the media, he should come talk to the class, too. She asks if she may call him at work to see if he will come. Mr. Treskoski asks if that will be a problem for him at work. "No," says Molly. "He's the personnel manager at the electronics parts factory, and he lets me call any time." Mr. Treskoski gives Molly permission to call, and Mr. Winters agrees to come.

35. In agreeing to allow Molly to invite her father, Mr. Treskoski demonstrates

    (A) an appreciation of a diversity of ideas.

    (B) an understanding of the importance of prior learning.

    (C) taking advantage of community resources.

    (D) stimulating curiosity in students.

When the Interlibrary Loan photocopies arrive from the community college, Mr. Treskoski assigns each student to one of six groups of four children each. He gives each group 5 of the 30 articles to examine for evidence of gangs in Texas and for signs of sensationalistic journalism. Each group will then present a report to the entire class. To each group he assigns one high-, two medium-, and one low-achieving student. The low-achieving student in one group is Lynn Stovall, a student who is involved in the district's full inclusion program for students with developmental disabilities. After three days, Mr. Treskoski receives a phone call from the mother of Carlita Rivas, the high-achieving student in Lynn's group. Ms. Rivas is upset because her daughter has been assigned to work in the same group as Lynn. "This boy can do nothing to help with the project," complains Ms. Rivas. "I'm sure that he is a nice boy, but I don't want my daughter to have to work with such a poor student. What is wrong with him, anyway? Is he retarded, or what?"

36. What should Mr. Treskoski do?

   (A) Tell Ms. Rivas that he understands her concern, and patiently explain to her that Lynn has fetal alcohol syndrome and is mentally retarded. Offer to send her a variety of materials about fetal alcohol syndrome so that she may better understand Lynn's problems and perhaps identify ways that Carlita may work with him in the group.

   (B) Explain that he understands her concern, and that he will move Lynn out of the group immediately.

   (C) Firmly explain that he has to make the instructional decisions about the class, and that since Lynn is mentally retarded, Carlita has the social obligation to help him. Explain to Ms. Rivas that unless students work together to build community, they will not learn the value of civic virtue, which is a main goal of social studies education.

   (D) Explain that throughout the year, students will be grouped in a variety of ways, and that a major goal of the class is for students to learn to work with others who are both very like and very unlike themselves in a number of ways. Explain that he is sorry, but he will not to be able to answer her questions about Lynn, since it would be unethical and illegal to do so.

◆◆◆◆◆◆◆◆

The Individuals with Disability Education Act (IDEA) provides for the placement of students in the "least restrictive environment" through an inclusion model.

37. In this inclusion model, who are the parties responsible for the implementation of the student's Individualized Education Plan (IEP)?

   (A) The special education teacher in collaboration with the Admission, Review, and Dismissal (ARD) committee will implement the IEP.

   (B) The special education teacher and the mainstream teacher will be responsible for the implementation of the IEP.

   (C) The special education teacher is the only responsible agent for the implementation of the IEP.

   (D) The ARD committee in collaboration with the regular mainstream teacher will implement the plan.

The State Compensatory Education program provides services to students in "at-risk situations."

38. Identify the students who qualify for services under this program.

    (A) Students who fail to meet expectations on TAKS or who are two or more years below grade level.

    (B) Students who fail to score at or above the 40th percentile on one of the state-approved standardized achievement tests.

    (C) Students who exhibit superior intellectual abilities and who might feel unchallenged by traditional teaching methods.

    (D) Students who are illegally in the United States.

39. Older students might benefit more from deductive teaching than younger children because younger children

    (A) prefer inductive teaching.

    (B) might not have the level of cognitive development needed to understand the principles or the generalizations presented through this method.

    (C) might get discouraged with the method.

    (D) might not have the intellectual capability to understand the examples presented through this method.

Mr. O'Brien is a high school communications teacher. At the end of the school year, he reviews the topics he has taught and the assignments he has given.

40. He then uses this review to direct his professional development activities over the summer months by

    (A) identifying areas not covered, or new topics to study and research during the summer months.

    (B) updating his files on each of the topics.

    (C) assessing the quality of the assignments received from students over the past school year.

    (D) revising student assignments by re-evaluating educational objectives for class.

Mr. O'Brien discovers that he spends virtually no class time discussing the differences in the ways females and males communicate, although he notes that several best-selling books by academic scholars have been written on this topic. Furthermore, he has observed some recurring gender differences among the students he has taught over the years, and he wonders if he should add this timely topic to the list of those he now teaches.

41.   He decides to discuss this possibility with other teachers at his school to

    (A)   demonstrate his knowledge of current professional and academic topics.

    (B)   solicit his peers' ideas and input on expanding and/or revising the curriculum in communication classes.

    (C)   determine if he should do any additional professional reading on this topic.

    (D)   ascertain any gender differences in communication styles among his colleagues.

When Mr. O'Brien brings up the topic of gender differences in styles of communication, he discovers that two of his colleagues have opposite views.

42.   Subsequently, he decides that the best course of action to take is to

    (A)   go immediately to the department chair or curricular supervisor and let that party know about the dissension in the ranks.

    (B)   drop the topic since it is clearly too controversial to pursue.

    (C)   invite both colleagues to help him develop lessons that would include both viewpoints on the topic.

    (D)   argue with both colleagues to clearly state his own view of the topic based on current research findings.

Mr. O'Brien reads Deborah Tannen's best-selling book *You Just Don't Understand: Women and Men in Conversation* and decides that he would like to use the book as a reference tool for introducing some gender-related ideas to his students.

43.   By selecting a best-seller as a reference, Mr. O'Brien is

    (A)   attempting to locate contemporary and relevant sources of information for his students.

(B)   expecting students to purchase an additional book for his course.

(C)   demonstrating to his colleagues that he is aware of contemporary research in his discipline.

(D)   requiring students to do more outside reading in the course.

The literature Mr. O'Brien surveys reveals that female students are less likely to participate in classroom discussions than male students. Some researchers cite this behavior as an illustration of females' lower self-esteem.

44.   In an effort to boost the self-esteem of female students in his class, Mr. O'Brien

(A)   endeavors to ask female students easier questions so they will get the answers right.

(B)   develops a question grid to enable him to call on all students in the class, both male and female, an equal number of times.

(C)   avoids calling on female students if the question is one requiring higher-order thinking skills.

(D)   avoids giving critical feedback to female students who give incorrect answers.

As Mr. O'Brien learns about female students' problems with self-esteem, he recalls a former student, Shonda Harris, who was a very shy, quiet student. Shonda never volunteered to answer questions or participate in class discussions, although she made the top grades in his class. Mr. O'Brien never called on her in class and now he wonders if he acted appropriately.

45.   In retrospect, he concludes that in the future he should

(A)   continue to call only on those students who raise their hands or otherwise indicate their willingness to respond, so as not to unduly pressure students.

(B)   gently tease to provoke shy, quiet students to participate in class discussions.

(C)   require students to participate in class discussions with the result of lowered grades if they fail to do so.

(D)   meet with the student privately and discuss why he, as the teacher, wants students to participate in class discussions and then listen to her or his reasons for not volunteering to do so.

Mr. O'Brien decides that he will require his students to participate in discussions and that class participation will account for a percentage of students' grades in his communications course.

46.   This new requirement will

    (A)   be an effective motivational tool for all students in his classes.

    (B)   motivate only some of the students in the course to participate.

    (C)   result in improved grades for all students in his classes.

    (D)   discourage the majority of students from participating in class discussions.

Before introducing the topic of gender differences in communication styles to his students, Mr. O'Brien asks the members of the class to individually brainstorm ten situations wherein each student would like to improve his or her communication skills. In each situation, students are then asked to identify the gender of their audience (or the receiver of the communication, the other party in the situation). Next, students are asked to tally the number of times there is a sex difference between themselves as the sender of the message and the receiver of the message.

47.   In this activity, Mr. O'Brien

    (A)   avoids a classroom activity that could deteriorate into an argument.

    (B)   utilizes a strategy to promote student learning.

    (C)   saves classroom time.

    (D)   finds a way to assess who is having trouble communicating and who is not.

As students tally their responses from the brainstorming activity, they indicate that many of the communication problems they routinely encounter involve members of the opposite sex.

48.   This discovery allows Mr. O'Brien to

    (A)   capitalize on students' self-motivation to learn how to communicate more effectively.

    (B)   skip over a formal introduction to the topic of gender differences in communication.

    (C)   pinpoint whether male or female students are having greater difficulty communicating.

(D)   dismiss students' concerns about their problems in communicating with others.

Mr. O'Brien asks students to form groups of three or four to describe some of the factors that are commonly associated with the "communication conflicts" involving members of the opposite sex.

49.   By asking students to work in groups, Mr. O'Brien's instructional strategy is to

(A)   avoid a tedious lecture.

(B)   encourage students to develop better social skills.

(C)   allow students to structure their own time in class.

(D)   give students opportunities to discover and clarify communication conflicts in a relaxed and supportive environment.

Mr. O'Brien ends the class by telling students that over the next few weeks they will be required to keep a communications journal. Every time they have an eventful exchange—either positive or negative—they are to record the details of the exchange in their journal.

50.   This assignment is given as

(A)   a way to help students improve their composition and rhetorical skills.

(B)   a way of understanding individual students, monitoring instructional effectiveness, and shaping instruction.

(C)   a way of helping students become more accountable for the way they manage their time.

(D)   the basis for giving daily grades to students.

Mr. George is a high school social studies teacher at Arlington High School. He believes that motivation is an important component of the learning process. One day, he brings cookies and milk as a focus activity to illustrate the concept of supply and demand of goods and services. Students eat the cookies and drink the milk, but find that approach to be awkward.

51.   Identify the statement that best describes the type of focus activity used by Mr. George.

(A)   The focus is funny and appropriate to students' cognitive development.

(B)   The focus is effective and right on target.

(C)   The focus is challenging and based on students' experiential background.

(D)   The focus is developmentally inappropriate for the students.

Ms. Jaynes is a secondary special education teacher and reading specialist. Her teaching assignment requires her to provide for the special needs of twelve students who are experiencing difficulties in reading.

52.   Her first action to establish a relationship with the students is to

(A)   interview the students' previous teachers to solicit their opinions and advice on meeting the educational needs of the students.

(B)   review school files on each student, including assessment and testing history.

(C)   meet students individually and informally discuss how they feel about school and reading.

(D)   administer a standardized reading test to determine their current reading performance.

In selecting a test to administer to students, Ms. Jaynes needs to be relatively certain that she has selected a test that is not biased.

53.   Test bias refers to whether or not

(A)   a test measures what it purports to measure.

(B)   a test consistently measures what it purports to measure.

(C)   the test discriminates between students who are intelligent or lacking in intelligence.

(D)   the test discriminates among students on the basis of race, ethnicity, gender, cultural or socio-economic background, or other ideographic characteristics.

Ms. Jaynes gives a standardized reading test to a student in her class on Friday afternoon (Test Time 1). The following Monday morning, Ms. Jaynes is absent and the substitute teacher gives the same form of the test to the student again (Test Time 2). The student's parents are surprised and pleased to learn that their child's grade level score improved significantly from Test Time 1 to Test Time 2. Ms. Jaynes subsequently has to explain the difference in scores to the parents; she explains the difference as a result of test-practice effects.

54. Test-practice effects are the phenomenon of

   (A) students' scores improving when they take the same form of a test shortly after the first testing.

   (B) students' scores improving as a result of having received adequate instruction and practice time with the skills being tested.

   (C) a test not measuring what it claims to measure.

   (D) students answering questions the way they think the examiner wants the question answered.

As a special education teacher, Ms. Jaynes has learned that an essential part of her job is to confer with her colleagues who teach core academic classes. She spends time giving her colleagues weekly reports on students' progress and learning about what the students are doing in their academic classes.

55. Ms. Jaynes believes that this practice is

   (A) an effective way of gaining popularity and respect among her colleagues.

   (B) an effective way to discipline students since they know she has influence among their other teachers.

   (C) an important part of her profession as a member of a community who must work effectively with all members of that community to reach common goals.

   (D) the only way to qualify for merit pay and salary increases.

Mr. Luna is a high school teacher at the Center for Innovation High School. He follows student-centered learning practices by leading students to construct their own knowledge. These techniques are sometimes called unguided discovery learning because students are allowed opportunities to select both the form and substance of the learning experience. Based on these foundations, Mr. Luna uses project-oriented teaching strategies. He provides general guidelines for the project, but avoids giving students direct or specific details. Instead, he expects students to analyze the information given, review the resources available (textbook and other printed materials distributed in class) to develop their own framework, and use creativity to complete the project. He expects students to define the concept and to construct their own knowledge. Mr. Luna follows what in the literature is known as indirect teaching practices.

56. Identify the students that might benefit the most from Mr. Luna's teaching style.

(A)   Students who prefer inductive teaching strategies

(B)   Students who prefer deductive teaching strategies

(C)   Students who are highly intelligent

(D)   Students from upper and middle class backgrounds

Mr. Holderman is a high school mathematics teacher in a low-income inner-city school. He is getting his students ready to take the advanced placement test in mathematics. He wants to demonstrate that students from low-income areas can also excel in mathematics. With this idea in mind, he has purchased with his own money a computer program to teach advanced calculus. He has installed the program on the 15 computers available in the school computer laboratory. Mr. Holderman is very satisfied with the program. The students are learning a lot with it, and Mr. Holderman is very pleased with the outcome and plans to make additional copies of the program so students can use it at home or at the community library.

57.   Identify the statement that best describes the behavior of the teacher.

(A)   He is a well-informed teacher that takes advantage of a law that allows poor schools the option of taking a one-time exemption from copyright restrictions.

(B)   He is a caring teacher, but he is violating copyright laws.

(C)   He is a caring teacher and deserves to receive credit for all the work done on behalf of the students.

(D)   He is a good model for the school and the district.

58.   Computer-assisted instruction can be classified into the following major categories:

(A)   Tutorials, simulations, and productivity tools

(B)   Presentation tools, tutorials, simulations, and instructional games

(C)   Problem-solving, drill-and-practice, simulations, and instructional games

(D)   Word processing, database, spread sheets, and presentation tools

Ms. Aljuhbar is an ESL teacher. She works with high school-aged students, typically with groups of six to twelve students who possess varying degrees of ability for understanding English. Her primary objective in working with her students is to help them understand the academic English spoken in their classes and to help them communicate more effectively in English with their other teachers and classmates. Her secondary objective is to create cultural awareness within her students and expose them to customs of the United States.

59. These objectives are examples of

   (A) behavioral objectives.

   (B) performance objectives.

   (C) instructional goals.

   (D) outcome-based education.

As Ms. Aljuhbar develops her weekly lesson plans, she identifies specific behavioral objectives for each class session.

60. By doing this, Ms. Aljuhbar

   (A) specifies exactly which instructional methods should be used.

   (B) lists the materials and equipment that will be needed.

   (C) describes what students will be able to do as a result of receiving instruction.

   (D) focuses attention on teacher-centered activities.

One of Ms. Aljuhbar's students, Lee Zhang, has been enthusiastic in class and has eagerly participated in class activities until the end of the fall semester. When the spring semester begins, Lee seems despondent. She no longer participates in class activities, and she stops turning in her homework or even doing assignments in class.

61. The best thing for Ms. Aljuhbar to do to help Lee is to

   (A) contact Lee's family to see if they are having family problems.

   (B) confer with other teachers at the school to determine if Lee is acting the same way in all of her classes.

   (C) ask Lee if something is wrong since her schoolwork is suffering and her performance in class has changed since the semester break.

   (D) give Lee extra credit work to help her catch-up and improve her grades.

One activity that Ms. Aljuhbar uses with her ESL students requires that each student choose a fable or folk tale that he or she learned as a child. The student is then privately videotaped telling the story in his or her native language. Next, the student is given the tape and allowed time to view it, critique it, and then translate it into English. Finally, at a second taping, the student is videotaped telling the story in English. The student is then given the tape with both versions.

62.   Ms. Aljuhbar has found that this is an effective instructional strategy because

    (A)   it is based on the premise that practice makes perfect.

    (B)   it allows the student to make choices and to move from the familiar to the novel or unfamiliar at his or her own pace.

    (C)   it permits the student to critique the tape in private.

    (D)   it is done in a non-threatening environment.

Reading teachers have to spend a lot of instructional time on pre-reading activities to meet the needs of culturally and linguistically diverse (CLD) students.

63.   Identify the rationale for this emphasis on pre-reading skills.

    (A)   Pre-reading can be used to explore the knowledge that children bring to the reading process and fill the cultural and linguistic gaps needed to facilitate reading comprehension.

    (B)   Pre-reading can be used to teach decoding and comprehension skills to ensure that students are able to decode and comprehend every word in the story prior to reading it.

    (C)   Pre-reading can be used to guide students to use graphic and pictorial clues and to write a summary of the story.

    (D)   Pre-reading can be used to answer comprehension questions and find details about the story.

Mr. Xiao is a second-year high school history teacher in a large urban school with a very diverse student body. He regularly divides his classes into small groups that work separately on the given assignments. Mr. Xiao would like to improve the functioning of the group work.

64.   The best way to do this is to

    (A)   permit students to choose the group to which they would like to belong.

(B)   make sure that in each group there is a student with above-average leadership skills.

(C)   assess how well the group worked together and use this as a basis for students' grades.

(D)   provide students with guidelines that enumerate what generates successful collaboration and help students review and evaluate their group work after the assignment is finished.

Mr. Winter is an ESL teacher who follows a unique method to promote second language development. He avoids negative statements when responding to students. Instead, he uses questioning techniques to lead the child to the expected answer. Students in his class feel comfortable trying to address questions because they know that Mr. Winter will never embarrass or interrupt them. Mr. Winter focuses his attention on the intended message and asks clarification questions only when the speech is unintelligible or the content of the communication is incorrect. When he needs to correct students, he does it indirectly by modeling the language structure in question. Mr. Winter exemplifies the principles teachers ought to promote in a student-centered language classroom.

65.   Identify the principles of language learning exemplified by Mr. Winter.

(A)   Children learn languages when teachers follow a grammar format that introduces language structures in sequential and systematic fashion.

(B)   Second language development is controlled by the left hemisphere of the brain.

(C)   Children learn languages in an environment in which risk-taking is encouraged and errors are allowed.

(D)   Children learn languages when good teachers do their job.

66.   Identify the only statement that *fails* to describe current principles for effective assessment of culturally and linguistically diverse (CLD) students.

(A)   The objective of assessment is to value the unique characteristics of each individual.

(B)   Students go through different stages of development, and these stages should be the criterion for evaluation.

(C)   CLD students might express potential differently, due to linguistic and cultural influences.

(D)   Since CLD students may have culture and language deficits, they are not required to take standardized achievement tests.

67.	The main purpose of family literacy programs is to

(A)	teach English to Spanish-speaking parents and to provide them with training in cross-cultural communication.

(B)	keep children busy while parents attend ESL classes.

(C)	empower parents to help and be involved in the education of their children.

(D)	empower adult English language learners by providing intensive English as second language instruction.

Ms. Chernev is a third-year teacher at Palo Verde Elementary. In her first-grade class are several students with serious academic needs.

68.	Which would be the best way for her to make sure these students understand learning expectations?

(A)	Provide them with the support they need to achieve learning goals set by students and the teacher together

(B)	 Frequently assign group work in heterogeneous groups

(C)	Avoid giving them tasks that may be especially challenging for them

(D)	Reward them even when their performance does not meet standards of acceptability

Mrs. Walker is thinking about developing a tenth-grade world history unit. The unit needs to emphasize Virgil's attempt to connect the origins of Rome to the events that followed the destruction of Troy by the Greeks. She wants the unit to be challenging, yet the students must be able to handle the work. She is aware that this is the semester the students will take their first college entrance exam. The information from a cooperative learning workshop taken during the summer should be included in the unit.

69.	What should be Mrs. Walker's first step in planning the unit?

(A)	Combining cooperative learning and the content

(B)	Deciding on an evaluation that will be fair to all students

(C)	Developing objectives for the unit

(D)	Finding available materials and resources

70. Mrs. Walker's understanding of human development is evident because her planning alludes to which statement about cognitive growth?

   (A)   Students will learn whatever they need to learn if they are given enough time and proper instruction.

   (B)   Students will use higher-order thinking skills in real-world situations.

   (C)   Students will develop a sense of involvement and responsibility in relation to the larger school community.

   (D)   Constant difficult schoolwork and demands will cause students to become interested.

71. Which of the following is an indication that Mrs. Walker is aware of the environmental factors that may affect learning?

   (A)   She is developing a tenth-grade world history unit.

   (B)   She wants to be sure that the students are challenged.

   (C)   She is aware that this is the semester the students will take their first college entrance exam.

   (D)   She decides to utilize group work for a large portion of the unit.

72. What might Mrs. Walker include in her planning to keep gifted students challenged?

   (A)   An extra report on the history of the Greeks

   (B)   Let them tutor students who are unmotivated

   (C)   Encourage them to plan learning activities of their own

   (D)   Create a tightly organized and well-designed unit for the student

Mrs. Gomez teaches a seventh-grade English class. As she plans for the semester, she designs a "Writers' Workshop." The workshop will be both a reading and writing experience for all the seventh-graders. Mrs. Gomez and the students will read the works of published authors and those of each other. The goal of the workshop is to improve one's own writing and to help one's peers become better writers.

The first element of writing to be introduced is a metaphor. To introduce the concept of a metaphor, Mrs. Gomez displays the definition and examples of a metaphor on an overhead projector. The display remains visible to the students as the reading of a poem follows. The students' task is to correctly identify the metaphors in the poem. The class further practices identifying metaphors through a paper-and-pencil exercise. Following the paper-and-pencil exercise, students develop their own metaphors and share them with the class. Initially, the metaphors are simple while gradually becoming complex. Then, Mrs. Gomez shows a filmstrip and asks the students to identify and discuss its metaphors.

To stimulate the students in writing their own poetry containing metaphors, Mrs. Gomez displays brightly colored transparencies of works of art. The students are instructed to write a poem about the art or an object found in the art transparency. Mrs. Gomez will evaluate students through a rubric containing class participation, completion of the steps of the writers' flowchart, special directions given in class, and a poem containing at least three metaphors.

73. The main purpose of the "Writers' Workshop" is to

   (A)   promote creative writing through a variety of instructional activities.

   (B)   use a variety of experiences to promote poetry and process writing.

   (C)   encourage all students to use a multi-sensory approach for creative writing.

   (D)   promote a sense of responsibility for one's own learning.

74. The multiple evaluation tools used by Mrs. Gomez exhibit her own competency in

   (A)   creative thinking.

   (B)   communication through the use of various media.

   (C)   being a reflective questioner.

   (D)   working with other teachers.

75. Identify the assessment principle represented by the rubric used to evaluate completion of the poem.

   (A)   Assessment should be concrete and objective.

   (B)   Assessment should be multidimensional.

   (C)   Assessment should be informal and based on students' performance.

   (D)   Assessment should be research-based.

Mr. Smith is a first-year teacher in the process of setting up classroom rules for his eighth-grade class.

76. Identify the first consideration he needs to take into account prior to developing classroom rules.

   (A) Rules must be stated clearly to avoid misinterpretations.

   (B) Rules must be long and specific enough to cover all possible behaviors typical of eighth-graders.

   (C) Rules must be consistent with district and school rules.

   (D) Rules must include a rationale to avoid the idea that they were arbitrarily set.

77. What is the main benefit of allowing students to have input in the selection of classroom rules?

   (A) It promotes a sense of ownership, which increases the likelihood that students will comply with them.

   (B) It emphasizes external locus of control, which leads to compliance.

   (C) It teaches students the process for setting up a classroom management program.

   (D) It treats students as moral thinkers and conditions them to obey rules without questioning their fairness.

Ms. Lawrence is a seventh-grade bilingual teacher in the Lone Star Middle School. Since she is fully aware of the importance of promoting active learning and the importance of motivation in learning, she leads her students in the process of discovery through fun activities. She teaches language and content through the use of games, songs, and hands-on activities. Some of her colleagues appear to be skeptical about her unorthodox approach. But they notice that children have fun in her class and they do well on state examinations. A lot of her colleagues ask themselves how she does it.

78. Find the answer to this question by identifying the statement that best describes Ms. Lawrence's approach to teaching.

   (A) She promotes the acquisition of language and content using a deductive approach.

   (B) She uses inductive learning and active learning to teach language and content.

(C)   She follows humanistic and behaviorist teaching practices to teach language and content.

(D)   She has very good students and good interpersonal skills.

79.   Identify the main benefit students get from cooperative learning activities.

(A)   Students are allowed to socialize and practice communication skills without the intrusion of the teacher.

(B)   Students assume responsibility for the learning process and work together with minimum teacher supervision.

(C)   Teachers function as facilitators of knowledge as opposed to dispensers of knowledge.

(D)   Students are allowed opportunities to be creative and plan the daily instructional activities.

80.   Identify the key benefits for using portfolios to document student progress.

(A)   It allows for the gathering of students' work completed during the year.

(B)   It provides confidential information for faculty and support personnel.

(C)   It provides students an opportunity to show the range of quality and breadth of their work over time for assessment.

(D)   It allows for the gathering of documents to report the data required in the accountability system.

Mr. Shah has given an assignment in which four students work together to present a reflection on an author and his/her works. Mr. Shah, through a survey, has realized that many students have not worked in such a group before, so he reviews the rules of participation.

81.   Which of the following are vital rules to achieve the desired outcome?

(A)   Allow people opportunities to communicate, talk in a low tone of voice, and criticize each other's work

(B)   Listen to each other's ideas and develop a fair system where students can compete for control of the group

(C)   Support each other during the interaction, take turns when talking, and listen to each other's ideas

(D)   Allow competition among members and guide students to assign grades to each other's work based on individual performance

82. Which part of the newspaper might easily prove a feasible area to teach mathematics for third-graders?

(A) Stock market reports   (C) Obituaries

(B) World news report   (D) Sports section

Ms. Dominguez is teaching a lesson on finding the area of irregular polygons. In her lesson, she uses illustrations and equations from the chalkboard, as well as large and moveable cardboard polygons.

83. What is Ms. Dominguez's intention in using the cardboard polygons?

(A) Incorporate visual and tactile learning styles into the lesson presentation

(B) Assess eye-hand coordination of the students when using the manipulatives

(C) Spice up her lesson

(D) Stress self-directed learning

Mr. Thacker has joined the staff of Edgemont High School. He will be teaching sophomore English, a course taught by four teachers who follow the same curriculum, but use their own ideas for instructional strategies. The first unit of study is a novel with which Mr. Thacker is not familiar—*Laughing Boy*. Since he has just completed his student teaching at the tenth-grade level, he is very familiar with *The Red Badge of Courage*, a novel often taught at the tenth-grade level in Texas. He would like to begin the school year with it, rather than the novel the other teachers are using.

As a football coach, his first weeks of school will be very busy. He also feels that the purpose of the unit—to study the structure of the novel—could be accomplished with either book equally well. However, when he mentions his idea and the reasons for it to his fellow sophomore English teachers, they are not in favor of his deviating from the set curriculum.

84. What steps should Mr. Thacker take next regarding the first unit of study?

(A) He should go ahead and teach the book he wants to teach.

(B) He should talk to the departmental chairperson and explain his position. If she approves of this change in titles, he will make the substitution. If she does not, he will teach *Laughing Boy*.

(C)   He should talk to the principal, who had the greatest influence in hiring him, and follow his advice.

(D)   He should send a note to his students' parents on the first day of school and see if they mind the substitution of one novel for the other. He will abide by their majority opinion.

Mr. Sánchez is an art teacher in a local elementary school. Occasionally, he takes home school materials and a laptop computer assigned to his classroom. He requested permission from the school principal to use art materials to prepare sample projects for his class and the computer to prepare lesson plans and to keep track of students' progress. Some of the teachers don't like the fact that Mr. Sánchez takes the computer home almost every weekend. They believe that his behavior is unethical.

85.   Identify the statements that best describe the Code of Ethic for Teachers that address this issue.

(A)   School materials and equipment should be used in school only; thus, Mr. Sánchez is at fault.

(B)   Teachers have the right to borrow school materials and equipment as long as they plan to return them.

(C)   Teachers can borrow the materials and equipment as long as these are used for "official school business" only.

(D)   Teachers can take school materials home, but they should never take equipment home.

In Fort Worth, an exhibit of Mayan artifacts is on display in the month of November. Mr. Méndez, a new eighth-grade Spanish teacher, has mentioned the exhibit to students in his two Spanish classes. The students have responded with many questions about Mayan people and culture, expressing more interest in this topic than any other concept studied thus far. Although Mr. Méndez has encouraged his students to attend the free exhibit, many lack transportation to the museum. Although warned by the other Spanish teacher about the trouble involved in setting up a field trip, his students' enthusiasm urges him to seek approval from the principal to make the necessary arrangements. With his principal's approval and warning to follow the guidelines for a field trip in the teacher's handbook, Mr. Méndez is ready to make plans for his students to view the Mayan exhibit in two weeks.

86.   Which of the following steps in planning for the trip is *faulty*?

(A)   Mr. Méndez has prepared a notice to let other teachers know the date the students will be missing afternoon classes when they attend the exhibit. He has alerted the students to prepare, prior to the field trip, any work due for classes missed.

(B)   Mr. Méndez has sent a note to each parent with information about the field trip plans, including learning objectives.

(C)   Mr. Méndez has received his principal's approval for the field trip.

(D)   Mr. Méndez has arranged for a school bus to transport students to and from the exhibit.

87.   When students are in middle school, they require more autonomy. Which of the following satisfies this need?

(A)   Activities and assignments that are designed to meet a variety of individual preferences

(B)   The use of democratic procedures to make decisions that will impact the entire class

(C)   The implementation of blocks of free time into the daily schedules of the students

(D)   The determination of grades based on self-evaluation of the students

Ms. Smith, a second-grade teacher, has been informed that a student with multiple disabilities, Michael, will soon become a member of her class. In order to be sure that Michael enters a positively-charged classroom, Ms. Smith has to prepare a strategy.

88.   Which of the following strategies will yield the desired effect?

(A)   Train students to uphold their civic responsibility and take turns helping Michael.

(B)   Clearly iterate a code of behavior that the students will have to adhere to upon Michael's arrival.

(C)   The teacher's behavior and attitude should serve as a paradigm for student behavior.

(D)   Upon Michael's arrival, conduct an information and question-and-answer session concerning his handicap.

Mr. Hayworth wants to teach his second-grade science class the following concept: "The student knows that systems may not work when necessary parts are missing from the whole."

89. Which strategy should Mr. Hayworth use in order to teach this concept effectively?

(A) Clearly articulate the definitions of key terms that will be used to describe the concept.

(B) Conceptual repetition, utilizing a variety of phrases to explain it.

(C) Illustrate the concept by referring to real-life situations that students are familiar with.

(D) Use the board to provide visual demonstration of how parts comprise a single system.

In preparation for a social studies unit, Ms. Brink makes plans to instruct her students via teacher presentations that include a video and a guest speaker, class discussions in both large and small groups, group activities, and a field trip.

90. One of the most significant benefits of this approach is that Ms. Brink

(A) can easily pace herself to accommodate the diverse learning needs of her students.

(B) will be able to organize the presentation of material in a logical and coherent way.

(C) can cover a significant amount of content in a time-effective way.

(D) can provide learning opportunities for students with varied learning styles.

ANSWER KEY

1.	(D)	24.	(D)	46.	(B)	68.	(A)
2.	(D)	25.	(B)	47.	(B)	69.	(C)
3.	(D)	26.	(B)	48.	(A)	70.	(A)
4.	(B)	27.	(C)	49.	(D)	71.	(C)
5.	(A)	28.	(A)	50.	(B)	72.	(C)
6.	(A)	29.	(B)	51.	(D)	73.	(A)
7.	(C)	30.	(B)	52.	(C)	74.	(B)
8.	(C)	31.	(B)	53.	(D)	75.	(B)
9.	(A)	32.	(B)	54.	(A)	76.	(C)
10.	(D)	33.	(C)	55.	(C)	77.	(A)
11.	(B)	34.	(B)	56.	(A)	78.	(B)
12.	(C)	35.	(A)	57.	(B)	79.	(B)
13.	(A)	36.	(D)	58.	(C)	80.	(C)
14.	(A)	37.	(B)	59.	(C)	81.	(C)
15.	(D)	38.	(A)	60.	(C)	82.	(D)
16.	(A)	39.	(B)	61.	(C)	83.	(A)
17.	(B)	40.	(A)	62.	(B)	84.	(B)
18.	(B)	41.	(B)	63.	(A)	85.	(C)
19.	(D)	42.	(C)	64.	(D)	86.	(B)
20.	(D)	43.	(A)	65.	(C)	87.	(A)
21.	(C)	44.	(B)	66.	(D)	88.	(C)
22.	(C)	45.	(D)	67.	(C)	89.	(C)
23.	(A)					90.	(D)

To determine in which domains your strengths and weaknesses lie, use the table on page 391.

TExES PPR EC–12

DETAILED EXPLANATIONS OF ANSWERS

1. **(D)** The correct response is (D). Comprehension is demonstrated when the reader questions his or her intent for reading. For example, one may be reading a story to find out what terrible things may befall the main character. Comprehension increases when students become aware of the focus and expectations for the activity. It also teaches students that we read for different purposes, i.e., skimming, scanning for information, to obtain the main idea, or to obtain details. The rationale for selecting a book may be an interesting bit of information (A), but it is not a major topic of discussion with the students. Sharing personal information (B) creates a certain bond, but this is not directly relevant to the question. It is also important that all students are on-task before the beginning of a lesson (C), but this is a smaller part of the skill modeled in response (D).
Competency 004

2. **(D)** The correct response is (D). A question testing whether or not a student can synthesize information will require students to generalize from given facts, draw conclusions, and use old ideas to create new ones. Students will use the information discussed in class to generate suggestions to save unwanted pets. An evaluation question (A) will require a judgment of the quality of an idea or solution. In order to be real analysis (B), the question would have to ask the student to analyze given information, draw a conclusion, or find support for a given idea. Comprehension questions (C) require one to rephrase the idea in one's own words, then use this for comparison.
Competency 007

3. **(D)** The correct response is (D). By having a mixed-level pair read together, the remedial student receives instruction, and the skilled student receives reinforcement. This peer support system constitutes one of the main principles of cooperative learning. It uses alternate teaching resources, the students themselves, to enhance the learning environment. A certain goal—comprehension—has been set (A), but this is not the most important outcome. The teacher will need to observe fewer groups (B), but it is unlikely that this will change the time needed to work with all groups as long as quality is to be maintained. Although the reading is done in pairs, each student should have a book (C), just as it would be impractical to permit another teacher to utilize the books while one teacher is using them.
Competency 003

4.   **(B)**   The correct response is (B). Students at this age do not have the cognitive skills required to realize how much they have actually learned, or how much they will actually be able to retain. For this reason, (A) must be incorrect. At this stage in their intellectual development, students cannot differentiate between material that is completely understood and material that they have not completely comprehended (C). Students will generally feel that they are capable of learning much more than they will actually retain (D).
    Competency 001

5.   **(A)**   The correct response is (A). By mapping out previous knowledge, information already known can be transferred to support new information. Although words on the board are visual (B), this is not the underlying motive. Semantic mapping done at the beginning of a story tests how much prior knowledge the students have about the topic from the outset (C). This does model proper use of words (D), but this is not the main intent of the exercise.
    Competency 004

6.   **(A)**   The correct response is (A). Parents can use flash cards with visuals or words to introduce vocabulary and concepts. (B) is incorrect because it does not explain how the game and television are going to be used to teach vocabulary. (C) and (D) do not meet the criteria of "fun and relaxed." Direct error correction and teaching vocabulary words through rote memorization is boring and probably ineffective.
    Competency 011

7.   **(C)**   The correct response is (C). Inviting friends home to read together is ineffective because it does not involve parents directly, and the activity can evolve into a social gathering. All the other statements provide examples of activities to promote literacy at home.
    Competency 011

8.   **(C)**   The correct response is (C). This response recognizes that children learn at different rates and suggests a structured method to limit the number of children per center. The teacher should make an effort to organize activities that will allow time for completion (A); however, it is impossible for all students to work at the same rate. Children who finish early should not be given extra work merely to keep them busy (B). Speed is not the primary goal of this activity (D).
    Competency 004

9.   **(A)**   The correct response is (A). When a teacher provides instruction as a facilitator, he or she adjusts the amount and type of help provided to each student based on individual needs and abilities. This creates independent learners. A supervisor oversees activities but does not necessarily offer assistance or support independent activities (B). Although a teacher often has to be a disciplinarian, this is not the primary goal of moving from group to group (C). A teacher moving from

group to group may also be informally assessing student work (D), but it is not the main goal of the activity.
   Competency 008

10.   **(D)**   The correct response is (D). A concluding activity should encourage students to summarize what they have learned and share this information with other students. A class party celebrating scientists is a valuable experience but does not allow students to share what they have learned (A). A topic for cumulative reviews should not be limited to only medical discoveries when the unit's topic was much broader (B). A test is considered an evaluation technique and should not be confused with a concluding activity (C).
   Competency 008

11.   **(B)**   The correct response is (B). Materials should represent a wide range of topics and people, thereby fostering an appreciation for diversity in the students. An appropriate reading level (A), related information (C), and a majority of interest (D) are all important, but cannot be called the main reason for selecting resource material.
   Competency 002

12.   **(C)**   The correct answer is (C). Hands-on activities lead students to discovery, inductive learning, and the development of higher-order thinking skills. The first part of (A) is correct, but the second part might be difficult to prove. There is no evidence to suggest that hands-on activities increase intelligence. (B) can lead to active learning and perhaps can promote collegiality among students; however, the development of collegiality is not the main purpose of the activity. (D) is incorrect because there is no connection between the activity and the promotion of equity and freedom.
   Competency 001

13.   **(A)**   The correct response is (A). Research on "wait time" indicates that when students are given more time to reflect on questions, the quality of the answer improves. (B) is incorrect because the main purpose of the activity is not to socialize, but to learn from each other. (C) and (D) are byproducts of the main activity.
   Competency 003

14.   **(A)**   The correct response is (A). The purpose of bringing materials and demonstrating the process of building the housing is to get students interested in the lesson. (B) is incorrect because evaluation is done after teaching the content. (C) is incorrect because enrichment usually expands on the content and is presented at the end of the formal lesson. (D) is incorrect because closing is done after teaching the content.
   Competency 003

15.   **(D)**   The correct answer is (D). One of the best ways of closing the lesson is by asking students about the content covered and learned. (A) is incorrect because motivation or focus usually happens at the beginning of the lesson. (B) is incorrect because there was no indication that students needed reteaching. Reteaching is done when students are having difficulties understanding the content. (C) is incorrect because the purpose of enrichment is to expand on the topic, not to revisit it.
     Competency 003

16.   **(A)**   The correct response is (A). Students are guided to analyze information and make decisions based on data. (B) and (C) are byproducts of the main activity. Study skills are barely mentioned in the scenario; thus, (D) is not the best answer.
     Competency 003

17.   **(B)**   The correct response is (B) because it contains the two main components of Constructivism: empowering students and leading them to assume responsibility of their own learning. (A) presents a humanistic view of education, but it fails to emphasize the main components of the Constructivism philosophy. (C) addresses a bilingual objective that is not necessarily part of Constructivism. (D) addresses an important component of language development and school success, but it has no direct connection with Constructivism.
     Competency 004

18.   **(B)**   The correct answer is (B). Students at this stage have a tendency to forget rules. These have to be taught and rehearsed to make sure students understand the expected behavior. (A) and (C) are good ideas, but fail to address the real intent of the question. (D) is unrealistic. It is impossible to raise students' self-image prior to exposing them to classroom rules.
     Competency 006

19.   **(D)**   The correct response is (D). The statements describe the typical behavior of five- to seven-year-old students. (A), (B), and (C) describe children ages eight and up. Older students have a better understanding of classroom routines and discipline. They are also more mature, independent thinkers, and often enjoy challenging authority.
     Competency 006

20.   **(D)**   The correct response is (D). In Assertive Discipline, students are given a set of specific behaviors and consequences for each behavior. Children are allowed to choose the behavior as long as they accept the consequences. In this system the teacher punishes the behavior, not the child. The rules are prominently displayed and kept to a minimum to make sure that students are able to remember them. (A) is incorrect because the program does not require an extensive list of rules, and students are not required to recite them. (B) is inaccurate because physical restraint or coercion is generally discouraged in Assertive Discipline. (C) is incorrect because

Assertive Discipline presents a short list of rules, but students are not required to produce specific behaviors daily; students are required to follow the rules.
  Competency 006

21. **(C)** The correct answer is (C). In these games, students are exposed to maps skills and problem-solving activities that guide them to make decisions. (A) is a byproduct of the main benefit. (B) is incorrect. The games are not designed to teach explicitly these language skills. (D) is incorrect because games by definition are designed to be enjoyed, not forced to enjoy.
  Competency 009

22. **(C)** The correct response is (C). Teachers often include too many animations and colors. Students are frequently impressed with the colorful approach and might not pay attention to the intended content. (A), (B), and (D) are incorrect because they describe atypical behavior for most children.
  Competency 009

23. **(A)** The correct answer is (A) because it is the only answer that refers to productivity tools. Teachers commonly use these productivity tools to facilitate classroom management and instruction. (B), (C), and (D) contain a combination of productivity and instructional tools and games.
  Competency 009

24. **(D)** The correct response is (D). Writing the alphabet simply as an exercise is an isolated act that will do little to create fluency and self-confidence in reading and writing. Reading in a comfortable atmosphere (A), modeling fluent reading for students (B), and using real-life skills to practice spelling and writing (C) present skills to enhance reading and writing in a manner that is neither threatening nor boring. By accepting invented spelling (C), the teacher is following developmentally appropriate and student-centered teaching practices. Children generally go through specific stages of writing, and inventive spelling is one of them.
  Competency 008

25. **(B)** The correct response is (B). All parent conferences should begin and end on a positive note and should avoid technical terms and educational jargon. Any problems should be discussed at once and not left for the second conference (A). English language learners should be encouraged to develop fluency in both languages, not exclusively English (C). A teacher is well-liked and appreciated if he or she speaks in a way that parents readily understand (D).
  Competency 011

26. **(B)** The correct response is (B). By reviewing the lessons, Ms. Treen is reflectively self-evaluating her teaching and reviewing ways she can improve to better fit the needs of the students. Although good ideas can be shared, all plans must be modified to fit the class and teacher style (A). "Community Helpers" is

a topic appropriate for kindergarten (C). Although a class visitor and filmstrip may increase motivation and enthusiasm, (D) does not address the need to evaluate the entire unit.

Competency 010

27.   **(C)**   The correct response is (C). Students between two and seven years of age are going through what Piaget called the Preoperational Stage of cognitive development. At this stage, students are still characterized by perceptual dominance and might have problems handling abstractions. (A) and (B) are probably valid statements, but they do not address the real educational principle of the activity. (D) is wrong because children might lack muscular coordination at this stage, but that should not interfere with their ability to handle objects of different shapes.

Competency 001

28.   **(A)**   The correct response is (A) because it describes possible benefits when involving parents in the education process. (B) and (C) present superficial and indirect consequences of the activity. The activity presented in (D) will definitely involve the community, but the activity is not designed to teach family members how things are done in the United States.

Competency 011

29.   **(B)**   The correct response is (B). There is no indication that suggests Sheba's parents do not speak English. Thus, it may not be necessary to involve a translator. Immigrant parents might feel insulted when teachers assume that they are not fluent in English. Developing an anecdotal record of the behavior and approaches to solve the problem (A) and checking the student's permanent records (D) indicate that the teacher has done her share to understand and solve the problem. Gathering information about the parents' background (C) might also be beneficial to avoid cross-cultural communication problems.

Competency 011

30.   **(B)**   The correct response is (B). The Texas State Bilingual Education law allows the use of two languages in grades pre-K through the elementary grades. In middle school, it allows either the two languages or English as a second language (ESL) only. After middle school, the law provides for the use of ESL or a special language program only.

Competency 013

31.   **(B)**   The correct response is (B). Mr. Treskoski's behavior demonstrates that he wants to study the gang issue further and reflect upon that research before he gives an answer to the class. This indicates that he knows how to promote his own growth. It also demonstrates that he is modeling behavior that creates a school culture that enhances learning. Mr. Treskoski's statement does not indicate that he will plan for a lesson, (A), but rather study in order to develop a reasoned opinion of his own. Mr. Treskoski clearly intends to share his opinion with the class after he has

formulated one (C); sharing his opinion will promote diversity, rather than inhibit it. Mr. Treskoski indicates that deferring to answer is not due to time constraints, but to his need to explore the issue further (D).

    Competency 012

32.   **(B)**   The correct response is (B). Mr. Treskoski demonstrates to Mr. Hinojosa that he considers the librarian an important source of advice by asking his recommendations. This is a step toward developing a collegial relationship and toward creating a mutually supportive learning environment. It would not take a great deal of time to find the information in the school's library, nor would it be difficult to ascertain the computer capability of the library (A). The question does not concern individual student development (C). Nothing suggests that Mr. Treskoski's actions could result from compliance with customary library regulations (D).

    Competency 012

33.   **(C)**   The correct response is (C). Rather than aborting the project because of the school's lack of computer capability, Mr. Treskoski seeks assistance from a community resource, the local community college. This will foster student growth in at least three ways: first, the students will receive materials that would not otherwise be available to them; second, the students will become aware of a source of local computer access that they may use later in their own endeavors; and third, students will become the beneficiaries of a close community tie between the school and the community college. Nothing in the question suggests that individual needs are being addressed (A). Indeed, until the material arrives, Mr. Treskoski has no way of knowing the difficulty or exact content of the articles; therefore, he has no way of knowing whether any of the articles will meet the needs of any particular student. The question does not address the various domains of student growth (B). While gathering materials can be considered part of the planning activity (D), the focus in this scenario is not on planning, but on the use of community resources.

    Competency 012

34.   **(B)**   The correct response is (B). Mr. Treskoski is developing a strong partnership with Casey's aunt when he demonstrates his interest in having her share a role in classroom instruction. The main benefit is not only the use of relatives as resources, but the use of the local community. Although having a guest speaker is an instructional strategy (A), the important issue is having Casey's aunt be the speaker. Since her aunt is editorial director, she may not be as well-qualified to address the issue of the newspaper's partisanship as some other member of the newspaper staff, such as the managing editor, would be. Therefore, Mr. Treskoski's interest would lie in fostering a strong parent-teacher relationship, rather than in instructional strategy. The emphasis is not on an individual talent and ability (C). The emphasis is on Casey's inviting her aunt and Mr. Treskoski's encouragement of the aunt's taking part in the classroom life. Nothing in the question addresses the issue of modalities (D).

    Competency 011

35. **(A)** The correct response is (A). By allowing Molly's father to come and express a dissenting opinion, Mr. Treskoski demonstrates that he appreciates diversity of ideas. This in turn creates an environment that celebrates the diversity of groups and the uniqueness of individuals. While Molly's prior learning is demonstrated by her telling Mr. Treskoski what her father has said (B), the emphasis is not on her prior learning, but on inviting Mr. Winters to share his unique perspective. Since Mr. Winters is the personnel manager at the electronics factory instead of an authority on either crime or the newspaper, he can not be considered a community resource on this issue (C). If the issue had to do with electronics or personnel matters, he would have been considered a community resource. While the students may be curious as to what Mr. Winters has to say, the emphasis is not on stimulating student curiosity (D), but on inviting Mr. Winters to come and share his perspective.
   Competency 002

36. **(D)** The correct response is (D). It is a violation of both legal and ethical guidelines to discuss a special education student's handicapped condition with another student's parent. The Family Right to Privacy Act (FRPA) assures the confidentiality of student records. Mr. Treskoski would violate ethical and legal guidelines if he discussed Lynn's disability with Ms. Rivas (A). Moving Lynn out of the group simply because Ms. Rivas did not want her daughter to be grouped with him (B) would violate the spirit of the Fourteenth Amendment, as it would segregate Lynn from his assigned group because he has a disability. While it is a major goal of social studies to instill civic virtue in students (C), Mr. Treskoski cannot violate the legal and ethical guidelines that protect Lynn.
   Competency 013

37. **(B)** The correct response is (B). In an inclusion environment, the mainstream teacher has to obtain a copy of the IEP and deliver it in collaboration with the special education teacher. The ARD committee in collaboration with the special education teacher will be involved in the design of the IEP.
   Competency 013

38. **(A)** Students who do not meet expectations on the state criterion-referenced test or who are below grade level qualify for assistance under the Compensatory Education law. The law does not use the results of norm-referenced standardized achievement tests (B) or immigration status (D) as a criterion for participation in the program. Students who exhibit intellectual abilities beyond their peers (C) are covered under the Gifted and Talented legislation.
   Competency 013

39. **(B)** The correct response is (B). In the deductive method, teachers present the rules or the generalization and ask students to apply them. Rules are often very abstract and young children might have difficulties understanding them. (A) and (C) are probably true statements, but they fail to provide a tangible reason for the prefer-

ence. (D) is incorrect because it describes the inductive method, not the deductive method. In the inductive method, teachers present examples or lead students in a hands-on activity, and later they are asked about the elements learned as a result of the activity.

Competency 001

40.   **(A)**   The correct response is (A). Since Mr. O'Brien's goal is his own professional development, the answer is (A). He would not assess the quality of students' assignments (C) or revise students' assignments (D) to enhance his own growth and development. Choices (B), (C), and (D) refer to instructional activities, not professional development activities.

Competency 012

41.   **(B)**   The correct response is (B). Mr. O'Brien is demonstrating that he is a reflective practitioner who can work cooperatively with others in his school. (A) describes a form of intellectual snobbery that does not lead to collegiality. Independent of others' views, Mr. O'Brien has a professional responsibility to keep pace with developments and issues in his teaching field (C). Finally, (D) is a poor answer because it would not necessarily help him reach his goal of improving instruction.

Competency 012

42.   **(C)**   The correct response is (C). Including both colleagues' viewpoints is an effort to bring students a balanced and fair presentation on the topic and to work effectively with other professionals at his school. (A) and (D) would neither promote collegiality nor demonstrate Mr. O'Brien's ability to work with other members of the teaching community; (B) would mean that Mr. O'Brien refuses to consider the issue carefully simply because it is not an issue with a singular point of view; however, many topics discussed at the secondary level are subject to multiple points of view.

Competency 012

43.   **(A)**   The correct response is (A). Mr. O'Brien is designing a supportive classroom for all students, both males and females. Using a particular book as a reference work for a course would not result in students having to buy the book (B) or having to read the reference book (D), nor would colleagues necessarily be aware of the practice (C). In conclusion, Mr. O'Brien would simply have access to Deborah Tannen's findings and her interpretation of her data.

Competency 006

44.   **(B)**   The correct response is (B). An effective and equitable practice is to give all students an opportunity to participate in class discussions. (A) and (C) are different ways of stating the same practice, in both cases treating the female students differently. (D) is incorrect; research does show that male students tend to receive more feedback when they answer questions, which enhances their self-esteem, whereas female students are seldom given positive or negative feedback.

Competency 005

45. **(D)** The correct response is (D). Sensitivity to students' self-esteem means that teachers take an interest in their students, visiting with them privately and trying to understand the reasons for their behavior in class. Taking an interest in the student may provide the encouragement the student needs to begin participating in class activities. (B) is a harassing behavior that is to be avoided. (A) and (C), although reasonable educational practices, would probably have little direct effect on changing the behavior of the students the teacher is concerned about helping.
Competency 005

46. **(B)** The correct response is (B). Some students, especially those who respond well to external validators, will be motivated to participate in class when their grades are affected by their participation. (A) is incorrect because this practice will not motivate all students. (C) is incorrect because there is nothing inherent to this practice that would result in all students earning higher grades—only those who participate would improve their grades. This practice of rewarding students for their participation would not be expected to discourage student participation (D).
Competency 008

47. **(B)** The correct response is (B). Mr. O'Brien's strategy involves everyone in class and encourages each student to discover the practical applications for the information to be learned in class. (A) is incorrect because in a communications class, discourse and discussions are encouraged, not avoided; in these classes, students learn to argue and disagree in a civil manner. (C) is incorrect because this strategy takes quite a bit of classroom time since it allows all students to be actively involved; thus, it is not a time-saving device. (D) is incorrect because brainstorming is a creative activity, not an activity aimed at assessing skills or knowledge.
Competency 008

48. **(A)** The correct response is (A). Mr. O'Brien has employed a brainstorming activity to allow students to uncover their own, personal communication problems and needs. Therefore, they will have more motivation and interest in learning about communication differences between men and women. (B) is incorrect; in fact, Mr. O'Brien may choose to introduce the topic formally at the next class meeting. (C) is incorrect in that at no point has Mr. O'Brien presented information to pit men and women against each other, nor is that the purpose of presenting this topic. (D) is incorrect as Mr. O'Brien's choice of activities will have the opposite effect of dismissing students' concerns as he recognizes and helps them to identify their problems.
Competency 008

49. **(D)** The correct response is (D). Group activities allow students to learn cooperatively. (A) is incorrect because it does not specify an instructional goal for the group work. (B) is incorrect because the goal is problem-solving, not merely improving social skills. (C) is incorrect because students are not structuring their own time in this example.
Competency 007

50.　**(B)**　The correct response is (B). Students often disclose more personal information in journals than when speaking in class. The teacher can also check for comprehension of content and the success or failure of class objectives. Journals typically are not graded with consideration to standard usage or grammatical constructions; therefore, (A) is incorrect. The assignment has no direct bearing on time-management skills; therefore, (C) is incorrect. (D) is irrelevant: no mention is made of giving daily grades on the journal writing.
　　Competency 010

51.　**(D)**　The correct response is (D). The use of milk and cookies as an activity to promote interest in the topic is more appropriate for students in primary grades. (A), (B) and (C) are incorrect. The activity is funny, but inappropriate for the cognitive development of high school students.
　　Competency 001

52.　**(C)**　The correct response is (C). Meeting with each student and informally determining individual needs is the best first step towards establishing rapport with each student. Subsequently, Ms. Jaynes will want to review school files (B), and administer tests (D). Ms. Jaynes has to be careful when she discusses students with other teachers (A), so as not to be influenced by biased opinions or stereotypes against students with learning disabilities or other special needs.
　　Competency 010

53.　**(D)**　The correct response is (D); this choice is a definition of test bias. (A) refers to test validity; (B) refers to test reliability; (C) is the objective of intelligence tests.
　　Competency 010

54.　**(A)**　The correct response is (A). Practice effects are seen when students are re-tested with the same instrument shortly after the first testing. It is assumed that students' scores will improve with subsequent exposure to the same material. (B) is not a practice effect, but the desired effect of improved skills or enhanced performance; indeed, it is the purpose of instruction. (C) pertains to the issue of test validity, and (D) refers to the issue of social desirability (that is, when students answer the way they believe is desired). Social desirability is an issue with opinion or attitude tests, not achievement or skills tests.
　　Competency 010

55.　**(C)**　The correct response is (C). Although (A), (B), and (D) are possible products of Ms. Jaynes' actions, they are not the particular reason she engages in this practice. Popularity, higher salaries, and better-disciplined students do not always accompany involved and caring instruction. However, many intangible rewards are products of being a team member of the learning community.
　　Competency 012

56. **(A)** The correct response is (A). Inductive learners enjoy the discovery approach to learning. They examine the data and derive generalizations based on what they see and experience. (B) describes the opposite, i.e., students who like direct and explicit instruction, deductive teaching. (C) is too generic. Highly intelligent students will probably do well with any kind of approach. (D) is incorrect because there is no guarantee that students from middle and upper class will do better with the inductive teaching.
Competency 007

57. **(B)** The correct response is (B). Mr. Holderman is violating the copyright laws by making multiple copies of the program. If he wants to copy the program to multiple computers, he has to buy a site license for the school. (A) is incorrect because the law alluded to does not exist. Instructional programs are not exempted from copyright laws, unless they become public domain. (C) might appear to be right, but the legal violation takes precedence over his good intentions. (D) is incorrect because he is violating copyright laws, an action that should be avoided in the district.
Competency 009

58. **(C)** The correct response is (C). (A) and (B) are incorrect because they include productivity tools. (D) includes productivity tools only.
Competency 009

59. **(C)** The correct response is (C). These broadly-stated goals for instruction are examples of instructional or educational goals. Behavioral objectives (A) must describe specific skills or knowledge that should be acquired and demonstrated by students. Performance objectives (B) include performance standards and other specific performance criteria. The question has nothing to do with outcome-based education (D).
Competency 004

60. **(C)** The correct response is (C). Behavioral objectives describe what students will be able to do as a result of having received appropriate instruction. A variety of teaching methods may be used to reach these objectives (A); student-centered or teacher-centered activities (D) are examples of methods that may be used. Materials and equipment lists (B) may or may not be given on lesson plans; however, they are separate from behavioral objectives.
Competency 003

61. **(C)** The correct response is (C). This action shows concern for and opens the door for dialogue with the student. For high school-aged students, a direct approach that recognizes the student's responsibility for his or her own learning and behavior is usually the best approach. (A) and (B) are indirect and could exacerbate the student's present problems. (D) fails to get at the cause of Lee's difficulties.
Competency 005

62.   **(B)**   The correct response is (B). The instructional principle illustrated here is that students can more easily learn new information (English) when linked with the familiar (their native language). Moreover, learning becomes more effective when students are allowed to make choices about the learning activities in which they engage. (A) and (C) are plausible, however, they are poor choices in comparison with (B). (D) is incorrect in as much as filming one's performance involves some level of risk.
   Competency 004

63.   **(A)**   The correct answer is (A). Teachers need to assess prior knowledge, present vocabulary words, idiomatic expressions, and any kind of cultural framework needed to provide the child with the schema needed to understand a story. (B) is incorrect because it is impossible to use pre-reading activities to introduce the decoding and comprehension skills needed to deal with every word used in the story. The use of pictorial clues is appropriate for pre-reading activity, but to write a summary of the story as part of the pre-reading activity is illogical. Based on this discrepancy, (C) is incorrect. (D) is obviously incorrect because it does not address pre-reading activities. Details about a story and comprehension questions are usually introduced as part of the formal reading process.
   Competency 002

64.   **(D)**   The correct response is (D). Providing students with guidelines for successful group work and giving them a chance to discuss their own group's performance will help improve the functioning of group work as a whole. Permitting students to pick their groups (A) often leads to an exclusive atmosphere, which can prevent a lesson from being effective. Making sure that each group has a student who can lead the group (B) also does not ensure the success of this group's collaboration. Basing students' grades on the success of their group work (C) does not consider learning processes and the factors that impact student learning.
   Competency 004

65.   **(C)**   The correct response is (C), because it emphasizes the Interactive/Experiential nature of language learning. In this approach, children learn languages in a natural and relaxed environment without direct error corrections. (A) describes a grammar-based approach for language learning not supported by the scenario. (B) describes a debatable statement not supported by the scenario. Language functions have been linked to the left hemisphere of the brain. However, both the left and right hemispheres of the brain are connected, thus it is virtually impossible to ascertain if the left hemisphere alone controls language development. (D) represents an opinion that is not substantiated in the scenario.
   Competency 005

66.   **(D)**   The correct response is (D), because it uses the term "language deficits," which implies that the child brings cultural and linguistic deficits to the learning process. This statement contradicts the main principle of the effective assessment

philosophy for CLD students. (A), (B), and (C) describe the main principles for assessing CLD students.
Competency 010

67. (C) The correct response is (C). The main purpose of family literacy programs is to empower parents to take an active role in the education of their children. (A), (B), and (D) are possible topics in a literacy program, but they are not the main focus of the program.
Competency 011

68. (A) The correct response is (A). Ms. Chernev allows her students to be involved in setting their learning goals. This helps students understand what is expected of them. By providing all the support that students need to be successful, Ms. Chernev also creates an environment in which students can be productive and feel comfortable. Group work (B) does not ensure each student's individual success. Ms. Chernev should modify tasks to make sure that they reflect students' academic abilities as much as possible. However, this does not mean that students with low-average abilities should receive an easier assignment (C). Ms. Chernev should make sure to offer constructive feedback after each assignment so that students understand what is expected from them and how they can improve their work. They should not be rewarded for performances that do not meet expectations (D).
Competency 005

69. (C) The correct response is (C). This question relates to planning processes to design outcome-oriented learning experiences. Developing objectives is the first step in planning. (A) is incorrect; cooperative learning and the content are used to reach the objectives. (B) is an incorrect choice; evaluation is the last step in the planning process. Finding materials and resources (D) is an important step in planning, but the incorrect choice for this situation.
Competency 003

70. (A) The correct response is (A). This question relates to an understanding of human developmental processes. This understanding nurtures student growth through developmentally appropriate instruction. (B) is not the best answer; higher-order thinking skills are important instructional strategies. (C) is incorrect; promoting the lifelong pursuit of learning is achieved through structuring and managing the learning environment. Understanding how learning occurs would show that constant difficult schoolwork causes students to become disinterested, which renders (D) an incorrect choice.
Competency 001

71. (C) The correct response is (C). This question relates to environmental factors. Being aware of external forces will help in the planning and designing of the unit to promote students' learning and self-esteem. (A) is incorrect because it relates to the development of the unit that requires choosing lessons and activities

that reflect the principles of effective instruction. Challenging students requires the teacher to be aware of the learners' interests while designing the instruction; (B) is part of the planning process and incorrect for this situation. (D), the grouping of students, is an instructional strategy and is incorrect.
   Competency 005

72.   **(C)**   The correct response is (C). This question relates to human diversity and the idea that each student brings to the classroom a constellation of personal and social characteristics related to a variety of factors such as exceptionality. (C) encourages the gifted learners to participate in their own learning. (A) is simply more of the same kind of schoolwork and not an acceptable answer. Being intrinsically motivated, exceptional students often find unmotivated students difficult to tutor; therefore, (B) is incorrect. Teacher-made, tightly organized units do not allow the exceptional student the opportunity to experience the learning situation; thus, (D) is incorrect.
   Competency 002

73.   **(A)**   The correct response is (A). The main purpose of the activity is to teach creative writing using a variety of strategies. (B), (C), and (D) present secondary reasons for designing in the "Writer's Workshop."
   Competency 002

74.   **(B)**   The correct response is (B). In the assessment, Mrs. Gomez has to communicate effectively with the students. To accomplish this, she uses various media. She is connecting the media to the different learning styles. Evaluation generates divergent thinking, but never creative thinking (A); thus, the statement is false. The evaluation tools are not to evaluate Mrs. Gomez' competency (C), but are designed to evaluate the students' competency in identifying and creating metaphors. Working with other colleagues (D) is not the issue; instead, using a variety of communication techniques in the evaluation is the goal.
   Competency 007

75.   **(B)**   The correct answer is (B). The multidimensional nature of the rubric used to assess the assignment is broad enough to allow for individual differences. (A), (C), and (D) present generic statements about assessment.
   Competency 010

76.   **(C)**   The correct response is (C). Since district and school-wide rules can supersede individual classroom rules, teachers must review them to avoid conflict. (A) and (D) represent sound practices in setting up the classroom rules, but they are not the first consideration. (B) is incorrect because it is virtually impossible to write rules to cover all possible behaviors of eighth-graders.
   Competency 006

77.   **(A)**   The correct response is (A). Sharing information about the rationale for

rules minimizes the idea that these are arbitrarily imposed on the students. It also makes students more responsible agents in the discipline management program. (B) is incorrect because the purpose of allowing students to have input in setting classroom rules is to promote an internal locus of control, as opposed to an external locus of control. (C) is incorrect because the activity is not designed to teach students how to set up a classroom management plan, but to be effective participants in the plan. (D) is incorrect because being a moral thinker is not compatible with conditioning to obey without thinking.
  Competency 006

78.   **(B)**   The correct response is (B). The scenario represents an example of inductive learning where students acquire knowledge subconsciously through active engagement in fun activities. (A) represents an opposing view, deductive learning. (C) is contradictory because it addresses two opposing schools of psychology. (D) represents an opinion about the students and the teacher that is not directly supported in the scenario.
  Competency 007

79.   **(B)**   The correct response is (B). Readers should not get distracted about the use of the "Jigsaw" as an example. The real question deals with cooperative learning in general. By participating in cooperative learning activities, students become active learners and take responsibility for the learning process. (A) represents a byproduct of the activity, not the main purpose. (C) is written from the teacher's point of view and fails to address the key benefit for students. (D) is incorrect because teachers, not students, are in charge of the planning.
  Competency 007

80.   **(C)**   The correct response is (C). The most important reason for using portfolio is to track students' progress and to give them a sense of ownership and participation in the assessment process. (A) represents a superficial view of how portfolio is implemented. (B) and (D) are inaccurate because Portfolio Assessment is not designed to have confidential information and, traditionally, portfolio documents are not used to report data for the accountability system.
  Competency 010

81.   **(C)**   The correct response is (C). When working in cooperative groups, it is important that members support each other, take turns in an orderly fashion, and listen to individual contributions. Based on these principles, (A) is incorrect because it requires students to criticize each other's work. (B) and (D) are incorrect because competition is not a desirable outcome of cooperative learning.
  Competency 006

82.   **(D)**   The correct answer is (D). The newspaper offers invaluable resource information and non-traditional learning opportunities. However, the sports section is probably more appropriate than any other part to teach mathematics to third-graders. The information provided in the stock market section (A) and the obituaries

(C) might not be developmentally appropriate or interesting for third-graders. The world news report (B) could probably be used, but it will require creativity to adapt the information to deal with mathematics.
Competency 009

83. **(A)** The correct response is (A). A good lesson contains opportunities for all types of learners. Assessing hand-eye coordination (B) is not an objective of this lesson. Manipulatives often spice up a lesson (C), but this is not the main objective of using the manipulative. The activity may become self-directed (D), but this is not specified in the question.
Competency 009

84. **(B)** The correct response is (B). For a yearlong cooperative working relationship, Mr. Thacker should probably go ahead and teach the novel specified in the curriculum guide. However, Mr. Thacker's sincere desire to get off to a strong start with his teaching by using *The Red Badge of Courage* may convince the chairperson to discuss the matter again with the other sophomore teachers and allow Mr. Thacker to teach the novel. If the curriculum is inviolate, the chairperson will know which of the other three sophomore English teachers will be the most helpful to Mr. Thacker and share teaching resources and strategies with him for the novel all are teaching. (A) is incorrect since Mr. Thacker is dooming himself to being the outcast on the sophomore English team by going against the usual team commitment regarding curriculum. (C) is incorrect since Mr. Thacker is showing that he does not understand the hierarchy of authority on the school campus. By not following the advice of the other teachers and by overlooking the departmental chairperson, he is politically unwise in his decision-making. (D) is incorrect since he is ignoring the total input from school professionals and co-workers about his teaching and instead asking the parents to make a curriculum decision. Actually, his permitting the parents to vote about the book to use with their children may well be an unfavorable action in the parents' perspective. He might have difficulty regaining their confidence in his effectiveness as a teacher.
Competency 013

85. **(C)** The correct response is (C). The Code of Ethics for Teachers allows the use of materials and equipment as long as it is used for "official school business" only. Borrowing school property under any other conditions is unethical.
Competency 013

86. **(B)** The correct response is (B). Mr. Méndez has made an attempt to notify all parents, but he has not verified that all parents received his notification. He must also have a signed statement from the parent of every child giving permission for the child to ride with Mr. Méndez or one of the parents driving a van. Such a release form is required in Texas public schools. Some school districts have even more rigid rules, not allowing students to attend a field trip unless a school employee is driving each vehicle used in transport. The handbook referred to by the principal will specify the regulations required by the Ft. Worth district. (A), (C), and (D) are all

correct because they contain steps that Mr. Méndez should take in arranging for the field trip. After obtaining the school administrator's approval for the field trip, he has considered the needs of other teachers of his students as well as of the parents who will assist him in transporting the students.

Competency 013

87. **(A)** The correct answer is (A). In order to cultivate autonomy in the classroom, the teacher should provide activities that encourage students to have input in what they will learn. In this way, students feel ownership of their lives and of what they learn—a feeling that will help to enhance the students' ability to take initiative, to be motivated, and to complete tasks with confidence and competence. (B) would be beneficial in producing a classroom environment that includes all students, but it would not aid in developing the individuality of each student. (C) is incorrect; without prescribed routines that are scheduled to be completed within a designated time frame, effective accomplishments will be slim. (D) would not provide students with the sort of autonomy that is considered to be the most valuable and healthy.

Competency 001

88. **(C)** The correct answer is (C). The teacher is responsible for modeling the behavior that should be directed towards a student with multiple disabilities. It is important for Michael to experience a positive classroom atmosphere, for it will contribute to the degree of his success in a new environment. In order to avert potential negative attention directed at Michael on the part of other students, Ms. Smith must set the standard for behavior. To iterate a code of behavior (B) and to conduct an information session (D) would only emphasize the fact that Michael is "different" and would separate him from his classmates, which is not desired. (A) is not the best answer because it advocates an improper attitude towards students with disabilities; neither Michael nor his classmates will benefit from this activity.

Competency 005

89. **(C)** The correct response is (C). Mr. Hayworth has to make sure he communicates his teaching objective in an effective way. Students will have an easier time grasping a concept in its entirety if they have familiar real-life situations as a reference. (A), (B), and (D) will help students understand the concept, however, they are not as effective and complete an approach as presented in (C).

Competency 007

90. **(D)** The correct answer is (D). Making sure that varied teaching methods appeal to students with different learning styles shows that Ms. Brink understands the diversity present in her classroom. Teachers should not be primarily motivated by what would make teaching easier for themselves, as suggested in (A) and (B); the needs of their students should come first. While covering a greater amount of material within a shorter time frame (C) is desirable, the first priority is to ensure that all students are stimulated by a variety of teaching methods.

Competency 002

Practice Test 4: PPR EC–12

Answers, Sorted by Competency

Question	Domain	Competency	Answer	Did You Answer Correctly?	Question	Domain	Competency	Answer	Did You Answer Correctly?
4	I	1	D		74	III	7	B	
12	I	1	C		78	III	7	B	
27	I	1	C		79	III	7	B	
39	I	1	B		89	III	7	C	
51	I	1	D		9	III	8	A	
70	I	1	A		10	III	8	D	
87	I	1	A		24	III	8	D	
11	I	2	B		46	III	8	B	
35	I	2	A		47	III	8	B	
63	I	2	A		48	III	8	A	
72	I	2	C		21	III	9	C	
73	I	2	A		22	III	9	C	
90	I	2	D		23	III	9	A	
3	I	3	D		57	III	9	B	
13	I	3	A		58	III	9	C	
14	I	3	A		82	III	9	D	
15	I	3	D		83	III	9	A	
16	I	3	A		26	III	10	B	
60	I	3	C		50	III	10	B	
61	I	3	C		52	III	10	C	
69	I	3	C		53	III	10	D	
1	I	4	D		54	III	10	A	
5	I	4	A		66	III	10	D	
8	I	4	C		75	III	10	B	
17	I	4	B		80	III	10	C	
59	I	4	C		6	III	11	A	
62	I	4	B		7	III	11	C	
64	I	4	D		25	III	11	B	
44	II	5	B		28	III	11	B	
45	II	5	D		34	III	11	B	
61	II	5	C		67	III	11	C	
65	II	5	C		31	IV	12	B	
68	II	5	A		32	IV	12	B	
71	II	5	C		33	IV	12	C	
88	II	5	C		40	IV	12	A	
18	II	6	B		41	IV	12	B	
19	II	6	D		42	IV	12	C	
20	II	6	D		55	IV	12	C	
43	II	6	A		30	IV	13	B	
76	II	6	C		36	IV	13	D	
77	II	6	A		37	IV	13	B	
81	II	6	C		38	IV	13	A	
2	III	7	D		84	IV	13	B	
49	III	7	D		85	IV	13	C	
56	III	7	A		86	IV	13	B	

TExES Practice Test 1: PPR EC–4
Answer Sheet

1. Ⓐ Ⓑ Ⓒ Ⓓ
2. Ⓐ Ⓑ Ⓒ Ⓓ
3. Ⓐ Ⓑ Ⓒ Ⓓ
4. Ⓐ Ⓑ Ⓒ Ⓓ
5. Ⓐ Ⓑ Ⓒ Ⓓ
6. Ⓐ Ⓑ Ⓒ Ⓓ
7. Ⓐ Ⓑ Ⓒ Ⓓ
8. Ⓐ Ⓑ Ⓒ Ⓓ
9. Ⓐ Ⓑ Ⓒ Ⓓ
10. Ⓐ Ⓑ Ⓒ Ⓓ
11. Ⓐ Ⓑ Ⓒ Ⓓ
12. Ⓐ Ⓑ Ⓒ Ⓓ
13. Ⓐ Ⓑ Ⓒ Ⓓ
14. Ⓐ Ⓑ Ⓒ Ⓓ
15. Ⓐ Ⓑ Ⓒ Ⓓ
16. Ⓐ Ⓑ Ⓒ Ⓓ
17. Ⓐ Ⓑ Ⓒ Ⓓ
18. Ⓐ Ⓑ Ⓒ Ⓓ
19. Ⓐ Ⓑ Ⓒ Ⓓ
20. Ⓐ Ⓑ Ⓒ Ⓓ
21. Ⓐ Ⓑ Ⓒ Ⓓ
22. Ⓐ Ⓑ Ⓒ Ⓓ
23. Ⓐ Ⓑ Ⓒ Ⓓ
24. Ⓐ Ⓑ Ⓒ Ⓓ
25. Ⓐ Ⓑ Ⓒ Ⓓ
26. Ⓐ Ⓑ Ⓒ Ⓓ
27. Ⓐ Ⓑ Ⓒ Ⓓ
28. Ⓐ Ⓑ Ⓒ Ⓓ
29. Ⓐ Ⓑ Ⓒ Ⓓ
30. Ⓐ Ⓑ Ⓒ Ⓓ

31. Ⓐ Ⓑ Ⓒ Ⓓ
32. Ⓐ Ⓑ Ⓒ Ⓓ
33. Ⓐ Ⓑ Ⓒ Ⓓ
34. Ⓐ Ⓑ Ⓒ Ⓓ
35. Ⓐ Ⓑ Ⓒ Ⓓ
36. Ⓐ Ⓑ Ⓒ Ⓓ
37. Ⓐ Ⓑ Ⓒ Ⓓ
38. Ⓐ Ⓑ Ⓒ Ⓓ
39. Ⓐ Ⓑ Ⓒ Ⓓ
40. Ⓐ Ⓑ Ⓒ Ⓓ
41. Ⓐ Ⓑ Ⓒ Ⓓ
42. Ⓐ Ⓑ Ⓒ Ⓓ
43. Ⓐ Ⓑ Ⓒ Ⓓ
44. Ⓐ Ⓑ Ⓒ Ⓓ
45. Ⓐ Ⓑ Ⓒ Ⓓ
46. Ⓐ Ⓑ Ⓒ Ⓓ
47. Ⓐ Ⓑ Ⓒ Ⓓ
48. Ⓐ Ⓑ Ⓒ Ⓓ
49. Ⓐ Ⓑ Ⓒ Ⓓ
50. Ⓐ Ⓑ Ⓒ Ⓓ
51. Ⓐ Ⓑ Ⓒ Ⓓ
52. Ⓐ Ⓑ Ⓒ Ⓓ
53. Ⓐ Ⓑ Ⓒ Ⓓ
54. Ⓐ Ⓑ Ⓒ Ⓓ
55. Ⓐ Ⓑ Ⓒ Ⓓ
56. Ⓐ Ⓑ Ⓒ Ⓓ
57. Ⓐ Ⓑ Ⓒ Ⓓ
58. Ⓐ Ⓑ Ⓒ Ⓓ
59. Ⓐ Ⓑ Ⓒ Ⓓ
60. Ⓐ Ⓑ Ⓒ Ⓓ

61. Ⓐ Ⓑ Ⓒ Ⓓ
62. Ⓐ Ⓑ Ⓒ Ⓓ
63. Ⓐ Ⓑ Ⓒ Ⓓ
64. Ⓐ Ⓑ Ⓒ Ⓓ
65. Ⓐ Ⓑ Ⓒ Ⓓ
66. Ⓐ Ⓑ Ⓒ Ⓓ
67. Ⓐ Ⓑ Ⓒ Ⓓ
68. Ⓐ Ⓑ Ⓒ Ⓓ
69. Ⓐ Ⓑ Ⓒ Ⓓ
70. Ⓐ Ⓑ Ⓒ Ⓓ
71. Ⓐ Ⓑ Ⓒ Ⓓ
72. Ⓐ Ⓑ Ⓒ Ⓓ
73. Ⓐ Ⓑ Ⓒ Ⓓ
74. Ⓐ Ⓑ Ⓒ Ⓓ
75. Ⓐ Ⓑ Ⓒ Ⓓ
76. Ⓐ Ⓑ Ⓒ Ⓓ
77. Ⓐ Ⓑ Ⓒ Ⓓ
78. Ⓐ Ⓑ Ⓒ Ⓓ
79. Ⓐ Ⓑ Ⓒ Ⓓ
80. Ⓐ Ⓑ Ⓒ Ⓓ
81. Ⓐ Ⓑ Ⓒ Ⓓ
82. Ⓐ Ⓑ Ⓒ Ⓓ
83. Ⓐ Ⓑ Ⓒ Ⓓ
84. Ⓐ Ⓑ Ⓒ Ⓓ
85. Ⓐ Ⓑ Ⓒ Ⓓ
86. Ⓐ Ⓑ Ⓒ Ⓓ
87. Ⓐ Ⓑ Ⓒ Ⓓ
88. Ⓐ Ⓑ Ⓒ Ⓓ
89. Ⓐ Ⓑ Ⓒ Ⓓ
90. Ⓐ Ⓑ Ⓒ Ⓓ

To determine in which domains your strengths and weaknesses lie, use the table on page 208.

TExES Practice Test 2: PPR 4–8
Answer Sheet

1. Ⓐ Ⓑ Ⓒ Ⓓ	31. Ⓐ Ⓑ Ⓒ Ⓓ	61. Ⓐ Ⓑ Ⓒ Ⓓ
2. Ⓐ Ⓑ Ⓒ Ⓓ	32. Ⓐ Ⓑ Ⓒ Ⓓ	62. Ⓐ Ⓑ Ⓒ Ⓓ
3. Ⓐ Ⓑ Ⓒ Ⓓ	33. Ⓐ Ⓑ Ⓒ Ⓓ	63. Ⓐ Ⓑ Ⓒ Ⓓ
4. Ⓐ Ⓑ Ⓒ Ⓓ	34. Ⓐ Ⓑ Ⓒ Ⓓ	64. Ⓐ Ⓑ Ⓒ Ⓓ
5. Ⓐ Ⓑ Ⓒ Ⓓ	35. Ⓐ Ⓑ Ⓒ Ⓓ	65. Ⓐ Ⓑ Ⓒ Ⓓ
6. Ⓐ Ⓑ Ⓒ Ⓓ	36. Ⓐ Ⓑ Ⓒ Ⓓ	66. Ⓐ Ⓑ Ⓒ Ⓓ
7. Ⓐ Ⓑ Ⓒ Ⓓ	37. Ⓐ Ⓑ Ⓒ Ⓓ	67. Ⓐ Ⓑ Ⓒ Ⓓ
8. Ⓐ Ⓑ Ⓒ Ⓓ	38. Ⓐ Ⓑ Ⓒ Ⓓ	68. Ⓐ Ⓑ Ⓒ Ⓓ
9. Ⓐ Ⓑ Ⓒ Ⓓ	39. Ⓐ Ⓑ Ⓒ Ⓓ	69. Ⓐ Ⓑ Ⓒ Ⓓ
10. Ⓐ Ⓑ Ⓒ Ⓓ	40. Ⓐ Ⓑ Ⓒ Ⓓ	70. Ⓐ Ⓑ Ⓒ Ⓓ
11. Ⓐ Ⓑ Ⓒ Ⓓ	41. Ⓐ Ⓑ Ⓒ Ⓓ	71. Ⓐ Ⓑ Ⓒ Ⓓ
12. Ⓐ Ⓑ Ⓒ Ⓓ	42. Ⓐ Ⓑ Ⓒ Ⓓ	72. Ⓐ Ⓑ Ⓒ Ⓓ
13. Ⓐ Ⓑ Ⓒ Ⓓ	43. Ⓐ Ⓑ Ⓒ Ⓓ	73. Ⓐ Ⓑ Ⓒ Ⓓ
14. Ⓐ Ⓑ Ⓒ Ⓓ	44. Ⓐ Ⓑ Ⓒ Ⓓ	74. Ⓐ Ⓑ Ⓒ Ⓓ
15. Ⓐ Ⓑ Ⓒ Ⓓ	45. Ⓐ Ⓑ Ⓒ Ⓓ	75. Ⓐ Ⓑ Ⓒ Ⓓ
16. Ⓐ Ⓑ Ⓒ Ⓓ	46. Ⓐ Ⓑ Ⓒ Ⓓ	76. Ⓐ Ⓑ Ⓒ Ⓓ
17. Ⓐ Ⓑ Ⓒ Ⓓ	47. Ⓐ Ⓑ Ⓒ Ⓓ	77. Ⓐ Ⓑ Ⓒ Ⓓ
18. Ⓐ Ⓑ Ⓒ Ⓓ	48. Ⓐ Ⓑ Ⓒ Ⓓ	78. Ⓐ Ⓑ Ⓒ Ⓓ
19. Ⓐ Ⓑ Ⓒ Ⓓ	49. Ⓐ Ⓑ Ⓒ Ⓓ	79. Ⓐ Ⓑ Ⓒ Ⓓ
20. Ⓐ Ⓑ Ⓒ Ⓓ	50. Ⓐ Ⓑ Ⓒ Ⓓ	80. Ⓐ Ⓑ Ⓒ Ⓓ
21. Ⓐ Ⓑ Ⓒ Ⓓ	51. Ⓐ Ⓑ Ⓒ Ⓓ	81. Ⓐ Ⓑ Ⓒ Ⓓ
22. Ⓐ Ⓑ Ⓒ Ⓓ	52. Ⓐ Ⓑ Ⓒ Ⓓ	82. Ⓐ Ⓑ Ⓒ Ⓓ
23. Ⓐ Ⓑ Ⓒ Ⓓ	53. Ⓐ Ⓑ Ⓒ Ⓓ	83. Ⓐ Ⓑ Ⓒ Ⓓ
24. Ⓐ Ⓑ Ⓒ Ⓓ	54. Ⓐ Ⓑ Ⓒ Ⓓ	84. Ⓐ Ⓑ Ⓒ Ⓓ
25. Ⓐ Ⓑ Ⓒ Ⓓ	55. Ⓐ Ⓑ Ⓒ Ⓓ	85. Ⓐ Ⓑ Ⓒ Ⓓ
26. Ⓐ Ⓑ Ⓒ Ⓓ	56. Ⓐ Ⓑ Ⓒ Ⓓ	86. Ⓐ Ⓑ Ⓒ Ⓓ
27. Ⓐ Ⓑ Ⓒ Ⓓ	57. Ⓐ Ⓑ Ⓒ Ⓓ	87. Ⓐ Ⓑ Ⓒ Ⓓ
28. Ⓐ Ⓑ Ⓒ Ⓓ	58. Ⓐ Ⓑ Ⓒ Ⓓ	88. Ⓐ Ⓑ Ⓒ Ⓓ
29. Ⓐ Ⓑ Ⓒ Ⓓ	59. Ⓐ Ⓑ Ⓒ Ⓓ	89. Ⓐ Ⓑ Ⓒ Ⓓ
30. Ⓐ Ⓑ Ⓒ Ⓓ	60. Ⓐ Ⓑ Ⓒ Ⓓ	90. Ⓐ Ⓑ Ⓒ Ⓓ

To determine in which domains your strengths and weaknesses lie, use the table on page 275.

TExES Practice Test 3: PPR 8–12
Answer Sheet

1. Ⓐ Ⓑ Ⓒ Ⓓ	31. Ⓐ Ⓑ Ⓒ Ⓓ	61. Ⓐ Ⓑ Ⓒ Ⓓ
2. Ⓐ Ⓑ Ⓒ Ⓓ	32. Ⓐ Ⓑ Ⓒ Ⓓ	62. Ⓐ Ⓑ Ⓒ Ⓓ
3. Ⓐ Ⓑ Ⓒ Ⓓ	33. Ⓐ Ⓑ Ⓒ Ⓓ	63. Ⓐ Ⓑ Ⓒ Ⓓ
4. Ⓐ Ⓑ Ⓒ Ⓓ	34. Ⓐ Ⓑ Ⓒ Ⓓ	64. Ⓐ Ⓑ Ⓒ Ⓓ
5. Ⓐ Ⓑ Ⓒ Ⓓ	35. Ⓐ Ⓑ Ⓒ Ⓓ	65. Ⓐ Ⓑ Ⓒ Ⓓ
6. Ⓐ Ⓑ Ⓒ Ⓓ	36. Ⓐ Ⓑ Ⓒ Ⓓ	66. Ⓐ Ⓑ Ⓒ Ⓓ
7. Ⓐ Ⓑ Ⓒ Ⓓ	37. Ⓐ Ⓑ Ⓒ Ⓓ	67. Ⓐ Ⓑ Ⓒ Ⓓ
8. Ⓐ Ⓑ Ⓒ Ⓓ	38. Ⓐ Ⓑ Ⓒ Ⓓ	68. Ⓐ Ⓑ Ⓒ Ⓓ
9. Ⓐ Ⓑ Ⓒ Ⓓ	39. Ⓐ Ⓑ Ⓒ Ⓓ	69. Ⓐ Ⓑ Ⓒ Ⓓ
10. Ⓐ Ⓑ Ⓒ Ⓓ	40. Ⓐ Ⓑ Ⓒ Ⓓ	70. Ⓐ Ⓑ Ⓒ Ⓓ
11. Ⓐ Ⓑ Ⓒ Ⓓ	41. Ⓐ Ⓑ Ⓒ Ⓓ	71. Ⓐ Ⓑ Ⓒ Ⓓ
12. Ⓐ Ⓑ Ⓒ Ⓓ	42. Ⓐ Ⓑ Ⓒ Ⓓ	72. Ⓐ Ⓑ Ⓒ Ⓓ
13. Ⓐ Ⓑ Ⓒ Ⓓ	43. Ⓐ Ⓑ Ⓒ Ⓓ	73. Ⓐ Ⓑ Ⓒ Ⓓ
14. Ⓐ Ⓑ Ⓒ Ⓓ	44. Ⓐ Ⓑ Ⓒ Ⓓ	74. Ⓐ Ⓑ Ⓒ Ⓓ
15. Ⓐ Ⓑ Ⓒ Ⓓ	45. Ⓐ Ⓑ Ⓒ Ⓓ	75. Ⓐ Ⓑ Ⓒ Ⓓ
16. Ⓐ Ⓑ Ⓒ Ⓓ	46. Ⓐ Ⓑ Ⓒ Ⓓ	76. Ⓐ Ⓑ Ⓒ Ⓓ
17. Ⓐ Ⓑ Ⓒ Ⓓ	47. Ⓐ Ⓑ Ⓒ Ⓓ	77. Ⓐ Ⓑ Ⓒ Ⓓ
18. Ⓐ Ⓑ Ⓒ Ⓓ	48. Ⓐ Ⓑ Ⓒ Ⓓ	78. Ⓐ Ⓑ Ⓒ Ⓓ
19. Ⓐ Ⓑ Ⓒ Ⓓ	49. Ⓐ Ⓑ Ⓒ Ⓓ	79. Ⓐ Ⓑ Ⓒ Ⓓ
20. Ⓐ Ⓑ Ⓒ Ⓓ	50. Ⓐ Ⓑ Ⓒ Ⓓ	80. Ⓐ Ⓑ Ⓒ Ⓓ
21. Ⓐ Ⓑ Ⓒ Ⓓ	51. Ⓐ Ⓑ Ⓒ Ⓓ	81. Ⓐ Ⓑ Ⓒ Ⓓ
22. Ⓐ Ⓑ Ⓒ Ⓓ	52. Ⓐ Ⓑ Ⓒ Ⓓ	82. Ⓐ Ⓑ Ⓒ Ⓓ
23. Ⓐ Ⓑ Ⓒ Ⓓ	53. Ⓐ Ⓑ Ⓒ Ⓓ	83. Ⓐ Ⓑ Ⓒ Ⓓ
24. Ⓐ Ⓑ Ⓒ Ⓓ	54. Ⓐ Ⓑ Ⓒ Ⓓ	84. Ⓐ Ⓑ Ⓒ Ⓓ
25. Ⓐ Ⓑ Ⓒ Ⓓ	55. Ⓐ Ⓑ Ⓒ Ⓓ	85. Ⓐ Ⓑ Ⓒ Ⓓ
26. Ⓐ Ⓑ Ⓒ Ⓓ	56. Ⓐ Ⓑ Ⓒ Ⓓ	86. Ⓐ Ⓑ Ⓒ Ⓓ
27. Ⓐ Ⓑ Ⓒ Ⓓ	57. Ⓐ Ⓑ Ⓒ Ⓓ	87. Ⓐ Ⓑ Ⓒ Ⓓ
28. Ⓐ Ⓑ Ⓒ Ⓓ	58. Ⓐ Ⓑ Ⓒ Ⓓ	88. Ⓐ Ⓑ Ⓒ Ⓓ
29. Ⓐ Ⓑ Ⓒ Ⓓ	59. Ⓐ Ⓑ Ⓒ Ⓓ	89. Ⓐ Ⓑ Ⓒ Ⓓ
30. Ⓐ Ⓑ Ⓒ Ⓓ	60. Ⓐ Ⓑ Ⓒ Ⓓ	90. Ⓐ Ⓑ Ⓒ Ⓓ

To determine in which domains your strengths and weaknesses lie, use the table on page 334.

TExES Practice Test 4: PPR EC–12
Answer Sheet

1. Ⓐ Ⓑ Ⓒ Ⓓ	31. Ⓐ Ⓑ Ⓒ Ⓓ	61. Ⓐ Ⓑ Ⓒ Ⓓ
2. Ⓐ Ⓑ Ⓒ Ⓓ	32. Ⓐ Ⓑ Ⓒ Ⓓ	62. Ⓐ Ⓑ Ⓒ Ⓓ
3. Ⓐ Ⓑ Ⓒ Ⓓ	33. Ⓐ Ⓑ Ⓒ Ⓓ	63. Ⓐ Ⓑ Ⓒ Ⓓ
4. Ⓐ Ⓑ Ⓒ Ⓓ	34. Ⓐ Ⓑ Ⓒ Ⓓ	64. Ⓐ Ⓑ Ⓒ Ⓓ
5. Ⓐ Ⓑ Ⓒ Ⓓ	35. Ⓐ Ⓑ Ⓒ Ⓓ	65. Ⓐ Ⓑ Ⓒ Ⓓ
6. Ⓐ Ⓑ Ⓒ Ⓓ	36. Ⓐ Ⓑ Ⓒ Ⓓ	66. Ⓐ Ⓑ Ⓒ Ⓓ
7. Ⓐ Ⓑ Ⓒ Ⓓ	37. Ⓐ Ⓑ Ⓒ Ⓓ	67. Ⓐ Ⓑ Ⓒ Ⓓ
8. Ⓐ Ⓑ Ⓒ Ⓓ	38. Ⓐ Ⓑ Ⓒ Ⓓ	68. Ⓐ Ⓑ Ⓒ Ⓓ
9. Ⓐ Ⓑ Ⓒ Ⓓ	39. Ⓐ Ⓑ Ⓒ Ⓓ	69. Ⓐ Ⓑ Ⓒ Ⓓ
10. Ⓐ Ⓑ Ⓒ Ⓓ	40. Ⓐ Ⓑ Ⓒ Ⓓ	70. Ⓐ Ⓑ Ⓒ Ⓓ
11. Ⓐ Ⓑ Ⓒ Ⓓ	41. Ⓐ Ⓑ Ⓒ Ⓓ	71. Ⓐ Ⓑ Ⓒ Ⓓ
12. Ⓐ Ⓑ Ⓒ Ⓓ	42. Ⓐ Ⓑ Ⓒ Ⓓ	72. Ⓐ Ⓑ Ⓒ Ⓓ
13. Ⓐ Ⓑ Ⓒ Ⓓ	43. Ⓐ Ⓑ Ⓒ Ⓓ	73. Ⓐ Ⓑ Ⓒ Ⓓ
14. Ⓐ Ⓑ Ⓒ Ⓓ	44. Ⓐ Ⓑ Ⓒ Ⓓ	74. Ⓐ Ⓑ Ⓒ Ⓓ
15. Ⓐ Ⓑ Ⓒ Ⓓ	45. Ⓐ Ⓑ Ⓒ Ⓓ	75. Ⓐ Ⓑ Ⓒ Ⓓ
16. Ⓐ Ⓑ Ⓒ Ⓓ	46. Ⓐ Ⓑ Ⓒ Ⓓ	76. Ⓐ Ⓑ Ⓒ Ⓓ
17. Ⓐ Ⓑ Ⓒ Ⓓ	47. Ⓐ Ⓑ Ⓒ Ⓓ	77. Ⓐ Ⓑ Ⓒ Ⓓ
18. Ⓐ Ⓑ Ⓒ Ⓓ	48. Ⓐ Ⓑ Ⓒ Ⓓ	78. Ⓐ Ⓑ Ⓒ Ⓓ
19. Ⓐ Ⓑ Ⓒ Ⓓ	49. Ⓐ Ⓑ Ⓒ Ⓓ	79. Ⓐ Ⓑ Ⓒ Ⓓ
20. Ⓐ Ⓑ Ⓒ Ⓓ	50. Ⓐ Ⓑ Ⓒ Ⓓ	80. Ⓐ Ⓑ Ⓒ Ⓓ
21. Ⓐ Ⓑ Ⓒ Ⓓ	51. Ⓐ Ⓑ Ⓒ Ⓓ	81. Ⓐ Ⓑ Ⓒ Ⓓ
22. Ⓐ Ⓑ Ⓒ Ⓓ	52. Ⓐ Ⓑ Ⓒ Ⓓ	82. Ⓐ Ⓑ Ⓒ Ⓓ
23. Ⓐ Ⓑ Ⓒ Ⓓ	53. Ⓐ Ⓑ Ⓒ Ⓓ	83. Ⓐ Ⓑ Ⓒ Ⓓ
24. Ⓐ Ⓑ Ⓒ Ⓓ	54. Ⓐ Ⓑ Ⓒ Ⓓ	84. Ⓐ Ⓑ Ⓒ Ⓓ
25. Ⓐ Ⓑ Ⓒ Ⓓ	55. Ⓐ Ⓑ Ⓒ Ⓓ	85. Ⓐ Ⓑ Ⓒ Ⓓ
26. Ⓐ Ⓑ Ⓒ Ⓓ	56. Ⓐ Ⓑ Ⓒ Ⓓ	86. Ⓐ Ⓑ Ⓒ Ⓓ
27. Ⓐ Ⓑ Ⓒ Ⓓ	57. Ⓐ Ⓑ Ⓒ Ⓓ	87. Ⓐ Ⓑ Ⓒ Ⓓ
28. Ⓐ Ⓑ Ⓒ Ⓓ	58. Ⓐ Ⓑ Ⓒ Ⓓ	88. Ⓐ Ⓑ Ⓒ Ⓓ
29. Ⓐ Ⓑ Ⓒ Ⓓ	59. Ⓐ Ⓑ Ⓒ Ⓓ	89. Ⓐ Ⓑ Ⓒ Ⓓ
30. Ⓐ Ⓑ Ⓒ Ⓓ	60. Ⓐ Ⓑ Ⓒ Ⓓ	90. Ⓐ Ⓑ Ⓒ Ⓓ

To determine in which domains your strengths and weaknesses lie, use the table on page 391.

References

"Action steps for schools." *Creating Safe and Drug-Free Schools: An Action Guide.* U.S. Department of Education. Sept. 1996
http://www.ed.gov/offices/OESE/SDFS/actguid/steps.html

Americans with Disabilities Act. U.S. Department of Justice, Civil Rights Division.
http://www.usdoj.gov/crt/ada

Balkom, S. "Cooperative Learning." U.S. Department of Education, Office of Education Research. June 1992
http://www.ed.gov/pubs/OR/ConsumerGuides/cooplear.html

Barbiero, D. "Tacit Knowledge." *Dictionary of Philosophy of Mind.* 2002
http://www.artsci.wustle.edu/~philos/MindDict/tacitknowledge.html

Baxter-Magolda, M. B. *Knowing and Reasoning in College: Gender-Based Patterns in Students' Intellectual Development.* San Francisco: Jossey-Bass, 1992.

Bloom, B. *Human Characteristics and School Learning.* New York: McGraw-Hill, 1976.

Bloom, B. "Major Categories in the Taxonomy of Educational Objectives." University of Washington, 2001.
http://faculty.washington.edu/krumme/guides/bloom.html

Brophy, J. "Synthesis of Research on Motivation." 2000.
http://carbon.cudenver.edu/~lsherry/cognition/brophy.html

Canfield, A. A. and Canfield, J. S. *Instructional Styles Inventory.* Los Angeles: Western Psychological Services, 1988.

CDC Youth Risk Behavior Surveillance Study. Centers for Disease Control and Prevention, 1997.
ftp://ftp.cdc.gov/pub/Publications/mmwr/ss/ss4703.pdf

"Code of Ethics in the Education Profession." National Association of Education, 2002.
http://www.nea.org/aboutnea/code.html

"Code of Ethics and Standard Practices for Texas Educators." Texas Administrative Code, State Board of Educator Certification, 2002.

Coles, R. "Point of View: When Earnest Volunteers are Sorely Tested." *Chronicle of Higher Education* (5 May 1993): A52.

Cross, K.P. and T. Angelo. *Classroom Assessment Techniques.* San Francisco: Jossey-Bass, 1994.

Deschenes, C., D. Ebeling, and J. Sprague. *Adapting Curriculum and Instruction in Inclusive Classrooms: A Teacher's Desk Reference*. Port Chester, NY: National Professional Resources, 1994.

DeVries, R. "Moral and Intellectual Development Through Play: How to Promote Children's Development Through Playing Group Games." University of Northern Iowa, College of Education's Regent Center, 2002.

Dillenbourg, P. and D. K. Schneider. "The Conditions for Effective Collaborative Learning." TECFA Education and Technologies, 8 February 1995.

Dunn, R. "The Productivity Environmental Preferences Scale (PEPS)." Paper presented at Learning Styles Institute, Lubbock, Texas, 5-9 June 1993.

Dunn, R., and K. Dunn. "Using Learning Styles Information to Enhance Teaching Effectiveness." Paper presented at Learning Styles Institute, Lubbock, Texas, 5-9 June 1993.

Elkind, D. "Egocentrism in Adolescence." *Child Development*, 38 (1967), 1025-34.

Ellis, D. *Becoming a Master Student*. New York: Houghton Mifflin, 2002.

Erikson, E. *Childhood and Society*. New York: Horton, 1963.

Flavell, J. H. "Metacognition and Cognitive Monitoring: A New Area of Cognitive-Developmental Inquiry." *American Psychologist*, 34 (1979), 21-30.

Flavell, J. H. "Speculations About the Nature and Development of Metacognition." In *Metacognition, Motivation, and Learning*, edited by R. H. Kluwe and F. E. Weinert. Hillsdale, NJ: Erlbaum, 1987.

Gagne, R. M., L. J. Briggs, and W. W. Wager. *Principles of Instructional Design*. New York: Wadsworth Thompson, 1992.

Gordon, T. *Parent Effectiveness Training: The Proven Program for Raising Responsible Children*. New York: Three Rivers Press, 2000.

Gregorc, A. *Inside Styles: Beyond the Basics*. Columbia, CT: Gregorc Associates, 1985.

Hunter, M.C. *Mastery Teaching*. Thousand Oaks, CA: Corwin Press, 1995.

Individuals with Disabilities Education Act. U.S. Department of Education, 1997. *http://www.ideapractices.org/law/regulations.regs*

Johnson, D. and R. Johnson. *Joining Together: Group Theory and Group Skills*. Englewood Cliffs, NJ: Prentice Hall, 1982.

Jukes, I., et al. The Committed Sardine: Facilitating Educational Change. 2002 *http://www.thecommittedsardine.net/*

Kaplan, S. "Theory and Practice: Curriculum and Instruction for Educators." University of Washington, 2001.
http://www-rcf.usc.edu/~skaplan/

"LD Basics." National Center for Learning Disabilities. 2002
http://www.ncld.org/info/index.cfm

"Major Categories in the Taxonomy of Educational Objectives." University of Washington, 2001.
http://faculty.washington.edu/krumme/guides/bloom.html

Maslow, A. *Toward a Psychology of Being*. New York: Van Nostrand Reinhold, 1968.

National Organization for Fetal Alcohol Syndrome (NOFAS).
http://www.nofas.org/main/what_is_FAS.htm

Nolting, P. "Meeting Learners' Special Needs." Paper presented at West Texas Regional TASP Workshop, Lubbock, Texas, 7 August 1993.

Palmer, P. J. *The Courage to Teach*. San Francisco: Jossey-Bass, 1998.

Paul, R. *Critical Thinking: How to Prepare Students for a Rapidly Changing World*. Santa Rosa, CA: Center for Critical Thinking, 1993.

Piaget, J. *The Psychology of Intelligence*. London: Routledge and Kegan Paul, 1950.

Sadker, M. and D. Sadker. *Failing at Fairness: How America's Schools Cheat Girls*. New York: Charles Scribner's Sons, 1994.

Slavin, R. E. *Educational Psychology: Theory and Practice*. London: Pearson Publishing, 1997.

"Speculations About the Nature and Development of Metacognition." In *Metacognition, Motivation, and Learning*, edited by R. H. Kluwe and F. E. Weinert. Hillsdale, NJ: Erlbaum, 1987.

Stahl, R. J. "Using 'Think-Time' and 'Wait-Time' Skillfully in the Classroom." ERIC Digest, ED370885, 1994.
http://www.ed.gov/databases/ERIC_Digests/ed370885.html

Sternberg, R. J. *Beyond IQ: A Triarchic Theory of Human Intelligence*. Cambridge: Cambridge University Press, 1985.

"Student Violence – Warning Signs." Adapted from *Reducing School Violence: Building a Framework for School Safety*. Southeastern Regional Vision for Education, 2002.
http://www.teachersfirst.com/crisis/warning/htm

Tavris, C. "Coping with Student Conflict Inside and Outside the Classroom." Paper presented at Texas Junior College Teachers' Conference, San Antonio, Texas, 25 February 1994.

Truehaft, J. "Multimedia Design Considerations." Using Technology in Education. Algonquin College, 1995.
http://www.algonquinc.on.ca/edtech/mmdesign.html

Tyler, R. W. *Basic Principles of Curriculum and Instruction.* Chicago: University of Chicago Press, 1994.

U.S. Congress. Children's Internet Protection Act. 106th Congress
http://www.cybertelecom.org/cda/cipatext.htm

U.S. Copyright Law. U.S. Copyright Office, Library of Congress
http://www.copyright.gov/title17/

Weinstein, C. E., A. C. Schulte, and D. R. Palmer. *The Learning and Study Strategies Inventory.* Clearwater, FL: H & H Publishing, 1988.

"What is Fetal Alcohol Syndrome?" National Organization on Fetal Alcohol Syndrome, 2002.
http://www.nofas.org/main/what_is_FAS.htm

Index

REA's Test Prep Books Are The Best!
(a sample of the <u>hundreds of letters</u> REA receives each year)

" I am writing to congratulate you on preparing an exceptional study guide. In five years of teaching this course I have never encountered a more thorough, comprehensive, concise and realistic preparation for this examination. "
Teacher, Davie, FL

" I have found your publications, *The Best Test Preparation...*, to be exactly that. "
Teacher, Aptos, CA

" I used your *CLEP Introductory Sociology* book and rank it 99% — thank you! "
Student, Jerusalem, Israel

" Your *GMAT* book greatly helped me on the test. Thank you. "
Student, Oxford, OH

" I recently got the *French SAT II* Exam book from REA. I congratulate you on first-rate French practice tests."
Instructor, Los Angeles, CA

" Your *AP English Literature and Composition* book is most impressive."
Student, Montgomery, AL

" This [REA] study guide was a tremendous help and I credit it with giving me the tools to help me pass the TASP. "
Student, Austin, TX

(more on front page)